The
Small To
in
American
Literature

C. David Mead

Professor of English, Michigan State University

ADVISORY EDITOR

The Small Town in American Literature

SECOND EDITION

Edited by

David M. Cook
Craig G. Swauger

Indiana University of Pennsylvania

Harper & Row, Publishers

New York   Hagerstown   San Francisco   London

Sponsoring Editor: George A. Middendorf
Project Editor: Robert Ginsberg
Designer: Andrea C. Goodman
Production Supervisor: Kewal K. Sharma
Compositor: Maryland Linotype Composition Company, Inc.
Printer and Binder: The Murray Printing Company

THE SMALL TOWN IN AMERICAN LITERATURE, Second Edition

Library of Congress Cataloging in Publication Data
Cook, David M   comp.
    The small town in American literature.

    Bibliography: p.
    1. College readers.   2. City and town life—
Literary collections.   I. Swauger, Craig G., joint comp.
II. Title.
PE1122.C59   1977   810'.8'032   76-26489
ISBN 0-06-041354-9

Contents

Preface

The small town in America is almost legend. As it has moved with this country through wars, depressions, and the years of peace and plenty, it has furnished the nation with leaders and heroes and a strain of humble, hardy people. In the small town many of this country's people have spent their formative years; here their visions and their ideals have taken shape. From it has come an important part of the history of America.

So it is fitting that our writers—poets, novelists, playwrights—have found inspiration in small-town life—some to extol it, some to question it, some simply to record it. The small town has proved to be rich in materials for writers of imaginative literature. Throughout our history countless writers have examined its religion, its culture, its economics, and its social and political roots. Philip Freneau and Washington Irving treated the villages of early America; today John Updike and Tennessee Williams write of the small town that still exists as a force in the rapidly changing mood of the country.

In part, literature shows the shaping influence of our environment upon our behavior. As this nation has changed, so has the character of the small town and its people. American writers have attempted to show that the small town has been at some times a positive influence and at other times an inhibiting one on a great segment of the American people. These two trends, in fact, have been pervasive in the history of American literature. The nineteenth century promoted the image of the romantic ideal, fostered to a degree by the isolation and self-sufficiency of the frontier. The frontier was seen as a healthy, happy place, where people were free from the ills of civilization. Writers then saw the small town as a desirable place in which to live and work and bring up a family; it provided a sense of security, a feeling of belonging. However, many writers in the last part of the nineteenth century and from that time on, influenced by realism and naturalism, reconsidered this romantic ideal. They began to see the frontier, and later the small town, as a place where people led the same dreary lives of people living elsewhere. The nostalgia associated with the small town began to fade, and the qualities extolled by earlier writers were severely examined by those later writers who saw behind the facade of the ideal the same tragic, frustrated lives that had earlier been associated with city environments.

To provide sources for research, the editors of *The Small Town in American Literature* have turned to the richness of the primary materials of American literature that deal with the small town. The sources included in this casebook provide opportunities for both literary and sociological investigations. A student interested in research from a literary point of view may, for example, consider the technique of satire or the small town as it is reflected in a particular literary genre. A student interested in research from a sociological point of view may choose from such a wide variety of topics as the morality of the small town, the education, the cultural poverty, the politics, the frustrations. As many of the selections as possible have been published in their entirety. The excerpts from longer works will be useful for certain types of research, however. While they will have limited value as an introduction to literary study, it is anticipated that students will be led to an examination of the complete work from which the selection is taken. In some instances, the paperback edition of the work, such as the novel *Main Street,* might be used in conjunction with the controlled research text. A teacher may wish to go beyond the primary sources, too, and require students to examine such secondary sources as critical and biographical studies of writers, studies in literary history such as Ima Honaker Herron's *The Small Town in American Literature* (1939), or sociological studies such as Arthur J. Vidich and Joseph Bensman's *Small Town in Mass Society* (1958).

The small town in America cannot be defined precisely. It ranges from the hamlet consisting of a few houses scattered around a country store and post office, through the village with one main street, to the growing, bustling town that is about to become a small city. All of these have certain characteristics in common, however. The population of the small town normally allows the majority of the inhabitants to know most of the town's business. The geographical size means that all of the neighbors and shops are usually within walking distance. Recreational facilities, transportation, and social activities are somewhat limited, and the attitudes of the citizenry tend to be conservative. Religious activity in the small town is of primary importance, and the townspeople, unless they are rich enough or have a high enough social standing to flout public opinion, conform, at least outwardly, to the values prescribed by the various religious groups. If they do not, they are frequently ostracized. Some towns are populated almost exclusively by certain ethnic or religious groups subscribing to a single set of mores. After graduating from high school, the young people frequently drift away, because the opportunities for employment are limited and the status quo of the community resists any changes the young might recommend.

A recent sociological focus has been on the role of women in American society. American writers have been concerned with restrictions on women from the beginning. The writer Anne Bradstreet, in the first century of America's existence, reacted against the attitudes of the people of her community, who felt she should be exclusively a housewife. In Nathaniel Hawthorne's *The Scarlet Letter,* the community rejects and punishes Hester Prynne for deviating from its standards. Writers in the nineteenth and twentieth centuries have explored community attitudes—both positive and negative—toward the spinster in the small town, from Edward Eggleston's Miss Nancy Sawyer to William Faulkner's Emily Grierson and Minnie Cooper. Sympathetic portrayals of women are presented by Sara Orne Jewett in "Miss Tempy's Watchers" and by Willa Cather in *My Ántonia.* The pioneer woman is shown in *My Ántonia* as well as in Edgar Lee Masters's "Lucinda Matlock." A woman trying desperately to break the bounds of society's restrictions is portrayed in Tennessee Williams's "The Case of the Crushed Petunias." Joyce Carol Oates, a contemporary woman writer, is concerned about the role of women in today's society.

Another concern of American literature during the past three decades has been the emergence of a black identity. White writers have treated blacks in literature with compassion. Harriet Beecher Stowe, while sympathetic, presented a stereotype. Samuel L. Clemens, and later Faulkner and Erskine Caldwell, describe the existing prejudice and hostility toward blacks. But the most honest treatment has been that of the black writer. James Baldwin, Richard Wright, Eldridge Cleaver, and Le Roi Jones are representative of this group. Ralph Ellison's treatment of the black man in *Invisible Man* clarifies the issues rationally and artistically.

The selections in this casebook move from the frontier villages of Eggleston and E. W. Howe to the more familiar towns described by Sinclair Lewis and John Updike to reveal the range in the treatment of the small town in American literature. The recreation of a locale, either real or mythical, has been the basis for much of the imaginative literature depicting the small town. Clemens (Mark Twain) uses local color in his detailing of Mississippi River towns. Mary E. Wilkins Freeman turns to the hilltowns of New England as the background for *A Humble Romance,* and Margaret Deland writes about western Pennsylvania in *Old Chester Tales.* Sherwood Anderson in *Winesburg, Ohio* and James Agee in *A Death in the Family* describe the small town at the turn of the century. Lewis creates the mythical town of Gopher Prairie as the setting for his most famous novel, *Main Street;* Faulkner gives the reader Yoknapatawpha County; Edwin Arlington

Robinson peoples Tilbury Town; John O'Hara creates Gibbsville out of his home town of Pottsville; and Masters's Spoon River defines a geographical area from his past. In short, the selections, arranged roughly in chronological order, are intended to show the effects of regional viewpoints, of changes in local conditions, of the individual lives, of the passing of time— as demonstrated in the poem, the short story, the play, and the novel. The last selection in this book, Richard Brautigan's *Trout Fishing in America,* questions whether a truly romantic idyll ever existed in America.

A list of suggested areas of research is included at the end of the book, along with a number of sample thesis statements. In addition, a bibliography of additional primary sources has been included to suggest other possibilities for exploration. A brief introduction to each primary source in the book is intended to provide pertinent facts about the writer and to make some comment on the relationship of the selection to the literature of the small town. The source of each selection may be found on the first page of the selection. Students should use this information in preparing both footnotes and bibliographical entries in their research papers. Each selection contains the original page numbers from the source cited. These page numbers are shown in brackets within the body of the work; all the material preceding a page number appears on that page in the original source.

DAVID M. COOK
CRAIG G. SWAUGER

The
Small Town
in
American
Literature

EDWARD EGGLESTON
1837–1902

In the Circle
of the School

from
THE HOOSIER
SCHOOL-MASTER

The *Hoosier School-Master* (1871) is an important literary document for
two reasons: it was a force in the development of American realistic fiction
and it is a monument in American regional writing. Eggleston's early years
were spent in Vevay, Indiana, a small river town serving the southeastern
corner of Indiana as a trading center. A change in family fortunes caused
Edward and his brother George to roam from place to place. Edward became a self-appointed circuit-riding preacher and later edited *Hearth and
Home*. In order to revive this failing journal he decided to write a serial
that would stir his readers. Since regional writing had just recently come
into vogue, he chose as his subject the actual doings of the backwoodsmen
of Indiana. The plot was suggested by George's experiences as a teacher
near Vevay when he was just 16. In his novel Eggleston not only offered
his protest to the contemporary writers' preoccupation with New England
but also recorded for posterity an accurate picture of a phase of American
civilization that was rapidly vanishing. The novel was a success as a serial
and greatly increased the circulation of *Hearth and Home*. It was then published in book form and widely pirated all over the world.

    The *Hoosier School-Master* tells the story of a beginning teacher in a
one-room schoolhouse. He soon learns that his position must be established
through physical force rather than intellectual superiority. Many entertain-
ing adventures befall him as he boards with various members of the community. Chapter I describes the teaching conditions; Chapter II discusses

the importance of the spelling bee, a major social event for the community; Chapters XII and XVI present some of the religious attitudes of the community; and Chapter XXI introduces a community type—the unmarried lady. These selections reflect Eggleston's strong interests in religion and in Indianian dialect, which are characteristic of the book as a whole.

Eggleston's best novels are *The Hoosier School-Master*, *The End of the World* (1872), *The Circuit Rider* (1874), *Roxy* (1878), *The Hoosier Schoolboy* (1883), and *The Graysons* (1888).

from THE HOOSIER SCHOOL-MASTER

CHAPTER 1

A PRIVATE LESSON FROM A BULLDOG

"Want to be a school-master, do you? You? Well, what would *you* do in Flat Crick deestrick, *I'd* like to know? Why, the boys have driv off the last two, and licked the one afore them like blazes. You might teach a summer school, when nothin' but children come. But I 'low it takes a right smart *man* to be school-master in Flat Crick in the winter. They'd pitch you out of doors, sonny, neck and heels, afore Christmas."

The young man, who had walked ten miles to get the school in this district, and who had been mentally reviewing his learning at every step he took, trembling lest the committee should find that he did not know enough, was not a little taken aback at this greeting from "old Jack Means," who was the first trustee that he lighted on. The impression made by these ominous remarks was emphasized by the glances which he received from Jack Means's two sons. The older one eyed him from the top of his brawny shoulders with that amiable look which a big dog turns on a little one before shaking him. Ralph Hartsook had never thought of being [9] measured by the standard of muscle. This notion of beating education into young savages in spite of themselves, dashed his ardor.

He had walked right to where Jack Means was at work shaving shingles in his own front yard. While Mr. Means was making the speech which we have set down above, and punctuating it with expectorations, a large brindle bull-dog had been sniffing at Ralph's heels, and a girl in a new linsey-woolsey dress, standing by the door, had nearly giggled her head off at the delightful prospect of seeing a new school-teacher eaten up by the ferocious brute.

Edward Eggleston, *The Hoosier School-Master* (New York: Orange Judd Company, 1892).

Between the disheartening words of the old man, the immense muscles of the young man who was to be his rebellious pupil, the jaws of the ugly bull-dog, and the heartless giggle of the girl, Ralph had a delightful sense of having precipitated himself into a den of wild beasts. Faint with weariness and discouragement, and shivering with fear, he sat down on a wheelbarrow.

"You, Bull!" said the old man to the dog, which was showing more and more a disposition to make a meal of the incipient pedagogue, "you, Bull! git aout, you pup!" The dog walked sullenly off, but not until he had given Ralph a look full of promise of what he meant to do when he got a good chance. Ralph wished himself back in the village of Lewisburg, whence he had come.

"You see," continued Mr. Means, spitting in a meditative sort of way, "you see, we a'n't none of you saft sort in these diggins. It takes a *man* to boss this deestrick. Howsumdever, ef you think you kin trust your hide in Flat Crick school-house I ha'n't got no 'bjection. But if you git licked don't come on us. Flat Crick don't pay no 'nsurance, you bet! Any other trustees? Wal, yes. But as I pay the most taxes, t'others jist let me [10] run the thing. You can begin right off a Monday. They a'n't been no other applications. You see it takes some grit to apply for this school. The last master had a black eye for a month. But, as I said, you can jist roll up and wade in. I 'low you've got pluck, may be, and that goes for a heap sight more'n sinnoo with boys. Walk in, and stay over Sunday with me. You'll hev to board roun', and I guess you better begin here."

Ralph did not go in, but sat out on the wheelbarrow, watching the old man shave shingles, while the boys split the blocks and chopped wood. Bull smelled of the new-comer again in an ugly way, and got a good kick from the older son for his pains. But out of one of his red eyes the dog warned the young school-master that *he* should yet suffer for all kicks received on his account.

"Ef Bull once takes a holt, heaven and yarth can't make him let go," said the older son to Ralph, by way of comfort.

It was well for Ralph that he began to "board roun'" by stopping at Mr. Means's. Ralph felt that Flat Creek was what he needed. He had lived a bookish life. But here was his lesson in the art of managing people. For who can manage the untamed and strapping youths of a winter school in Hoopole County has gone far toward learning one of the hardest of lessons. And twenty-five years ago, in Ralph's time, things were worse than they are now. The older son of Mr. Means was called Bud Means. What his real name was Ralph could not find out, for in many of these families the nickname of "Bud" given to the oldest boy, and that of "Sis" which is the birthright of the oldest girl, completely bury the proper Christian name. Ralph was a general. He saw his first strategic point, which was to capture Bud Means.

After supper the boys began to get ready for [12] something. Bull stuck up his ears in a dignified way, and the three or four yellow curs who were Bull's satellites yelped delightedly and discordantly.

"Bill," said Bud Means to his brother, "ax the master ef he'd like to hunt coons. I'd like to take the starch out uv the stuck-up fellow."

" 'Nough said," was Bill's reply.

"You durn't do it," said Bud.

"I don't take no sech a dare," returned Bill, and walked down to the gate, on which Ralph stood watching the stars come out, and wishing he had never seen Flat Creek.

"I say, mister," began Bill, "mister, they's a coon what's been a eatin' our chickens lately, and we're goin' to try ketch the varmint. You wouldn't like to take a coon hunt nor nothin', would you?"

"Why, yes," said Ralph, "there's nothing I should like better, if I could only be sure Bill wouldn't mistake me for the coon."

And so, as a matter of policy, Ralph dragged his tired legs eight or ten miles, on hill and in hollow, after Bud, and Bill, and Bull, and the coon. But the raccoon climbed a tree. The boys got into a quarrel about whose business it was to have brought the ax, and who was to blame that the tree could not be felled. Now, if there was anything Ralph's muscles were good for, it was to climb. So, asking Bud to give him a start, he soon reached the limb above the one on which the raccoon was. Ralph did not know how ugly a customer a raccoon can be, and so got credit for more courage than he had. With much peril to his legs from the raccoon's teeth, he succeeded in shaking the poor creature off among the yelping brutes and yelling boys. Ralph could not help sympathizing with the hunted animal, which sold its life as dearly as possible, giving the dogs [13] many a scratch and bit. It seemed to him that he was like the raccoon, precipitated into the midst of a party of dogs who would rejoice in worrying *his* life out, as Bull and his crowd were destroying the poor raccoon. When Bull at last seized the raccoon and put an end to it, Ralph could not but admire the decided way in which he did it, calling to mind Bud's comment: "Ef Bull once takes a holt, heaven and yarth can't make him let go."

But as they walked home, Bud carrying the raccoon by the tail, Ralph felt that his hunt had not been in vain. He fancied that even red-eyed Bull, walking uncomfortably close to his heels, respected him more since he had climbed that tree.

"Purty peart kind of a master," remarked the old man to Bud after Ralph had gone to bed. "Guess you better be a little easy on him. Hey?"

But Bud deigned no reply. Perhaps because he knew that Ralph heard the conversation through the thin partition.

Ralph woke delighted to find it raining. He did not want to hunt or fish on Sunday, and this steady rain would enable him to make friends with Bud. I do not know how he got started, but after breakfast he began to tell stories. Out of all the books he had ever read he told story after story. And "old man Means," and "old *Miss* Means," and Bud Means, and Bill Means, and Sis Means, listened with great eyes while he told of Sinbad's adventures, of the Old Man of the Sea, of Robinson Crusoe, of Captain Gulliver's experiences in Lilliput, and of Baron Munchausen's exploits.

Ralph had caught his fish. The hungry minds of these backwoods people, sick and dying of their own commonplace, were refreshed with the new life that came to their imaginations in these stories. For there was but one book in the Means library, and that, a well-thumbed copy of "Cap-[14]tain Riley's Narrative," had long since lost all freshness.

"I'll be dog-on'd," said Bill emphatically, "ef I hadn't ruther hear the master tell them whoppin' yarns, than to go to a circus the best day I ever seed!" Bill could pay no higher compliment.

What Ralph wanted was to make a friend of Bud. It's a nice thing to have the seventy-four-gun ship on your own side, and the more Hartsook admired the knotted muscles of Bud Means, the more he desired to attach him to himself. So, whenever he struck out a peculiarly brilliant passage, he anxiously watched Bud's eye. But the young Philistine kept his own counsel. He listened but said nothing, and the eyes under his shaggy brow gave no sign. Ralph could not tell whether those eyes were deep and inscrutable, or only stolid. Perhaps a little of both. When Monday morning came Ralph was nervous. He walked to school with Bud.

"I guess you're a little skeered by what the old man said, a'n't you?"

Ralph was about to deny it, but on reflection concluded that it was always best to speak the truth. He said that Mr. Means's description of the school had made him feel a little down-hearted.

"What will you do with the tough boys? You a'n't no match for 'em." And Ralph felt Bud's eyes not only measuring his muscles, but scrutinizing his countenance. He only answered:

"I don't know."

"What would you do with me, for instance?" and Bud stretched himself up as if to shake out the reserve power coiled up in his great muscles.

"I shan't have any trouble with you."

"Why, I'm the worst chap of all. I thrashed the last master myself."

And again the eyes of Bud Means looked out [15] sharply from his shadowing brows to see the effect of this speech on the slender young man.

"You won't thrash me, though," said Ralph.

"Pshaw! I 'low I could whip you in an inch of your life with my left hand and never half try," said young Means with a threatening sneer.

"I know that as well as you do."

"Well, a'n't you afraid of me then?" and again he looked sidewise at Ralph.

"Not a bit," said Ralph, wondering at his own courage.

They walked on in silence a minute. Bud was turning the matter over. "Why a'n't you afraid of me?" he said presently.

"Because you and I are going to be friends."

"And what about t'others?"

"I am not afraid of all the other boys put together."

"You a'n't! The mischief! How's that?"

"Well, I'm not afraid of them because you and I are going to be friends, and you can whip all of them together. You'll do the fighting and I'll do the teaching.

The diplomatic Bud only chuckled a ilttle at this; whether he assented to the alliance or not Ralph could not tell.

When Ralph looked round on the faces of the scholars—the little faces full of mischief and curiosity, the big faces full of an expression which was not further removed than second-cousin from contempt—when young Hartsook looked into these faces, his heart palpitated with stage-fright. There is no audience so hard to face as one of school-children, as many a man has found to his cost. Perhaps it is that no conventional restraint can keep down their laughter when you do or say anything ridiculous.

Hartsook's first day was hurried and unsatisfac-[16]tory. He was not master of himself, and consequently not master of anybody else. When evening came there were symptoms of insubordination through the whole school. Poor Ralph was sick at heart. He felt that if there had ever been the shadow of an alliance between himself and Bud, it was all "off" now. It seemed to Hartsook that even Bull had lost his respect for the teacher. Half that night the young man lay awake. At last comfort came to him. A reminiscence of the death of the raccoon flashed on him like a vision. He remembered that quiet and annihilating bite which Bull gave. He remembered Bud's certificate, that "Ef Bull once takes a holt, heaven and yarth can't make him let go." He thought that what Flat Creek needed was a bull-dog. He would be a bull-dog, quiet but invincible. He would take hold in such a way that nothing should make him let go. And then he went to sleep.

In the morning Ralph got out of bed slowly. He put his clothes on slowly. He pulled on his boots in a bull-dog mood. He tried to move as he thought Bull would move if he were a man. He ate with deliberation, and looked everybody in the eyes with a manner that made Bud watch him curiously. He found himself continually comparing himself with Bull. He found Bull possessing a strange fascination for him. He walked to school alone, the rest having gone on before. He entered the school-room preserving a cool and dogged manner. He saw in the eyes of the boys that there was mischief brewing. He did not dare sit down in his chair for fear of a pin. Everybody looked solemn. Ralph lifted the lid of his desk. "Bow-wow! wow-wow!" It was the voice of an imprisoned puppy, and the school giggled and then roared. Then everything was quiet. [17]

The scholars expected an outburst of wrath from the teacher. For they had come to regard the whole world as divided into two classes, the teacher on the one side representing lawful authority, and the pupils on the other in a state of chronic rebellion. To play a trick on the master was an evidence of spirit; to "lick" the master was to be the crowned hero of Flat Creek district. Such a hero was Bud Means, and Bill, who had less muscle, saw a chance to distinguish himself on a teacher of slender frame. Hence the puppy in the desk.

Ralph Hartsook grew red in the face when he saw the puppy. But the cool, repressed, bull-dog mood in which he had kept himself saved him. He lifted the dog into his arms and stroked him until the laughter subsided. Then, in a solemn and set way, he began:

"I am sorry," and he looked round the room with a steady, hard eye— everybody felt that there was a conflict coming—"I am sorry that any scholar in this school could be so mean"—the word was uttered with a sharp emphasis, and all the big boys felt sure that there would be a fight with Bill Means, and perhaps with Bud—"could be so *mean*—as to—shut up his *brother* in such a place as that!"

There was a long, derisive laugh. The wit was indifferent, but by one stroke Ralph had carried the whole school to his side. By the significant glances of the boys, Hartsook detected the perpetrator of the joke, and with the hard and dogged look in his eyes, with just such a look as Bull would give a puppy, but with the utmost suavity in his voice, he said:

"William Means, will you be so good as to put this dog out of doors?"
[18]

CHAPTER II

A SPELL COMING

There was a moment of utter stillness; but the magnetism of Ralph's eye was too much for Bill Means. The request was so polite, the master's look was so innocent and yet so determined. Bill often wondered afterward that he had not "fit" rather than obeyed the request. But somehow he put the dog out. He was partly surprised, partly inveigled, partly awed into doing just what he had not intended to do. In the week that followed, Bill had to fight half a dozen boys for calling him "Puppy Means." Bill said he wished he'd a licked the master on the spot. 'Twould 'a saved five fights out of the six.

And all that day and the next, the bull-dog in the master's eye was a terror to evil-doers. At the close of school on the second day Bud was heard to give it as his opinion that "the master wouldn't be much in a tussle, but he had a heap of thunder and lightning in him."

Did he inflict corporal punishment? inquires some philanthropic friend. Would you inflict corporal punishment if you were tiger-trainer in Van Amburgh's happy family? But poor Ralph could never satisfy his constituency in this regard.

"Don't believe he'll do," was Mr. Pete Jones's comment to Mr. Means. "Don't thrash enough. [19] Boys won't larn 'less you thrash 'em says I. Leastways, mine won't. Lay it on good, is what I says to a master. Lay it on good. Don't do no harm. Lickin' and larnin' goes together. No lickin', no larnin', says I. Lickin' and larnin', lickin' and larnin', is the good ole way."

And Mr. Jones, like some wiser people, was the more pleased with his formula that it had an alliterative sound. Nevertheless, Ralph was master from this time until the spelling-school came. If only it had not been for that spelling-school! Many and many a time after the night of the fatal spelling-school Ralph used to say: "If only it had not been for the spelling-school!"

There had to be a spelling-school. Not only for the sake of my story, which would not have been worth the telling if the spelling-school had not taken place, but because Flat Creek district had to have a spelling-school. It is the only public literary exercise known in Hoopole County. It takes the place of lyceum lecture and debating club. Sis Means, or, as she wishes now to be called, Mirandy Means, expressed herself most positively in favor of it. She said that she 'lowed the folks in that district couldn't in no wise do without it. But it was rather to its social than its intellectual benefits that she referred. For all the spelling-schools ever seen could not enable her to stand anywhere but at the foot of the class. There is one branch diligently taught in a backwoods school. The public mind seems impressed with the difficulties of English orthography, and there is a solemn conviction that the chief end of man is to learn to spell. " 'Know Webster's Elementary' came down from Heaven," would be the backwoods version of the Greek saying but that, unfortunately for the Greeks, their fame has not reached so far. It often happens [20] that the pupil does not know the meaning of a single word in the lesson. That is of no consequence. What do you want to know the meaning of a word for? Words were made to be spelled, and men were created that they might spell them. Hence the necessity for sending a pupil through the spelling-book five times before you allow him to begin to read, or indeed to do anything else. Hence the necessity for those long spelling-classes at the close of each forenoon and afternoon session of the school, to stand at the head of which is the cherished ambition of every scholar. Hence, too, the necessity for devoting the whole of the afternoon session of each Friday to a "spelling-match." In fact, spelling is the "national game" in Hoopole County. Baseball and croquet matches are as unknown as Olympian chariot-races. Spelling and shucking are the only public competitions.

So that the fatal spelling-school had to be appointed for the Wednesday of the second week of the session, just when Ralph felt himself master of the situation. Not that he was without his annoyances. One of Ralph's troubles in the week before the spelling-school was that he was loved. The other that he was hated. . . . [21]

CHAPTER XII

THE HARDSHELL PREACHER

"They's preachin' down to Bethel Meetin'-house to-day," said the Squire at breakfast. Twenty years in the West could not cure Squire Hawkins of saying "to" for "at." "I rather guess as how the old man Bosaw will give pertickeler fits to our folks to-day." For Squire Hawkins, having been expelled from the "Hardshell" church of which Mr. Bosaw was pastor, for the grave offense of joining a temperance society, had become a member of the "Reformers," the very respectable people who now call themselves "Disciples," but whom the profane will persist in calling "Campbellites." They had a church in the village of Clifty, three miles away.

I know that explanations are always abominable to story readers, as they are to story writers, but as so many of my readers have never had the inestimable privilege of sitting under the gospel as it is ministered in enlightened neighborhoods like Flat Creek, I find myself under the necessity—need-cessity the Rev. Mr. Bosaw would call it—of rising to explain. Some people think the "Hardshells" a myth, and some sensitive Baptist people at the East resent all allusion to them. But the "Hardshell Baptists," or, as they are otherwise called, the "Whisky Baptists," and the "Forty-gallon Baptists," exist in all the old Western and South-west-[97]ern States. They call themselves "Anti-means Baptists" from their Antinomian tenets. Their confession of faith is a caricature of Calvinism, and is expressed by their preachers about as follows: "Ef you're elected you'll be saved; ef you a'n't, you'll be damned. God'll take keer of his elect. It's a sin to run Sunday-schools, or temp'rince s'cieties, or to send missionaries. You let God's business alone. What is to be will be, and you can't hender it." This writer has attended a Sunday-school, the superintendent of which was solemnly arraigned and expelled from the Hardshell Church for "meddling with God's business" by holding a Sunday-school. Of course the Hardshells are prodigiously illiterate, and often vicious. Some of their preachers are notorious drunkards. They sing their sermons out sometimes for three hours at a stretch.

Ralph found that he was to ride the "clay-bank mare," the only one of the horses that would "carry double," and that consequently he would have to take Miss Hawkins behind him. If it had been Hannah instead, Ralph might not have objected to this "young Lochinvar" mode of riding with a lady on "the croup," but Martha Hawkins was another affair. He had only this consolation; his keeping the company of Miss Hawkins might serve to disarm the resentment of Bud. At all events, he had no choice. What designs the Squire had in this arrangement he could not tell; but at any rate the clay-bank mare carried him to meeting on that December morning, with Martha Hawkins behind. And as Miss Hawkins was not used to this mode of locomotion, she was in a state of delightful fright every time the horse sank to the knees in the soft, yellow Flat Creek clay.

"We don't go to church so at the East," she said. "The mud isn't so deep at the East. When I was to Bosting—" but Ralph never heard what [98] happened when she was to Bosting, for just as she said Bosting the mare put her foot into a deep hole molded by the foot of the Squire's horse, and already full of muddy water.

As the mare's foot went twelve inches down into this track, the muddy water spurted higher than Miss Hawkins's head, and mottled her dress with golden spots of clay. She gave a little shriek, and declared that she had never "seen it so at the East."

The journey seemed a little long to Ralph, who found that the subjects upon which he and Miss Hawkins could converse were few; but Miss Martha was determined to keep things going, and once, when the conversation had died out entirely, she made a desperate effort to renew it by remarking, as they met a man or horseback, "That horse switches his tail just as they do at the East. When I was to Bosting I saw horses switch their tails just that way."

What surprised Ralph was to see that Flat Creek went to meeting. Everybody was there—the Meanses, the Joneses, the Bantas, and all the rest. Everybody on Flat Creek seemed to be there, except the old wooden-legged basket-maker. His family was represented by Shocky, who had come, doubtless, to get a glimpse of Hannah, not to hear Mr. Bosaw preach. In fact, few were thinking of the religious service. They went to church as a common resort to hear the news, and find out what was the current sensation.

On this particular morning there seemed to be some unusual excitement. Ralph perceived it as he rode up. An excited crowd, even though it be at a church-door on Sunday morning, can not conceal its agitation. Ralph deposited Miss Hawkins on the stile, and then got down himself, and paid her the closest attention to the door. This atten-[99]tion was for Bud's benefit. But Bud only stood with his hands in his pockets, scowling worse than ever. Ralph did not go in at the door. It was not the Flat Creek custom. The men gossiped outside, while the women chatted within. Whatever may have been the cause of the excitement, Ralph could not get at it. When he entered a little knot of people they became embarrassed, and the group dissolved itself, and its component parts joined other companies. What had the current of conversation to do with him? He overheard Pete Jones saying that the blamed old wooden leg was in it anyhow. He'd been seen goin' home at two in the mornin'. And he could name somebody else ef he choosed. But it was best to clean out one at a time. And just then there was a murmur: "Meetin's took up." And the masculine element filled the empty half of the "hewed-log" church.

When Ralph saw Hannah looking utterly dejected, his heart smote him, and the great struggle set in again. Had it not been for the thought of the other battle, and the comforting presence of the Helper, I fear Bud's interests would have fared badly. But Ralph, with the spirit of a martyr, resolved to wait until he knew what the result of Bud's suit should be, and whether, indeed, the young Goliath had prior claims, as he evidently thought he had. He turned hopefully to the sermon, determined to pick up any crumbs of comfort that might fall from Mr. Bosaw's meager table.

In reporting a single specimen passage of Mr. Bosaw's sermon, I shall not take the liberty which Thucydides and other ancient historians did, of making the sermon and putting it in the hero's mouth, but shall give that which can be vouched for.

"You see, my respective hearers," he began—but [100] alas! I can never picture to you the rich red nose, the see sawing gestures, the nasal resonance, the sniffle, the melancholy minor key, and all that. "My respective hearers-ah, you see-ah as how-ah as my tex'-ah says that the ox-ah knoweth his owner-ah, and-ah the ass-ah his master's crib-ah. A-h-h! Now, my respective hearers-ah, they're a mighty sight of resemblance-ah atwext men-ah and oxen-ah" [Ralph could not help reflecting that there was a mighty sight of resemblance between some men and asses. But the preacher did not see this analogy. It lay too close to him], "bekase-ah, you see, men-ah is mighty like oxen-ah. For they's a tremengious defference-ah atwixt defferent oxen-ah, jest as thar is atwext defferent men-ah; fer the ox knoweth-ah his owner-ah, and the ass-ah, his master's crib-ah. Now, my respective hearers-ah" [the preacher's voice here grew mellow, and the succeeding sentences were in the most pathetic and lugubrious voice], "you all know-ah that your humble speaker-ah has got-ah jest the best yoke of steers-ah in the township-ah." [Here Betsey Short shook the floor with a suppressed titter.] "They a'n't no sech steers as them air two of mine-ah in this whole kedentry-ah. Them crack oxen over at Clifty-ah ha'n't a patchin' to mine'-ah. Fer the ox knoweth his owner-ah, and the ass-ah his master's crib-ah.

"Now, my respective hearers-ah, they's a right smart sight of defference-ah atwext them air two oxen-ah, jest like they is atwext defferent men-ah. Fer-ah" [here the speaker grew earnest, and sawed the air, from this to the close, in a most frightful way], "fer-ah, you see-ah, when I go out-ah in the mornin'-ah to yoke-ah up-ah them steers-ah, and I says-ah, 'Wo, Berry-ah! *Wo, Berry-ah!* Wo, BERRY-AH!' why Berry-ah jest stands stock still-ah and don't hardly breath-ah while I put on the yoke-[101]ah, and put in the bow-ah, and put in the key-ah, fer, my brethering-ah and sistering-ah, the ox knoweth his owner-ah, and the ass-ah his master's crib-ah. Hal-le-lu-ger-ah!

"But-ah, my hearers-ah, but-ah when I stand at t'other eend of the yoke-ah, and say, 'Come, Buck-ah! *Come, Buck-ah!* COME, BUCK-AH! COME, BUCK-AH!' why what do you think-ah? Buck-ah, that ornery ole Buck-ah, 'stid of comin' right along-ah and puttin' his neck under-ah, acts jest like some men-ah what is fools-ah. Buck-ah jest kinder [102] sorter stands off-ah, and kinder sorter puts his head down-ah this ere way-ah, and kinder looks mad-ah, and says, Boo-*oo*-oo-OO-*ah!*"

Alas! Hartsook found no spiritual edification there, and he was in no mood to be amused. And so, while the sermon drew on through two dreary hours, he forgot the preacher in noticing a bright green lizard which, having taken up its winter quarters behind the tin candlestick that hung just back of the preacher's head, had been deceived by the genial warmth coming from the great box-stove, and now ran out two or three feet from his shelter, looking down upon the red-nosed preacher in a most confidential and amusing manner. Sometimes he would retreat behind the candlestick, which was not twelve inches from the preacher's head, and then rush out again. At each reappearance Betsey Short would stuff her handkerchief into her mouth and shake in a most distressing way. Shocky wondered what the lizard was winking at the preacher about. And Miss Martha thought that it reminded her of a lizard that she see at the East, the time she was to Bosting, in a jar of alcohol in the Natural History Rooms. The Squire was not disappointed in his anticipation that Mr. Bosaw would attack his denomination with some fury. In fact, the old preacher outdid himself in his violent indignation at "these people that follow Campbell-ah, that thinks-ah that obejience-ah will save 'em-ah, and that belongs-ah to temp'rince societies-ah and Sunday-schools-ah, and them air things-ah, that's not ortherized in the Bible-ah, but comes of the devil-ah, and takes folks as belongs to 'em to hell-ah."

As they came out the door Ralph rallied enough to remark: "He did attack your people, Squire."

"Oh! yes," said the Squire. "Didn't you see the Sarpent inspirin' him?" [103]

But when the long, long hours were ended Ralph got on the clay-bank mare and rode up alongside the stile whence Miss Martha mounted. And as he went away with a heavy heart, he overheard Pete Jones call out to somebody:

"We'll tend to his case a Christmas." Christmas was two days off.

And Miss Martha remarked with much trepidation that poor Pearson would have to leave. She'd always been afraid that would be the end of it. It reminded her of something she heard at the East the time she was down to Bosting.[104]

CHAPTER XVI

THE CHURCH MILITANT

Bud was doubly enlisted on the side of John Pearson, the basket-maker. In the first place, he knew that this persecution of the unpopular old man was only a blind to save somebody else; that they were thieves who cried "Stop thief!" And he felt consequently that this was a chance to put his newly-formed resolutions into practice. The Old Testament religious life, which consists in fighting the Lord's enemies, suited Bud's temper and education. It might lead to something better. It was the best possible to him, now. But I am afraid I shall have to acknowledge that there was a second motive that moved Bud to this championship. The good heart of Martha Hawkins having espoused the cause of the basket-maker, the heart of Bud Means could not help feeling warmly on the same side. Blessed is that man in whose life the driving of duty and the drawing of love impel the same way! But why speak of the driving of duty? For already Bud was learning the better lesson of serving God for the love of God.

The old basket-maker was the most unpopular man in Flat Creek district. He had two great vices. He would go to Clifty and have a "spree" once in three months. And he would tell the truth in a most unscrupulous manner. A man given to plain speak-[122]ing was quite as objectionable in Flat Creek as he would have been in France under the Empire, the Commune, or the Republic, and almost as objectionable as he would be in any refined community in America. People who live in glass houses have a horror of people who throw stones. And the old basket-maker, having no friends, was a good scape-goat. In driving him off, Pete Jones would get rid of a dangerous neighbor and divert attention from himself. The immediate crime of the basket-maker was that he had happened to see too much.

"Mr. Hartsook," said Bud, when they got out into the road, "you'd better go straight home to the Squire's. Bekase ef this lightnin' strikes a second time it'll strike awful closte to you. You hadn't better be seen with us. Which way did you come, Shocky?"

"Why, I tried to come down the holler, but I met Jones right by the big road, and he sweared at me and said he'd kill me ef I didn't go back and stay. And so I went back to the house and then slipped out through the graveyard. You see I was bound to come ef I got skinned. For Mr. Pearson's stuck to me and I mean to stick to him, you see."

Bud led Shocky through the graveyard. But when they reached the forest path from the graveyard he thought that perhaps it was not best to "show his hand," as he expressed it, too soon.

"Now, Shocky," he said, "do you run ahead and tell the ole man that I want to see him right off down by the Spring-in-rock. I'll keep closte behind you, and ef anybody offers to trouble you, do you let off a yell and I'll be thar in no time."

When Ralph left the school-house he felt mean. There were Bud and Shocky gone on an errand of mercy, and he, the truant member of the Church of the Best Licks, was not with them. The more he [123] thought of it the more he seemed to be a coward, and the more he despised himself; so, yielding as usual to the first brave impulse, he leaped nimbly over the fence and started briskly through the forest in a direction intersecting the path on which were Bud and Shocky. He came in sight just in time to see the first conflict of the Church in the Wilderness with her foes.

For Shocky's little feet went more swiftly on their eager errand than Bud anticipated. He got farther out of Bud's reach than the latter intended he should, and he did not discover Pete Jones until Pete, with his hog-drover's whip, was right upon him.

Shocky tried to halloo for Bud, but he was like one in a nightmare. The yell died into a whisper which could not have been heard ten feet.

I shall not repeat Mr. Jones's words. They were frightfully profane. But he did not stop at words. He swept his whip round and gave little Shocky one terrible cut. Then the voice was released, and the piercing cry of pain brought Bud down the path flying.

"You good-for-nothing scoundrel," growled Bud, "you're a coward and a thief to be a-beatin' a little creetur like him!" and with that Bud walked up on Jones, who prudently changed position in such a way as to get the upper side of the hill.

"Well, I'll gin you the upper side, but come on," cried Bud, "ef you a'n't afeared to fight somebody besides a poor, little, sickly baby or a crippled soldier. Come on!"

Pete was no insignificant antagonist. He had been a great fighter, and his well-seasoned arms were like iron. He had not the splendid set of Bud, but he had more skill and experience in the rude tournament of fists to which the backwoods is so [124] much given. Now, being out of sight of witnesses and sure that he could lie about the fight afterwards, he did not scruple to take advantages which would have disgraced him forever if he had taken them in [125] a public fight on election day or at a muster. He took the uphill side, and he clubbed his whip-stalk, striking Bud with all his force with the heavy end, which, coward-like, he had loaded with lead. Bud threw up his strong left arm and parried the blow, which, however, was so fierce that it fractured one of the bones of the arm. Throwing away his whip Pete rushed upon Bud furiously, intending to overpower him, but Bud slipped quickly to one side and let Jones pass down the hill, and as Jones came up again Means dealt him one crushing blow that sent him full length upon the ground. Nothing but the leaves saved him from a most terrible fall. Jones sprang to his feet more angry than ever at being whipped by one whom he regarded as a boy, and drew a long dirk-knife.

But he was blind with rage, and Bud dodged the knife, and this time gave Pete a blow on the nose which marred the homeliness of that feature, and doubled the fellow up against a tree ten feet away.

Ralph came in sight in time to see the beginning of the fight, and he arrived on the ground just as Pete Jones went down under the well-dealt blow from the only remaining fist of Bud Means.

While Ralph tied up Bud's disabled left arm Pete picked himself up slowly, and, muttering that he felt "consid'able shuck up like," crawled away like a whipped puppy. To every one whom he met, Pete, whose intellect seemed to have weakened in sympathy with his frame, remarked feebly that he was consid'able shuck up like, and vouchsafed no other explanation. Even to his wife he only said that he felt purty consid'able shuck up like, and that the boys would have to get on to-night without him. There are some scoundrels whose very malignity is shaken out of them for the time being by a thorough drubbing. [126]

"I'm afraid you're going to have trouble with your arm, Bud," said Ralph tenderly.

"Never mind; I put in my best licks fer *Him,* that air time, Mr. Hartsook." Ralph shivered a little at thought of this, but if it was right to knock Jones down at all, why might not Bud do it "heartily as unto the Lord"?

Gideon did not feel any more honest pleasure in chastising the Midianites than did Bud in sending Pete Jones away purty consid'able shuck up like. [127]

CHAPTER XXI

MISS NANCY SAWYER

In a little old cottage in Lewisburg, on one of the streets which was never traveled except by a solitary cow seeking pasture or a countryman bringing wood to some one of the half-dozen families living in it, and which in summer was decked with a profusion of the yellow and white blossoms of the dog-fennel—in this unfrequented street, so generously and unnecessarily broad, lived Miss Nancy Sawyer and her younger sister Semantha. Miss Nancy was a providence, one of those old maids that are benedictions to the whole town; one of those in whom the mother-love, wanting the natural objects on which to spend itself, overflows all bounds and lavishes itself on every needy thing, and grows richer and more abundant with the spending, a fountain of inexhaustible blessing. There is no nobler life possible to any one than to an unmarried woman. The more shame that some choose a selfish one, and thus turn to gall all the affection with which they are endowed. Miss Nancy Sawyer had been Ralph's Sunday-school teacher, and it was precious little, so far as information went, that he learned from her; for she never could conceive of Jerusalem as a place in any essential regard very different from Lewisburg, where she had spent her life. But Ralph learned [147] from her what most Sunday-school teachers fail to teach, the great lesson of Christianity, by the side of which all antiquities and geographies and chro-[148]nologies and exegetics and other niceties are as nothing.

And now he turned the head of the roan toward the cottage of Miss Nancy Sawyer as naturally as the roan would have gone to his own stall in the stable at home. The snow had gradually ceased to fall, and was eddying round the house, when Ralph dismounted from his foaming horse, and, carrying the still form of Shocky as reverently as though he had been something heavenly, knocked at Miss Nancy Sawyer's door.

With natural feminine instinct that lady started back when she saw Hartsook, for she had just built a fire in the stove, and she now stood at the door with unwashed face and uncombed hair.

"Why, Ralph Hartsook, where did you drop down from—and what have you got?"

"I came from Flat Creek this morning, and I brought you a little angel who has got out of heaven, and needs some of your motherly care."

Shocky was brought in. The chill shook him now by fits only, for a fever had spotted his cheeks already.

"Who are you?" said Miss Nancy, as she unwrapped him.

"I'm Shocky, a little boy as God forgot, and then thought of again." [149]

E. W. HOWE
1853–1937

A New Look
at the Frontier

from

THE STORY
OF A COUNTRY TOWN

E. W. Howe's *The Story of a Country Town* (1882) is more important for its sociological implications than for its literary merits. Its style and structural weaknesses greatly lessen any emotional or intellectual impact it might have on the reader. Howe's view of pioneer life in the frontier small town is not the romantic view of James Fennimore Cooper, on whose frontier man can prove himself through heroic action. Howe pictures the pioneer as depressed and defeated by the conditions imposed upon him by his environment. The people in his novel lead unrewarding lives and, for the most part, become mean, narrow, discontented, or complacent.

Howe's view that agrarian and village society contains the same vices and weaknesses found in urban society is a break from the then existing myth of the innocence and rejuvenating quality of life that supposedly existed the farther one got from the city, and it looks ahead to such writers as Edgar Lee Masters, Sherwood Anderson, Sinclair Lewis, and, more recently, Grace Metalious and James Gould Cozzens.

Three social groups placed in juxtaposition from the social milieu of Howe's novel—the farm community of Fairview and the surrounding territory, the country town of Twin Mounds, and an imagined eastern genteel society which frequently influences or measures the actions of the people in the frontier communities. The brief excerpts that follow describe the two pioneer settlements and give clear details of the religious experience there. The story is narrated by young Ned Westlock, whose father is a

minister in Fairview who moves to Twin Mounds to become editor of
its newspaper. Throughout the novel Howe exposes a great number of
skeletons in the closet, but the most shattering revelation, for Ned at least,
is that the Reverend Westlock, while for eight years preaching against sin,
had been sporting with the widow Mrs. Tremaine.

Howe, a newspaper editor by profession, is known today for the novel
excerpted here, which was his first novel and one of the earliest examples
of realism in American fiction. He wrote other, trivial novels as well as
several collections of editorials and aphorisms, including *Country Town
Sayings* (1911) and *The Anthology of Another Town* (1920).

from THE STORY
OF A COUNTRY TOWN

CHAPTER I

FAIRVIEW

Ours was the prairie district out West, where we had gone to grow up
with the country.

I believe that nearly every farmer for miles around moved to the
neighborhood at the same time, and that my father's wagons headed the
procession. I have heard that most of them gathered about him on the way,
and as he preached from his wagon wherever night overtook him, and held
camp meetings on Sundays, he attracted a following of men traveling the
same road who did not know themselves where they were going, although
a few of the number started with him, among them my mother's father
and his family. When he came to a place that suited him, he picked out
the land he wanted—which any man was free to do at that time—and the
others settled about him.

In the dusty tramp of civilization westward—which seems to have
always been justified by a tradition that men grow up by reason of it—
our section was not a favorite, and remained new and unsettled after countries and States farther west had grown old. Every one who came there
seemed favorably impressed with the steady fertility of the soil, and expressed surprise that the lands were not all occupied; but no one in the
great outside [1] world talked about it, and no one wrote about it, so that
those who were looking for homes went to the West or the North, where
others were going.

There were cheap lands farther on, where the people raised a crop

E. W. Howe, *The Story of a Country Town* (Boston: Houghton Mifflin Company, 1882).

one year, and were supported by charity the next; where towns sprang up on credit, and farms were opened with borrowed money; where the people were apparently content, for our locality did not seem to be far enough west, nor far enough north, to suit them; where no sooner was one stranger's money exhausted than another arrived to take his place; where men mortgaged their possessions at full value, and thought themselves rich, notwithstanding, so great was their faith in the country; where he who was deepest in debt was the leading citizen, and where bankruptcy caught them all at last. On these lands the dusty travelers settled, where there were churches, schoolhouses, and bridges—but little rain—and railroads to carry out the crops should any be raised; and when anyone stopped in our neighborhood, he was too poor and tired to follow the others.

I became early impressed with the fact that our people seemed to be miserable and discontented, and frequently wondered that they did not load their effects on wagons again, and move away from a place which made all the men surly and rough, and the women pale and fretful. Although I had never been to the country they had left, except as a baby in arms, I was unfavorably impressed with it, thinking it must have been a very poor one that such a lot of people left it and considered their condition bettered by the change, for they never talked of going back, and were therefore probably better satisfied than they had ever been before. A road ran by our house, and when I first began to think about it at all, I thought that [2] the covered wagons traveling it carried people moving from the country from which those in our neighborhood came, and the wagons were so numerous that I was led to believe that at least half the people of the world had tried to live there, and moved away after an unfortunate experience.

On the highest and bleakest point in the county, where the winds were plenty in winter because they were not needed, and scarce in summer for an opposite reason, the meeting-house was built, in a corner of my father's field. This was called Fairview, and so the neighborhood was known. There was a graveyard around it, and cornfields next to that, but not a tree or shrub attempted its ornament, and as the building stood on the main road where the movers' wagons passed, I thought that, next to their ambition to get away from the country which had been left by those in Fairview, the movers were anxious to get away from Fairview church, and avoid the possibility of being buried in its ugly shadow, for they always seemed to drive faster after passing it.

High up in a steeple which rocked with every wind was a great bell, the gift of a missionary society, and when there was a storm this tolled with fitful and uncertain strokes, as if the ghosts from the grave lot had crawled up there, and were counting the number to be buried the coming year, keeping the people awake for miles around. Sometimes, when the wind was particularly high, there were a great number of strokes on the bell in quick succession, which the pious said was an alarm to the wicked, sounded by the devil, a warning relating to the conflagration which could never be put out, else Fairview would never have been built.

When anyone died it was the custom to toll the bell once for every year of the deceased's age, and as deaths [3] usually occur at night, we were frequently wakened from sleep by its deep and solemn tones. When I was yet a very little boy I occasionally went with my father to toll the bell when news came that someone was dead, for we lived nearer the place than any of the others, and when the strokes ran up to forty and fifty it was very dreary work, and I sat alone in the church wondering who would ring for me, and how many strokes could be counted by those who were shivering at home in their beds.

The house was built the first year of the settlement, and the understanding was that my father contributed the little money necessary, and superintended the work, in which he was assisted by anyone who volunteered his labor. It was his original intention to build it alone, and the little help he received only irritated him, as it was not worth the boast that he had raised to temple to the Lord single-handed. All the carpenter's work, and all the plasterer's work, he performed without assistance except from members of his own household, but I believe the people turned out to the raising, and helped put up the frames.

Regularly after its completion he occupied the rough pulpit (which he built with especial reference to his own size), and every Lord's Day morning and evening preached a religion to the people which I think added to their other discomforts, for it was hard and unforgiving. There were two or three kinds of Baptists among the people of Fairview when the house was completed, and a few Presbyterians, but they all became Methodists without revolt or question when my father announced in his first preaching that Fairview would be of that denomination.

He did not solicit them to join him, though he probably intimated in a way which admitted of no discussion that the few heretics yet remaining out in the world had better [4] save themselves before it was too late. It did not seem to occur to him that men and women who had grown up in a certain faith renounced it with difficulty; it was enough that they were wrong, and that he was forgiving enough to throw open the doors of the accepted church. If they were humiliated, he was glad of it, for that was necessary to condone their transgression; if they had arguments to excuse it, he did not care to hear them, as he had taken God into partnership, and built Fairview, and people who worshiped there would be expected to throw aside all doctrinal nonsense. . . . [5] . . .

The only remarkable thing I ever did in my life—I may [7] as well mention it here, and be rid of it—was to learn to read letters when I was five years old, and as the ability to read even print was by no means a common accomplishment in Fairview, this circumstance gave me great notoriety. I no doubt learned to read from curiosity as to what the books and papers scattered about were for, as no one took the pains to teach me, for I remember that they were all greatly surprised when I began to spell words, and pronounce them, and yet I am certain I was never encouraged in it. . . . [8] . . .

The house where we lived, and into which we moved on the day when my recollection begins, was the largest in the settlement; a square house of two stories, painted so white that after night it looked like a ghost. It was built on lower ground than Fairview church, though the location was sightly, and not far away ran a stream fringed with thickets of brush, where I found the panting cattle and sheep on hot days, and thought they gave me more of a welcome than my father and Jo did in the field; for [10] they were not busy, but idle like me, and I hoped it was rather a relief to them to look at me in mild-eyed wonder.

Beyond the little stream and the pasture was the great dusty road, and in my loneliness I often sat on the high fence beside it to watch for the coming of the movers' wagons, and to look curiously at those stowed away under the cover bows, tumbled together with luggage and effects of every kind. If one of the drivers asked me how far it was to the country town I supposed he had heard of my wonderful learning, and took great pains to describe the road, as I had heard my father do a hundred times in response to similar inquiries from movers. Sometimes I climbed up to the driver's seat, and drove with him out to the prairie, and I always noticed that the women and children riding behind were poorly dressed, and tired-looking, and I wondered if only the unfortunate traveled our way, for only that kind of people lived in Fairview, and I had never seen any other kind in the road.

When I think of the years I lived in Fairview, I imagine that the sun was never bright there (although I am certain that it was), and I cannot relieve my mind of the impression that the cold, changing shadow of the gray church has spread during my long absence and enveloped all the houses where the people lived. When I see Fairview in my fancy now, it is always from a high place, and looking down upon it, the shadow is denser around the house where I lived than anywhere else, so that I feel to this day that should I visit it, and receive permission from the new owners to walk through the rooms, I should find the walls damp and mouldy because the bright sun and the free air of Heaven had deserted them as a curse. [11]

CHAPTER IV

THE RELIGION OF FAIRVIEW

Although the people of Fairview frequently did not dress comfortably, and lived in the plainest manner, they never failed to attend the services at the church, to which everybody belonged, with the exception of my grandfather, and Jo, and myself. I have often wondered since that we were not made the subject of a special series of meetings, and frightened into repentance; but for some unaccountable reason we were left alone. They even discussed Jo's situation, laying it to contrariness, and saying that if all the rest of them were wicked, he would be religious; but they said nothing at all to me about the subject. I often attended the revivals, and sang the songs as loudly as the rest of them, but when I thought that I was one of those whose terrible condition the hymns described, it gave me such a turn that I left that part of the house where the excitement ran highest, and joined Jo on the back seats, who took no other interest in the novel performance than that of looker-on.

As soon as a sufficient number of children reached a suitable age to make their conversion a harvest, a revival was commenced for their benefit, and they were called upon to make a full confession with such energy, and warned to cling to the cross for safety with such earnestness, that they generally did it, and but few escaped. If there was one so stubborn that he would not yield from [32] worldly pride, of which he had not a particle— no one ever supposed it possible that he lacked faith, though they all did—the meetings were continued from Sunday until Monday, and kept up every night of the week at the house where the owner of the obdurate heart lived, so that he finally gave in; for peace and quiet, if for nothing else.

If two or three, or four or five, would not relent within a reasonable time, the people gave up every other work, and gathered at the church in great alarm, in response to the ringing of the bell, and there they prayed and shouted the livelong day for the Lord to come down among them. At these times Jo and I were usually left at home to work in the field, and if we heard the people coming home in the evening shouting and singing, we knew that the lost sheep had been recovered, and I often feared they would form a ring around us in the field, and compel a full surrender. A young woman who lived at our house to help my mother, the daughter of a neighboring farmer, once engaged their attention for nearly a week, but she gave up one hot afternoon, and came down the path which led through the cornfields from the church shouting and going on like mad, followed by those that had been present when the Lord finally came down, who were singing and proclaiming the event as loudly as they could. This frightened me so much that I ran into the house, and hid under the bed, supposing they would soon go away, and that then I could come out; but they immediately began a prayer-meeting to give the new convert opportunity to face a frowning world by relating her experience, and thus they kept me in my uncomfortable position until I thought I must smother from the heat.

My father received little aid in the conduct of these meetings except from a very good farmer, but very bad [33] exhorter, named Theodore

Meek, whose name had been gradually shortened by neighborhood familiarity until he was known as The. Meek; and for a long time I thought he was meant when reference was made to "The Meek and lowly," supposing that Lowly was an equally good man living in some of the adjoining settlements. This remarkable man laughed his religion rather than preached, or prayed, or shouted, or sang it. His singing would be regarded at this day as a very expert rendering or a laughing song, but to us it was an impressive performance, as were his praying and occasional preaching, though I wonder we were not amused. The. Meek was, after my father, the next best man in Fairview; the next largest farmer, and the next in religion and thrift. In moving to the country I think his wagons were next to ours, which headed the procession. He sat nearest the pulpit at the meetings, was the second to arrive—my father coming first—and always took up the collections. If there was a funeral, he stood next my father, who conducted the services; at the school-meetings he was the second to speak; and if a widow needed her corn gathered, or her winter's wood chopped, my father suggested it, and The. Meek immediately said it should have been attended to before. He also lived nearer our house than any of the others, and was oftener there; and his house was built so much like ours that only experts knew it was cheaper, and not quite so large. His family, which consisted of a fat wife by a second marriage, and so many children that I never could remember all of their names—there was always a new baby whenever its immediate predecessor was old enough to name—were laughers like him, and to a stranger it would have seemed that they found jokes in the Bible, for they were always reading the Bible, and always laughing. [34]

Another assistant was Mrs. Tremaine, the miller's widowed sister, who had lived in the country before we came, a waxed-faced woman who apparently had no other duty to attend to than religion; for although she lived a considerable distance from Fairview church, she was always at the meetings, and I have thought of her as being constantly occupied in coming from or going to church, finding it time to start back again as soon as she reached home. The only assistance she afforded was to pray whenever called upon in a voice so low that there was always doubt when she had finished; but this made little difference, as it gave the others opportunity to be heard in short exclamations concerning the kindness of the Lord if sinners would really renounce the world and make a full confession. Her speeches in the experience meetings were of the same order, and when she sat down the congregation invariably began a song descriptive of a noble woman always battling for the right, and sure to conquer in the end; from which grew an impression that she was a very sainted person, and that the sins of her brother, the miller, were much on her mind. It is certain that he thought little of them himself, never attending the services, or sending his regrets.

It was usually a part of my duty on Sunday to take one of the wagons,

Jo taking the other, and to drive about collecting infirm and unfortunate people who would otherwise be unable to attend church; for my father believed in salvation for all who were willing to accept it, though they were poor, and unable to walk, or hear, or see, or understand; and he was kinder to the unfortunate people than to any of the others, favoring them out of his strength and abundance in a hundred ways.

There was always a suspicion in my mind, which may have been an unjust one, that they shouted and went on [35] in response to his preaching because he was their friend, and wanted them to do so. In any event, he could throw them into the greatest excitement, and cause them to exhibit themselves in the most remarkable way, whenever he saw fit, so that they got on very well together.

One of these unfortunates was Mr. Winter, the lame shoemaker, who wheeled himself around in a low buggy. Pushing this into my wagon with the assistance of his wife, after we had first made a run-way of boards, I hauled him to Fairview, where we unloaded him in the same manner. He was a very devout man, and a shouter, and during the revivals he wheeled himself up and down the aisles in his buggy, which frequently squeaked and rattled in a very uncomfortable manner, to shake hands with the people. I suppose that at first this performance was a little odd to people, but they got used to it; for I have noticed that while strangers regarded Mr. Winter as a great curiosity, he attracted no more attention at home than a man unobjectionable in the matter of legs. There was a good deal of talk from time to time of holding special services to restore Mr. Winter's shrivelled legs by prayer, but if ever it was tried, it was in secret, for I never heard of it. There were probably half a dozen of these unfortunates altogether, and they were always given the best corner, which was near the pulpit, where their piety could be easily seen and heard.

With the addition of a blind woman who cried and lamented a great deal, and whom I also went after nearly every Sunday, those I have mentioned were the ones most conspicuous in the meetings; for while the others were very devout, they had nothing to offer for the general good except their presence and a capacity to rise to their feet and confess the Lord in a few words. My father was the leader, of course, and occupied the time [36] himself when others could not be induced to occupy it, which was often the case after those I have mentioned had appeared in what might be called their specialties.

This, coupled with the unforgiving doctrines of Rev. John Westlock, was the religion to which I was accustomed, and which I believe added greatly to the other miseries of Fairview, for Fairview was afflicted with a melancholy that could have resulted from nothing else. There was little visiting, and there were no public gatherings except those at the church already mentioned, where the business of serving the Lord was dispatched as soon as possible to allow the people to return home and nurse their misery. The people were all overworked, and I still remember how the pale, unhappy women spoke in low and trembling tones at the experience meetings of heavy crosses to bear, and sat down crying as though their hearts were breaking. I was always touched by this pitiful proceeding, and I doubt not their petitions went further into heaven than any of the others. [37]

CHAPTER XVI

MORE OF THE VILLAGE OF TWIN MOUNDS

In Twin Mounds the citizens spent their idle time in religious discussions, and although I lived there a great many years I do not remember that any of the questions in dispute were ever settled. They never discussed politics with any animation, and read but little, except in the Bible to find points to dispute; but of religion they never tired, and many of them could quote the sacred word by the page. No two of them ever exactly agreed in their ideas, for men who thought alike on baptism violently quarreled when the resurrection was mentioned, and two of them who engaged a hell-redemptionist one night would in all probability fail to agree themselves the next, on the atonement. The merchants neglected their customers, when they had them, to discuss points in the Bible which I used to think were not of the slightest consequence, and in many instances the men who argued the most were those who chased deer with hounds on Sunday, and ran horse races, for they did not seem to discuss the subject so much on account of its importance as because of its fitness as a topic to quarrel about.

There was always a number of famous discussions going on, as between the lawyer and the storekeeper, or the blacksmith and the druggist, or the doctor and the carpenter, and whenever I saw a crowd gathering hurriedly in the evening I knew that two of the disputants had got together again to renew their old difficulty, which they [165] kept up until a late hour, in the presence of half the town.

There was a certain man who kept a drug store, who was always in nervous excitement from something a fat blacksmith had said to him in their discussions, and who had a habit of coming in on him suddenly in the middle of the day; and whenever I went into the place of business of either one of them I heard them telling those present how they had triumphed the night before, or intended to triumph on a future occasion. Some of the greatest oaths I have ever heard were uttered by these men while discussing religion, and frequently the little and nervous drug-store-keeper had to be forcibly prevented from jumping at his burly opponent and striking him. The drug store was not far away from the office where I worked, and whenever loud and boisterous talking was heard in that direction a smile went round, for we knew the blacksmith had suddenly come upon his enemy, and attacked him with something he had thought up while at his work. I never knew exactly what the trouble between them was, though I heard enough of it; but I remembered that it had some reference to a literal resurrection, and a new body; and I often thought it queer that each one was able to take the Bible and establish his position so clearly. Whenever I heard the blacksmith talk I was sure that the druggist was wrong, but when the druggist called upon the blacksmith to stop right there, and began his argument, I became convinced that, after all, there were two sides to the question.

These two men, as well as most of the others, were members of a church known then as the Campbellite, for I do not remember that there was an infidel or unbeliever in the place. There were a great many backsliders, but none of them ever questioned religion itself, though [166] they could never agree on doctrine. It has occurred to me since that if one of them had thought to dispute the inspiration of the Bible, and argued about that, the people would have been entirely happy, for the old discussions in time became very tiresome.

The people regarded religion as a struggle between the Campbellite church and the Devil, and a sensation was developed one evening when my father remarked to the druggist, in the presence of the usual crowd— he happened to be in the place on an errand, as he never engaged in the amusement of the town—that sprinkling answered every purpose of baptism. The druggist became very much excited immediately and prepared for a discussion, but my father only laughed at him and walked away. The next Sunday, however, he preached a sermon on the subject in the courthouse, and attacked the town's religion with so much vigor that the excitement was very intense.

Most of the citizens of Twin Mounds came from the surrounding country, and a favorite way of increasing the population was to elect the county officers from the country, but after their terms expired a new set moved in, for it was thought they became so corrupt by a two years' residence that they could not be trusted to a re-election. The town increased in size a little in this manner, for none of these men ever went back to their farms again, though they speedily lost standing after they retired from their positions. Many others who left their farms to move to the town said in excuse that the school advantages were better, and seemed very anxious for a time that their children should be educated, but once they were established in Twin Mounds they abused the school a great deal, and said it was not satisfactory, and allowed their children to remain away if they were so inclined. [167]

There was the usual number of merchants, professional men, mechanics, etc., who got along well enough, but I never knew how at least one half the inhabitants lived. Some of them owned teams, and farmed in the immediate vicinity; others "hauled," and others did whatever offered, but they were all poor, and were constantly changing from one house to another. These men usually had great families of boys, who grew up in the same indifferent fashion, and drifted off in time nobody knew where, coming back occasionally, after a long absence, well-dressed, and with money to rattle in their pockets. But none of them ever came back who had business of sufficient importance elsewhere to call them away again, for they usually remained until their good clothes wore out, the delusion of their respectability was broken, and they became town loafers again, or engaged in the hard pursuits of their fathers. The only resident of Twin Mounds who ever distinguished himself ran away with a circus and never came back, for although he was never heard of it was generally believed that he must have become famous in some way to induce him to forego the pleasure of returning home in good clothes, and swaggering up and down the street to allow the people to shake his hand.

This class of men never paid their debts, and to get credit for an amount was equal to earning it, to their way of thinking, and a new merchant who came in did a great business until he found them out. I have said they never paid; they did sometimes, but if they paid a dollar on account they bought three or four times that amount to go on the books.

They always seemed to me to be boys yet, surprised at being their own masters, and only worked when they had to, as boys do. They engaged in boys' amusements too, for most of them owned packs of dogs, and a short-distance [168] racehorses, and it was one of their greatest accomplishments to drive a quarter-horse to a wood-wagon to some out-of-the-way neighborhood, match it against a farmer's horse threatened with speed, and come back with all the money owned in that direction. I suppose they came West to grow up with the country, like the rest of us, but they were idle where they came from, and did not improve in the West, because work was necessary, whereupon the thought no doubt occurred to them that they could have grown rich in that way anywhere.

A few of them were away most of the time—I never knew where, but so far away that they seldom came home—and their families supported themselves as best they could, but were always expecting the husbands and fathers to return and take them away to homes of luxury. Occasionally news came that they were killed by Indians, and occasionally this was contradicted by the certainty that they were locked up for disreputable transactions, or hanged. Whenever a Twin Mounds man died away from home otherwise than honorably, it was always said that he had been killed by the Indians.

All of this, and much more, I learned during the first three years of my residence there, which were generally uneventful and without incident, save that on rare occasions I was permitted to visit Jo and Agnes at Fairview, who made so such of me that I dreaded to come away. I had long since displaced Adams, and Jo was out of his time at the mill, and for more than a year had been receiving wages enabling him to save considerable money, which he invested in his enterprise at the Ford with a steadfastness for which I, his best friend, did not give him credit. He was engaged now to be married to Mateel Shepherd, and he worked and studied to make himself worthy of her. Barker had been known to confess that [169] Jo was the better miller of the two—I believe he really was—and when he came to town he spent more of his time in examining the machinery in the mills on the river than in visiting me, and it was plain that the old-fashioned establishment on Bull River would not satisfy him when he began the building of his own.

Dad Erring's hands had improved somewhat during the three years, and the great piles of framed timbers lying at the Ford now were his work, but Jo had paid him from his earnings as much as he would take. These were hauled from the woods, where they were fashioned by Jo himself on odd occasions, with ox teams and low wagons, assisted by the cheap labor which abounded in winter.

While the creek was low, he had laid a broad foundation for his dam, with stones so large that a great many men were necessary to handle them, which were sunk into the creek, and the succeeding layers fastened to them by a process he had invented. I think he worked there a little every week during the three years, assisted by young men he hired for almost nothing, and there was system and order in everything he did. Occasionally it happened that the water at Barker's was too high or too low to run the mill, when he worked on his own enterprise from daylight until dark, living at his father's house. Barker often gave him the half of one day, and all of the next, when trade was dull, and these opportunities he improved to the very best advantage; every time I went to Fairview I visited the mill, and it was always growing.

Jo made a good deal of money every month by running extra time, which opportunity Barker delighted to give him, and often after he had worked all night or all day he would commence again and work half of his employer's time, studying his books when everything was running smoothly. [170]

His ambition had become noised about, and partly because a mill was needed in that part of the country, and partly because the people had lately grown to admire Jo, they proposed to raise him a certain sum of money, to be returned at any time within five years after the mill should commence running. My recollection is that the amount was three or four hundred dollars, and I have always believed that Damon Barker paid Lytle Biggs out of his own pocket to solicit subscriptions to the fund, for he seemed to have something to do with it.

During this time I had mastered the mystery of the boxes so well that I wondered how it was possible I had puzzled my brain over them, they seemed so simple and easy, and if I improved the time well, I am sure it was due to the kindly encouragement and help of Martin, who was not only a very clever printer, but an intelligent man besides. It had always been a part of his work, I believe, to write the few local items of the town, and he taught me to help him; making me do it my way first, and then, after he had explained the errors, I wrote them all over again. If I employed a bad sentence, or an inappropriate word, he explained his objections at length, and I am certain that had I been less dull I should have become a much better writer than I am, for he was very competent to teach me.

My father, as an editor, was earnest and vigorous, and the subjects of which he wrote required columns for expression, so that his page of the paper was always full. I spent a quite recent rainy holiday in a dusty attic looking over an old file of the "Union of States" when he was its editor, and was surprised at the ability he displayed. The simple and honest manner in which he discussed the questions of the day became very popular, for he always advocated that which was right, and there was always more presswork to do every week, which he seemed to re-[171]gard as an imposition on Martin, who had formerly had that hard part of the work to perform, and on the plea of needing exercise he early began to run the press himself, and in the history of the business at that time no man was known who could equal him in the rapid and steady manner in which he went about it.

Soon after my introduction into the office I had learned to ink the forms so acceptably with a hand roller that I was forced to keep at it, for a suitable successor could not be found, but at last we found a young man who had a passion for art (it was none other than my old enemy, Shorty Wilkinson; I fought him regularly every week during the first year of my residence in town, but we finally agreed to become friends), and after that Martin and I spent a portion of the two press days of the week in adorning our page with paragraphs of local happenings; or rather in rambling through the town hunting for them. Sometimes we invented startling things at night, and spent the time given us in wandering through the woods like idle boys, bathing and fishing in the streams in summer, and visiting the sugar camps in early spring, where we heard many tales of adventure which afterwards appeared in print under great headings.

By reason of the fact that it was conducted by a careful and industrious man, and the great number of law advertisements which came in from that and two of the adjoining counties, the "Union of States" made a good deal of money, and certainly it was improved under my father's proprietorship. Before it came into his possession it was conducted by a man who had ideas, but not talents, beyond a country newspaper, who regarded it as a poor field in which to expect either reputation or money; but my father made it as readable as he could, and worked every day and night at something designed to improve it. The [172] result was that its circulation rapidly extended, and the business was very profitable.

His disposition had not changed with his residence, except that he turned me over entirely to Martin, and a room had been fitted up in the building where the paper was printed for our joint occupancy, where we spent our evenings as we saw fit, but always to some purpose, for the confidence reposed in Martin was deserved.

From my mother, who was more lonely than ever in the stone house in which we lived, I learned occasionally that the Rev. John Westlock still read and thought far into every night. Into the room in which he slept was brought every evening the dining-table, and sitting before this, spread out to its full size, he read, wrote, or thought until he went to bed, which was always at a late hour.

It occurred to me once or twice, in an indifferent sort of way, that a man who had no greater affairs than a country printing office, and a large amount of wild land constantly increasing in value, had reason to think so much as he did, but I never suspected what his trouble was until it was revealed to me, as I shall presently relate.

When I rambled through the town at night, and passed that way, if I looked in at his window, which was on the ground floor, he was oftener thinking than reading or writing, leaning back in his chair, with a scowl on his face which frightened me. Whether the procession of forbidden pictures was still passing before him, and the figures accompanying them were still beckoning, will never be known until the Great Book of Men's Actions, said to be kept in Heaven, is opened, and I hope that those who are permitted to look at the writing under the head of John Westlock will be able to read, through the mercy of God: "Tempted and tried; but forgiven." [173]

Almost every Saturday afternoon he drove away into the country without explanation, and did not return until Sunday night or early Monday morning. Where he went we never knew, but we supposed he had gone to preach in some of the country churches or school-houses, for persons who came into the office through the week spoke in a way which led us to believe that such was the case, although he was not often at Fairview, Jo told me, but he heard of him frequently in the adjoining neighborhoods.

During the latter part of the second year of our residence in Twin Mounds, my father came home one Monday in an unusually bad humor, and though he went away occasionally after that, it was usually late in the evening, and I came to understand somehow that he did not preach any more, the result of some sort of a misunderstanding. Even had I been anxious to know the particulars, there was no one to inform me, as no one seemed to know, and in a little while I ceased to think about it entirely, for he at once gave me more to do by teaching me the details of the business. The men who came to the office to see him after that annoyed him, and made him more irritable, therefore he taught me the routine of his affairs, that I might relieve him of them. We all usually worked together, but after this he took whatever he had to do into the room where Martin had his bed, and when the people came in I was expected to attend to them. From my going into the bedroom to ask him questions about his land business, which I did not so well understand, it came to be believed that he was failing in health, and his old friends frequently expressed the hope that he would soon be better. If I had trouble in settling with any-one, he came out impatiently, and acted as if he would like to pitch the man into the street, [174] for his affairs were always straight and honest, and there was no occasion for trouble. Frequently he would propose to work in my place if I would go out in town, and solicit business, and when there were bills to collect, I was put about it, so that for weeks at a time he did not see any one, and trusted almost everything to me.

When my father was away, I was expected to stay at home, and I could not help noticing that my mother was growing paler and weaker, and that the old trouble of which she had spoken to Jo was no better. The house in which we lived was built of square blocks of stone, and the walls were so thick, and the windows so small, that I used to think of her as a prisoner shut up in it. The upper part was not used, except when I went there to sleep, and it was such a dismal and lonely place that I was often awakened in the night with bad dreams, but I always had company, for I found her sleeping on a pallet by the side of my bed, as though she was glad to be near me. I never heard her come, or go away, but if I awoke in the night I was sure to find her by my side.

"There is a great change in you, Ned," she said to me one evening when I had gone to stay with her, "since coming to town."

I replied that I was very glad to hear her say so, as I was very ignorant when I went into the office to work.

"The rest of us are unchanged," she said. "We are no happier here than in Fairview; just the same, I think."

It was the only reference she had ever made to the subject to me, and I did not press it, for I feared she would break down and confess the sor-row which filled her life. A great many times afterwards I could have led her up to talk about it, fully and freely, I think, but I dreaded to hear from her own lips how unhappy she really was. [175] Had I those days to live over—how often are those words said and written, as though there is a consciousness with every man of having been unwise as well as unhappy in his youth—I would pursue a different course, but it never occurred to me then that I could be of more use to her than I was, or that I could in any way lessen her sorrow. She never regretted that I no longer slept in the house, nor that I was growing as cold toward her as my father, which must have been the case, so I never knew that she cared much about it. Indeed, I interpreted her unhappiness as indifference toward me, and it had been that way since I could remember. Had she put her arms around me, and asked me to love her because no one else did, I am sure I should have been devoted to her, but her quietness convinced me that she was so troubled in other ways that there was no time to think of me, and while I believe I was kind and thoughtful of her, I fear I was never affectionate. [176]

SAMUEL L. CLEMENS
1835–1910

The Mississippi River Towns

from

THE ADVENTURES OF HUCKLEBERRY FINN

John Erskine, says Samuel L. Clemens, provided us "with our first and still our best account of Main Street—of the small community, narrow as to their virtues and starved in their imaginations. . . ."

The small communities that Clemens knew so well were the villages along the Mississippi River in the middle 1800s. Clemens—born in Florida, Missouri, in 1835—spent his boyhood and youth in the little frontier town of Hannibal, Missouri, where his family had moved when he was four. Later, after a variety of experiences—as printer, prospector, and correspondent—Clemens returned to the Mississippi to become one of the best steamboat pilots on the river. He guided the big steamers through the channels between St. Louis and New Orleans and came to know all the little river towns along the way.

Clemens, better known as Mark Twain, was truly the product of a frontier society. His pseudonym came from the rivermen's expression that meant safe water—a depth of two fathoms. He rose from the poverty and obscurity of the little town of Hannibal to fame and literary immortality. Clemens began as a reporter on the Hannibal *Courier* and later worked as a journeyman printer in St. Louis, New York, Philadelphia, and Cincinnati. He developed his writing talent while a reporter, especially for the *Territorial Enterprise* in Virginia City, Nevada. The literary attention came suddenly in 1865 with the publication of his story "The Celebrated Jumping Frog of Calaveras County." For the rest of his life Clemens produced works of remarkable versatility and scope—autobiography, travel books, boyhood fiction, historical romances, melodrama, and novels and essays of social protest. By 1885 he was the most widely read of American writers and possibly, in his time, the most famous man in the world. This eminence was still with him when he died in 1910. On a hill above Hannibal stands today the bronze figure of Mark Twain with the inscription: "His religion was humanity, and the whole world mourned for him when he died."

The Mississippi River locales gave Clemens the material for some of his best works—*The Adventures of Tom Sawyer* (1876), *Life on the Mississippi* (1883), and *The Adventures of Huckleberry Finn* (1885). In *Huckleberry Finn,* Pikeville, Bricksville, and Peter Wilk's town are reflections of Hannibal and the other river towns. Clemens viewed the small town as a satirist, attacking the meanness and narrowness of life there. In emphasizing the dark side of the small town, he often showed that the only relief from boredom came in displays of violence. Clemens himself was actual witness to four murders. In *The Adventures of Huckleberry Finn* Clemens's attitudes toward religion, superstition, aristocracy, slavery, and tradition reach the reader through the simple, backwood narration of Huck Finn.

In the story, Huck—son of the town drunk of St. Petersburg, Missouri—runs away to escape the women who would "sivilize" him and the father who would beat him. On nearby Jackson Island in the Mississippi he encounters Jim, a runaway slave. Together they flee down the Mississippi on a raft, traveling 1100 miles to Pikeville, Arkansas. It is this trip down the river that provides the narrative focus that allows Clemens to make his observations about life in the small river towns.

In Huck Finn, Clemens creates a narrator who uses a salty vernacular characteristic of native American humor. But Clemens uses a number of other American dialects, as he points out in the author's statement at the beginning of the book. The satire emerges through exaggeration and deadpan seriousness; Huck's oversimplification of people and problems thus allows Clemens to disengage himself from direct authorial outbursts. It is Huck Finn who questions the conventional morality of society, who satirizes that which by tradition has been held sacrosanct. As a skeptic and a realist, Huck is eminently equipped to make just and honest evaluations of the people and villages he encounters on the river journey.

The following excerpts from *The Adventures of Huckleberry Finn* begin with Chapters I and II, in which Huck complains of his restrictive, "sivilized" life in St. Petersburg and in which attitudes toward religion and prayer, susperstition, and frontier puritanism are revealed. Chapters XXI and XXII describe the typical Mississippi River town and its people and relate the cold-blooded shooting down of a man.

from THE ADVENTURES OF HUCKLEBERRY FINN

CHAPTER I

You don't know about me, without you have read a book by the name of
"The Adventures of Tom Sawyer," but that ain't no matter. That book
was made by Mr. Mark Twain, and he told the truth, mainly. There was
things which he stretched, but mainly he told the truth. That is nothing.
I never seen anybody but lied, one time or another, without it was Aunt
Polly, or the widow, or maybe Mary. Aunt Polly—Tom's Aunt Polly, she
is—and Mary, and the Widow Douglas, is all told about in that book—
which is mostly a true book; with some stretchers, as I said before.

Now the way that the book winds up, is this: Tom and me found the
money that the robbers hid in the cave, and it made us rich. We got six
thousand dollars apiece—all gold. It was an awful sight of money when it
was piled up. Well, Judge Thatcher, he took it and put it out at interest,
and it fetched us a dollar a day apiece, all the year round—more than a
body could tell what to do with. The Widow Douglas, she took me for her
son, and allowed she would sivilize me; but it was rough living in the house
all the time, considering how dismal regular and decent the widow was in
all her ways; and so when I couldn't stand it no longer, I lit out. I got into
my old rags, and my sugar-hogshead again, and was free and satisfied. But
[17] Tom Sawyer, he hunted me up and said he was going to start a band
of robbers, and I might join if I would go back to the widow and be
respectable. So I went back.

The widow she cried over me, and called me a poor lost lamb, and she
called me a lot of other names, too, but she never meant no harm by it.
She put me in them new clothes again, and I couldn't do nothing but sweat
and sweat, and feel all cramped up. Well, then, the old thing commenced
again. The widow rung a bell for supper, and you had to come to time.
When you got to the table you couldn't go right to eating, but you had to
wait for the widow to tuck down her head and grumble a little over the
victuals, though there weren't really anything the matter with them. That
is, nothing only everything was cooked by itself. In a barrel of odds and
ends it is different; things get mixed up, and the juice kind of swaps
around, and the things go better.

After supper she got out her book and learned me about Moses and the

Samuel L. Clemens, *The Adventures of Huckleberry Finn* (New York: Charles L. Webster and Company, 1885).

Bulrushers; and I was in a sweat to find out all about him; but by-and-by she let it out that Moses had been dead a considerable long time; so then I didn't care no more about him; because I don't take no stock in dead people.

Pretty soon I wanted to smoke, and asked the widow to let me. But she wouldn't. She said it was a mean practice and wasn't clean, and I must try to not do it any more. That is just the way with some people. They [18] get down on a thing when they don't know nothing about it. Here she was a bothering about Moses, which was no kin to her, and no use to anybody, being gone, you see, yet finding a power of fault with me for doing a thing that had some good in it. And she took snuff too; of course that was all right, because she done it herself.

Her sister, Miss Watson, a tolerable slim old maid, with goggles on, had just come to live with her, and took a set at me now, with a spelling-book. She worked me middling hard for about an hour, and then the widow made her ease up. I couldn't stood it much longer. Then for an hour it was deadly dull, and I was fidgety. Miss Watson would say, "Don't put your feet up there, Huckleberry"; and "don't scrunch up like that, Huckleberry —set up straight"; and pretty soon she would say, "Don't gap and stretch like that, Huckleberry—why don't you try to behave?" Then she told me all about the bad place, and I said I wished I was there. She got mad, then, but I didn't mean no harm. All I wanted was to go somewheres; all I wanted was a change, I warn't particular. She said it was wicked to say what I said; said she wouldn't say it for the whole world; *she* was going to live so as to go to the good place. Well, I couldn't see no advantage in going where she was going, so I made up my mind I wouldn't try for it. But I never said so, because it would only make trouble, and wouldn't do no good.

Now she had got a start, and she went on and told me all about the good place. She said all a body would have to do there was to go around all day long with a harp and sing, forever and ever. So I didn't think [19] much of it. But I never said so. I asked her if she reckoned Tom Sawyer would go there, and, she said, not by a considerable sight. I was glad about that, because I wanted him and me to be together.

Miss Watson she kept pecking at me, and it got tiresome and lonesome. By-and-by they fetched the niggers in and had prayers, and then everybody was off to bed. I went up to my room with a piece of candle and put it on the table. Then I set down in a chair by the window and tried to think of something cheerful, but it warn't no use. I felt so lonesome I most wished I was dead. The stars was shining, and the leaves rustled in the woods ever so mournful; and I heard an owl, away off, who-whooing about somebody that was dead, and a whippowill and a dog crying about somebody that was going to die; and the wind was trying to whisper something to me and I couldn't make out what it was, and so it made the cold shivers run over me.

Then away out in the woods I heard that kind of a sound that a ghost makes when it wants to tell about something that's on its mind and can't make itself understood, and so can't rest easy in its grave and has to go about that way every night grieving. I got so down-hearted and scared, I did wish I had some company. Pretty soon a spider went crawling up my shoulder, and I flipped it off and it lit in the candle; and before I could budge it was all shriveled up. I didn't need anybody to tell me that that was an awful bad sign and would fetch me some bad luck, so I was scared and most shook the clothes off of me. I got up and turned around in my tracks three times and crossed my breast every time; and then I tied up a little lock of my hair with a thread to keep witches away. But I hadn't no confidence. You do that when you've lost a horse-shoe that you've found, instead of nailing it up over the door, but I hadn't ever heard anybody say it was any way to keep off bad luck when you'd killed a spider.

I set down again, a shaking all over, and got out my pipe for a smoke; for the house was all as still as death, now, and so the widow wouldn't know. Well, after a long time I heard the clock away off in the town go boom—boom—boom—twelve licks—and all still again—stiller than ever. Pretty soon I heard a twig snap, down in the dark amongst the [20] trees—something was a stirring. I set still and listened. Directly I could just barely hear a *"me-yow! me-yow!"* down there. That was good! Says I, *"me-yow! me-yow!"* as soft as I could, and then I put out the light and scrambled out of the window onto the shed. Then I slipped down to the ground and crawled in amongst the trees, and sure enough there was Tom Sawyer waiting for me. [21]

CHAPTER II

We went tip-toeing along the path amongst the trees back towards the end of the widow's garden, stooping down so as the branches wouldn't scrape our heads. When we was passing by the kitchen I fell over a root and made a noise. We scrouched down and laid still. Miss Watson's big nigger, named Jim, was setting in the kitchen door; we could see him pretty clear, because there was a light behind him. He got up and stretched his neck out about a minute, listening. Then he says,

"Who dah?"

He listened some more; then he come tip-toeing down and stood right between us; we could a touched him, nearly. Well, likely it was minutes and minutes that there warn't a sound, and we all there so close together. There was a place on my ankle that got to itching; but I dasn't scratch it; and then my ear began to itch; and next my back, right between my shoulders. Seemed like I'd die if I couldn't scratch. Well, I've noticed that thing plenty of times since. If you are with the quality, or at a funeral, or trying to go to sleep when you ain't sleepy—if you are anywheres [22] where it won't do for you to scratch, why you will itch all over in upwards of a thousand places. Pretty soon Jim says:

"Say—who is you? War is you? Dog my cats ef I didn't hear sumf'n. Well, I knows what I's gwyne to do. I's gwyne to set down here and listen tell I hears it agin."

So he set down on the ground betwixt me and Tom. He leaned his back up against a tree, and stretched his legs out till one of them most touched one of mine. My nose begun to itch. It itched till the tears come into my eyes. But I dasn't scratch. Then it begun to itch on the inside. Next I got to itching underneath. I didn't know how I was going to set still. This miserableness went on as much as six or seven minutes; but it seemed a sight longer than that. I was itching in eleven different places now. I reckoned I couldn't stand it more'n a minute longer, but I set my teeth hard and got ready to try. Just then Jim begun to breathe heavy; next he begun to snore—and then I was pretty soon comfortable again.

Tom he made a sign to me—kind of a little noise with his mouth—and we went creeping away on our hands and knees. When we was ten foot off, Tom whispered to me and wanted to tie Jim to the tree for fun; but I said no; he might wake and make a disturbance, and then they'd find out I warn't in. Then Tom said he hadn't got candles enough, and he would slip in the kitchen and get some more. I didn't want him to try. I said Jim might wake up and come. But Tom wanted to resk it; so we slid in there and got three candles, and Tom laid five cents on the table for pay. Then we got out, and I was in a sweat to get away; but nothing would do Tom but he must crawl to where Jim was, on his hands and knees, and play something on him. I waited, and it seemed a good while, everything was so still and lonesome.

As soon as Tom was back, we cut along the path, around the garden fence, and by-and-by fetched up on the steep top of the hill the other side of the house. Tom said he slipped Jim's hat off of his head and hung it on a limb right over him, and Jim stirred a little, but he didn't wake. After-wards Jim said the witches bewitched him and put him in a trance, and rode him all over the State, and then set him under the trees again and hung his hat on a limb to show who done it. And next time Jim told it he said they rode him down to New Orleans; [23] and after that, every time he told it he spread it more and more, till by-and-by he said they rode him all over the world, and tired him most to death, and his back was all over saddle-boils. Jim was monstrous proud about it, and he got so he wouldn't hardly notice the other niggers. Niggers would come miles to hear Jim tell about it, and he was more looked up to than any nigger in that country. Strange niggers would stand with their mouths open and look him all over, same as if he was a wonder. Niggers is always talking about witches in the dark by the kitchen fire; but whenever one was talking and letting on to know all about such things, Jim would happen in and say, "Hm!

What you know 'bout witches?" and that nigger was corked up and had to take a back seat. Jim always kept that five-center piece around his neck with a string and said it was a charm the devil give to him with his own hands and told him he could cure anybody with it and fetch witches whenever he wanted to, just by saying something to it; but he never told what it was he said to it. Niggers would come from all around there and give Jim anything they had, just for a sight of that five-center piece; but they wouldn't touch it, because the devil had had his hands on it. Jim was most ruined, for a servant, because he got so stuck up on account of having seen the devil and been rode by witches.

Well, when Tom and me got to the edge of the hill-top, we looked away down into the village and could see three or four lights twinkling, where there was sick folks, may be; and the stars over us was sparkling ever so fine; and down by the village was the river, a whole mile broad, and awful still and grand. We went down the hill and found Jo Harper, and Ben Rogers, and two or three more of the boys, hid in the old tanyard. So we unhitched a skiff and pulled down the river two mile and a half, to the big scar on the hillside, and went ashore. [24]

We went to a clump of bushes, and Tom made everybody swear to keep the secret, and then showed them a hole in the hill, right in the thickest part of the bushes. Then we lit the candles and crawled in on our hands and knees. We went about two hundred yards, and then the cave opened up. Tom poked about amongst the passages and pretty soon ducked under a wall where you wouldn't a noticed that there was a hole. We went along a narrow place and got into a kind of room, all damp and sweaty and cold, and there we stopped. Tom says:

"Now we'll start this band of robbers and call it Tom Sawyer's Gang. Everybody that wants to join has got to take an oath, and write his name in blood."

Everybody was willing. So Tom got out a sheet of paper that he had wrote the oath on, and read it. It swore every boy to stick to the band, and never tell any of the secrets; and if anybody done anything to any boy in the band, whichever boy was ordered to kill that person and his family must do it, and he mustn't eat and he mustn't sleep till he had killed them and hacked a cross in [25] their breasts, which was the sign of the band. And nobody that didn't belong to the band could use that mark, and if he did he must be sued; and if he done it again he must be killed. And if anybody that belonged to the band told the secrets, he must have his throat cut, and then have his carcass burnt up and the ashes scattered all around, and his name blotted off of the list with blood and never mentioned again by the gang, but have a curse put on it and be forgot, forever.

Everybody said it was a real beautiful oath, and asked Tom if he got it out of his own head. He said, some of it, but the rest was out of pirate books, and robber books, and every gang that was high-toned had it.

Some thought it would be good to kill the *families* of boys that told the secrets. Tom said it was a good idea, so he took a pencil and wrote it in. Then Ben Rogers says:

"Here's Huck Finn, he hain't got no family—what you going to do 'bout him?"

"Well, hain't he got a father?" says Tom Sawyer.

"Yes, he's got a father, but you can't never find him, these days. He used to lay drunk with the hogs in the tanyard, but he hain't been seen in these parts for a year or more."

They talked it over, and they was going to rule me out, because they said every boy must have a family or somebody to kill, or else it wouldn't be fair and square for the others. Well, nobody could think of anything to do—everybody was stumped, and set still. I was most ready to cry; but all at once I thought of a way, and so I offered them Miss Watson—they could kill her. Everybody said: "Oh, she'll do, she'll do. That's all right. Huck can come in."

Then they all stuck a pin in their fingers to get blood to sign with, and I made my mark on the paper.

"Now," says Ben Rogers, "what's the line of business of this Gang?"

"Nothing only robbery and murder," Tom said.

"But who are we going to rob? houses—or cattle—or——"

"Stuff! stealing cattle and such things ain't robbery, it's burglary," says Tom Sawyer. "We ain't burglars. That ain't no sort of style. We are high-[26]waymen. We stop stages and carriages on the road, with masks on, and kill the people and take their watches and money."

"Must we always kill the people?"

"Oh, certainly. It's best. Some authorities think different, but mostly it's considered best to kill them. Except some that you bring to the cave here and keep them till they're ransomed."

"Ransomed? What's that?"

"I don't know. But that's what they do. I've seen it in books; and so of course that's what we've got to do."

"But how can we do it if we don't know what it is?"

"Why blame it all, we've *got* to do it. Don't I tell you it's in the books? Do you want to go to doing different from what's in the books, and get things all muddled up?"

"Oh, that's all very fine to *say*, Tom Sawyer, but how in the nation are these fellows going to be ransomed if we don't know how to do it to them? that's the thing *I* want to get at. Now what do you *reckon* it is?"

"Well I don't know. But per'aps if we keep them till they're ransomed, it means that we keep them till they're dead."

"Now, that's something *like*. That'll answer. Why couldn't you said that before? We'll keep them till they're ransomed to death—and a bothersome lot they'll be, too, eating up everything and always trying to get loose."

"How you talk, Ben Rogers. How can they get loose when there's a guard over them, ready to shoot them down if they move a peg?"

"A guard. Well, that *is* good. So somebody's got to set up all night and never get any sleep, just so as to watch them. I think that's foolishness. Why can't a body take a club and ransom them as soon as they get here?"

"Because it ain't in the books so—that's why. Now Ben Rogers, do you want to do things regular, or don't you?—that's the idea. Don't you reckon that the people that made the books knows what's the correct thing to do? Do you reckon *you* can learn 'em anything? Not by a good deal. No, sir, we'll just go on and ransom them in the regular way."

"All right. I don't mind; but I say it's a fool way, anyhow. Say—do we kill the women, too?" [27]

"Well, Ben Rogers, if I was as ignorant as you I wouldn't let on. Kill the women? No—nobody ever saw anything in the books like that. You fetch them to the cave, and you're always as polite as pie to them; and by-and-by they fall in love with you and never want to go home any more."

"Well, if that's the way, I'm agreed, but I don't take no stock in it. Mighty soon we'll have the cave so cluttered up with women, and fellows waiting to be ransomed, that there won't be no place for the robbers. But go ahead, I ain't got nothing to say."

Little Tommy Barnes was asleep, now, and when they waked him up he was scared, and cried, and said he wanted to go home to his ma, and didn't want to be a robber any more.

So they all made fun of him, and called him cry-baby, and that made him mad, and he said he would go straight and tell all the secrets. But Tom give him five cents to keep quiet, and said we would all go home and meet next week and rob somebody and kill some people.

Ben Rogers said he couldn't get out much, only Sundays, and so he wanted to begin next Sunday; but all the boys said it would be wicked to do it on Sunday, and that settled the thing. They agreed to get together and fix a day as soon as they could, and then we elected Tom Sawyer first captain and Jo Harper second captain of the Gang, and so started home.

I clumb up the shed and crept into my window just before day was breaking. My new clothes was all greased up and clayey, and I was dog-tired. [28]

[Huck Finn, weary of the attempts to "sivilize" him and fearful of his drunken father's treatment of him, fakes his own death and runs away to Jackson's Island. Here he joins Jim, the slave, in his search for freedom. The two flee aboard a raft, floating down the Mississippi River. Huck, as narrator, recounts their adventures on the water and the land. At one point they are joined by two rogues—the king and the duke. The following section tells of their going ashore to put on a perform-

ance in a river town. It offers a good description of the town and its people, particularly in relation to the murder of a man and the citizens' inability to act against the murderer.]

CHAPTER XXI

It was after sun-up, now, but we went right on, and didn't tie up. The king and the duke turned out, by-and-by, looking pretty rusty; but after they'd jumped overboard and took a swim, it chippered them up a good deal. After breakfast the king he took a seat on a corner of the raft, and pulled off his boots and rolled up his britches, and let his legs dangle in the water, so as to be comfortable, and lit his pipe, and went to getting his Romeo and Juliet by heart. When he had got it pretty good, him and the duke begun to practice it together. The duke had to learn him over and over again, how to say every speech; and he made him sigh, and put his hand on his heart, and after while he said he done it pretty well; "only," he says, "you mustn't bellow out *Romeo!* that way, like a bull!—you must say it soft, and sick, and languishly, so—R-o-o-meo! that is the idea; for Juliet's a dear sweet mere child of a girl, you know, and she don't bray like a jackass."

Well, next they got out a couple of long swords that the duke made out of oak laths, and begun to practice the sword-fight—the duke called himself Richard III.; and the way they laid on, and pranced around the raft was grand to see. But by-and-by the king tripped and fell overboard, and after that they [177] took a rest, and had a talk about all kinds of adventures they'd had in other times along the river.

After dinner, the duke says:

"Well, Capet, we'll want to make this a first-class show, you know, so I guess we'll add a little more to it. We want a little something to answer encores with, anyway."

"What's onkores, Bilgewater?"

The duke told him, and then says:

"I'll answer by doing the Highland fling or the sailor's hornpipe; and you—well, let me see—oh, I've got it—you can do Hamlet's soliloquy."

"Hamlet's which?"

"Hamlet's soliloquy, you know; the most celebrated thing in Shakespeare. Ah, it's sublime, sublime! Always fetches the house. I haven't got it in the book—I've only got one volume—but I reckon I can piece it out from memory. I'll just walk up and down a minute, and see if I can call it back from recollection's vaults."

So he went to marching up and down, thinking, and frowning horrible every now and then; then he would hoist up his eyebrows; next he would squeeze his hand on his forehead and stagger back and kind of moan; next he would sigh, and next he'd let on to drop a tear. It was beautiful to see him. By-and-by he got it. He told us to give attention. Then he strikes a most noble attitude, with one leg shoved forwards, [178] and his arms stretched away up, and his head tilted back, looking up at the sky; and then he begins to rip and rave and grit his teeeth; and after that, all through his speech he howled, and spread around, and swelled up his chest, and just knocked the spots out of any acting ever *I* see before. . . .

Well, the old man he liked that speech, and he mighty soon got it so he could do it first rate. It seemed like he was just born for it; and when he had his hand in and was excited, it was perfectly lovely the way he would rip and tear and rair up behind when he was getting it off. [179]

The first chance we got, the duke he had some show bills printed; and after that, for two or three days as we floated along, the raft was a most uncommon lively place, for there warn't nothing but sword-fighting and rehearsing—as the duke called it—going on all the time. One morning, when we was pretty well down the State of Arkansaw, we come in sight of a little one-horse town in a big bend; so we tied up about three-quarters of a mile above it, in the mouth of a crick which was shut in like a tunnel by the cypress trees, and all of us but Jim took the canoe and went down there to see if there was any chance in that place for our show.

We struck it mighty lucky; there was going to be a circus there that afternoon, and the country people was already beginning to come in, in all kinds of old shackly wagons, and on horses. The circus would leave before night, so our show would have a pretty good chance. The duke he hired the court house, and we went around and stuck up our bills. . . . [180]

Then we went loafing around the town. The stores and houses was most all old shackly dried-up frame concerns that hadn't ever been painted; they was set up three or four foot above ground on stilts, so as to be out of reach of the water when the river was overflowed. The houses had little gardens around them, but they didn't seem to raise hardly anything in them but jimpson weeds, and sunflowers, and ash-piles, and old curled-up boots and shoes, and pieces of bottles, and rags, and played-out tin-ware. The fences was made of different kinds of boards, nailed on at different times; and they leaned every which-way, and had gates that didn't generly have but one hinge—a leather one. Some of the fences had been whitewashed, some time or another, but the duke said it was in Clumbus's time, like enough. There was generly hogs in the garden, and people driving them out.

All the stores was along one street. They had white-domestic awnings in front, and the country people hitched their horses to the awning-posts. There was empty dry-goods boxes under the awnings, and loafers roosting on them all day long, whittling them with their Barlow knives; and chawing tobacco, and gaping and yawning and stretching—a mighty ornery lot. They generly had on yellow straw hats most as wide as an umbrella, but

didn't wear no coats nor waistcoats; they called one another Bill, and Buck,
[181] and Hank, and Joe, and Andy, and talked lazy and drawly, and used
considerable many cuss-words. There was as many as one loafer leaning up
against every awning-post, an he most always had his hands in his britches
pockets, except when he fetched them out to lend a chaw of tobacco or
scratch. What a body was hearing amongst them, all the time was—

"Gimme a chaw 'v tobacker, Hank."

"Cain't—I hain't got but one chaw left. Ask Bill."

Maybe Bill he gives him a chaw; maybe he lies and says he ain't got none.
Some of them kinds of loafers never has a cent in the world, nor a chaw of
tobacco of their own. They get all their chawing by borrowing—they say to
a fellow, "I wisht you'd len' me a chaw, Jack, I jist this minute give Ben
Thompson the last chaw I had"—which is a lie, pretty much every time; it
don't fool nobody but a stranger; but Jack ain't no stranger, so he says—

"*You* give him a chaw, did you? so did your sister's cat's grandmother. You
pay me back the chaws you've awready borry'd off'n me, Lafe Buckner, then
I'll loan you one or two ton of it, and won't charge you no back intrust,
nuther."

"Well, I *did* pay you back some of it wunst."

"Yes, you did—'bout six chaws. You borry'd store tobacker and paid
back nigger-head." [182]

Store tobacco is flat black plug, but these fellows mostly chaws the
natural leaf twisted. When they borrow a chaw, they don't generly cut it off
with a knife, but they set the plug in between their teeth, and gnaw with
their teeth and tug at the plug with their hands till they get it in two—then
sometimes the one that owns the tobacco looks mournful at it when it's
handed back, and says, sarcastic—

"Here, gimmie the *chaw*, and you take the *plug.*"

All the streets and lanes was just mud, they warn't nothing else *but*
mud—mud as black as tar, and nigh about a foot deep in some places; and
two or three inches deep in *all* the places. The hogs loafed and grunted
around, everywheres. You'd see a muddy sow and a litter of pigs come lazy-
ing along the street and whollop herself right down in the way, where folks
had to walk around her, and she'd stretch out, and shut her eyes, and wave
her ears, whilst the pigs was milking her, and looks as happy as if she was
on salary. And pretty soon you'd hear a loafer sing out, "Hi! *so* boy! sick
him, Tige!" and away the sow would go, squealing most horrible, with a
dog or two swinging to each ear, and three or four dozen more a-coming;
and then you would see all the loafers get up and watch the thing out of
sight, and laugh at the fun and look grateful for the noise. Then they'd
settle back again till there was a dog-fight. There couldn't anything wake
them up all over, and make them happy all over, like a dog-fight—unless it
might be putting turpentine on a stray dog and setting fire to him, or tying
a tin pan to his tail and see him run himself to death.

On the river front some of the houses was sticking out over the bank, and they was bowed and bent, and about ready to tumble in. The people had moved out of them. The bank was caved away under one corner of some others, and that corner was hanging over. People lived in them yet, but it was dangersome, because sometimes a strip of land as wide as a house caves in at a time. Sometimes a belt of land a quarter of a mile deep will start in and cave along and cave along till it all caves into the river in one summer. Such a town as that has to be always moving back, and back, and back, because the river's always gnawing at it. [183]

The nearer it got to noon that day, the thicker and thicker was the wagons and horses in the streets, and more coming all the time. Families fetched their dinners with them, from the country, and eat them in the wagons. There was considerable whiskey drinking going on, and I seen three fights. By-and-by somebody sings out—

"Here comes old Boggs!—in from the country for his little old monthly drunk—here he comes, boys!"

All the loafers looked glad—I reckoned they was used to having fun out of Boggs. One of them says—

"Wonder who he's a gwyne to chaw up this time. If he'd a chawed up all the men he's ben a gwyne to chaw up in the last twenty year, he'd have considerable ruputation, now."

Another one says, "I wisht old Boggs 'd threaten me, 'cuz then I'd know I warn't gwyne to die for a thousan' year."

Boggs comes a-tearing along on his horse, whooping and yelling like an Injun, and singing out—

"Cler the track, thar. I'm on the waw-path, and the price uv coffins is a gwyne to raise."

He was drunk, and weaving about in his saddle; he was over fifty year old, and had a very red face. Everybody yelled at him, and laughed at him, and sassed him, and he sassed back, and said he'd attend to them and lay them out in their regular turns, but he couldn't wait now, because he'd come to town to kill old Colonel Sherburn, and his motto was, "meat first, and spoon vittles to top off on."

He see me, and rode up and says—

"Whar'd you come f'm, boy? You prepared to die?"

Then he rode on. I was scared; but a man says—

"He don't mean nothing; he's always a carryin' on like that, when he's drunk. He's the best-naturedest old fool in Arkansaw—never hurt nobody, drunk nor sober."

Boggs rode up before the biggest store in town and bent his head down so he could see under the curtain of the awning, and yells—[184]

"Come out here, Sherburn! Come out and meet the man you've swindled. You're the houn' I'm after, and I'm gwyne to have you, too!"

And so he went on, calling Sherburn everything he could lay his tongue to, and the whole street packed with people listening and laughing and going on. By-and-by a proud-looking man about fifty-five—and he was a heap the best dressed man in that town, too—steps out of the store, and the crowd drops backs on each side to let him come. He says to Boggs, mighty ca'm and slow—he says:

"I'm tired of this; but I'll endure it till one o'clock. Till one o'clock, mind—no longer. If you open your mouth against me only once, after that time, you can't travel so far but I will find you."

Then he turns and goes in. The crowd looked mighty sober; nobody stirred, and there warn't no more laughing. Boggs rode off blackguarding Sherburn as loud as he could yell, all down the street; and pretty soon back he comes and stops before the store, still keeping it up. Some men crowded around him and tried to get him to shut up, but he wouldn't; they told him it would be one o'clock in about fifteen minutes, and so he *must* go home—he must go right away. But it didn't do no good. He cussed away, with all his might, and [185] throwed his hat down in the mud and rode over it, and pretty soon away he went a-raging down the street again, with his gray hair a-flying. Everybody that could get a chance at him tried their best to coax him off of his horse so they could lock him up and get him sober; but it warn't no use—up the street he would tear again, and give Sherburn another cussing. By-and-by somebody says—

"Go for his daughter!—quick, go for his daughter; sometimes he'll listen to her. If anybody can persuade him, she can."

So somebody started on a run. I walked down street a ways, and stopped. In about five or ten minutes, here comes Boggs again—but not on his horse. He was a-reeling across the street towards me, bareheaded, with a friend on both sides of him aholt of his arms and hurrying him along. He was quiet, and looked uneasy; and he warn't hanging back any, but was doing some of the hurrying himself. Somebody sings out—

"Boggs!"

I looked over there to see who said it, and it was that Colonel Sherburn. He was standing perfectly still, in the street, and had a pistol raised in his right hand—not aiming it, but holding it out with the barrel tilted up towards the sky. The same second I see a young girl coming on the run, and two men with her. Boggs and the men turned round, to see who called him, and when they see the pistol the men jumped to one side, and the pistol barrel come down slow and steady to a level—both barrels cocked. Boggs throws up both of his hands, and says, "O Lord, don't shoot!" Bang! goes the first shot, and he staggers back clawing at the air—bang! goes the second one, and he tumbles backwards onto the ground, heavy and solid, with his arms spread out. That young girl screamed out, and comes rushing, and down she throws herself on her father, crying, and saying, "Oh, he's killed him, he's killed him!" The crowd closed up around them, and shouldered and jammed one another, with their necks stretched, trying to see, and people on the inside trying to shove them back, and shouting, "Back, back! give him air, give him air!"

Colonel Sherburn he tossed his pistol onto the ground, and turned around on his heels and walked off. [186]

They took Boggs to a little drug store, the crowd pressing around, just the same, and the whole town following, and I rushed and got a good place at the window, where I was close to him and could see in. They laid him on the floor, and put one large Bible under his head, and opened another one and spread it on his breast—but they tore open his shirt first, and I seen where one of the bullets went in. He made about a dozen long gasps, his breast lifting the Bible up when he drawed in his breath, and letting it down again when he breathed it out—and after that he laid still; he was dead. Then they pulled his daughter away from him, screaming and crying, and took her off. She was about sixteen, and very sweet and gentle-looking, but awful pale and scared.

Well, pretty soon the whole town was there, squirming and scrouging and pushing and shoving to get at the window and have a look, but people that had the places wouldn't give them up, and folks behind them was saying all the time, "Say, now, you've looked enough, you fellows! 'taint right and 'taint fair, for you to stay thar all the time, and never give nobody a chance; other folks has their right as well as you."

There was considerable jawing back, so I slid out, thinking maybe there was going to be trouble. The streets was full, and everybody was excited. Everybody that seen the shooting was telling how it happened, and there was a big [187] crowd packed around each one of these fellows, stretching their necks and listening. One long lanky man, with long hair and a big white fur stove-pipe hat on the back of his head, and a crooked-handled cane, marked out the places on the ground where Boggs stood, and where Sherburn stood, and the people following him around from one place to t'other and watching everything he done, and bobbing their heads to show they understood, and stooping a little and resting their hands on their thighs to watch him mark the places on the ground with his cane; and then he stood up straight and stiff where Sherburn had stood, frowning and having his hat-brim down over his eyes, and sung out, "Boggs!" and then fetched his cane down slow to a level, and says "Bang!" staggered backwards, says "Bang!" again, and fell down flat on his back. The people that had seen the thing said he done it perfect; said it was just exactly the way it all happened. Then as much as a dozen people got out their bottles and treated him.

Well, by-and-by somebody said Sherburn ought to be lynched. In about a minute everybody was saying it; so away they went, mad and yelling, and snatching down every clothes-line they come to, to do the hanging with. [188]

CHAPTER XXII

They swarmed up the street towards Sherburn's house, a-whooping and yelling and raging like Injuns, and everything had to clear the way or get run over and tromped to mush, and it was awful to see. Children was heeling it ahead of the mob, screaming and trying to get out of the way; and every window along the road was full of women's heads, and there was nigger boys in every tree, and bucks and wenches looking over every fence; and as soon as the mob would get nearly to them they would break and skaddle back out of reach. Lots of the women and girls was crying and taking on, scared most to death.

They swarmed up in front of Sherburn's palings as thick as they could jam together, and you couldn't hear yourself think for the noise. It was a little twenty-foot yard. Some sung out "Tear down the fence! tear down the fence!" Then there was a racket of ripping and tearing and smashing, and down she goes, and the front wall of the crowd begins to roll in like a wave.

Just then Sherburn steps out on to the roof of his little front porch, with a [189] double-barrel gun in his hand, and takes his stand, perfectly ca'm and deliberate, not saying a word. The racket stopped, and the wave sucked back.

Sherburn never said a word—just stood there, looking down. The stillness was awful creepy and uncomfortable. Sherburn run his eye slow along along the crowd; and wherever it struck, the people tried a little to outgaze him, but they couldn't; they dropped their eyes and looked sneaky. Then pretty soon Sherburn sort of laughed; not the pleasant kind, but the kind that makes you feel like when you are eating bread that's got sand in it.

Then he says, slow and scornful:

"The idea of *you* lynching anybody! It's amusing. The idea of you thinking you had pluck enough to lynch a *man!* Because you're brave enough to tar and feather poor friendless cast-out women that come along here, did that make you think you had grit enough to lay your hands on a *man?* Why, a *man's* safe in the hands of ten thousand of your kind—as long as it's daytime and you're not behind him.

"Do I know you? I know you clear through. I was born and raised in the South, and I've lived in the North; so I know the average all around. The average man's a coward. In the North he lets anybody walk over him that wants to, and goes home and prays for a humble spirit to bear it. In the South one man, all by himself, has stopped a stage full of men, in the day-time, and robbed the lot. Your newspapers call you a brave people so much that you think you *are* braver than any other people—whereas you're just *as* brave, and no braver. Why don't your juries hang murderers? Because they're afraid the man's friends will shoot them in the back, in the dark—and it's just what they *would* do.

"So they always acquit; and then a *man* goes in the night, with a hundred masked cowards at his back, and lynches the rascal. Your mistake is, that you didn't bring a man with you; that's one mistake, and the other is that you didn't come in the dark, and fetch your masks. You brought *part* of a man—Buck Harkness, there—and if you hadn't had him to start you, you'd a taken it out in blowing.

"You didn't want to come. The average man don't like trouble and danger. *You* don't like trouble and danger. But if only *half* a man—like Buck Hark-[190]ness, there—shouts 'Lynch him, lynch him!' you're afraid to back down—afraid you'll be found out to be what you are—*cowards*— and so you raise a yell, and hang yourselves onto that half-a-man's coat tail, and come raging up here, swearing what big things you're going to do. The pitifulest thing out is a mob; that's what an army is—a mob; they don't fight with courage that's born in them, but with courage that's bor- rowed from their mass, and from their officers. But a mob without any *man* at the head of it, is *beneath* pitifulness. Now the thing for *you* to do, is to droop your tails and go home and crawl in a hole. If any real lynching's going to be done, it will be done in the dark, Southern fashion; and when they come they'll bring their masks, and fetch a *man* along. Now *leave*— and take your half-a-man with you"—tossing his gun up across his left arm and cocking it, when he says this.

The crowd washed back sudden, and then broke all apart and went tearing off every which way, and Buck Harkness he heeled it after them, looking tolerable cheap. I could a staid, if I'd a wanted to, but I didn't want to.

I went to the circus, and loafed around the back side till the watch- man went by, and then dived in under the tent. I had my twenty-dollar gold piece and some other money, but I reckoned I better save it, because ther ain't no telling [191] how soon you are going to need it, away from home and amongst strangers, that way. You can't be too careful. I ain't opposed to spending money on circuses, when there ain't no other way, but there ain't no use in *wasting* it on them.

It was a real bully circus. It was the splendidest sight that ever was, when they all come riding in, two and two, a gentleman and lady, side by side, the men just in their drawers and under-shirts, and no shoes nor stir- rups, and resting their hands on their thighs, easy and comfortable—there must a' been twenty of them—and every lady with a lovely complexion, and perfectly beautiful, and looking just like a gang of real sure-enough queens, and dressed in clothes that cost millions of dollars, and just littered with diamonds. It was a powerful fine sight; I never see anything so lovely. And then one by one they got up and stood, and went a-weaving around the ring so gentle and wavy and graceful, the men looking ever so tall and airy and straight, with their heads bobbing and skimming along, away up there under the tent-roof, and every lady's rose-leafy dress flapping soft and silky around her hips, and she looking like the most loveliest parasol.

And then faster and faster they went, all of them dancing, first one foot stuck out in the air and then the other, the horses leaning more and more, and the ring-master going round and round the centre-pole, cracking his whip and shouting "hi!—hi!" and the clown cracking jokes behind him; and by-and-by all hands dropped the reins, and every lady put her knuckles on her hips and every gentleman folded his arms, and then how the horses did lean over and hump themselves! And so, one after the other they all skipped off into the ring, and made the sweetest bow I ever see, and then scampered out, and everybody clapped their hands and went just about wild.

Well, all through the circus they done the most astonishing things; and all the time that clown carried on so it most killed the people. The ring-master couldn't ever say a word to him but he was back at him quick as a wink with the funniest things a body ever said; and how he ever *could* think of so many of them, and so sudden and so pat, was what I couldn't noway understand. Why, I couldn't a thought of them in a year. And by-and-by a drunk man tried to get into the ring—said he wanted to ride; said he could ride as well as anybody [192] that ever was. They argued and tried to keep him out, but he wouldn't listen, and the whole show come to a standstill. Then the people begun to holler at him and make fun of him, and that made him mad, and he begun to rip and tear; so that stirred up the people, and a lot of men begun to pile down off of the benches and swarm towards the ring, saying, "Knock him down! throw him out!" and one or two women begun to scream. So, then, the ring-master he made a little speech, and said he hoped there wouldn't be no disturbance, and if the man would promise he wouldn't make no more trouble, he would let him ride, if he thought he could stay on the horse. So everybody laughed and said all right, and the man got on. The minute he was on, the horse begun to rip and tear and jump and cavort around, with two circus men hanging onto his bridle trying to hold him, and the drunk man hanging onto his neck, and his heels flying in the air every jump, and the whole crowd of people standing up shouting and laughing till the tears rolled down. And at last, sure enough, all the circus men could do, the horse broke loose, and away he went like the very nation, round and round the ring, with that sot laying down on him and hanging to his neck, with first one leg hanging most to the ground on one side, and then t'other side, and the people just crazy. It warn't funny to me, though; I was all of a tremble to see his danger. But [193] pretty soon he struggled up astraddle and grabbed the bridle, a-reeling this way and that; and the next minute he sprung up and dropped the bridle and stood! and the horse agoing like a house afire too. He just stood up there, a-sailing around as easy and comfortable as if he warn't ever drunk in his life—and then he begun to pull off his clothes and sling them. He shed them so thick they kind of clogged up the air, and altogether he shed seventeen suits. And then, there he was, slim and handsome, and dressed the gaudiest and prettiest you ever saw, and he lit into that horse

with his whip and made him fairly hum—and finally skipped off, and made
his bow and danced off to the dressing-room, and everybody just a-howling
with pleasure and astonishment.

Then the ring-master he see how he had been fooled, and he *was* the
sickest ring-master you ever see, I reckon. Why, it was one of his own men!
He had got up that joke all out of his own head, and never let on to nobody.
Well, I felt sheepish enough, to be took in so, but I wouldn't a been in that
ring-master's place, not for a thousand dollars. I don't know; there may be
bullier circuses than what that one was, but I never struck them yet. Anyways it was plenty good enough for *me;* and wherever I run across it, it can
have all of *my* custom, every time.

Well, that night we had *our* show; but there warn't only about twelve
people there; just enough to pay expenses. And they laughed all the time,
and that made the duke mad; and everybody left, anyway, before the show
was over, but one boy which was asleep. So the duke said these Arkansaw
lunkheads couldn't come up to Shakespeare; what they wanted was low
comedy—and may be something ruther worse than low comedy, he reckoned. He said he could size their style. So next morning he got some big
sheets of wrapping-paper and some black paint, and drawed off some hand-
bills and struck them up all over the village. The bills said: [194]

AT THE COURT HOUSE!
For 3 nights only!

The World-Renowned Tragedians
DAVID GARRICK THE YOUNGER!
and
EDMUND KEAN THE ELDER!
Of the London and Continental
Theatres,

In their Thrilling Tragedy of
THE KING'S CAMELOPARD
or
THE ROYAL NONESUCH!!!
Admission 50 cents.

Then at the bottom was the biggest line of all—which said:

LADIES AND CHILDREN NOT ADMITTED

"There," says he, "if that line don't fetch them I don't know Arkansaw!"
[195]

SARAH ORNE JEWETT
1849–1909

Men and Women of Old New England

"MISS TEMPY'S WATCHERS"

Sarah Orne Jewett was born in 1849 in the village of South Berwick, Maine, and many of her stories depict the life that she knew in this community. Her materials came from the legends of the townspeople, one of them her grandfather, who had known the town when it had flourished. Jewett wrote chiefly of the decline of South Berwick. The daughter of a country doctor, she profited much from traveling with her father as he made his rounds along the coast of Maine. She owed much of her education to him, for he was an intelligent, cultivated man.

In writing of the decline of her own town, Jewett wanted to stress how glorious the past had been. Certainly she witnessed what was happening as the children began leaving, the old people remaining behind—with the disappearing farms and the decaying town offering mute evidence of the change. Early on she had observed the coming of the workers to the textile mills, and she declared her intention of defending the people she knew. "When I was perhaps fifteen," she wrote, "the first city boarders began to make their appearance near Berwick, and the way they misconstrued the country people and made game of their peculiarities fired me with indignation. I determined to teach the world that country people were not the awkward, ignorant set those people seemed to think. I wanted the world to know their grand simple lives; and, so far as I had a mission, when I first began to write, I think that was it."

There are no grotesques among her characters; instead she concentrates on the admirable figures she knew. The men and women she created, many of them shrewd and quick-witted, are genuine and realistically presented.

Characterization—as well as background and atmosphere—are emphasized above plot. While essentially a realist, Jewett recorded the lives of the ordinary people with a touch of romanticism. Certainly there is nothing coarse or common in her sketches of the old-time village and farm life.

Jewett was first published in The *Atlantic* in 1869. Then followed *Deephaven* (1877), *Tales of New England* (1879), and *The Country of the Pointed Firs* (1896). "Miss Tempy's Watchers," which first appeared in *Tales of New England,* demonstrates her power of characterization and her use of regional dialect. The two women, who sit through the night while Miss Tempy's body lies upstairs, reveal much about themselves and their community.

"MISS TEMPY'S WATCHERS"

The time of year was April; the place was a small farming town in New Hampshire, remote from any railroad. One by one the lights had been blown out in the scattered houses near Miss Tempy Dent's; but as her neighbors took a last look out-of-doors, their eyes turned with instinctive curiosity toward the old house, where a lamp burned steadily. They gave a little sigh. "Poor Miss Tempy!" said more than one bereft acquaintance; for the good woman lay dead in her north chamber, and the light was a watcher's light. The funeral was set for the next day, at one o'clock.

The watchers were two of the oldest friends, Mrs. Crowe and Sarah Ann Binson. They were sitting in the kitchen, because it seemed less awesome than the unused best room, and they beguiled the long hours by steady conversation. One would think that [7] neither topics nor opinions would hold out, at that rate, all through the long spring night; but there was a certain degree of excitement just then, and the two women had risen to an unusual level of expressiveness and confidence. Each had already told the other more than one fact that she had determined to keep secret; they were again and again tempted into statements that either would have found impossible by daylight. Mrs. Crowe was knitting a blue yarn stocking for her husband; the foot was already so long that it seemed as if she must have forgotten to narrow it at the proper time. Mrs. Crowe knew exactly what she was about, however; she was of a much cooler disposition than Sister Binson, who made futile attempts at some sewing, only to drop her work into her lap whenever the talk was most engaging.

Sarah Orne Jewett, "Miss Tempy's Watchers," from *Tales of New England* (Boston: Houghton Mifflin Company) 1894.

Their faces were interesting,—of the dry, shrewd, quick-witted New England type, with thin hair twisted neatly back out of the way. Mrs. Crowe could look vague and benignant, and Miss Binson was, to quote her neighbors, a little too sharp-set; but the world knew that she had need to be, with the load she must carry of supporting an ineffi-[8]cient widowed sister and six unpromising and unwilling nieces and nephews. The eldest boy was at last placed with a good man to learn the mason's trade. Sarah Ann Binson, for all her sharp, anxious aspect, never defended herself, when her sister whined and fretted. She was told every week of her life that the poor children never would have had to lift a finger if their father had lived, and yet she had kept her steadfast way with the little farm, and patiently taught the young people many useful things, for which, as everybody said, they would live to thank her. However pleasureless her life appeared to outward view, it was brimful of pleasure to herself.

Mrs. Crowe, on the contrary, was well to do, her husband being a rich farmer and an easy-going man. She was a stingy woman, but for all that she looked kindly; and when she gave away anything, or lifted a finger to help anybody, it was thought a great piece of beneficence, and a compliment, indeed, which the recipient accepted with twice as much gratitude as double the gift that came from a poorer and more generous acquaintance. Everybody liked to be on good terms with Mrs. Crowe. Socially she stood much [9] higher than Sarah Ann Binson. They were both old schoolmates and friends of Temperance Dent, who had asked them, one day, not long before she died, if they would not come together and look after the house, and manage everything, when she was gone. She may have had some hope that they might become closer friends in this period of intimate partnership, and that the richer woman might better understand the burdens of the poorer. They had not kept the house the night before; they were too weary with the care of their old friend, whom they had not left until all was over.

There was a brook which ran down the hillside very near the house, and the sound of it was much louder than usual. When there was silence in the kitchen, the busy stream had a strange insistence in its wild voice, as if it tried to make the watchers understand something that related to the past.

"I declare, I can't begin to sorrow for Tempy yet. I am so glad to have her at rest," whispered Mrs. Crowe. "It is strange to set here without her, but I can't make it clear that she has gone. I feel as if she had got easy and dropped off to sleep, and I'm more scared about waking her up than knowing any other feeling." [10]

"Yes," said Sarah Ann, "it's just like that, ain't it? But I tell you we are goin' to miss her worse than we expect. She's helped me through with many a trial, has Temperance. I ain't the only one who says the same, neither."

These words were spoken as if there were a third person listening; somebody beside Mrs. Crowe. The watchers could not rid their minds of the feeling that they were being watched themselves. The spring wind whistled in the window crack, now and then, and buffeted the little house in a gusty way that had a sort of companionable effect. Yet, on the whole, it was a very still night, and the watchers spoke in a half-whisper.

"She was the freest-handed woman that ever I knew," said Mrs. Crowe, decidedly. "According to her means, she gave away more than anybody. I used to tell her 't wa'n't right. I used really to be afraid that she went with out too much, for we have a duty to ourselves."

Sister Binson looked up in a half-amused, unconscious way, and then recollected herself.

Mrs. Crowe met her look with a serious face. "It ain't so easy for me to give as it [11] is for some," she said simply, but with an effort which was made possible only by the occasion. "I should like to say, while Tempy is laying here yet in her own house, that she has been a constant lesson to me. Folks are too kind, and shame me with thanks for what I do. I ain't such a generous woman as poor Tempy was, for all she had nothin' to do with, as one may say."

Sarah Binson was much moved at this confession, and was even pained and touched by the unexpected humility. "You have a good many calls on you"—she began, and then left her kind little compliment half finished.

"Yes, yes, but I've got means enough. My disposition's more of a cross to me as I grow older, and I made up my mind this morning that Tempy's example should be my pattern henceforth." She began to knit faster than ever.

"'T ain't no use to get morbid: that's what Tempy used to say her-self," said Sarah Ann, after a minute's silence. "Ain't it strange to say 'used to say'? and her own voice choked a little. "She never did like to hear folks git goin' about themselves."

"'T was only because they're apt to do it [12], so as other folks will say 't wasn't so, an' praise 'em up," humbly replied Mrs. Crowe, "and that ain't my object. There wa'n't a child but what Tempy set herself to work to see what she could do to please it. One time my brother's folks had been stop-ping here in the summer, from Massachusetts. The children was all little, and they broke up a sight of toys, and left 'em when they were going away. Tempy come right up after they rode by, to see if she couldn't help me set the house to rights, and she caught me just as I was going to fling some of the clutter into the stove. I was kind of tired out, starting 'em off in season. 'Oh, give me them!' says she, real pleading; and she wropped 'em up and took 'em home with her when she went, and she mended 'em up and stuck 'em together, and made some young one or other happy with every blessed one. You'd thought I'd done her the biggest favor. 'No thanks to me. I should ha' burnt 'em, Tempy,' says I."

"Some of 'em came to our house, I know," said Miss Binson. "She'd take a lot o' trouble to please a child, 'stead o' shoving of it out o' the way, like the rest of us when we're drove." [13]

"I can tell you the biggest thing she ever done, and I don't know's there's anybody left but me to tell it. I don't want it forgot," Sarah Binson went on, looking up at the clock to see how the night was going. "It was that pretty-looking Trevor girl, who taught the Corners school, and married so well afterwards, out in New York State. You remember her, I dare say?"

"Certain," said Mrs. Crowe, with an air of interest.

"She was a splendid scholar, folks said, and give the school a great start; but she'd overdone herself getting her education, and working to pay for it, and she all broke down one spring, and Tempy made her come and stop with her a while,—you remember that? Well, she had an uncle, her mother's brother, out in Chicago, who was well off and friendly, and used to write to Lizzie Trevor, and I dare say make her some presents; but he was a lively, driving man, and didn't take time to stop and think about his folks. He hadn't seen her since she was a little girl. Poor Lizzie was so pale and weakly that she just got through the term o' school. She looked as if she was just going straight off in a decline. Tempy, she [14] cosseted her up a while, and then, next thing folks knew, she was tellin' round how Miss Trevor had gone to see her uncle, and meant to visit Niagray Falls on the way, and stop over night. Now I happened to know, in ways I won't dwell on to explain, that the poor girl was in debt for her schoolin' when she come here, and her last quarter's pay had just squared it off at last, and left her without a cent ahead, hardly; but it had fretted her thinking of it, so she paid it all; those might have dunned her that she owed it to. An' I taxed Tempy about the girl's goin off on such a journey till she owned up, rather'n have Lizzie blamed, that she'd given her sixty dollars, same's if she was rolling in riches, and sent her off to have a good rest and vacation."

"Sixty dollars!" exclaimed Mrs. Crowe. "Tempy only had ninety dollars a year that came in to her; rest of her livin' she got by helpin' about, with what she raised off this little piece o' ground, sand one side an' clay the other. An' how often I've heard her tell, years ago, that she'd rather see Niagary than any other sight in the world!"

The women looked at each other in silence; the magnitude of the generous sacri-[15]fice was almost too great for their comprehension.

"She was just poor enough to do that'" declared Mrs. Crowe at last, in an abandonment of feeling. "Say what you may, I feel humbled to the dust," and her companion ventured to say nothing. She never had given away sixty dollars at once, but it was simply because she never had it to give. It came to her very lips to say in explanation, "Tempy was so situated;" but she checked herself in time, for she would not betray her own loyal guarding of a dependent household.

"Folks say a great deal of generosity, and this one's being public-sperited, and that one free-handed about giving," said Mrs. Crowe, who was a little nervous in the silence. "I suppose we can't tell the sorrow it would be to some folks not to give, same's 't would be to me not to save. I seem

kind of made for that, as if 't was what I'd got to do. I should feel sights
better about it if I could make it evident what I was savin' for. If I had a
child, now, Sarah Ann," and her voice was a little husky,—"if I had a child,
I should think I was heapin' of it up because he was the one [16] trained by
the Lord to scatter it again for good. But here's Mr. Crowe and me, we
can't do anything with money, and both of us like to keep things same's
they've always been. Now Priscilla Dance was talking away like a mill-
clapper, week before last. She'd think I would go right off and get one o'
them new-fashioned gilt-and-white papers for the best room, and some new
furniture, an' a marble-top table. And I looked at her, all struck up. 'Why,'
says I, 'Priscilla, that nice old velvet paper ain't hurt a mite. I shouldn't feel
't was my best room without it. Dan'el says 't is the first thing he can remember rubbin' his little baby fingers on to it, and how splendid he thought
them red roses was.' I maintain," continued Mrs. Crowe stoutly, "that folks
wastes sights o' good money doin' just just foolish things. Tearin' out the
insides o' meetin'-houses, and fixin' the pews different; 't was good enough
as 't was with mendin'; then times come, an' they want to put it all back
same's 't was before."

This touched upon an exciting subject to active members of that
parish. Miss Binson and Mrs. Crowe belonged to opposite parties, and had
at one time come as near hard [17] feelings as they could, and yet escape
them. Each hastened to speak of other things and to show her untouched
friendliness.

"I do agree with you," said Sister Binson, "that few of us know what
use to make of money, beyond every-day necessities. You've seen more o' the
world than I have, and know what's expected. When it comes to taste and
judgment about such things, I ought to defer to others;" and with this
modest avowal the critical moment passed when there might have been an
improper discussion.

In the silence that followed, the fact of their presence in a house of
death grew more clear than before. There was something disturbing in the
noise of a mouse gnawing at the dry boards of a closet wall near by. Both the
watchers looked up anxiously at the clock; it was almost the middle of
the night, and the whole world seemed to have left them alone with their
solemn duty. Only the brook was awake.

"Perhaps we might give a look up-stairs now," whispered Mrs. Crowe,
as if she hoped to hear some reason against their going just then to the
chamber of death; but Sister Binson rose, with a serious and yet [18] satisfied countenance, and lifted the small lamp from the table. She was much
more used to watching than Mrs. Crowe, and much less affected by it. They
opened the door into a small entry with a steep stairway; they climbed the
creaking stairs, and entered the cold upper room on tiptoe. Mrs. Crowe's
heart began to beat very fast as the lamp was put on a high bureau, and
made long, fixed shadows about the walls. She went hesistatingly toward the

solemn shape under its white drapery, and felt a sense of remonstrance as Sarah Ann gently, but in a business-like way, turned back the thin sheet.

"Seems to me she looks pleasanter and pleasanter," whispered Sarah Ann Binson impulsively, as they gazed at the white face with its wonderful smile. "To-morrow 't will all have faded out. I do believe they kind of wake up a day or two after they die, and it's then they go." She replaced the light covering, and they both turned quickly away; there was a chill in this upper room.

"'T is a great thing for anybody to have got through, ain't it?" said Mrs. Crowe softly, as she began to go down the stairs on tiptoe. The warm air from the kitchen [19] beneath met them with a sense of welcome and shelter.

"I don' know why it is, but I feel as near again to Tempy down here as I do up there," replied Sister Binson. "I feel as if the air was full of her, kind of. I can sense things, now and then, that she seems to say. Now I never was one to take up with no nonsense of sperits and such, but I declare I felt as if she told me just now to put some more wood into the stove."

Mrs. Crowe preserved a gloomy silence. She had suspected before this that her companion was of a weaker and more credulous disposition than herself. "'T is a great thing to have got through," she repeated, ignoring definitely all that had last been said. "I suppose you know as well as I that Tempy was one that always feared death. Well, it's all put behind her now; she knows what 't is." Mrs. Crowe gave a little sigh, and Sister Binson's quick sympathies were stirred toward this other old friend, who also dreaded the great change.

"I'd never like to forgit almost those last words Tempy spoke plain to me," she said gently, like the comforter she truly was. "She looked up at me once or twice, that [20] last afternoon after I come to set by her, and let Mis' Owen go home; and I says, 'Can I do anything to ease you Tempy?' and the tears come into my eyes so I couldn't see what kind of a nod she give me. 'No, Sarah Ann, you can't, dear,' says she; and then she got her breath again, and says she, looking at me real meanin', I'm only a-gettin' sleepier and sleepier; that's all there is,' says she, and smiled up at me kind of wishful, and shut her eyes. I knew well enough all she meant. She'd been lookin' out for a chance to tell me, and I don' know's she ever said much afterwards."

Mrs. Crowe was not knitting; she had been listening too eagerly. "Yes, 't will be a comfort to think of that sometimes," she said, in acknowledgment.

"I know that old Dr. Prince said once, in evenin' meetin', that he'd watched by many a dyin' bed, as we well knew, and enough o' his sick folks had been scared o' dyin' their whole lives through; but when they come to the last, he'd never seen one but was willin', and most were glad, to go. ''T is as natural as bein' born or livin' on,' he said. I don't know what had moved him to speak that night. You know he wa'n't [21] in the habit of it, and 't was the monthly concert of prayer for foreign missions anyways," said Sarah Ann; "but 't was a great stay to the mind to listen to his words of experience."

"There never was a better man," responded Mrs. Crowe, in a really cheerful tone. She had recovered from her feeling of nervous dread, the kitchen was so comfortable with lamplight and firelight; and just then the old clock began to tell the hour of twelve with leisurely whirring strokes.

Sister Binson laid aside her work, and rose quickly and went to the cupboard. "We'd better take a little to eat," she explained. "The night will go fast after this. I want to know if you went and made some o' your nice cupcake, while you was home to-day?" she asked, in a pleased tone; and Mrs. Crowe acknowledged such a gratifying piece of thoughtfulness for this humble friend who denied herself all luxuries. Sarah Ann brewed a generous cup of tea, and the watchers drew their chairs up to the table presently, and quelled their hunger with good country appetites. Sister Binson put a spoon into a small, old-fashioned glass of preserved quince, and passed it to [22] her friend. She was most familiar with the house, and played the part of hostess. "Spread some o' this on your bread and butter," she said to Mrs. Crowe. "Tempy wanted me to use some three or four times, but I never felt to. I know she'd like to have us comfortable now, and would urge us to make a good supper, poor dear."

"What excellent preserves she did make!" mourned Mrs. Crowe. "None of us has got her light hand at doin' things tasty. She made the most o' everything, too. Now, she only had that one old quince-tree down in the far corner of the piece, but she'd go out in the spring and tend to it, and look at it so pleasant, and kind of expect the old thorny thing into bloomin'."

"She was just the same with folks," said Sarah Ann. "And she'd never git mor'n a little apernful o' quinces, but she'd have every mite o' good-ness out o' those, and set the glasses up onto her best-room closet shelf, *so* pleased. 'T wa'n't but a week ago to-morrow mornin' I fetched her a little taste o' jelly in a teaspoon; and she says 'Thank ye,' and took it, an' the minute she tasted it she looked up at me as worried as could be. 'Oh, I don't want to eat that,' says she, [23] 'I always keep that in case o' sickness.' 'You're goin' to have the good o' one tumbler yourself,' says I. 'I'd just like to know who's sick now, if you ain't!' An' she couldn't help laughin', I spoke up so smart. Oh, dear me, how I shall miss talkin' over things with her! She always sensed things, and got just the p'int you meant."

"She didn't begin to age until two or three years ago, did she?" asked Mrs. Crowe. "I never saw anybody keep her looks as Tempy did. She looked young long after I begun to feel like an old woman. The doctor used to say 't was her young heart, and I don't know but what he was right. How she did do for other folks! There was one spell she wasn't at home a day to a fortnight. She got most of her livin' so, and that made her own potatoes and things last her through. None o' the young folks could get married without her, and all the old ones was disappointed if she wa'n't round when they was down with sickness and had to go. An' cleanin', or tailorin' for boys, or rug-hookin',—there was nothing' but what she could do as handy as most. 'I do love to work,'—ain't you heard her say that twenty times a week?" [24]

Sarah Ann Binson nodded, and began to clear away the empty plates. "We may want a taste o' somethin' more towards mornin'," she said. "There's plenty in the closet here; and in case some comes from a distance to the funeral, we'll have a little table spread after we get back to the house."

"Yes, I was busy all the mornin'. I've cooked up a sight o' things to bring over," said Mrs. Crowe. "I felt 't was the last I could do for her."

They drew their chairs near the stove again, and took up their work. Sister Binson's rocking-chair creaked as she rocked; the brook sounded louder than ever. It was more lonely when nobody spoke, and presently Mrs. Crowe returned to her thoughts of growing old.

"Yes, Tempy aged all of a sudden. I remember I asked her if she felt as well as common, one day, and she laughed at me good. There, when Mr. Crowe begun to look old, I couldn't help feeling as if somethin' ailed him, and like as not 't was somethin' he was goin' to git right over, and I dosed him for it stiddy, half of one summer."

"How many things we shall be wanting to ask Tempy!" exclaimed Sarah Ann [25] Binson, after a long pause. "I can't make up my mind to doin' without her. I wish folks could come back just once, and tell us how 't is where they've gone. Seems then we could do without 'em better."

The brook hurried on, the wind blew about the house now and then; the house itself was a silent place, and the supper, the warm fire, and an absence of any new topics for conversation made the watchers drowsy. Sister Binson closed her eyes first, to rest them for a minute; and Mrs. Crowe glanced at her compassionately, with a new sympathy for the hard-worked little woman. She made up her mind to let Sarah Ann have a good rest, while she kept watch alone; but in a few minutes her own knitting was dropped, and she, too, fell asleep. Overhead, the pale shape of Tempy Dent, the outworn body of that generous, loving-hearted, simple soul, slept on also in its white raiment. Perhaps Tempy herself stood near, and saw her own life and its surroundings with new understanding. Perhaps she herself was the only watcher.

Later, by some hours, Sarah Ann Binson woke with a start. There was a pale light [26] of dawn outside the small windows. Inside the kitchen, the lamp burned dim. Mrs. Crowe awoke, too.

"I think Tempy'd be the first to say 't was just as well we both had some rest," she said, not without a guilty feeling.

Her companion went to the outer door, and opened it wide. The fresh air was none too cold, and the brook's voice was not nearly so loud as it had been in the midnight darkness. She could see the shapes of the hills, and the great shadows that lay across the lower country. The east was fast growing bright.

" 'T will be a beautiful day for the funeral," she said, and turned again, with a sigh, to follow Mrs. Crowe up the stairs. [27]

MARY E. WILKINS FREEMAN
1852-1930

Puritan Restraints

"TWO OLD LOVERS"

A local colorist of the highest order, Mary E. Wilkins Freeman wrote chiefly of country life in Massachusetts. Her early life was spent in the restricted atmosphere of New England villages, in an environment marked by puritan restraints. Certainly it was not an easy life: she was handicapped by ill health in her early years, her parents died when she was young, and her schooling was severely limited. She wrote to earn a living, using her home town of Randolph, Massachusetts, and the people she knew there as material for her stories. She was quite successful as a short-story writer, her stories—episodic in form—consisting of careful studies of characters who lived in the rigid New England environment.

Her writing is marked by objectivity and detachment. The reality of her dialect, the simplicity of her style, and the verisimilitude of her settings permit her to portray honestly and realistically the decline of New England. She acknowledges that the greatness of New England lies in its past; yet she deals with its decline without sentimental overtones. Her characters are the men and women who remained in New England after the West was opened. They are the humble, ordinary figures—the old, the helpless, and at times the abnormal—whose lives are the product of repression. There is no romanticism in her writing. The portrayals of the towns and the people are grim and stark, showing the harsh environment and the unfortunate people in a variety of small-town locales.

Her best work appeared when she was Mary Wilkins. At 49, she married Dr. Charles M. Freeman, and after that her achievement fell off, her writing becoming more sophisticated and self-conscious. In this later period she turned out serials for women's magazines, but these pieces of writing are of little worth.

Her two important works are *A Humble Romance and Other Stories* (1887) and *A New England Nun and Others Stories* (1891). "Two Old Lovers," which is from *A Humble Romance,* shows the remarkable economy of Freeman's early work. The hamlet of Leyden is treated with accuracy and the characters represent the villagers who cling to tradition, though tense and repressed by the environment.

"TWO OLD LOVERS"

Leyden was emphatically a village of cottages, and each of them built after one of two patterns: either the front door was on the right side, in the corner of a little piazza extending a third of the length of the house, with the main roof jutting over it, or the piazza stretched across the front, and the door was in the centre.

The cottages were painted uniformly white, and had blinds of a bright spring-green color. There was a little flower-garden in front of each; the beds were laid out artistically in triangles, hearts, and rounds, and edged with box; boys'-love, sweet-williams, and pinks were the fashionable and prevailing flowers.

There was a general air of cheerful though humble prosperity about the place, which it owed, and indeed its very existence also, to the three old weather-beaten boot-and-shoe factories which arose stanchly and importantly in the very midst of the natty little white cottages.

Years before, when one Hiram Strong put up his three factories for the manufacture of the rough shoe which the working-man of America wears, he hardly thought he was also gaining for himself the honor of founding Leyden. He chose the site for his buildings mainly because they would be easily accessible to the railway which stretched [25] to the city, sixty miles distant. At first the workmen came on the cars from the neighboring towns, but after a while they became tired of that, and one after another built for himself a cottage, and established his family and his household belongings near the scene of his daily labors. So gradually Leyden grew. A built his cottage like C, and B built his like D. They painted them white, and hung the green blinds, and laid out their flower-beds in front and their vegetable-beds at the back. By and by came a church and a store and a post-office to pass, and Leyden was a full-fledged town.

That was a long time ago. The shoe-factories had long passed out of the hands of Hiram Strong's heirs; he himself was only a memory on the earth. The business was not quite as wide-awake and vigorous as when in its first youth; it droned a little now; there was not quite so much bustle

Mary E. Wilkins, "Two Old Lovers," from *A Humble Romance and Other Stories* (New York: Harper & Brothers, Publishers, 1887). Used by permission of Harper & Row, Publishers, Incorporated.

and hurry as formerly. The factories were never lighted up of an evening on account of over-work, and the workmen found plenty of time for pleasant and salutary gossip over their cutting and pegging. But this did not detract in the least from the general cheerfulness and prosperity of Leyden. The inhabitants still had all the work they needed to supply the means necessary for their small comforts, and they were contented. They too had begun to drone a little like the factories. "As slow as Leyden" was the saying among the faster-going towns adjoining theirs. Every morning at seven the old men, young men, and boys, in their calico shirt-sleeves, their faces a ilttle pale—perhaps from their in-door life—filed unquestioningly out of the back doors of the white cottages, treading still deeper the well-worn foot-paths stretching around the sides of the houses, and entered the factories. They were great, [26] ugly wooden buildings, with wings which they had grown in their youth jutting clumsily from their lumbering shoulders. Their outer walls were black and grimy, streaked and splashed and patched with red paint in every variety of shade, accordingly as the original hue was tempered with smoke or the beatings of the storms of many years.

The men worked peacefully and evenly in the shoe-shops all day; and the women stayed at home and kept the little white cottages tidy, cooked the meals, and washed the clothes, and did the sewing. For recreation the men sat on the piazza in front of Barker's store of an evening, and gossiped or discussed politics; and the women talked over their neighbors' fences, or took their sewing into their neighbors' of an afternoon.

People died in Leyden as elsewhere; and here and there was a little white cottage whose narrow foot-path leading round to its back door its master would never tread again.

In one of these lived Widow Martha Brewster and her daughter Maria. Their cottage was one of those which had its piazza across the front. Every summer they trained morning-glories over it, and planted their little garden with the flower-seeds popular in Leyden. There was not a cottage in the whole place whose surroundings were neater and gayer than theirs, for all they were only two women, and two old women at that; for Widow Martha Brewster was in the neighborhood of eighty, and her daughter, Maria Brewster, near sixty. The two had lived alone since Jacob Brewster died and stopped going to the factory, some fifteen years ago. He had left them this particular white cottage, and a snug little sum in the savings-bank besides, for the whole Brewster family had [27] worked and economized all their long lives. The women had corded boots at home, while the man had worked in the shop, and never spent a cent without thinking of it overnight.

Leyden folks all thought that David Emmons would marry Maria Brewster when her father died. "David can rent his house, and go to live with Maria and her mother," said they, with an affectionate readiness to arrange matters for them. But he did not. Every Sunday night at eight o'clock punctually, the form of David Emmons, arrayed in his best clothes, with his stiff white dickey, and a nosegay in his button-hole, was seen to advance up the road towards Maria Brewster's, as he had been seen to advance every Sunday night for the last twenty-five years, but that was all. He manifested not the slightest intention of carrying out people's judicious plans for his welfare and Maria's.

She did not seem to pine with hope deferred; people could not honestly think there was any occasion to pity her for her lover's tardiness. A cheerier woman never lived. She was literally bubbling over with jollity. Round-faced and black-eyed, with a funny little bounce of her whole body when she walked, she was the merry feature of the whole place.

Her mother was now too feeble, but Maria still corded boots for the factories as of old. David Emmons, who was quite sixty, worked in them, as he had from his youth. He was a slender, mild-faced old man, with a fringe of gray yellow beard around his chin; his head was quite bald. Years ago he had been handsome, they said, but somehow people had always laughed at him a little, although they all liked him. "The slowest of all the slow Leydenites" [28] outsiders called him, and even the "slow Leydenites" poked fun at this exaggeration of themselves. It was an old and well-worn remark that it took David Emmons an hour to go courting, and that he was always obliged to leave his own home at seven in order to reach Maria's at eight, and there was a standing joke that the meeting-house passed him one morning on his way to the shop.

David heard the chaffing of course—there is a very little delicacy in matters of this kind among country people—but he took it all in good part. He would laugh at himself with the rest, but there was something touching in his deprecatory way of saying sometimes, "Well, I don't know how 'tis, but it don't seem to be in my natur' to do any other way. I suppose I was born without the faculty of gittin' along quick in this world. You'll have to git behind and push me a leetle, I reckon."

He owned his little cottage, which was one of the kind which had the piazza on the right side. He lived entirely alone. There was a half-acre or so of land beside his house, which he used for a vegetable garden. After and before shop hours, in the dewy evenings and mornings, he dug and weeded assiduously between the green ranks of corn and beans. If David Emmons was slow, his vegetables were not. None of the gardens in Leyden surpassed his in luxuriant growth. His corn tasselled out and his potato patch was white with blossoms as soon as anybody's.

He was almost a vegetarian in his diet; the products of his garden spot were his staple articles of food. Early in the morning would the gentle old bachelor set his spot of green things boiling, and dine gratefully at noon, like mild Robert Herrick, on pulse and herbs. His garden supplied also his sweetheart and her mother with all the vegetables [29] they could use. Many times in the course of a week could David have been seen slowly moving towards the Brewster cottage with a basket on his arm well stocked with the materials for an innocent and delicious repast.

But Maria was not to be outdone by her old lover in kindly deeds. Not a Saturday but a goodly share of her weekly baking was deposited, neatly covered with a white crash towel, on David's little kitchen table. The surreptitious air with which the back-door key was taken from its hiding-place (which she well knew) under the kitchen blind, the door unlocked and entered, and the good things deposited, was charming, although highly ineffectual. "There goes Maria with David's baking," said the women, peering out of their windows as she bounced, rather more gently and cautiously than usual, down the street. And David himself knew well the ministering angel to whom these benefits were due when he lifted the towel and discovered with tearful eyes the brown loaves and flaky pies—the proofs of his Maria's love and culinary skill.

Among the younger and more irreverent portions of the community there was considerable speculation as to the mode of courtship of these old lovers of twenty-five years' standing. Was there ever a kiss, a tender clasp of the hand, those usual expressions of affection between sweethearts?

Some of the more daring spirits had even gone so far as to commit the manifest impropriety of peeping in Maria's parlor windows; but they had only seen David sitting quiet and prim on the little slippery horse-hair sofa, and Maria by the table, rocking slowly in her little cane-seated rocker. Did Maria ever leave her rocker and sit on that slippery horse-hair sofa by David's side? They never knew; but [30] she never did. There was something laughable, and at the same time rather pathetic, about Maria and David's courting. All the outward appurtenances of "keeping company" were as rigidly observed as they had been twenty-five years ago, when David Emmons first cast his mild blue eyes shyly and lovingly on red-cheeked, quick-spoken Maria Brewster. Every Sunday evening, in the winter, there was a fire kindled in the parlor, the parlor lamp was lit at dusk all the year round, and Maria's mother retired early, that the young people might "sit up." The "sitting up" was no very formidable affair now, whatever it might have been in the first stages of the courtship. The need of sleep overbalanced sentiment in those old lovers, and by ten o'clock at the latest Maria's lamp was out, and David had wended his solitary way to his own home.

Leyden people had a great curiosity to know if David had ever actually popped the question to Maria, or if his natural slowness was at fault in this as in other things. Their curiosity had been long exercised in vain, but Widow Brewster, as she waxed older, grew loquacious, and one day told a neighbor, who had called in her daughter's absence, that "David had never reely come to the p'int. She supposed he would some time; for her part, she thought he had better; but then, after all, she knowed Maria didn't care, and maybe 'twas jest as well as 'twas, only sometimes she was afeard she should never live to see the weddin' if they wasn't spry." Then there had been hints concerning a certain pearl-colored silk which Maria, having a good chance to get at a bargain, had purchased some twenty years ago, when she thought, from sundry remarks, that David was coming to the point; and it was further intimated that the silk had been privately made up ten years [31] since, when Maria had again surmised that the point was about being reached. The neighbor went home in a state of great delight, having by skilful manœuvring actually obtained a glimpse of the pearl-colored silk.

It was perfectly true that Maria did not lay David's tardiness in putting the important question very much to heart. She was too cheerful, too busy, and too much interested in her daily duties to fret much about anything. There was never at any time much of the sentimental element in her composition, and her feeling for David was eminently practical in its nature. She, although the woman, had the stronger character of the two, and there was something rather mother-like than lover-like in her affection for him. It was through the protecting care which chiefly characterized her love that the only pain to her came from their long courtship and postponement of marriage. It was true that, years ago, when David had led her to think, from certain hesitating words spoken at parting one Sunday night, that he would certainly ask the momentous question soon, her heart had gone into a happy flutter. She had bought the pearl-colored silk then.

Years after, her heart had fluttered again, but a little less wildly this time. David almost asked her another Sunday night. Then she had made up the pearl-colored silk. She used to go and look at it fondly and admiringly from time to time; once in a while she would try it on and survey herself in the glass, and imagine herself David's bride—a faded bride, but a happy and a beloved one.

She looked at the dress occasionally now, but a little sadly, as the conviction that she should never wear it was forcing itself upon her more and more. But the sadness was always more for David's sake than her own. She saw [32] him growing an old man, and the lonely, uncared-for life that he led filled her heart with tender pity and sorrow for him. She did not confine her kind offices to the Saturday baking. Every week his little house was tidied and set to rights, and his mending looked after.

Once, on a Sunday night, when she spied a rip in his coat, that had grown long from the want of womanly fingers constantly at hand, she had a good cry after he had left and she had gone into her room. There was something more pitiful to her, something that touched her heart more deeply, in that rip in her lover's Sunday coat than in all her long years of waiting.

As the years went on, it was sometimes with a sad heart that Maria stood and watched the poor lonely old figure moving slower than ever down the street to his lonely home; but the heart was sad for him always, and never for herself. She used to wonder at him a little sometimes, though always with the most loyal tenderness, that he should choose to lead the solitary, cheerless life that he did, to go back to his dark, voiceless home, when he might be so sheltered and cared for in his old age. She firmly believed that it was only owing to her lover's incorrigible slowness, in this as in everything else. She never doubted for an instant that he loved her. Some women might have tried hastening matters a little themselves, but Maria, with the delicacy which is sometimes more inherent in a steady, practical nature like hers than in a more ardent one, would have lost her self-respect forever if she had done such a thing.

So she lived cheerfully along, corded her boots, though her fingers were getting stiff, humored her mother, who was getting feebler and more childish every year, and did the best she could for her poor, foolish old lover. [33]

When David was seventy, and she sixty-eight, she gave away the pearl-colored silk to a cousin's daughter who was going to be married. The girl was young and pretty and happy, but she was poor, and the silk would make over into a grander wedding dress for her than she could hope to obtain in any other way.

Poor old Maria smoothed the lustrous folds fondly with her withered hands before sending it away, and cried a little, with a patient pity for David and herself. But when a tear splashed directly on to the shining surface of the silk, she stopped crying at once, and her sorrowful expression changed into one of careful scrutiny as she wiped the salt drop away with her handkerchief, and held the dress up to the light to be sure that it was not spotted. A practical nature like Maria's is sometimes a great boon to its possessor. It is doubtful if anything else can dry a tear as quickly.

Somehow Maria always felt a little differently towards David after she had given away her wedding dress. There had always been a little tinge of consciousness in her manner towards him, a little reserve and caution before people. But after the wedding dress had gone, all question of marriage had disappeared so entirely from her mind, that the delicate considerations born of it vanished. She was uncommonly hale and hearty for a woman of her age; there was apparently much more than two years' difference between her and her lover. It was not only the Saturday's bread and pie that she carried now and deposited on David's little kitchen table, but, openly and boldly, not caring who should see her, many a warm dinner. Every day, after her own house-work was done, David's house was set to rights. He should have all the comforts he needed in [34] his last years, she determined. That they were his last years was evident. He coughed, and now walked so slowly from feebleness and weakness that it was a matter of doubt to observers whether he could reach Maria Brewster's before Monday evening.

One Sunday night he stayed a little longer than usual—the clock struck ten before he started. Then he rose, and said, as he had done every Sunday evening for so many years. "Well, Maria, I guess it's about time for me to be goin'."

She helped him on with his coat, and tied on his tippet. Contrary to his usual habit he stood in the door, and hesitated a minute—there seemed to be something he wanted to say.

"Maria."

"Well, David?"

"I'm gittin' to be an old man, you know, an' I've allus been slow-goin'; I couldn't seem to help it. There has been a good many things I haven't got around to." The old cracked voice quavered painfully.

"Yes, I know, David, all about it; you couldn't help it. I wouldn't worry a bit about it if I were you."

"You don't lay up anything agin me, Maria?"

"No, David."

"Good-night, Maria."

"Good-night, David. I will fetch you over some boiled dinner to-morrow."

She held the lamp at the door till the patient, tottering old figure was out of sight. She had to wipe the tears from her spectacles in order to see to read her Bible when she went in.

Next morning she was hurrying up her housework to go [35] over to David's—somehow she felt a little anxious about him this morning—when there came a loud knock at her door. When she opened it, a boy stood there, panting for breath; he was David's next neighbor's son.

"Mr. Emmons is sick," he said, "an' wants you. I was goin' for milk, when he rapped on the window. Father an' mother's in thar, an' the doctor. Mother said, tell you to hurry."

The news had spread rapidly; people knew what it meant when they saw Maria hurrying down the street, without her bonnet, her gray hair flying. One woman cried when she saw her. "Poor thing!" she sobbed, "poor thing!"

A crowd was around David's cottage when Maria reached it. She went straight in through the kitchen to his little bedroom, and up to his side. The doctor was in the room, and several neighbors. When he saw Maria, poor old David held out his hand to her and smiled feebly. Then he looked imploringly at the doctor, then at the others in the room. The doctor understood, and said a word to them, and they filed silently out. Then he turned to Maria. "Be quick," he whispered.

She leaned over him. "Dear David," she said, her wrinkled face quivering, her gray hair straying over her cheeks.

He looked up at her with a strange wonder in his glazing eyes. "Maria" —a thin, husky voice, that was more like a wind through dry corn-stalks, said—"Maria, I'm—dyin', an'—I allers meant to—have asked you—to—marry me." [36]

MARGARET DELAND
1857–1945

In Western Pennsylvania

from

THE PROMISES OF DOROTHEA

One significant trend in American fiction in the second half of the nine-teenth century was the development of the story of local color. The Civil War had intensified a sectional awareness throughout the nation, and fol-lowing the war the local-color story became the staple of American writing. However, the majority of the local colorists, most of whom were women, made no worthwhile contributions to fiction with their mere descriptions of unfamiliar peoples and localities, their exploitation of dialects, customs, scenery, and out-of-the-way places of American culture. The best of these writers—including Bret Harte, G. W. Cable, M. N. Murfree, Ambrose Bierce, Sarah Orne Jewett, Mary E. Wilkins Freeman, and Margaret Deland —attempt to go beyond mere local color; they try to point out the re-lationships between the locales they describe and the people who live there. Local color is generally subordinate to the characters; details of setting explain character and add a touch of realism. Sarah Orne Jewett shows the influence of the rocky country of her beloved Maine on the people who live there. Bert Harte and Ambrose Bierce both use the setting of the frontier— its isolation and loneliness—in their exploration of human behavior.

Margaret Deland was brought up in a little Pennsylvania town, Man-chester, now incorporated into the city of Pittsburgh. At the age of 16 she went to New York to study and later taught there. But in her writing she returns to the days of her youth, naming her Pennsylvania home town "Old

Chester." It was a town composed of old, genteel English and Scotch and Irish families, a place of strong tradition and deep religious prejudices, and narrow yet wholesome and kindly ideals. Old Chester is clearly the author's native town, yet it could be any number of small towns across the United States. *Old Chester Tales* (1898) deals with universal types and themes. The setting is less important than the people in these stories. The action of the stories revolves around a central character, Dr. Lavendar, the elderly rector who appears in a number of Deland's books. The brief passage printed here is the opening section of the first tale and presents the background of old Chester.

Old Chester Tales is Deland's best-known work today; other books drawn from early memories are *Around Old Chester* (1915), *New Friends in Old Chester* (1924), *Old Chester Days* (1935), *If This Be I (As I Suppose It Be)* (1935), and *Golden Yesterdays* (1941). Her best novel, *John Ward, Preacher* (1888), deals with religious life in the small town, showing the conflict a minister faces between his love of a liberal-thinking wife and a rather narrow religious faith.

from THE PROMISES OF DOROTHEA

Old Chester was always very well satisfied with itself. Not that that implies conceit; Old Chester merely felt that satisfaction with the conditions as well as the station into which it had pleased God to call it which is said to be a sign of grace. Such satisfaction is sad also to be at variance with progress, but it cannot be denied that it is comfortable; as for progress, everybody knows it is accompanied by growing-pains. Besides, if people choose to burn lamps and candles instead of gas; if they prefer to jog along the turnpike in stage-coaches instead of whizzing past in a cloud of dust and cinders in a railroad car; if they like to hear the old parson who married them—or baptized some of them, for that matter—mumbling and droning through his old, old sermons; if they like to have him rejoice with them, and advise them, and weep with them beside their open graves—if people deliberately choose this sort of thing, the outside world may wonder, but it has no right to condemn. And if it had condemned, Old Chester would not have cared in the very least. It looked down upon the outside world. Not unkindly, indeed, but pityingly; and it pursued its [3] contented way, without restlessness, and without aspirations.

Margaret Deland, "The Promises of Dorothea," from *Old Chester Tales* (New York: Grosset and Dunlap, 1898).

In saying "Old Chester" one really means the Dales, the Wrights, the Lavendars—that includes Susan Carr, who married Joey Lavendar when she was old enough to have given up all ideas of that kind of thing; it means the Temple connection, though only Jane Temple lives in Old Chester now, and she is Mrs. Dove; at least that is her name, but hardly any one remembers it, and she is always spoken of as "Jane Temple"; the Dove is only an incident, so to speak, for one scarcely feels that her very respectable little husband is part of "Old Chester." The term includes the Jay girls, of course, and the Barkleys; though in my time only Mrs. Barkley was left; her sons had gone out into the world, and her husband—it must have been somewhere in the early sixties that Barkley senior, Old Chester's blackest sheep, took his departure for a Place (his orthodox relatives were inclined to believe) which, in these days, is even more old-fashioned than Old Chester itself. The Kings are of Old Chester, and the two Miss Ferrises; and the Steeles, and the John Smiths. The Norman Smiths, who own a great mill in the upper village, have no real connection with Old Chester, though the John Smiths are always very much afraid of being confounded with them; the two families are generally referred to as the "real Smiths" and the "rich Smiths." The real Smiths might with equal accuracy have been called the poor Smiths, except that Old Chester could not have been so impolite. The rich Smiths were one of several families who went to make up what the geographies call the "popula-[4]tion" of the village, but they were never thought of when one said "Old Chester." The Macks were in this class, and the Hayeses, and a dozen others. Old Chester had nothing to say against these people; they were rich, but it did not follow that they had not made their money honestly; and their sons and daughters, having had time to get used to wealth, had reasonably good manners. But they were not "Old Chester." The very fact that they were not always satisfied with the existing order proved that. One by one these outsiders had bought or built in the village, because they had interests in the new rolling-mills in Upper Chester; and they had hardly come before they began to make a stir, and try to "improve" things. Then it was that Old Chester arose in its might; Heaven and the town vote were invoked for protection against a branch railroad to connect the two villages; and the latter, at least, answered with decision. The proposition that gas should be brought from the mill town destroyed itself because of its cost; even the rich Smiths felt that it would be too expensive.

So Old Chester pursued its own satisfied path; it had a habit of alluding to any changes that the younger generation or the new people might advocate as "airs." Sam Wright said, gruffly, that what had been good enough for his father was good enough for him. This was when his eldest son suggested that a connection with Upper Chester's water supply would be a good thing. "Young man," said Sam, "I've pumped many a bucket of water in my day, and it won't hurt you to do the same." "It isn't a question of hurting," said young Sam, impatiently; "it's a question of saving time." "Saving your [5] grandmother!" interrupted his father; "since when has your time been so valuable, sir? Come, now, don't put on airs! I guess what was good enough for my father is good enough for you."

This satisfaction with the Past was especially marked in church matters. When Helen Smith—pretty, impulsive, and a dear good child, too, if she was "new"—told Dr. Lavendar that she thought it would be a good thing to have a girls' club at St. Michael's, the old minister said, his kind eyes twinkling at her," "The best club for girls is their mothers' firesides, my dear!"

At which Miss Smith pressed her lips together, and said, shortly: "Well, if you feel that way about a girls' club, I suppose you won't approve of a debating society for the boys?"

"Ho!" said Dr. Lavendar, "boys don't wait for their parson's approval to debate! There is too much debating already. If our boys here in Old Chester would talk less and do more, if they would stop discussing things they know nothing about, and listen to the opinions of their elders and betters, they might amount to something. No, we don't want any debating societies in Old Chester. They may have their place in big city parishes— but here! Why, there are only a dozen or two boys, anyhow, and I know their fathers, every one of them; they wouldn't thank me for making the boys bigger blatherskites than they are already—being boys."

"But, Dr. Lavendar," Helen protested, with heightened color, "you can't say the fathers' influence is always good. Look at Job Todd; his eldest boy is fourteen, and what a home to spend his evenings in! And there are the two Rice boys—no mother, [6] and a half-crazy father; surely some harmless entertainment—"

"They come to Sunday-school; and the young fry have my collect class on Saturdays," said Dr. Lavendar; "and the boys in Maria Welwood's class, or Jane Temple's, get all the pleasant evenings they need."

"Well," Helen said, trying to keep the irritation out of her voice, "I suppose there is no use in saying anything more, only it does seem to me that we are behind the times."

"I hope so, I hope so," said Dr. Lavendar, cheerfully.

But in spite of snubs like this the new people had their opinions in matters ecclesiastical as well as civil. The Hayeses said that they thought a "more ornate ritual would bring in the lower classes;" and they added that they did wish Dr. Lavendar would have Weekly Celebration. The Macks, who, before they got their money, had been United Presbyterians, said that they could not understand why Dr. Lavendar wouldn't have an altar and a cross. He was very little of a churchman, they said, to just have the old wooden communion-table; which, indeed, never had any other decoration than the "fair white linen cloth" on the first Sunday of the month.

"I said so to poor, dear old Dr. Lavendar," said Mrs. Mack, "and he said, 'We have no dealing with the Scarlet Woman, ma'am, at St. Michael's! Isn't he a queer old dear? So narrow-minded!"

And it must be admitted that the dear old man was a little short with ex-Presbyterian Mrs. Mack. The fact was, at that particular time, he happened to have enough to think of besides the whims of the [7] new people. It was that year that Old Chester—the real Old Chester—had such deep disturbances: There was Miss Welwood's financial catastrophe; and the distressing behavior of young Robert Smith (he was one of the "real Smiths") ; and the elder Miss Ferris's illness, and the younger Miss Ferris's recovery—both caused by Oscar King's extraordinary conduct; conduct in which, it must be admitted, Dr. Lavendar was very much mixed up. [8]

EDWIN ARLINGTON ROBINSON
1868–1950

People of
Tilbury Town

from

THE CHILDREN
OF THE NIGHT

On the public green in Gardiner, Maine, is a monument erected to the
town's most famous citizen, Edwin Arlington Robinson, who lived there
as a boy and who in turn made Gardiner famous as the model for his
Tillbury Town. His somber books of poems include *The Torrent and the
Night Before* (1896), *The Children of the Night* (1897), *Captain Craig*
(1902), *The Town Down the River* (1910), *The Man Against the Sky*
(1916), and *The Three Taverns* (1920).

When Robinson's family settled there shortly after the boy's birth in
1869, Gardiner was a country village serenely reposing on the banks of
the Kennebec. Never much more than a very small town during the poet's
youth (it is a small town still), Gardiner was chiefly a marketplace for farm
and dairy products and a center for the lumbering trade. Tote roads and
the river road led into it; and weathered New England farmers and lum-
berjacks, trappers, and craftsmen of various kinds assembled there to barter
and gossip.

The town had sophistication, of a kind, and pride, and something of
this the poet suggests in the name he gives to it in his verse. "Tilbury"
brings to mind the smart, two-wheeled carriage of the turn of the century
and therefore, ironically, aristocratic character and polish. Tilbury Town
itself Robinson peopled with a gallery of unforgettable characters.

Most of these people are sufferers, and for most of them Robinson, himself all his life a desperately lonely man, felt a sympathetic affection. There is Luke Havergal, the distraught and bereaved lover; there is Cliff Klingenhagen, who has learned how to be happy on wormwood; there is John Evereldown, the God-abandoned lecher whom Robinson most likely drew from John Tarbox, a familiar reprobate of the Gardiner of his youth; there is Richard Cory, whose condition the Tilbury townsfolk mistake; there is Reuben Bright the butcher, who so loved his wife that life without her is meaningless; there is the melancholy Charles Carville, who draws a blank for his life; there is the miser Aaron Stark, a "loveless exile" cynically amused by expressions of alien pity.

All are failures—"children of the night." But in Tilbury Town they have dignity and distinction, for each is regarded as an individual and significant human being, submitted as he is to the penetrating psychological examination of a keenly sensitive and sympathetic poet.

It is the "little man" of the American lower middle class whom Robinson has immortalized—the farmer, the lumberjack, the craftsman, the drifter. He writes in one lyric poignantly of a deserted village, where "there is nothing but the ghosts of things," of a dead village that God has shut from his sight. But Richard Cory and Reuben Bright and Aaron Stark shall walk the streets of Tilbury Town forever.

The despair of the people of Tilbury Town was Robinson's own despair. He was unable to complete an undergraduate course at Harvard because of his father's failing health; he was most of the time financially insecure, lonely, and depressed, often turning to alcohol. Although he received a Pulitzer Prize in 1921 for his first book, *Collected Poems,* and although he is now recognized as a major American poet, he depended greatly on his friends for a means of living.

from THE CHILDREN
OF THE NIGHT

JOHN EVERELDOWN

"Where are you going to-night, to-night,—
   Where are you going, John Evereldown?
There's never the sign of a star in sight,
   Nor a lamp that's nearer than Tilbury Town.
Why do you stare as a dead man might?
Where are you pointing away from the light?
And where are you going to-night, to-night,—
   Where are you going, John Evereldown?"

"Right through the forest, where none can see,
   There's where I'm going, to Tilbury Town.
The men are asleep,—or awake, may be,—
   But the women are calling John Evereldown.
Ever and ever they call for me,
And while they call can a man be free?
So right through the forest, where none can see,
   There's where I'm going, to Tilbury Town." [30]

"But why are you going so late, so late,—
   Why are you going, John Evereldown?
Though the road be smooth and the way be straight,
   There are two long leagues to Tilbury Town.
Come in by the fire, old man, and wait!
Why do you chatter out there by the gate?
And why are you going so late, so late,—
   Why are you going, John Evereldown?"

"I follow the women wherever they call,—
   That's why I'm going to Tilbury Town.
God knows if I pray to be done with it all,
   But God is no friend to John Evereldown.
So the clouds may come and the rain may fall,
The shadows may creep and the dead men crawl,—
But I follow the women wherever they call,
   And that's why I'm going to Tilbury Town." [31]

Edwin Arlington Robinson, *The Children of the Night* (Boston: R. G. Badger & Co., 1897).
"The Dead Village," "Richard Cory," 'Reuben Bright," "Aaron Stark," "Charles
Carville's Eyes," "Cliff Klingenhagen," and "John Evereldown" are reprinted with the
permission of Charles Scribner's Sons.

LUKE HAVERGAL

Go to the western gate, Luke Havergal,
There where the vines cling crimson on the wall,
And in the twilight wait for what will come.
The leaves will whisper there of her, and some,
Like flying words, will strike you as they fall;
But go, and if you listen she will call.
Go to the western gate, Luke Havergal—
Luke Havergal.

No, there is not a dawn in eastern skies
To rift the fiery night that's in your eyes;
But there, where western glooms are gathering,
The dark will end the dark, if anything:
God slays Himself with every leaf that flies,
And hell is more than half of paradise.
No, there is not a dawn in eastern skies—
In eastern skies. [32]

Out of a grave to tell you this,
Out of a grave I come to quench the kiss
That flames upon your forehead with a glow
That blinds you to the way that you must go.
Yes, there is yet one way to where she is,
Bitter, but one that faith may never miss.
Out of a grave I come to tell you this—
To tell you this.

There is the western gate, Luke Havergal,
There are the crimson leaves upon the wall.
Go, for the winds are tearing them away,—
Nor think to riddle the dead words they say,
Nor any more to feel them as they fall;
But go, and if you trust her she will call.
There is the western gate, Luke Havergal—
Luke Havergal. [33]

RICHARD CORY

Whenever Richard Cory went down town,
We people on the pavement looked at him:
He was a gentleman from sole to crown,
Clean favored, and imperially slim.

And he was always quietly arrayed,
And he was always human when he talked;
But still he fluttered pulses when he said,
"Good-morning," and he glittered when he walked.

And he was rich—yes, richer than a king—
And admirably schooled in every grace:
In fine, we thought that he was everything
To make us wish that we were in his place.

So on we worked, and waited for the light,
And went without the meat, and cursed the bread;
And Richard Cory, one calm summer night,
Went home and put a bullet through his head. [35]

AARON STARK

Withal a meagre man was Aaron Stark,
Cursed and unkempt, shrewd, shrivelled, and morose.
A miser was he, with a miser's nose,
And eyes like little dollars in the dark.
His thin, pinched mouth was nothing but a mark;
And when he spoke there came like sullen blows
Through scattered fangs a few snarled words and close,
As if a cur were chary of its bark.

Glad for the murmur of his hard renown,
Year after year he shambled through the town,
A loveless exile moving with a staff;
And oftentimes there crept into his ears
A sound of alien pity, touched with tears,—
And then (and only then) did Aaron laugh. [46]

CLIFF KLINGENHAGEN

Cliff Klingenhagen had me in to dine
With him one day; and after soup and meat,
And all the other things there were to eat,
Cliff took two glasses and filled one with wine
And one with wormwood. Then, without a sign
For me to choose at all, he took the draught
Of bitterness himself, and lightly quaffed
It off, and said the other one was mine.

And when I asked him what the deuce he meant
By doing that, he only looked at me
And smiled, and said it was a way of his.
And though I know the fellow, I have spent
Long time a-wondering when I shall be
As happy as Cliff Klingenhagen is. [48]

CHARLES CARVILLE'S EYES

A melancholy face Charles Carville had,
But not so melancholy as it seemed,
When once you knew him, for his mouth redeemed
His insufficient eyes, forever sad:

In them there was no life-glimpse, good or bad,
Nor joy nor passion in them ever gleamed;
His mouth was all of him that ever beamed,
His eyes were sorry, but his mouth was glad.

He never was a fellow that said much,
And half of what he did say was not heard
By many of us: we were out of touch
With all his whims and all his theories
Till he was dead, so those blank eyes of his
Might speak them. Then we heard them, every word. [49]

THE DEAD VILLAGE

Here there is death. But even here, they say,
Here where the dull sun shines this afternoon
As desolate as ever the dead moon
Did glimmer on dead Sardis, men were gay;
And there were little children here to play,
With small soft hands that once did keep in tune
The strings that stretch from heaven, till too soon
The change came, and the music passed away.

Now there is nothing but the ghosts of things,—
No life, no love, no children, and no men;
And over the forgotten place there clings
The strange and unrememberable light
That is in dreams. The music failed, and then
God frowned, and shut the village from His sight. [50]

REUBEN BRIGHT

Because he was a butcher and thereby
Did earn an honest living (and did right),
I would not have you think that Reuben Bright
Was any more a brute than you or I;
For when they told him that his wife must die,
He stared at them, and shook with grief and fright,
And cried like a great baby half that night,
And made the women cry to see him cry.

And after she was dead, and he had paid
The singers and the sexton and the rest,
He packed a lot of things that she had made
Most mournfully away in an old chest
Of hers, and put some chopped-up cedar boughs
In with them, and tore down the slaughter-house. [60]

WILLA CATHER
1873–1947

Artist
on the Frontier

"THE SCULPTOR'S FUNERAL"

Willa Cather, in her fiction, was one of the first American writers interested in exploring the influence of the new immigrants on the rich cultural past of the Midwest. Born in Virginia on December 7, 1873, Willa Cather moved with her family to a farm near Red Cloud, Nebraska, when she was only ten years old. She grew up observing firsthand the conflict between the materialists of the frontier and the Bohemians and Scandinavians who brought a cultural heritage from other lands.

After Cather graduated from the University of Nebraska in 1895, she turned to journalism and teaching. In time she gave her full attention to the writing of poetry, novels, and short stories. Her first collection of stories, *The Troll Garden* (1905), contained "The Sculptor's Funeral," a story of revolt against the drabness and materialism of frontier life. She became known as the historian of Nebraska chiefly because of three novels: *O Pioneers!* (1913), *The Song of the Lark* (1915), and *My Antonia* (1918). Later she turned to the Southwest and produced *Death Comes for the Archbishop* (1927) and *Shadows on the Rock* (1931), both of which reveal her interest in Catholicism.

In "The Sculptor's Funeral" Cather presents the bleak, cheerless background of a Kansas town—its streets and its people. Here she uses the theme of the gifted individual in conflict with social prejudice and convention, the yearning of a sensitive person "cast ashore upon a desert of newness and ugliness and sordidness, for all that is chastened and old, and noble with traditions." As a boy, Harvey Merrick realized he could never conform to the manners of his town; his artistic temperament was very early chilled by the insensitivity of his native town. This much about his early life is guessed at by the friend who accompanies Harvey's corpse from the East. At the same time we are given the views of the townspeople who were never able to appreciate Harvey as a sensitive, perceptive person who had to seek out broader, more cultured world.

"THE SCULPTOR'S FUNERAL"

A group of the townspeople stood on the station siding of a little Kansas town, awaiting the coming of the night train, which was already twenty minutes overdue. The snow had fallen thick over everything; in the pale starlight the line of bluffs across the wide, white meadows south of the town made soft, smoke-colored curves against the clear sky. The men on the siding stood first on one foot and then on the other, their hands thrust deep into their trousers pockets, their overcoats open, their shoulders screwed up with the cold; and they glanced from time to time toward the southwest, where the railroad track wound along the river shore. They conversed in low tones and moved about restlessly, seeming uncertain as to what was expected of them. There was but one of the company who looked as though he knew exactly why he was there, and he kept conspicuously apart, walking to the far end of the platform, returning to the station door, then pacing up the track again, his chin sunk in the high collar of his overcoat, his burly shoulders drooping forward, his gait heavy and dogged. Presently he was approached by a tall, spare grizzled man clad in a faded Grand Army suit, who shuffled out from the group and advanced with a certain deference, craning his neck forward until his back made the angle of a jack-knife three-quarters open.

"I reckon she's a-goin' to be pretty late again to-night, Jim," he remarked in a squeaky falsetto. "S'pose it's the snow?"

"I don't know," responded the other man with a shade of annoyance, speaking from out an astonishing cataract of red beard that grew fiercely and thickly in all directions.

The spare man shifted the quill toothpick he was chewing to the other side of his mouth. "It ain't likely that anybody from the East will come with the corpse, I'spose," he went on reflectively.

"I don't know," responded the other, more curtly than before.

"It's too bad he didn't belong to some lodge or other. I like an order funeral myself. They seem more appropriate for people of some repytation," the spare man continued, with an ingratiating concession in his shrill voice, as he carefully placed his toothpick in his vest pocket. He always carried the flag at the G. A. R. funerals in the town.

The heavy man turned on his heel without replying, and walked up the siding. The spare man shuffled back to the uneasy group. "Jim's ez full ez a tick, ez ushel," he commented commiseratingly.

Just then a distant whistle sounded, and there was a shuffling of feet on the platform. A number of lanky boys of all ages appeared as suddenly and slimily as eels wakened by the crack of thunder; some came from the waiting-room, where they had been warming themselves by the red stove, or half asleep on the slat benches; others uncoiled themselves from baggage trucks or slid out of express wagons. Two clambered down from the driver's seat of a hearse that stood backed up against the siding. They straightened their stooping shoulders and lifted their heads, and a flash of momentary animation kindled their dull eyes at that cold, vibrant scream, the world-wide call for men. It stirred them like the note of a trumpet, just as it had often stirred in his boyhood the man who was coming home to-night.

The night express shot, red as a rocket, from out the eastward marsh lands and wound along the river shore under the long lines of shivering poplars that sentinelled the meadows, the escaping steam hanging in grey masses against the pale sky and blotting out the Milky Way. In a moment the red glare from the headlight streamed [329] up the snow-covered track before the siding and glittered on the wet, black rails. The burly man with the dishevelled red beard walked swiftly up the platform toward the approaching train, uncovering his head as he went. The group of men behind him hesitated, glanced questioningly at one another, and awkwardly followed his example. The train stopped, and the crowd shuffled up to the express car just as the door was thrown open, the spare man in the G. A. R. suit thrusting his head forward with curiosity. The express messenger appeared in the doorway, accompanied by a young man in a long ulster and traveling-cap.

"Are Mr. Merrick's friends here?" inquired the young man.

The group on the platform swayed and shuffled uneasily. Philip Phelps, the banker, responded with dignity: "We have come to take charge of the body. Mr. Merrick's father is very feeble and can't be about."

"Send the agent out here," growled the express messenger, "and tell the operator to lend a hand."

The coffin was got out of its rough box and down on the snowy platform. The townspeople drew back enough to make room for it and then formed a close semicircle about it, looking curiously at the palm-leaf which lay across the black cover. No one said anything. The baggage man stood by his truck, waiting to get at the trunks. The engine panted heavily, and the fireman dodged in and out among the wheels with his yellow torch and long oil-can, snapping the spindle boxes. The young Bostonian, one of the dead sculptor's pupils who had come with the body, looked about him helplessly. He turned to the banker, the only one of that black, uneasy, stoop-shouldered group who seemed enough of an individual to be addressed.

"None of Mr. Merrick's brothers are here?" he asked uncertainly.

The man with the red beard for the first time stepped up and joined the group. "No, they have not come yet; the family is scattered. The body will be taken directly to the house." He stooped and took hold of one of the handles of the coffin.

"Take the long hill road up, Thompson, it will be easier on the horses," called the liveryman as the undertaker snapped the door of the hearse and prepared to mount to the driver's seat.

Laird, the red-bearded lawyer, turned again to the stranger: "We didn't know whether there would be any one with him or not," he explained. "It's a long walk, so you'd better go up in the hack." He pointed to a single battered conveyance, but the young man replied stiffly: "Thank you, but I think I will go up with the hearse. If you don't object," turning to the undertaker, "I'll ride with you."

They clambered up over the wheels and drove off in the starlight up the long, white hill toward the town. The lamps in the still village were shining from under the low, snow-burdened roofs; and beyond, on every side, the plains reached out into emptiness, peaceful and wide as the soft sky itself, and wrapped in a tangible, white silence.

When the hearse backed up to a wooden sidewalk before a naked, weather-beaten frame house, the same composite, ill-defined group that had stood upon the station siding was huddled about the gate. The front yard was an icy swamp, and a couple of warped planks, extending from the sidewalk to the door, made a sort of rickety footbridge. The gate hung on one hinge, and was opened wide with difficulty. Steavens, the young stranger, noticed that something black was tied to the knob of the front door.

The grating sound made by the casket, as it was drawn from the hearse, was answered by a scream from the house; the front door was wrenched open, and a tall, corpulent woman rushed out bareheaded into the snow and flung herself upon the coffin, shrieking: "My boy, my boy! And this is how you've come home to me!"

As Steavens turned away and closed his eyes with a shudder of unutterable repulsion, another woman, also tall, but flat and angular, dressed entirely in black, darted out of the house and caught Mrs. Merrick by the shoulders, crying sharply: "Come, come, mother; you mustn't go on like this!" Her tone changed to one of obsequious solemnity as she turned to the banker: "The parlor is ready, Mr. Phelps."

The bearers carried the coffin along the narrow boards, while the undertaker ran ahead with the coffin-rests. They bore it into a large, un-

heated room that smelled dampness and disuse and furniture polish, and
set it down under a hanging lamp ornamented with jingling glass prisms
and before a "Rogers group" of John Alden and Priscilla, wreathed with
smilax. Henry Steavens stared about him with the sickening [330] conviction that there had been some horrible mistake, and that he had somehow
arrived at the wrong destination. He looked painfully about over the
clover-green Brussels, the fat plush upholstery; among the hand-painted
china plaques and panels, and vases, for some mark of identification, for
something that might once conceivably have belonged to Harvey Merrick.
It was not until he recognized his friend in the crayon portrait of a little
boy in kilts and curls hanging above the piano, that he felt willing to
let any of these people approach the coffin.

"Take the lid off, Mr. Thompson; let me see my boy's face," wailed
the elder women between her sobs. This time Steavens looked fearfully,
almost beseechingly into her face, red and swollen under its masses of
strong, black, shiny hair. He flushed, dropped his eyes, and then, almost
incredulously, looked again. There was a kind of power about her face—
a kind of brutal handsomeness, even; but it was scarred and furrowed by
violence, and so colored and coarsened by fiercer passions that grief
seemed never to have laid a gentle finger there. The long nose was dis-
tended and knobbed at the end, and there were deep lines on either side
of it; her heavy, black brows almost met across her forehead, her teeth
were large and square, and set far apart—teeth that could tear. She filled
the room; the men were obliterated, seemed tossed about like twigs in an
angry water, and even Steavens felt himself being drawn into the whirlpool.

The daughter—the tall, raw-boned woman in crêpe, with a mourning
comb in her hair which curiously lengthened her long face—sat stiffly upon
the sofa, her hands, conspicuous for their large knuckles, folded in her lap,
her mouth and eyes drawn down, solemnly awaiting the opening of the
coffin. Near the door stood a mulatto woman, evidently a servant in the
house, with a timid bearing and an emaciated face pitifully sad and gentle.
She was weeping silently, the corner of her calico apron lifted to her eyes,
occasionally suppressing a long, quivering sob. Steavens walked over and
stood beside her.

Feeble steps were heard on the stairs, and an old man, tall and frail,
odorous of pipe smoke, with shaggy, unkept grey hair and a dingy beard,
tobacco-stained about the mouth, entered uncertainly. He went slowly up
to the coffin and stood rolling a blue cotton handkerchief between his
hands, seeming so pained and embarrassed by his wife's orgy of grief that he
had no consciousness of anything else.

"There, there, Annie, dear, don't take on so," he quavered timidly,
putting out a shaking hand and awkwardly patting her elbow. She turned
with a cry, and sank upon his shoulder with such violence that he tottered
a little. He did not even glance toward the coffin, but continued to look

at her with a dull, frightened, appealing expression, as a spaniel looks at the whip. His sunken cheeks slowly reddened and burned with miserable shame. When his wife rushed from the room, her daughter strode after her with set lips. The servant stole up to the coffin, bent over it for a moment, and then slipped away to the kitchen, leaving Steavens, the lawyer and the father to themselves. The old man stood trembling and looking down at his dead son's face. The sculptor's splendid head seemed even more noble in its rigid stillness than in life. The dark hair had crept upon the wide forehead; the face seemed strangely long, but in it there was not that beautiful and chaste repose which we expect to find in the faces of the dead. The brows were so drawn that there were two deep lines above the beaked nose, and the chin was thrust forward defiantly. It was as though the strain of life had been so sharp and bitter that death could not at once wholly relax the tension and smooth the countenance into perfect peace—as though he were still guarding something precious and holy which might even yet be wrested from him.

The old man's lips were working under his stained beard. He turned to the lawyer with timid deference: "Phelps and the rest are comin' back to set up with Harve, ain't they?" he asked. "Thank 'ee, Jim, thank 'ee." He brushed the hair back gently from his son's forehead. "He was a good boy, Jim; always a good boy. He was ez gentle ez a child and the kindest of 'em all—only we didn't none of us ever onderstand him." The tears trickled slowly down his beard and dropped upon the sculptor's coat.

"Martin, Martin—Oh, Martin! come here," his wife wailed from the top of the stairs. The old man started timorously: "Yes, Annie, I'm coming." He turned away, hesitated, stood for a moment in miserable indecision; then reached back [331] and patted the dead man's hair softly, and stumbled from the room.

"Poor old man, I didn't think he had any tears left. Seems as if his eyes would have gone dry long ago. At his age nothing cuts very deep," remarked the lawyer.

Something in his tone made Steavens glance up. While the mother had been in the room, the young man had scarcely seen any one else; but now, from the moment he first glanced into Jim Laird's florid face and blood-shot eyes, he knew that he had found what he had been heart-sick at not finding before—the feeling, the understanding, that must exist in some one, even here.

The man was red as his beard, with features swollen and blurred by dissipation, and a hot, blazing blue eye. His face was strained—that of a man who is controlling himself with difficulty—and he kept plucking at his beard with a sort of fierce resentment. Steavens, sitting by the window, watched him turn down the glaring lamp, still its jangling pendants with an angry gesture, and then stand with his hands locked behind him, staring down into the master's face. He could not help wondering what link there could have been between the porcelain vessel and so sooty a lump of potter's clay.

From the kitchen an uproar was sounding; when the dining-room door opened, the import of it was clear. The mother was abusing the maid for having forgotten to make the dressing for the chicken salad which had been prepared for the watchers. Steavens had never heard anything in the least like it; it was injured, emotional, dramatic abuse, unique and masterly in its excruciating cruelty, as violent and unrestrained as had been her grief of twenty minutes before. With a shudder of disgust the lawyer went into the dining-room and closed the door into the kitchen.

"Poor Roxy's getting it now," he remarked when he came back. "The Merricks took her out of the poor-house years ago; and if her loyalty would let her, I guess the poor old thing could tell tales that would curdle your blood. She's the mulatto woman who was standing in here a while ago, with her apron to her eyes. The old woman is a fury; there never was anybody like her for demonstrative piety and ingenious cruelty. She made Harvey's life a hell for him when he lived at home; he was so sick ashamed of it. I never could see how he kept himself so sweet."

"He was wonderful," said Steavens slowly, "wonderful; but until to-night I have never known how wonderful."

"That is the true and eternal wonder of it, anyway; that it can come even from such a dung-heap as this," the lawyer cried, with a sweeping gesture which seemed to indicate much more than the four walls within which they stood.

"I think I'll see whether I can get a little air. The room is so close I am beginning to feel rather faint," murmured Steavens, struggling with one of the windows. The sash was stuck, however, and would not yield, so he sat down dejectedly and began pulling at his collar. The lawyer came over, loosened the sash with one blow of his red fist and sent the window up a few inches. Steavens thanked him, but the nausea which had been gradually climbing into his throat for the last half hour left him with but one desire—a desperate feeling that he must get away from this place with what was left of Harvey Merrick. Oh, he comprehended well enough now the quiet bitterness of the smile that he had seen so often on his master's lips!

He remembered that once, when Merrick returned from a visit home, he brought with him a singularly feeling and suggestive bas-relief of a thin, faded old woman, sitting and sewing something pinned to her knee; while a full-lipped, full-blooded little urchin, his trousers held up by a single gallows, stood beside her, impatiently twitching her gown to call her attention to a butterfly he had caught. Steavens, impressed by the tender and delicate modeling of the thin, tired face, had asked him if it were his mother. He remembered the dull flush that had burned up in the sculptor's face.

The lawyer was sitting in a rocking-chair beside the coffin, his head thrown back and his eyes closed. Steavens looked at him earnestly, puzzled at the line of the chin, and wondering why a man should conceal a feature of such distinction under that disfiguring shock of beard. Suddenly, as though he felt the young sculptor's keen glance, he opened his eyes.

"Was he always a good deal of an oyster?" he asked abruptly. "He was terribly shy as a boy."

"Yes, he was an oyster, since you put it so," rejoined Steavens. "Although he could be very fond of people, he always gave one [332] the impression of being detached. He disliked violent emotion; he was reflective, and rather distrustful of himself—except, of course, as regarded his work. He was sure-footed enough there. He distrusted men pretty thoroughly and women even more, yet somehow without believing ill of them. He was determined, indeed, to believe the best, but he seemed afraid to investigate."

"A burnt dog dreads the fire," said the lawyer grimly, and closed his eyes.

Steavens went on and on, reconstructing that whole miserable boyhood. All this raw, biting ugliness had been the portion of the man whose tastes were refined beyond the limits of the reasonable—whose mind was an exhaustless gallery of beautiful impressions, and so sensitive that the mere shadow of a poplar leaf flickering against a sunny wall would be etched and held there forever. Surely, if ever a man had the magic word in his finger tips, it was Merrick. Whatever he touched, he revealed its holiest secret; liberated it from enchantment and restored it to its pristine loveliness, like the Arabian prince who fought the enchantress spell for spell. Upon whatever he had come in contact with, he had left a beautiful record of the experience—a sort of ethereal signature; a scent, a sound, a color that was his own.

Steavens understood now the real tragedy of his master's life; neither love nor wine, as many had conjectured, but a blow which had fallen earlier and cut deeper than these could have done—a shame not his, and yet so unescapably his, to hide in his heart from his very boyhood. And without, the frontier warfare; the yearning of a boy, cast ashore upon a desert of newness and ugliness and sordidness, for all that is chastened and old, and noble with traditions.

At eleven o'clock the tall, flat woman in black crêpe entered and announced that the watchers were arriving, and asked them "to step into the dining-room." As Steavens rose, the lawyer said dryly: "You go on— it'll be a good experience for you, doubtless; as for me, I'm not equal to that crowd to-night; I've had twenty years of them."

As Steavens closed the door after him he glanced back at the lawyer, sitting by the coffin in the dim light, with his chin resting on his hand.

The same misty group that had stood before the door of the express car shuffled into the dining-room. In the light of the kerosene lamp they separated and became individuals. The minister, a pale, feeble-looking man with white hair and blond chin-whiskers, took his seat beside a small side table and placed his Bible upon it. The Grand Army man sat down behind the stove and tilted his chair back comfortably against the wall, fishing his quill toothpick from his waistcoat pocket. The two bankers, Phelps and Elder, sat off in a corner behind the dinner-table, where they could finish their discussion of the new usury law and its effect on chattel security loans. The real estate agent, an old man with a smiling, hypocritical face, soon joined them. The coal and lumber dealer and the cattle shipper sat on opposite sides of the hard coal-burner, their feet on the nickel-work. Steavens took a book from his pocket and began to read. The talk around him ranged through various topics of local interest while the house was quieting down. When it was clear that the members of the family were in bed, the Grand Army man hitched his shoulders and, untangling his long legs, caught his heels on the rounds of his chair.

"S'pose there'll be a will, Phelps?" he queried in his weak falsetto.

The banker laughed disagreeably, and began trimming his nails with a pearl-handled pocket-knife.

"There'll scarcely be any need for one, will there?" he queried in his turn.

The restless Grand Army man shifted his position again, getting his knees still nearer his chin. "Why, the ole man says Harve's done right well lately," he chirped.

The other banker spoke up. "I reckon he means by that Harve ain't asked him to mortgage any more farms lately so as he could go on with his education."

"Seems like my mind don't reach back to a time when Harve wasn't bein' edycated," tittered the Grand Army man.

There was a general chuckle. The minister took out his handkerchief and blew his nose sonorously. Banker Phelps closed his knife with a snap. "It's too bad the old man's sons didn't turn out better," he remarked with reflective authority. "They never hung together. He spent money enough on Harve to stock a dozen cattle-farms and he might as well have poured it into Sand Creek. If Harve had stayed at home and helped nurse what little they had, and gone into stock on the old man's bottom farm, they might all have been well [333] fixed. But the old man had to trust everything to tenants and was cheated right and left."

"Harve never could have handled stock none," interposed the cattleman. "He hadn't it in him to be sharp. Do you remember when he bought Sander's mules for eight-year olds, when everybody in town knew that Sander's father-in-law give 'em to his wife for a wedding present eighteen years before, an' they was full-grown mules then."

Every one chuckled, and the Grand Army man rubbed his knees with a spasm of childish delight.

"Harve never was much account for anything practical, and he shore was never fond of work," began the coal and lumber dealer. "I mind the last time he was home; the day he left, when the old man was out to the barn helpin' his hand hitch up to take Harve to the train, and Cal. Moots was patchin' up the fence, Harve, he come out on the step and sings out, in his lady-like voice: 'Cal. Moots, Cal. Moots! please come cord my trunk.' "

"That's Harve for you," approved the Grand Army man gleefully. "I kin hear him howlin' yet when he was a big feller in long pants, and his his mother used to whale him with a rawhide in the barn for lettin' the cows git foundered in the cornfield when he was drivin' 'em home from pasture. He killed a cow of mine that-a-way onct—a pure Jersey and the best milker I had, an' the ole man had to put up for her. Harve, he was watchin' the sun set acrost the marshes when the anamile got away; he argued that sunset was oncommon fine."

"Where the old man made his mistake was in sending the boy East to schools," said Phelps, stroking his goatee and speaking in a deliberate, judicial tone. "There was where he got his head full of traipsing to Paris and all such folly. What Harve needed, of all people, was a course in some first-class Kansas City business college."

The letters were swimming before Steavens's eyes. Was it possible that these men did not understand, that the palm on the coffin meant nothing to them? The very name of their town would have remained forever buried in the postal guide had it not been now and again mentioned in the world in connection with Harvey Merrick's. He remembered what his master had said to him on the day of his death, after the congestion of both lungs had shut off any probability of recovery, and the sculptor had asked his pupil to send his body home. "It's not a pleasant place to be lying while the world is moving and doing and bettering," he had said with a feeble smile, "but it rather seems as though we ought to go back to the place we came from in the end. The townspeople will come in for a look at me; and after they have had their say I shan't have much to fear from the judgment of God. The wings of the Victory, in there"—with a weak gesture toward his studio—"will not shelter me."

The cattleman took up the comment. "Forty's young for a Merrick to cash in; they usually hang on pretty well. Probably he helped it along with whisky."

"His mother's people were not long-lived, and Harvey never had a robust constitution," said the minister mildly. He would have liked to say more. He had been the boy's Sunday-school teacher, and had been fond of him; but he felt that he was not in a position to speak. His own sons had turned out badly, and it was not a year since one of them had made his last trip home in the express car, shot in a gambling-house in the Black Hills.

"Nevertheless, there is no disputin' that Harve frequently looked upon the wine when it was red, also variegated, and it shore made an oncommon fool of him," moralized the cattleman.

Just then the door leading into the parlor rattled loudly and every one started involuntarily, looking relieved when only Jim Laird came out. His red face was convulsed with anger, and the Grand Army man ducked his head when he saw the spark in his blue, blood-shot eye. They were all afraid of Jim; he was a drunkard, but he could twist the law to suit his client's needs as no other man in all western Kansas could do; and there were many who tried. The lawyer closed the door gently behind him, leaned back against it and folded his arms, cocking his head a little to one side. When he assumed this attitude in the courtroom, ears were always pricked up, as it usually foretold a flood of withering sarcasm.

"I've been with you gentlemen before," he began in a dry, even tone, "when you've sat by the coffins of boys born and raised in this town; and, if I remember rightly, you were never any too well satisfied when you checked them up. What's the matter, [334] anyhow? Why is it that reputable young men are as scarce as millionaires in Sand City? It might almost seem to a stranger that there was some way something the matter with your progressive town. Why did Ruben Sayer, the brightest young lawyer you ever turned out, after he had come home from the university as straight as a die, take to drinking and forge a check and shoot himself? Why did Bill Merrit's son die of the shakes in a saloon in Omaha? Why was Mr. Thomas's son, here, shot in a gambling-house? Why did young Adams burn his mill to beat the insurance companies and go to the pen?"

The lawyer paused and unfolded his arms, laying one clenched fist quietly on the table. "I'll tell you why. Because you drummed nothing but money and knavery into their ears from the time they wore knickerbockers; because you carped away at them as you've been carping here to-night, holding our friends Phelps and Elder up to them for their models, as our grandfathers held up George Washington and John Adams. But the boys, worse luck, were young, and raw at the business you put them to; and how could they match coppers with such artists as Phelps and Elder? You wanted them to be successful rascals; they were only unsuccessful ones—that's all the difference. There was only one boy ever raised in this borderland between ruffianism and civilization, who didn't come to grief, and you hated Harvey Merrick more for winning out than you hated all the other boys who got under the wheels. Lord, Lord, how you did hate him! Phelps, here, is fond of saying that he could buy and sell us all out any time he's a mind to; but he knew Harve wouldn't have given a tinker's damn for his bank and all his cattle-farms put together; and a lack of appreciation, that way, goes hard with Phelps.

"Old Nimrod, here, thinks Harve drank too much; and this from such as Nimrod and me!

"Brother Elder says Harve was too free with the old man's money—fell short in filial consideration, maybe. Well, we can all remember the very tone in which brother Elder swore his own father was a liar, in the county court; and we all know that the old man came out of that partnership with his son as bare as a sheared lamb. But maybe I'm getting personal, and I'd better be driving ahead at what I want to say."

The lawyer paused a moment, squared his heavy shoulders, and went on: "Harvey Merrick and I went to school together, back East. We were dead in earnest, and we wanted you all to be proud of us some day. We meant to be great men. Even I, and I haven't lost my sense of humor, gentlemen, I meant to be a great man. I came back here to practise, and I found you didn't in the least want me to be a great man. You wanted me to be a shrewd lawyer—oh, yes! Our veteran here wanted me to get him an increase of pension, because he had dyspepsia; Phelps wanted a new county survey that would put the widow Wilson's little bottom farm inside his south line; Elder wanted to lend money at 5 per cent a month and get it collected; Old Stark here wanted to wheedle old women up in Vermont into investing their annuities in real-estate mortgages that are not worth the paper they are written on. Oh, you needed me hard enough, and you'll go on needing me; and that's why I'm not afraid to plug the truth home to you this once.

"Well, I came back here and became the damned shyster you wanted me to be. You pretend you have some sort of respect for me; and yet you'll stand up and throw mud at Harvey Merrick, whose soul you couldn't dirty, and whose hands you couldn't tie. Oh, you're a discriminating lot of Christians! There have been times when the sight of Harvey's name in some Eastern paper has made me hang my head like a whipped dog; and, again, times when I liked to think of him off there in the world, away from all this hog-wallow, doing his great work and climbing the big, clean up-grade he'd set for himself.

"And we? Now that we've fought and lied and sweated and stolen, and hated as only the disappointed strugglers in a bitter, dead little Western town know how to do, what have we got to show for it? Harvey Merrick wouldn't have given one sunset over your marshes for all you've got put together, and you know it. It's not for me to say why, in the inscrutable wisdom of God, a genius should ever have been called from his place of hatred and bitter waters; but I want this Boston man to know that the drivel he's been hearing here to-night is the only tribute any truly great man could ever have from such a lot of sick, side-tracked, burnt-dog, land-poor sharks as the here-present financiers of Sand [335] City—upon which town may God have mercy!"

The lawyer thrust out his hand to Steavens as he passed him, caught up his overcoat in the hall, and had left the house before the Grand Army man had had time to lift his ducked head and crane his long neck about at his fellows.

Next day Jim Laird was drunk and unable to attend the funeral services. Steavens called twice at his office, but was compelled to start East without seeing him. He had a presentiment that he would hear from him again, and left his address on the lawyer's table; but if Laird found it, he never acknowledged it. The thing in him that Harvey Merrick had loved must have gone under ground with Harvey Merrick's coffin; for it never spoke again, and Jim got the cold he died of driving-across the Colorado mountains to defend one of Phelps's sons who had got into trouble out there by cutting government timber. [336]

WILLA CATHER
1873–1947

Midwest Pioneers

from

MY ÁNTONIA

On the title page of *My Ántonia* (1918) appears the Latin quotation *Optima dies . . . prima fugit*—"The best days are the first to flee." At the end of the novel Jim Burden, the narrator, finds the old trail that many years before had brought Ántonia and the boy Jim to their homes in Nebraska. He says: "I had the sense of coming home to myself, and of having found what a little circle man's experience is . . . the same road was to bring us together again. Whatever we had missed, we possessed together the precious, the incommunicable past."

Despite the nostalgic touch suggested by Jim's words at the end, *My Ántonia* was one of the first novels to portray realistically the Middle West. In it Willa Cather presents the pioneer life, describing many of the experiences that produced the simple, natural people of the region.

Cather, who as a child had come from Virginia to Nebraska in the 1880s, reproduced some of her own experiences for this novel. Just as Cather herself grew up on a remote Nebraska farm, the heroine, suggested by a Bohemian girl the author once knew, develops and discovers herself in the pioneer country. *My Ántonia* traces sympathetically the lives of Ántonia Shimerda, the Bohemian girl who immigrated to the prairies of Nebraska, and Jim Burden, who, after the death of his parents, moved there from Virginia to be with his grandparents.

The Shimerdas first live in a dugout in the earth as they develop their farm. Ántonia seems almost to become a part of the prairie as she adjusts to its rough, primitive environment. In his recollection Jim observes: "More than any other person we remembered, this girl [Ántonia] seemed to mean to us the country, the conditions, the whole adventure of our childhood."

Jim tells the story of Ántonia—the suicide of her sensitive immigrant father, her working like a man in the fields, her employment as a hired girl in the town of Black Hawk, her enthusiasm for life. Jim must also tell of her unwed pregnancy, her return in shame to her family and the fields. But it is in a real sense Jim's story too—of his growing up in the small town, his introduction to literature and art in the university at Lincoln, and his career as a lawyer in the East.

Through Jim's eyes the reader sees Ántonia as a gay, healthy child, as a working girl, as a prairie woman, and finally as a mother, never ashamed of the child she bore out of wedlock. Twenty years pass and Jim, on a trip west, visits Ántonia on her farm. She has become a housewife, a mother of 14 children, married to a Czech. She is the ideal wife and mother, devoted to her family and the farming life and the open spaces.

The following passages from Book Two, "The Hired Girls," describe many aspects of life in Black Hawk (modeled on Red Cloud, Nebraska, where Cather attended high school after her family had retired from farming). The reader learns of Ántonia's coming to the Harleys as a hired girl and of the activities of the family—washday, preserving day, house cleaning, and gardening in the spring. Country funerals and weddings are important events. In Chapter II Mrs. Harley visits the Shimerdas to see "what the girl came from." In Chapter IX class distinction comes in for comment in the contrasting of the daughters of the Black Hawk merchants with the country girls who came to the town as hired girls. Chapter XII treats the social life in Black Hawk—the dances, the entertainers, the theatrical companies, the gathering places. Together these selections give us a picture of life in a small pioneer town in the 1880s.

(For additional biographical information on Cather, see the introduction to the preceding selection.)

from MY ÁNTONIA

CHAPTER II

Grandmother often said that if she had to live in town, she thanked God she lived next to Harlings. They had been farming people, like ourselves, and their place was like a little farm, with a big barn and a garden, and an orchard and grazing lots—even a windmill. The Harlings were Norwegians, and Mrs. Harling had lived in Christiania until she was ten years old. Her husband was born in Minnesota. He was a grain merchant and cattle-buyer, and was generally considered the most enterprising business

Willa Sibert Cather, *My Ántonia* (Boston: Houghton Mifflin Company 1918). Reprinted by permission of Houghton Mifflin Company.

man in our county. He controlled a line of grain elevators in the little
towns along the railroad to the west of us, and was away from home a great
deal. In his absence his wife was the head of the household.

Mrs. Harling was short and square and sturdy-looking, like her house.
Every inch of her was charged with an energy that made itself felt the
moment she entered a room. Her face was rosy and solid, with bright,
twinkling eyes and a stubborn little chin. She [168] was quick to anger,
quick to laughter, and jolly from the depths of her soul. How well I remember her laugh; it had in it the same sudden recognition that flashed into her
eyes, was a burst of humour, short and intelligent. Her rapid footsteps shook
her own floors, and she routed lassitude and indifference wherever she came.
She could not be negative or perfunctory about anything. Her enthusiasm,
and her violent likes and dislikes, asserted themselves in all the everyday
occupations of life. Wash-day was interesting, never dreary, at the Harlings'.
Preserving-time was a prolonged festival, and house-cleaning was like a revo-
lution. When Mrs. Harling made garden that spring, we could feel the stir
of her undertaking through the willow hedge that separated our place
from hers.

Three of the Harling children were near me in age. Charley, the only
son,—they had lost an older boy,—was sixteen; Julia, who was known as
the musical one, was fourteen when I was; and Sally, the tomboy with short
hair, was a year younger. She was nearly as strong as I, and uncannily clever
at all boys' sports. Sally was a wild thing, with sunburned yellow hair,
bobbed about her ears, [169] and a brown skin, for she never wore a hat.
She raced all over town on one roller skate, often cheated at "keeps," but
was such a quick shot one couldn't catch her at it.

The grown-up daughter, Frances, was a very important person in our
world. She was her father's chief clerk, and virtually managed his Black
Hawk office during his frequent absences. Because of her unusual business
ability, he was stern and exacting with her. He paid her a good salary, but
she had few holidays and never got away from her responsibilities. Even on
Sundays she went to the office to open the mail and read the markets. With
Charley, who was not interested in business, but was already preparing for
Annapolis, Mr. Harling was very indulgent; bought him guns and tools and
electric batteries, and never asked what he did with them.

Frances was dark, like her father, and quite as tall. In winter she wore
a sealskin coat and cap, and she and Mr. Harling used to walk home together in the evening, talking about grain-cars and cattle, like two men.
Sometimes she came over to see grandfather after supper, and her visits
flattered him. More than once they put their wits together to [170] rescue
some unfortunate farmer from the clutches of Wick Cutter, the Black Hawk
moneylender. Grandfather said Frances Harling was as good a judge of
credits as any banker in the county. The two or three men who had tried
to take advantage of her in a deal acquired celebrity by their defeat. She

knew every farmer for miles about; how much land he had under cultivation, how many cattle he was feeding, what his liabilities were. Her interest in these people was more than a business interest. She carried them all in her mind as if they were characters in a book or a play.

When Frances drove out into the country on business, she would go miles out of her way to call on some of the old people, or to see the women who seldom got to town. She was quick at understanding the grandmothers who spoke no English, and the most reticent and distrustful of them would tell her their story without realizing they were doing so. She went to country funerals and weddings in all weathers. A farmer's daughter who was to be married could count on a wedding present from Frances Harling.

In August the Harlings' Danish cook had [171] to leave them. Grandmother entreated them to try Ántonia. She cornered Ambrosch the next time he came to town, and pointed out to him that any connection with Christian Harling would strengthen his credit and be of advantage to him. One Sunday Mrs. Harling took the long ride out to the Shimerdas' with Frances. She said she wanted to see "what the girl came from" and to have a clear understanding with her mother. I was in our yard when they came driving home, just before sunset. They laughed and waved to me as they passed, and I could see they were in great humour. After supper, when grandfather set off to church, grandmother and I took my short cut through the willow hedge and went over to hear about the visit to the Shimerdas.

We found Mrs. Harling with Charley and Sally on the front porch, resting after her hard drive. Julia was in the hammock—she was fond of repose—and Frances was at the piano, playing without a light and talking to her mother through the open window.

Mrs. Harling laughed when she saw us coming. "I expect you left your dishes on the table to-night, Mrs. Burden," she called. [172] Frances shut the piano and came out to join us.

They had liked Ántonia from their first glimpse of her; felt they knew exactly what kind of girl she was. As for Mrs. Shimerda, they found her very amusing. Mrs. Harling chuckled whenever she spoke of her. "I expect I am more at home with that sort of bird than you are, Mrs. Burden. They're a pair, Ambrosch and that old woman!"

They had had a long argument with Ambrosch about Ántonia's allowance for clothes and pocket-money. It was his plan that every cent of his sister's wages should be paid over to him each month, and he would provide her with such clothing as he thought necessary. When Mrs. Harling told him firmly that she would keep fifty dollars a year for Ántonia's own use, he declared they wanted to take his sister to town and dress her up and make a fool of her. Mrs. Harling gave us a lively account of Ambrosch's behaviour throughout the interview; how he kept jumping up and putting on his cap as if he were through with the whole business, and how his mother tweaked his coat-tail and prompted him in Bohemian. Mrs. Harling finally agreed

[173] to pay three dollars a week for Ántonia's services—good wages in those days—and to keep her in shoes. There had been hot dispute about the shoes, Mrs. Shimerda finally saying persuasively that she would send Mrs. Harling three fat geese every year to "make even." Ambrosch was to bring his sister to town next Saturday.

"She'll be awkward and rough at first, like enough," grandmother said anxiously, "but unless she's been spoiled by the hard life she's led, she has it in her to be a real helpful girl."

Mrs. Harling laughed her quick, decided laugh. "Oh, I'm not worrying, Mrs. Burden! I can bring something out of that girl. She's barely seventeen, not too old to learn new ways. She's good-looking, too!" she added warmly.

Frances turned to grandmother. "Oh, yes, Mrs. Burden, you didn't tell us that! She was working in the garden when we got there, barefoot and ragged. But she has such fine brown legs and arms, and splendid colour in her cheeks—like those big dark red plums."

We were pleased at this praise. Grandmother spoke feelingly. "When she first came to this country, Frances, and had that gen-[174]teel old man to watch over her, she was as pretty a girl as ever I saw. But, dear me, what a life she's led, out in the fields with those rough threshers! Things would have been very different with poor Ántonia if her father had lived."

The Harlings begged us to tell them about Mr. Shimerda's death and the big snowstorm. By the time we saw grandfather coming home from church, we had told them pretty much all we knew of the Shimerdas.

"The girl will be happy here, and she'll forget those things," said Mrs. Harling confidently, as we rose to take our leave. [175]

CHAPTER IX

There was a curious social situation in Black Hawk. All the young men felt the attraction of the fine, well-set-up country girls who had come to town to earn a living, and, in nearly every case, to help the father struggle out of debt, or to make it possible for the younger children of the family to go to school.

Those girls had grown up in the first bitter-hard times, and had got little schooling themselves. But the younger brothers and sisters, for whom they made such sacrifices and who have had "advantages," never seem to me, when I meet them now, half as interesting or as well educated. The older girls, who helped to break up the wild sod, learned so much from life, from poverty, from their mothers and grandmothers; they had all, like Ántonia, been early awakened and made observant by coming at a tender age from an old country to a new. I can remember a score of these country girls who were in service in Black Hawk during the few years I lived there, and [225] I can remember something unusual and engaging about each of them. Physically they were almost a race apart, and out-of-door work had given them a vigour which, when they got over their first shyness on coming to town, developed into a positive carriage and freedom of movement, and made them conspicuous among Black Hawk women.

That was before the day of High-School athletics. Girls who had to walk more than half a mile to school were pitied. There was not a tennis court in the town; physical exercise was thought rather inelegant for the daughters of well-to-do families. Some of the High-School girls were jolly and pretty, but they stayed indoors in winter because of the cold, and in the summer because of the heat. When one danced with them, their bodies never moved inside their clothes; their muscles seemed to ask but one thing —not to be disturbed. I remember those girls merely as faces in the schoolroom, gay and rosy, or listless and dull, cut off below the shoulders, like cherubs, by the ink-smeared tops of the high desks that were surely put there to make us round-shouldered and hollow-chested.

The daughters of Black Hawk merchants [226] had a confident, unenquiring belief that they were "refined," and that the country girls, who "worked out," were not. The American farmers in our county were quite as hard-pressed as their neighbours from other countries. All alike had come to Nebraska with little capital and no knowledge of the soil they must subdue. All had borrowed money on their land. But no matter in what straits the Pennsylvanian or Virginian found himself, he would not let his daughters go out into service. Unless his girls could teach a country school, they sat at home in poverty. The Bohemian and Scandinavian girls could not get positions as teachers, because they had had no opportunity to learn the language. Determined to help in the struggle to clear the homestead from debt, they had no alternative but to go into service. Some of them, after they came to town, remained as serious and as discreet in behaviour as they had been when they ploughed and herded on their father's farm. Others, like the three Bohemian Marys, tried to make up for the years of youth they had lost. But every one of them did what she had set out to do, and sent home those hard-earned dollars. The girls I knew were always [227] helping to pay for ploughs and reapers, brood-sows, or steers to fatten.

One result of this family solidarity was that the foreign farmers in our country were the first to become prosperous. After the fathers were out of debt, the daughters married the sons of neighbours—usually of like nationality—and the girls who once worked in Black Hawk kitchens are to-day managing big farms and fine families of their own; their children are better off than the children of the town women they used to serve.

I thought the attitude of the town people toward these girls very stupid. If I told my schoolmates that Lena Lingard's grandfather was a clergyman, and much respected in Norway, they looked at me blankly. What did it matter? All foreigners were ignorant people who couldn't speak English. There was not a man in Black Hawk who had the intelligence or cultivation, much less the personal distinction, of Ántonia's father. Yet people saw no difference between her and the three Marys; they were all Bohemians, all "hired girls."

I always knew I should live long enough to see my country girls come into their own, and I have. To-day the best that a harassed Black [228] Hawk merchant can hope for is to sell provisions and farm machinery and automobiles to the rich farms where that first crop of stalwart Bohemian and Scandinavian girls are now the mistresses.

The Black Hawk boys looked forward to marrying Black Hawk girls, and living in a brand-new little house with best chairs that must not be sat upon, and hand-painted china that must not be used. But sometimes a young fellow would look up from his ledger, or out through the grating of his father's bank, and let his eyes follow Lena Lingard, as she passed the window with her slow, undulating walk, or Tiny Soderball, tripping by in her short skirt and striped stockings.

The country girls were considered a menace to the social order. Their beauty shone out too boldly against a conventional background. But anxious mothers need have felt no alarm. They mistook the mettle of their sons. The respect for respectability was stronger than any desire in Black Hawk youth.

Our young man of position was like the son of a royal house; the boy who swept out his office or drove his delivery wagon might frolic with the jolly country girls, but he himself [229] must sit all evening in a plush parlour where conversation dragged so perceptibly that the father often came in and made blundering efforts to warm up the atmosphere. On his way home from his dull call, he would perhaps meet Tony and Lena, coming along the sidewalk whispering to each other, or the three Bohemian Marys in their long plush coats and caps, comporting themselves with a dignity that only made their eventful histories the more piquant. If he went to the hotel to see a travelling man on business, there was Tiny, arching her shoulders at him like a kitten. If he went into the laundry to get his collars, there were the four Danish girls, smiling up from their ironing-boards, with their white throats and their pink cheeks.

The three Marys were the heroines of a cycle of scandalous stories, which the old men were fond of relating as they sat about the cigar-stand in the drugstore. Mary Dusak had been housekeeper for a bachelor rancher from Boston, and after several years in his service she was forced to retire from the world for a short time. Later she came back to town to take the place of her friend, Mary Svoboda, who was similarly embarrassed. The three Marys [230] were considered as dangerous as high explosives to have about the kitchen, yet they were such good cooks and such admirable housekeepers that they never had to look for a place.

The Vannis' tent brought the town boys and the country girls together on neutral ground. Sylvester Lovett, who was cashier in his father's bank, always found his way to the tent on Saturday night. He took all the dances

Lena Lingard would give him, and even grew bold enough to walk home with her. If his sisters or their friends happened to be among the onlookers on "popular nights," Sylvester stood back in the shadow under the cotton-wood trees, smoking and watching Lena with a harassed expression. Several times I stumbled upon him there in the dark, and I felt rather sorry for him. He reminded me of Ole Benson, who used to sit on the draw-side and watch Lena herd her cattle. Later in the summer, when Lena went home for a week to visit her mother, I heard from Ántonia that young Lovett drove all the way out there to see her, and took her buggy-riding. In my ingenuousness I hoped that Sylvester would marry Lena, and thus give all the country girls a better position in the town.[231]

Sylvester dallied about Lena until he began to make mistakes in his work; had to stay at the bank until after dark to make his books balance. He was daft about her, and everyone knew it. To escape from his predica-ment he ran away with a widow six years older than himself, who owned a half-section. This remedy worked, apparently. He never looked at Lena again, nor lifted his eyes as he ceremoniously tipped his hat when he hap-pened to meet her on the sidewalk.

So that was what they were like, I thought, these white-handed, high-collared clerks and bookkeepers! I used to glare at young Lovett from a distance and only wished I had some way of showing my contempt for him. [232]

CHAPTER XII

After Ántonia went to live with the Cutters, she seemed to care about nothing but picnics and parties and having a good time. When she was not going to a dance, she sewed until midnight. Her new clothes were the sub-ject of caustic comment. Under Lena's direction she copied Mrs. Gardener's new party dress and Mrs. Smith's street costume so ingeniously in cheap materials that those ladies were greatly annoyed, and Mrs. Cutter, who was jealous of them, was secretly pleased.

Tony wore gloves now, and high-heeled shoes and feathered bonnets, and she went downtown nearly every afternoon with Tiny and Lena and the Marshalls' Norwegian Anna. We High-School boys used to linger on the playground at the afternoon recess to watch them as they came trip-ping down the hill along the board sidewalk, two and two. They were grow-ing prettier every day, but as they passed us, I used to think with pride that Ántonia, like Snowwhite in the fairy tale, was still "fairest of them all." [244]

Being a Senior now, I got away from school early. Sometimes I overtook the girls downtown and coaxed them into the ice-cream parlour, where they would sit chattering and laughing, telling me all the news from the country.

I remember how angry Tiny Soderball made me one afternoon. She declared she had heard grandmother was going to make a Baptist preacher of me. "I guess you'll have to stop dancing and wear a white necktie then. Won't he look funny, girls?"

Lena laughed. "You'll have to hurry up, Jim. If you're going to be a preacher, I want you to marry me. You must promise to marry us all, and then baptize the babies."

Norwegian Anna, always dignified, looked at her reprovingly.

"Baptists don't believe in christening babies, do they, Jim?"

I told her I didn't know what they believed, and didn't care, and that I certainly wasn't going to be a preacher.

"That's too bad," Tiny simpered. She was in a teasing mood. "You'd make such a good one. You're so studious. Maybe you'd like to be a professor. You used to teach Tony, didn't you?" [245]

Ántonia broke in. "I've set my heart on Jim being a doctor. You'd be good with sick people, Jim. Your grandmother's trained you up so nice. My papa always said you were an awful smart boy."

I said I was going to be whatever I pleased. "Won't you be surprised, Miss Tiny, if I turn out to be a regular devil of a fellow?"

They laughed until a glance from Norwegian Anna checked them; the High-School Principal had just come into the front part of the shop to buy bread for supper. Anna knew the whisper was going about that I was a sly one. People said there must be something queer about a boy who showed no interest in girls of his own age, but who could be lively enough when he was with Tony and Lena or the three Marys.

The enthusiasm for the dance, which the Vannis had kindled, did not at once die out. After the tent left town, the Euchre Club became the Owl Club, and gave dances in the Masonic Hall once a week. I was invited to join, but declined. I was moody and restless that winter, and tired of the people I saw every day. Charley Harling was already at Annapo-[246]lis, while I was still sitting in Black Hawk, answering to my name at roll-call every morning, rising from my desk at the sound of a bell and marching out like the grammar-school children. Mrs. Harling was a little cool toward me, because I continued to champion Ántonia. What was there for me to do after supper? Usually I had learned next day's lessons by the time I left the school building, and I couldn't sit still and read forever.

In the evening I used to prowl about, hunting for diversion. There lay the familiar streets, frozen with snow or liquid with mud. They led to the houses of good people who were putting the babies to bed, or simply sitting still before the parlor stove, digesting their supper. Black Hawk had two saloons. One of them was admitted, even by the church people, to be as respectable as a saloon could be. Handsome Anton Jelinek, who had rented his homestead and come to town, was the proprietor. In his saloon there were long tables where the Bohemian and German farmers could eat the lunches they brought from home while they drank their beer. Jelinek kept rye bread on hand and smoked fish and strong imported cheeses to please the foreign [247] palate. I liked to drop into his bar-room and listen to the talk. But one day he overtook me on the street and clapped me on the shoulder.

"Jim," he said, "I am good friends with you and I always like to see you. But you know how the church people think about saloons. Your grandpa has always treated me fine, and I don't like to have you come into my place, because I know he don't like it, and it puts me in bad with him."

So I was shut out of that.

One could hang about the drugstore, and listen to the old men who sat there every evening, talking politics and telling raw stories. One could go to the cigar factory and chat with the old German who raised canaries for sale, and look at his stuffed birds. But whatever you began with him, the talk went back to taxidermy. There was the depot, of course; I often went down to see the night train come in, and afterwards sat awhile with the disconsolate telegrapher who was always hoping to be transferred to Omaha or Denver, "where there was some life." He was sure to bring out his pictures of actresses and dancers. He got them with cigarette coupons, [248] and nearly smoked himself to death to possess these desired forms and faces. For a change, one could talk to the station agent; but he was another malcontent; spent all his spare time writing letters to officials requesting a transfer. He wanted to get back to Wyoming where he could go trout-fishing on Sundays. He used to say "there was nothing in life for him but trout streams," ever since he'd lost his twins.

These were the distractions I had to choose from. There were no other lights burning downtown after nine o'clock. On starlight nights I used to pace up and down those long, cold streets, scowling at the little, sleeping houses on either side, with their storm-windows and covered back porches. They were flimsy shelters, most of them poorly built of light wood, with spindle porchposts horribly mutilated by the turning-lathe. Yet for all their frailness, how much jealousy and envy and unhappiness some of them managed to contain! The life that went on in them seemed to me made up of evasions and negations; shifts to save cooking, to save washing and cleaning, devices to propitiate the tongue of gossip. This guarded mode of existence was [249] like living under a tyranny. People's speech, their voices, their very glances, became furtive and repressed. Every individual taste, every natural appetite, was bridled by caution. The people asleep in those houses, I thought, tried to live like the mice in their own kitchens; to make no noise, to leave no trace, to slip over the surface of things in the dark. The growing piles of ashes and cinders in the back yards were the only evidence that the wasteful, consuming process of life went on at all. On Tuesday nights the Owl Club danced; then there was a little stir in the streets, and here and there one could see a lighted window until midnight. But the next night all was dark again.

After I refused to join "the Owls," as they were called, I made a bold resolve to go to the Saturday night dances at Firemen's Hall. I knew it would be useless to acquaint my elders with any such plan. Grandfather didn't approve of dancing, anyway; he would only say that if I wanted to dance I could go to the Masonic Hall, among "the people we knew." It was just my point that I saw altogether too much of the people we knew.

My bedroom was on the ground floor, and as [250] I studied there, I had a stove in it. I used to retire to my room early on Saturday night, change my shirt and collar and put on my Sunday coat. I waited until all was quiet and the old people were asleep, then raised my window, climbed out, and went softly through the yard. The first time I deceived my grandparents I felt rather shabby, perhaps even the second time, but I soon ceased to think about it.

The dance at the Firemen's Hall was the one thing I looked forward to all the week. There I met the same people I used to see at the Vannis' tent. Sometimes there were Bohemians from Wilber, or German boys who came down on the afternoon freight from Bismarck. Tony and Lena and Tiny were always there, and the three Bohemian Marys, and the Danish laundry girls.

The four Danish girls lived with the laundryman and his wife in their house behind the laundry, with a big garden where the clothes were hung out to dry. The laundryman was a kind, wise old fellow, who paid his girls well, looked out for them, and gave them a good home. He told me once that his own daughter died just as she was getting old enough to [251] help her mother, and that he had been "trying to make up for it ever since." On summer afternoons he used to sit for hours on the sidewalk in front of his laundry, his newspaper lying on his knee, watching his girls through the big open window while they ironed and talked in Danish. The clouds of white dust that blew up the street, the gusts of hot wind that withered his vegetable garden, never disturbed his calm. His droll expression seemed to say that he had found the secret of contentment. Morning and evening he drove about in his spring wagon, distributing freshly ironed clothes, and collecting bags of linen that cried out for his suds and sunny drying-lines. His girls never looked so pretty at the dances as they did standing by the ironing board, or over the tubs, washing the fine pieces, their white arms and throats bare, their cheeks bright as the brightest wild roses, their gold hair moist with the steam or the heat and curling in little damp spirals about their ears. They had not learned much English, and were not so ambitious as Tony or Lena; but they were kind, simple girls and they were always happy. When one danced with them, one smelled their clean, freshly ironed clothes that [252] had been put away with rosemary leaves from Mr. Jensen's garden.

There were never girls enough to go around at those dances, but everyone wanted a turn with Tony and Lena. Lena moved without exertion, rather indolently, and her hand often accented the rhythm softly on her partner's shoulder. She smiled if one spoke to her, but seldom answered. The music seemed to put her into a soft, waking dream, and her violet-coloured eyes looked sleepily and confidingly at one from under her long lashes. When she sighed she exhaled a heavy perfume of sachet powder. To dance "Home, Sweet Home," with Lena was like coming in with the tide. She danced every dance like a waltz, and it was always the same waltz— the waltz of coming home to something, of inevitable, fated return. After a while one got restless under it, as one does under the heat of a soft, sultry summer day.

When you spun out into the floor with Tony, you didn't return to anything. You set out every time upon a new adventure. I liked to schottische with her; she had so much spring and variety, and was always putting in new steps and slides. She taught me to [253] dance against and around the hard-and-fast beat of the music. If, instead of going to the end of the railroad, old Mr. Shimerda had stayed in New York and picked up a living with his fiddle, how different Ántonia's life might have been!

Ántonia often went to the dances with Larry Donovan, a passenger conductor who was a kind of professional ladies' man, as we said. I remember how admiringly all the boys looked at her the night she first wore her velveteen dress, made like Mrs. Gardener's black velvet. She was lovely to see, with her eyes shining, and her lips always a little parted when she danced. That constant, dark colour in her cheeks never changed.

One evening when Donovan was out on his run, Ántonia came to the hall with Norwegian Anna and her young man, and that night I took her home. When we were in the Cutters' yard, sheltered by the evergreens, I told her she must kiss me good night.

"Why, sure, Jim." A moment later she drew her face away and whispered indignantly, "Why, Jim! You know you ain't right to kiss me like that. I'll tell your grandmother on you!" [254]

"Lena Lingard lets me kiss her," I retorted, "and I'm not half as fond of her as I am of you."

"Lena does?" Tony gasped. "If she's up to any of her nonsense with you, I'll scratch her eyes out!" She took my arm again and we walked out of the gate and up and down the sidewalk. "Now, don't you go and be a fool like some of these town boys. You're not going to sit around here and whittle store-boxes and tell stories all your life. You are going away to school and make something of yourself. I'm just awful proud of you. You won't go and get mixed up with the Swedes, will you?"

"I don't care anything about any of them but you," I said. "And you'll always treat me like a kid, I suppose."

She laughed and threw her arms around me. "I expect I will, but you're a kid I'm awful fond of, anyhow! You can like me all you want to, but if I see you hanging around with Lena much, I'll go to your grandmother, as sure as your name's Jim Burden! Lena's all right, only—well, you know yourself she's soft that way. She can't help it. It's natural to her."

If she was proud of me, I was so proud of her [255] that I carried my head high as I emerged from the dark cedars and shut the Cutters' gate softly behind me. Her warm, sweet face, her kind arms, and the true heart in her; she was, oh, she was still my Ántonia! I looked with contempt at the dark, silent little houses about me as I walked home, and thought of the stupid young men who were asleep in some of them. I knew where the real women were, though I was only a boy; and I would not be afraid of them, either!

I hated to enter the still house when I went home from the dances, and it was long before I could get to sleep. Toward morning I used to have pleasant dreams: sometimes Tony and I were out in the country, sliding down straw-stacks as we used to do; climbing up the yellow mountains over and over, and slipping down the smooth sides into soft piles of chaff.

One dream I dreamed a great many times, and it was always the same. I was in a harvest-field full of shocks, and I was lying against one of them. Lena Lingard came across the stubble barefoot, in a short skirt, with a curved reaping-hook in her hand, and she was flushed like the dawn, with a kind of luminous rosiness all about her. She sat down beside me, turned to [256] me with a soft sigh and said, "Now they are all gone, and I can kiss you as much as I like."

I used to wish I could have this flattering dream about Ántonia, but I never did. [257]

WILLIAM FAULKNER
1897–1962

Time and Tradition in the South

"A ROSE FOR EMILY"

William Faulkner, who stands at the forefront of modern American fiction, was born, grew up, and lived in Mississippi until his death. Most of his novels and short stories depict his mythical Yoknapatawpha County—with its 2,400 square miles and its 15,611 inhabitants—measured and peopled as a microcosm not only of southern life but of the human condition. In Yoknapatawpha County he creates the towns of Jefferson and Frenchman's Bend; the families of Sartoris, Compson, de Spain, and Snopes; the Indians and Negroes; and the backwoodsmen—all now a very real part of American literature. His most important novels are *The Sound and the Fury* (1929), *As I Lay Dying* (1930), *Absalom, Absalom!* (1936), *Light in August* (1932), and *The Hamlet* (1940).

Faulkner is no less skilled in the short story, and some critics hold that his reputation is enhanced by his short fiction, which appears in such collections as *These 13* (1931), *Doctor Martino and Other Stories* (1934), *Go Down, Moses, and Other Stories* (1942), and *Collected Stories of William Faulkner* (1950).

In "A Rose for Emily" Faulkner considers many facets of small-town life—its moral code, its tradition, its social levels, its legends, and its conventions—by relating the story of Miss Emily Grierson. The setting for "A Rose for Emily" is the small town of Jefferson, county seat of Yoknapatawpha County. Faulkner tells his story through the eyes of an unnamed narrator—a member of the community—a device that limits the point of view. The reader will observe the emphasis on "we" in the story. Emily Grierson is seen as a young girl, as a spinster, and finally as an aged recluse. But she is always a force in the community—"dear, inescapable, impervious, tranquil, and perverse."

The chronology of the story places special emphasis upon tradition by the many contrasts Faulkner makes between the old (the past) and the new (the present). The new generation of leaders takes over in the community and the customs change gradually but surely over the years. Yet Miss Emily, who, in her pride and independence, and perhaps her contempt, represents the past, is Faulkner's protagonist. Time, then, is Faulkner's chief concern in "A Rose for Emily," and the story deals with how the town and Miss Emily contend with it.

"A ROSE FOR EMILY"

I

When Miss Emily Grierson died, our whole town went to her funeral: the men through a sort of respectful affection for a fallen monument, the women mostly out of curiosity to see the inside of her house, which no one save an old man servant—a combined gardener and cook—had seen in at least ten years.

It was a big, squarish frame house that had once been white, decorated with cupolas and spires and scrolled balconies in the heavily lightsome style of the seventies, set on what had once been our most select street. But garages and cotton gins had encroached and obliterated even the august names of that neighborhood; only Miss Emily's house was left, lifting its stubborn and coquettish decay above the cotton wagons and the gasoline pumps—an eyesore among eyesores. And now Miss Emily had gone to join the representatives of those august names where they lay in the cedar-bemused cemetery among the ranked and anonymous graves of Union and Confederate soldiers who fell at the battle of Jefferson.

Alive, Miss Emily had been a tradition, a duty, and a care; a sort of hereditary obligation upon the town, dating from that day in 1894 when Colonel Sartoris, the mayor—he who fathered the edict that no Negro woman should appear on [119] the streets without an apron—remitted her taxes, the dispensation dating from the death of her father on into perpetuity. Not that Miss Emily would have accepted charity. Colonel Sartoris invented an involved tale to the effect that Miss Emily's father had loaned money to the town, which the town, as a matter of business, preferred this way of repaying. Only a man of Colonel Sartoris' generation and thought could have invented it, and only a woman could have believed it.

When the next generation, with its more modern ideas, became mayors and aldermen, this arrangement created some little dissatisfaction. On the first of the year they mailed her a tax notice. February came, and there was no reply. They wrote her a formal letter, asking her to call at the sheriff's office at her convenience. A week later the mayor wrote her himself, offering to call or to send his car for her, and received in reply a note on paper of an archaic shape, in a thin, flowing calligraphy in faded ink, to the effect that she no longer went out at all. The tax notice was also enclosed, without comment.

They called a special meeting of the Board of Aldermen. A deputation waited upon her, knocked at the door through which no visitor had passed since she ceased giving china-painting lessons eight or ten years earlier. They were admitted by the old Negro into a dim hall from which a stairway mounted into still more shadow. It smelled of dust and disuse—a close, dank smell. The Negro led them into the parlor. It was furnished in heavy, leather-covered furniture. When the Negro opened the blinds of one window, they could see that the leather was cracked; and when they sat down, a faint dust rose sluggishly about their thighs, spinning with slow motes in the single sun-ray. On a tarnished gilt easel before the fireplace stood a crayon portrait of Miss Emily's father. [120]

They rose when she entered—a small, fat woman in black, with a thin gold chain descending to her waist and vanishing into her belt, leaning on an ebony cane with a tarnished gold head. Her skeleton was small and spare; perhaps that was why what would have been merely plumpness in another was obesity in her. She looked bloated, like a body long submerged in motionless water, and of that pallid hue. Her eyes, lost in the fatty ridges of her face, looked like two small pieces of coal pressed into a lump of dough as they moved from one face to another while the visitors stated their errand.

She did not ask them to sit. She just stood in the door and listened quietly until the spokeman came to a stumbling halt. Then they could hear the invisible watch ticking at the end of the gold chain.

Her voice was dry and cold. "I have no taxes in Jefferson. Colonel Sartoris explained it to me. Perhaps one of you can gain access to the city records and satisfy yourselves."

"But we have. We are the city authorities, Miss Emily. Didn't you get a notice from the sheriff, signed by him?"

"I received a paper, yes," Miss Emily said. "Perhaps he considers himself the sheriff . . . I have no taxes in Jefferson."

"But there is nothing on the books to show that, you see. We must go by the—"

"See Colonel Sartoris. I have no taxes in Jefferson."

"But, Miss Emily—"

"See Colonel Sartoris." (Colonel Sartoris had been dead almost ten years.) "I have no taxes in Jefferson. Tobe!" The Negro appeared. "Show these gentlemen out."

II

So she vanquished them, horse and foot, just as she had vanquished their fathers thirty years before about the smell. [121] That was two years after her father's death and a short time after her sweetheart—the one we believed would marry her—had deserted her. After her father's death she went out very little; after her sweetheart went away, people hardly saw her at all. A few of the ladies had the temerity to call, but were not received, and the only sign of life about the place was the Negro man—a young man then—going in and out with a market basket.

"Just as if a man—any man—could keep a kitchen properly," the ladies said; so they were not surprised when the smell developed. It was another link between the gross, teeming world and the high and mighty Griersons.

A neighbor, a woman, complained to the mayor, Judge Stevens, eighty years old.

"But what will you have me to do about it, madam?" he said.

"Why, send her word to stop it," the woman said. "Isn't there a law?"

"I'm sure that won't be necessary," Judge Stevens said. "It's probably just a snake or a rat that nigger of hers killed in the yard. I'll speak to him about it."

The next day he received two more complaints, one from a man who came in diffident deprecation. "We really must do something about it, Judge. I'd be the last one in the world to bother Miss Emily, but we've got to do something." That night the Board of Aldermen met—three gray-beards and one younger man, a member of the rising generation.

"It's simple enough," he said. "Send her word to have her place cleaned up. Give her a certain time to do it in, and if she don't . . ."

"Dammit sir," Judge Stevens said, "will you accuse a lady to her face of smelling bad?"

So the next night, after midnight, four men crossed Miss Emily's lawn and slunk about the house like burglars, sniffing along the base of the brick-work and at the cellar openings [122] while one of them performed a regular sowing motion with his hand out of a sack slung from his shoulder. They broke open the cellar door and sprinkled lime there, and in all the out-buildings. As they recrossed the lawn, a window that had been dark was lighted and Miss Emily sat in it, the light behind her, and her upright torso motionless as that of an idol. They crept quietly across the lawn and into the shadow of the locusts that lined the street. After a week or two the smell went away.

That was when people had begun to feel really sorry for her. People in our town, remembering how old lady Wyatt, her great-aunt, had gone completely crazy at last, believed that the Griersons held themselves a little too high for what they really were. None of the young men were quite good enough for Miss Emily and such. We had long thought of them as a tableau, Miss Emily a slender figure in white in the background, her father a spraddled silhouette in the foreground, his back to her and clutching a horsewhip, the two of them framed by the back-flung front door. So when she got to be thirty and was still single, we were not pleased exactly, but vindicated; even with insanity in the family she wouldn't have turned down all of her chances if they had really materialized.

When her father died, it got about that the house was all that was left to her; and in a way, people were glad. At last they could pity Miss Emily. Being left alone, and a pauper, she had become humanized. Now she too would know the old thrill and the old despair of a penny more or less.

The day after his death all the ladies prepared to call at the house and offer condolence and aid, as is our custom. Miss Emily met them at the door, dressed as usual and with no trace of grief on her face. She told them that her father was not dead. She did that for three days, with the ministers [123] calling on her, and the doctors, trying to persuade her to let them dispose of the body. Just as they were about to resort to law and force, she broke down, and they buried her father quickly.

We did not say she was crazy then. We believed she had to do that. We remembered all the young men her father had driven away, and we knew that with nothing left, she would have to cling to that which had robbed her, as people will.

III

She was sick for a long time. When we saw her again, her hair was cut short, making her look like a girl, with a vague resemblance to those angels in colored church windows—sort of tragic and serene.

The town had just let the contracts for paving the sidewalks, and in the summer after her father's death they began the work. The construction company came with niggers and mules and machinery, and a foreman named Homer Barron, a Yankee—a big, dark, ready man, with a big voice and eyes lighter than his face. The little boys would follow in groups to hear him cuss the niggers, and the niggers singing in time to the rise and fall of picks. Pretty soon he knew everybody in town. Whenever you heard a lot of laughing anywhere about the square, Homer Barron would be in the center of the group. Presently we began to see him and Miss Emily on Sunday afternoons driving in the yellow-wheeled buggy and the matched team of bays from the livery stable.

At first we were glad that Miss Emily would have an interest, because the ladies all said, "Of course a Grierson would not think seriously of a Northerner, a day laborer." But there were still others, older people, who said that even grief could not cause a real lady to forget *noblesse oblige*—[124] without calling it *noblesse oblige*. They just said, "Poor Emily. Her kinsfolk should come to her." She had some kin in Alabama; but years ago her father had fallen out with them over the estate of old lady Wyatt, the crazy woman, and there was no communication between the two families. They had not even been represented at the funeral.

And as soon as the old people said, "Poor Emily," the whispering began. "Do you suppose it's really so?" they said to one another. "Of course it is. What else could . . ." This behind their hands; rustling of craned silk and satin behind jalousies closed upon the sun of Sunday afternoon as the thin, swift clop-clop-clop of the matched team passed: "Poor Emily."

She carried her head high enough—even when we believed that she was fallen. It was as if she demanded more than ever the recognition of her dignity as the last Grierson; as if it had wanted that touch of earthiness to reaffirm her imperviousness. Like when she bought the rat poison, the arsenic. That was over a year after they had begun to say "Poor Emily," and while the two female cousins were visiting her.

"I want some poison," she said to the druggist. She was over thirty then, still a slight woman, though thinner than usual, with cold, haughty black eyes in a face the flesh of which was strained across the temples and about the eye-sockets as you imagine a lighthouse-keeper's face ought to look. "I want some poison," she said.

"Yes, Miss Emily. What kind? For rats and such? I recom—"

"I want the best you have. I don't care what kind."

The druggist named several. "They'll kill anything up to an elephant. But what you want is—"

"Arsenic," Miss Emily said. "Is that a good one?"

"Is . . . arsenic? Yes, ma'am. But what you want—"

"I want arsenic." [125]

The druggist looked down at her. She looked back at him, erect, her face like a strained flag. "Why, of course," the druggist said. "If that's what you want. But the law requires you to tell what you are going to use it for."

Miss Emily just stared at him, her head tilted back in order to look him eye for eye, until he looked away and went and got the arsenic and wrapped it up. The Negro delivery boy brought her the package; the druggist didn't come back. When she opened the package at home there was written on the box, under the skull and bones: "For rats."

IV

So the next day we all said, "She will kill herself"; and we said it would be the best thing. When she had first begun to be seen with Homer Barron, we had said, "She will marry him." Then we said, "She will persuade him yet," because Homer himself had remarked—he liked men, and it was known that he drank with the younger men in the Elks' Club—that he was not a marrying man. Later we said, "Poor Emily" behind the jalousies as they passed on Sunday afternoon in the glittering buggy, Miss Emily with her head high and Homer Barron with his hat cocked and a cigar in his teeth, reins and whip in a yellow glove.

Then some of the ladies began to say that it was a disgrace to the town and a bad example to the young people. The men did not want to interfere, but at last the ladies forced the Baptist minister—Miss Emily's people were Episcopal—to call upon her. He would never divulge what happened during that interview, but he refused to go back again. The next Sunday they again drove about the streets, and the following day the minister's wife wrote to Miss Emily's relations in Alabama. [126]

So she had blood-kin under her roof again and we sat back to watch developments. At first nothing happened. Then we were sure that they were to be married. We learned that Miss Emily had been to the jeweler's and ordered a man's toilet set in silver, with the letters H.B. on each piece. Two days later we learned that she had bought a complete outfit of men's clothing, including a nightshirt, and we said, "They are married." We were really glad. We were glad because the two female cousins were even more Grierson than Miss Emily had ever been.

So we were not surprised when Homer Barron—the streets had been finished some time since—was gone. We were a little disappointed that there was not a public blowing-off, but we believed that he had gone on to prepare for Miss Emily's coming, or to give her a chance to get rid of the cousins. (By that time it was a cabal, and we were all Miss Emily's allies to help circumvent the cousins.) Sure enough, after another week they departed. And, as we had expected all along, within three days Homer Barron was back in town. A neighbor saw the Negro man admit him at the kitchen door at dusk one evening.

And that was the last we saw of Homer Barron. And of Miss Emily for some time. The Negro man went in and out with the market basket, but the front door remained closed. Now and then we would see her at a window for a moment, as the men did that night when they sprinkled the lime, but for almost six months she did not appear on the streets. Then we knew that this was to be expected too; as if that quality of her father which had thwarted her woman's life so many times had been too virulent and too furious to die.

When we next saw Miss Emily, she had grown fat and her hair was turning gray. During the next few years it grew grayer and grayer until it attained an even pepper-and-salt iron-gray, when it ceased turning. Up to the day of her [127] death at seventy-four it was still that vigorous iron-gray, like the hair of an active man.

From that time on her front door remained closed, save for a period of six or seven years, when she was about forty, during which she gave lessons in china-painting. She fitted up a studio in one of the downstairs rooms, where the daughters and granddaughters of Colonel Sartoris' contemporaries were sent to her with the same regularity and in the same spirit that they were sent to church on Sundays with a twenty-five-cent piece for the collection plate. Meanwhile her taxes had been remitted.

Then the newer generation became the backbone and the spirit of the town, and the painting pupils grew up and fell away and did not send their children to her with boxes of color and tedious brushes and pictures cut from the ladies' magazines. The front door closed upon the last one and remained closed for good. When the town got free postal delivery, Miss Emily alone refused to let them fasten the metal numbers above her door and attach a mailbox to it. She would not listen to them.

Daily, monthly, yearly we watched the Negro grow grayer and more stooped, going in and out with the market basket. Each December we sent her a tax notice, which would be returned by the post office a week later, unclaimed. Now and then we would see her in one of the downstairs window—she had evidently shut up the top floor of the house—like the carven torso of an idol in a niche, looking or not looking at us, we could never tell which. Thus she passed from generation to generation—dear, inescapable, impervious, tranquil, and perverse.

And so she died. Fell ill in the house filled with dust and shadows, with only a doddering Negro man to wait on her. We did not even know she was sick; we had long since given up trying to get any information from the Negro. [128] He talked to no one, probably not even to her, for his voice had grown harsh and rusty, as if from disuse.

She died in one of the downstairs rooms, in a heavy walnut bed with a curtain, her gray head propped on a pillow yellow and moldy with age and lack of sunlight.

V

The Negro met the first of the ladies at the front door and let them in, with their hushed, sibilant voices and their quick, curious glances, and then he disappeared. He walked right through the house and out the back and was not seen again.

The two female cousins came at once. They held the funeral on the second day, with the town coming to look at Miss Emily beneath a mass of bought flowers, with the crayon face of her father musing profoundly above the bier and the ladies sibilant and macabre; and the very old men—some in their brushed Confederate uniforms—on the porch and the lawn, talking of Miss Emily as if she had been a contemporary of theirs, believing that they had danced with her and courted her perhaps, confusing time with its mathematical progression, as the old do, to whom all the past is not a diminishing road but, instead, a huge meadow which no winter ever quite touches, divided from them now by the narrow bottle-neck of the most re-cent decade of years.

Already we knew that there was one room in that region above stairs which no one had seen in forty years, and which would have to be forced. They waited until Miss Emily was decently in the ground before they opened it.

The violence of breaking down the door seemed to fill this room with pervading dust. A thin, acrid pall as of the tomb seemed to lie everywhere upon this room decked and furnished as for a bridal: upon the valance curtains of faded rose color, upon the rose-shaded lights, upon the dressing [129] table, upon the delicate array of crystal and the man's toilet things backed with tarnished silver, silver so tarnished that the monogram was obscured. Among them lay a collar and tie, as if they had just been removed, which, lifted, left upon the surface a pale crescent in the dust. Upon a chair hung the suit, carefully folded; beneath it the two mute shoes and the discarded socks.

The man himself lay in the bed.

For a long while we just stood there, looking down at the profound and fleshless grin. The body had apparently once lain in the attitude of an embrace, but now the long sleep that outlasts love, that conquers even the grimace of love, had cuckolded him. What was left of him rotted beneath what was left of the nightshirt, had become inextricable from the bed in which he lay; and upon him and upon the pillow beside him lay that even coating of the patient and biding dust.

Then we noticed that in the second pillow was the indentation of a head. One of us lifted something from it, and leaning forward, that faint and invisible dust dry and acrid in the nostrils, we saw a long strand of iron-gray hair. [130]

WILLIAM FAULKNER
1897–1962

Furious Repudiation of Truth

"DRY SEPTEMBER"

Again and again William Faulkner turned to the small town of Jefferson in Yoknapatawpha County as the setting for his stories. He knew the atmosphere, the customs and traditions, and the people and their thoughts and tensions. In "Dry September," the story of the lynching of a Negro for an attack on a white woman, Faulkner is dealing with an issue much larger than the lynching itself. The story is not simply an argument against the general treatment of blacks. Instead it is as if Faulkner wants us to see the people of Jefferson—in their lynch-mob psychology—as representative of the predicament of modern man.

The story opens in the barbershop where the men of the town gather and the attitudes of the townspeople are expressed. It is here that the rumor of the attack spreads. It is the white woman's word against the black man's. Yet it becomes clear to the reader that the attack on Minnie Cooper never took place.

The title is important and apt, offering both a literal and a symbolic meaning. Particularly to be noted are the images of the opening sentence—the blood, the dryness, the fall, the fire—all of which suggest death and sterility.

With great skill Faulkner sets the dramatic action of the first, third, and fifth sections against the quiet recounting in the second and fourth sections of the character of Minnie Cooper, a victim of her own sexual frustration. It is this frustration and loneliness that literally has driven her to hysteria and madness.

The story centers on the repudiation of truth. We note acts of passion without reason, and we see lives of people warped by insecurity, rigidity, and violence. Their reaction to the supposed attack reveals the mob psychology, with its need to assert itself and to strike out without purpose or justification.

"DRY SEPTEMBER"

I

Through the bloody September twilight, aftermath of sixty-two rainless days, it had gone like a fire in dry grass—the rumor, the story, whatever it was. Something about Miss Minnie Cooper and a Negro. Attacked, insulted, frightened: none of them, gathered in the barber shop on that Saturday evening where the ceiling fan stirred, without freshening it, the vitiated air, sending back upon them, in recurrent surges of stale pomade and lotion, their own stale breath and odors, knew exactly what had happened.

"Except it wasn't Will Mayes," a barber said. He was a man of middle age; a thin, sand-colored man with a mild face, who was shaving a client. "I know Will Mayes. He's a good nigger. And I know Miss Minnie Cooper, too."

"What do you know about her?" a second barber said.

"Who is she?" the client said. "A young girl?"

"No," the barber said. "She's about forty, I reckon. She aint married. That's why I dont believe—"

"Believe, hell!" a hulking youth in a sweat-stained silk shirt said. "Wont you take a white woman's word before a nigger's?"

"I dont believe Will Mayes did it," the barber said. "I know Will Mayes." [169]

"Maybe you know who did it, then. Maybe you already got him out of town, you damn niggerlover."

"I dont believe anybody did anything. I dont believe anything happened. I leave it to you fellows if them ladies that get old without getting married dont have notions that a man cant—"

"Then you are a hell of a white man," the client said. He moved under the cloth. The youth had sprung to his feet.

"You dont?" he said. "Do you accuse a white woman of lying?"

The barber held the razor poised above the half-risen client. He did not look around.

"It's this durn weather," another said. "It's enough to make a man do anything. Even to her."

Nobody laughed. The barber said in his mild, stubborn tone: "I aint accusing nobody of nothing. I just know and you fellows know how a woman that never—"

William Faulkner, "Dry September," from *Collected Stories of William Faulkner* (New York: Random House, 1950). Copyright 1930 and renewed 1958 by William Faulkner. Reprinted by permission of Random House, Inc.

"You damn niggerlover!" the youth said.

"Shut up, Butch," another said. "We'll get the facts in plenty of time to act."

"Who is? Who's getting them?" the youth said. "Facts, hell! I—"

"You're a fine white man," the client said. "Aint you?" In his frothy beard he looked like a desert rat in the moving pictures. "You tell them, Jack," he said to the youth. "If there aint any white men in this town, you can count on me, even if I aint only a drummer and a stranger."

"That's right, boys," the barber said. "Find out the truth first. I know Will Mayes."

"Well, by God!" the youth shouted. "To think that a white man in this town—"

"Shut up, Butch," the second speaker said. "We got plenty of time."

The client sat up. He looked at the speaker. "Do you [170] claim that anything excuses a nigger attacking a white woman? Do you mean to tell me you are a white man and you'll stand for it? You better go back North where you came from. The South dont want your kind here."

"North what?" the second said. "I was born and raised in this town."

"Well, by God!" the youth said. He looked about with a strained, baffled gaze, as if he was trying to remember what it was he wanted to say or to do. He drew his sleeve across his sweating face. "Damn if I'm going to let a white woman—"

"You tell them, Jack," the drummer said. "By God, if they—"

The screen door crashed open. A man stood in the floor, his feet apart and his heavy-set body poised easily. His white shirt was open at the throat; he wore a felt hat. His hot, bold glance swept the group. His name was McLendon. He had commanded troops at the front in France and had been decorated for valor.

"Well," he said, "are you going to sit there and let a black son rape a white woman on the streets of Jefferson?"

Butch sprang up again. The silk of his shirt clung flat to his heavy shoulders. At each armpit was a dark halfmoon. "That's what I been telling them! That's what I—"

"Did it really happen?" a third said. "This aint the first man scare she ever had, like Hawkshaw says. Wasn't there something about a man on the kitchen roof, watching her undress, about a year ago?"

"What?" the client said. "What's that?" The barber had been slowly forcing him back into the chair; he arrested himself reclining, his head lifted, the barber still pressing him down.

McLendon whirled on the third speaker. "Happen? What [171] the hell difference does it make? Are you going to let the black sons get away with it until one really does it?"

"That's what I'm telling them!" Butch shouted. He cursed, long and steady, pointless.

"Here, here," a fourth said. "Not so loud. Dont talk so loud."

"Sure," McLendon said; "no talking necessary at all. I've done my talking. Who's with me?" He poised on the balls of his feet, roving his gaze.

The barber held the drummer's face down, the razor poised. "Find out the facts first, boys. I know Willy Mayes. It wasn't him. Let's get the sheriff and do this thing right."

McLendon whirled upon him his furious, rigid face. The barber did not look away. They looked like men of different races. The other barbers had ceased also above their prone clients. "You mean to tell me," McLendon said, "that you'd take a nigger's word before a white woman's? Why, you damn niggerloving—"

The third speaker rose and grasped McLendon's arm; he too had been a soldier. "Now, now. Let's figure this thing out. Who knows anything about what really happened?"

"Figure out hell!" McLendon jerked his arm free. "All that're with me get up from there. The ones that aint—" He roved his gaze, dragging his sleeve across his face.

Three men rose. The drummer in the chair sat up. "Here," he said, jerking at the cloth about his neck; "get this rag off me. I'm with him. I dont live here, but by God, if our mothers and wives and sisters—" He smeared the cloth over his face and flung it to the floor. McLendon stood in the floor and cursed the others. Another rose and moved toward him. The remainder sat uncomfortable, not looking at one another, then one by one they rose and joined him.

The barber picked the cloth from the floor. He began to [172] fold it neatly. "Boys, dont do that. Will Mayes never done it. I know."

"Come on," McLendon said. He whirled. From his hip pocket protruded the butt of a heavy automatic pistol. They went out. The screen door crashed behind them reverberant in the dead air.

The barber wiped the razor carefully and swiftly, and put it away, and ran to the rear, and took his hat from the wall. "I'll be back as soon as I can," he said to the other barbers. "I can't let—" He went out, running. The two other barbers followed him to the door and caught it on the rebound, leaning out and looking up the street after him. The air was flat and dead. It had a metallic taste at the base of the tongue.

"What can he do?" the first said. The second one was saying Jees Christ, Jees Christ," under his breath. "I'd just as lief be Will Mayes as Hawk, if he gets McLendon riled."

"Jees Christ, Jees Christ," the second whispered.

"You reckon he really done it to her?" the first said.

II

She was thirty-eight or thirty-nine. She lived in a small frame house with her invalid mother and a thin, shallow, unflagging aunt, where each morning between ten and eleven she would appear on the porch in a lace-trimmed boudoir cap, to sit swinging in the porch swing until noon. After dinner she lay down for a while, until the afternoon began to cool. Then, in one of the three or four new voile dresses which she had each summer, she would go downtown to spend the afternoon in the stores with the other ladies, where they would handle the goods and haggle over the prices in cold, immediate voices, without any intention of buying.

She was of comfortable people—not the best in Jefferson, [173] but good people enough—and she was still on the slender side of ordinary looking, with a bright, faintly haggard manner and dress. When she was young she had had a slender, nervous body and a sort of hard vivacity which had enabled her for a time to ride upon the crest of the town's social life as exemplified by the high school party and church social period of her contemporaries while still children enough to be unclassconscious.

She was the last to realize that she was losing ground; that those among whom she had been a little brighter and louder flame than any other were beginning to learn the pleasure of snobbery—male—and retaliation—female. That was when her face began to wear that bright, haggard look. She still carried it to parties on shadowy porticoes and summer lawns, like a mask or a flag, with that bafflement of furious repudiation of truth in her eyes. One evening at a party she heard a boy and two girls, all schoolmates, talking. She never accepted another invitation.

She watched the girls with whom she had grown up as they married and got homes and children, but no man ever called on her steadily until the children of the other girls had been calling her "aunty" for several years, the while their mothers told them in bright voices about how popular Aunt Minnie had been as a girl. Then the town began to see her driving on Sunday afternoons with the cashier in the bank. He was a widower of about forty—a high-colored man, smelling always faintly of the barber shop or of whisky. He owned the first automobile in town, a red runabout; Minnie had the first motoring bonnet and veil the town ever saw. Then the town began to say: "Poor Minnie." "But she is old enough to take care of herself," others said. That was when she began to ask her old schoolmates that their children call her "cousin" instead of "aunty."

It was twelve years now since she had been relegated into [174] adultery by public opinion, and eight years since the cashier had gone to a Memphis bank, returning for one day each Christmas, which he spent at an annual bachelor's party at a hunting club on the river. From behind their curtains the neighbors would see the party pass, and during the over-the-way Christmas day visiting they would tell her about him, about how well he looked, and how they heard that he was prospering in the city, watching with bright, secret eyes her haggard, bright face. Usually by that hour there would be the scent of whisky on her breath. It was supplied her by a youth, a clerk at the soda fountain: "Sure; I buy it for the old gal. I reckon she's entitled to a little fun."

Her mother kept to her room altogether now; the gaunt aunt ran the house. Against that background Minnie's bright dresses, her idle and empty days, had a quality of furious unreality. She went out in the evenings only with women now, neighbors, to the moving pictures. Each afternoon she dressed in one of the new dresses and went downtown alone, where her young "cousins" were already strolling in the late afternoons with their delicate, silken heads and thin, awkward arms and conscious hips, clinging to one another or shrieking and giggling with paired boys in the soda fountain when she passed and went on along the serried store fronts, in the doors of which the sitting and lounging men did not even follow her with their eyes any more.

III

The barber went swiftly up the street where the sparse lights, insect-swirled, glared in rigid and violent suspension in the lifeless air. The day had died in a pall of dust; above the darkened square, shrouded by the spent dust, the sky was as clear as the inside of a brass bell. Below the east was a rumor of the twice-waxed moon. [175]

When he overtook them McLendon and three others were getting into a car parked in an alley. McLendon stooped his thick head, peering out beneath the top. "Changed your mind, did you?" he said. "Damn good thing; by God, tomorrow when this town hears about how you talked to-night—"

"Now, now," the other ex-soldier said. "Hawkshaw's all right. Come on, Hawk; jump in."

"Will Mayes never done it, boys," the barber said. "If anybody done it. Why, you all know well as I do there aint any town where they got better niggers than us. And you know how a lady will kind of think things about men when there aint any reason to, and Miss Minnie anyway—"

"Sure, sure," the soldier said. "We're just going to talk to him a little; that's all."

"Talk hell!" Butch said. "When we're through with the—"

"Shut up, for God's sake!" the soldier said. "Do you want everybody in town—"

"Tell them, by God!" McLendon said. "Tell every one of the sons that's let a white woman—"

"Let's go; let's go: here's the other car." The second car slid squealing out of a cloud of dust at the alley mouth. McLendon started his car and took the lead. Dust lay like fog in the street. The street lights hung nim-bused as in water. They drove on out of town.

A rutted lane turned at right angles. Dust hung above it too, and above all the land. The dark bulk of the ice plant, where the Negro Mayes was night watchman, rose against the sky. "Better stop here, hadn't we?" the soldier said. McLendon did not reply. He hurled the car up and slammed to a stop, the headlights glaring on the blank wall.

"Listen here, boys," the barber said; "if he's here, dont that prove he never done it? Dont it? If it was him, he [176] would run. Dont you see he would?" The second car came up and stopped. McLendon got down; Butch sprang down beside him. "Listen, boys," the barber said.

"Cut the lights off!" McLendon said. The breathless dark rushed down. There was no sound in it save their lungs as they sought air in the parched dust in which for two months they had lived; then the diminish-ing crunch of McLendon's and Butch's feet, and a moment later McLen-don's voice:

"Will! . . . Will!"

Below the east the wan hemorrhage of the moon increased. It heaved above the ridge, silvering the air, the dust, so that they seemed to breathe, live, in a bowl of molten lead. There was no sound of nightbird nor insect, no sound save their breathing and a faint ticking of contracting metal about the cars. Where their bodies touched one another they seemed to sweat dryly, for no more moisture came. "Christ!" a voice said; "let's get out of here."

But they didn't move until vague noises began to grow out of the darkness ahead; then they got out and waited tensely in the breathless dark. There was another sound: a blow, a hissing expulsion of breath and McLendon cursing in undertone. They stood a moment longer, then they ran forward. They ran in a stumbling clump, as though they were fleeing something. "Kill him, kill the son," a voice whispered. McLendon flung them back.

"Not here," he said. "Get him into the car." "Kill him, kill the black son!" the voice murmured. They dragged the Negro to the car. The barber had waited beside the car. He could feel himself sweating and he knew he was going to be sick at the stomach.

"What is it, captains?" the Negro said. "I aint done nothing. 'Fore God, Mr. John." Someone produced handcuffs. They worked busily about the Negro as though he were a post, quiet, intent, getting in one another's way. He sub-[177]mitted to the handcuffs, looking swiftly and constantly from dim face to dim face. "Who's here, captains?" he said, leaning to peer into the faces until they could feel his breath and smell his sweaty reek. He spoke a name or two. "What you all say I done, Mr. John?"

McLendon jerked the car door open. "Get in!" he said.

The Negro did not move. "What you all going to do with me, Mr.

John? I aint done nothing. White folks, captains, I aint done nothing: I swear 'fore God." He called another name.

"Get in!" McLendon said. He struck the Negro. The others expelled their breath in a dry hissing and struck him with random blows and he whirled and cursed them, and swept his manacled hands across their faces and slashed the barber upon the mouth, and the barber struck him also. "Get him in there," McLendon said. They pushed at him. He ceased struggling and got in and sat quietly as the others took their places. He sat between the barber and the soldier, drawing his limbs in so as not to touch them, his eyes going swiftly and constantly from face to face. Butch clung to the running board. The car moved on. The barber nursed his mouth with his handkerchief.

"What's the matter, Hawk?" the soldier said.

"Nothing," the barber said. They regained the highroad and turned away from town. The second car dropped back out of the dust. They went on, gaining speed; the final fringe of houses dropped behind.

"Goddamn, he stinks!" the soldier said.

"We'll fix that," the drummer in front beside McLendon said. On the running board Butch cursed into the hot rush of air. The barber leaned suddenly forward and touched McLendon's arm.

"Let me out, John," he said.

"Jump out, niggerlover," McLendon said without turning [178] his head. He drove swiftly. Behind them the sourceless lights of the second car glared in the dust. Presently McLendon turned into a narrow road. It was rutted with disuse. It led back to an abandoned brick kiln—a series of reddish mounds and weed- and vine-choked vats without bottom. It had been used for pasture once, until one day the owner missed one of his mules. Although he prodded carefully in the vats with a long pole, he could not even find the bottom of them.

"John," the barber said.

"Jump out, then," McLendon said, hurling the car along the ruts. Beside the barber the Negro spoke:

"Mr. Henry."

The barber sat forward. The narrow tunnel of the road rushed up and past. Their motion was like an extinct furnace blast: cooler, but utterly dead. The car bounded from rut to rut.

"Mr. Henry," the Negro said.

The barber began to tug furiously at the door. "Look out, there!" the soldier said, but the barber had already kicked the door open and swung onto the running board. The soldier leaned across the Negro and grasped at him, but he had already jumped. The car went on without checking speed.

The impetus hurled him crashing through dust-sheathed weeds, into the ditch. Dust puffed about him, and in a thin, vicious crackling of sapless stems he lay choking and retching until the second car passed and died away. Then he rose and limped on until he reached the highroad and turned toward town, brushing at his clothes with his hands. The moon was higher, riding high and clear of the dust at last, and after a while the town began to glare beneath the dust. He went on, limping. Presently he heard cars and the glow of them grew in the dust behind him and he left the road and crouched again in the weeds until they passed. Mc-[179]Lendon's car came last now. There were four people in it and Butch was not on the running board.

They went on; the dust swallowed them; the glare and the sound died away. The dust of them hung for a while, but soon the eternal dust absorbed it again. The barber climbed back onto the road and limped on toward town.

IV

As she dressed for supper on that Saturday evening, her own flesh felt like fever. Her hands trembled among the hooks and eyes, and her eyes had a feverish look, and her hair swirled crisp and crackling under the comb. While she was still dressing the friends called for her and sat while she donned her sheerest underthings and stockings and a new voile dress. "Do you feel strong enough to go out?" they said, their eyes bright too, with a dark glitter. "When you have had time to get over the shock, you must tell us what happened. What he said and did; everything."

In the leafed darkness, as they walked toward the square, she began to breathe deeply, something like a swimmer preparing to dive, until she ceased trembling, the four of them walking slowly because of the terrible heat and out of solicitude for her. But as they neared the square she began to tremble again, walking with her head up, her hands clenched at her sides, their voices about her murmurous, also with that feverish, glittering quality of their eyes.

They entered the square, she in the center of the group, fragile in her fresh dress. She was trembling worse. She walked slower and slower, as children eat ice cream, her head up and her eyes bright in the haggard banner of her face, passing the hotel and the coatless drummers in chairs along the curb looking around at her: "That's the one: see? The one in pink in the middle." "Is that her? What did they [180] do with the nigger? Did they—?" "Sure. He's all right." "All right, is he?" "Sure. He went on a little trip." Then the drug store, where even the young men lounging in the doorway tipped their hats and followed with their eyes the motion of her hips and legs when she passed.

They went on, passing the lifted hats of the gentlemen, the suddenly ceased voices, deferent, protective. "Do you see?" the friends said. Their voices sounded like long, hovering sighs of hissing exultation. "There's not a Negro on the square. Not one."

They reached the picture show. It was like a miniature fairyland with its lighted lobby and colored lithographs of life caught in its terrible and beautiful mutations. Her lips began to tingle. In the dark, when the picture began, it would be all right; she could hold back the laughing so it would not waste away so fast and so soon. So she hurried on before the turning faces, the undertones of low astonishment, and they took their accustomed places where she could see the aisle against the silver glare and the young men and girls coming in two and two against it.

The lights flicked away; the screen glowed silver, and soon life began to unfold, beautiful and passionate and sad, while still the young men and girls entered, scented and sibilant in the half dark, their paired backs in silhouette delicate and sleek, their slim, quick bodies awkward, divinely young, while beyond them the silver dream accumulated, inevitably on and on. She began to laugh. In trying to suppress it, it made more noise than ever; heads began to turn. Still laughing, her friends raised her and led her out, and she stood at the curb, laughing on a high, sustained note, until the taxi came up and they helped her in.

They removed the pink voile and the sheer underthings and the stockings, and put her to bed, and cracked ice for her temples, and sent for the doctor. He was hard to locate, [181] so they ministered to her with hushed ejaculations, renewing the ice and fanning her. While the ice was fresh and cold she stopped laughing and lay still for a time, moaning only a little. But soon the laughing welled again and her voice rose screaming.

"Shhhhhhhhhhhh! Shhhhhhhhhhhhhhhh!" they said, freshening the ice-pack, smoothing her hair, examining it for gray; "poor girl!" Then to one another: "Do you suppose anything really happened?" their eyes darkly aglitter, secret and passionate. "Shhhhhhhhhh! Poor girl! Poor Minnie!"

V

It was midnight when McLendon drove up to his neat new house. It was trim and fresh as a birdcage and almost as small, with its clean, green-and-white paint. He locked the car and mounted the porch and entered. His wife rose from a chair beside the reading lamp. McLendon stopped in the floor and stared at her until she looked down.

"Look at that clock," he said, lifting his arm, pointing. She stood before him, her face lowered, a magazine in her hands. Her face was pale, strained, and weary-looking. "Haven't I told you about sitting up like this, waiting to see when I come in?"

"John," she said. She laid the magazine down. Poised on the balls of his feet, he glared at her with his hot eyes, his sweating face.

"Didn't I tell you?" He went toward her. She looked up then. He caught her shoulder. She stood passive, looking at him.

"Don't, John. I couldn't sleep . . . The heat; something. Please, John. You're hurting me."

"Didn't I tell you?" He released her and half struck, half flung her across the chair, and she lay there and watched him quietly as he left the room. [182]

He went on through the house, ripping off his shirt, and on the dark, screened porch at the rear he stood and mopped his head and shoulders with the shirt and flung it away. He took the pistol from his hip and laid it on the table beside the bed, and sat on the bed and removed his shoes, and rose and slipped his trousers off. He was sweating again already, and he stopped and hunted furiously for the shirt. At last he found it and wiped his body again, and, with his body pressed against the dusty screen, he stood panting. There was no movement, no sound, not even an insect. The dark world seemed to lie stricken beneath the cold moon and the lidless stars. [183]

EDGAR LEE MASTERS
1868–1950

Voices
from the Grave

from

SPOON RIVER
ANTHOLOGY

"All, all are sleeping on the hill"—these are the residents of Spoon River. They are sleeping but they are not silent, for each has his story to tell from the grave. In *Spoon River Anthology* (1915) Edgar Lee Masters uses the form of the epitaph to permit the residents of the mythical small town of Spoon River to tell of the time of their living. There are 244 poetic monologues, although numerous ones combine to present various views of single incidents (19 stories are developed by the interrelated participants). Masters shows considerable skill in incorporating living speech into these monologues. While the rather blunt free verse he uses is considered a weakness by some critics, others feel that the form heightens the meaning that emerges from the lines. The town is populated primarily by tragic figures who are unable to cope with the mysteries and paradoxes that fate offers them. They are generally hypocrites, reprobates, and outcasts. The pioneer spirit of Lucinda Matlock, one of the few strong characters in Spoon River, reveals the essential problem faced by the rest. She tells them: "Life is too strong for you—it takes life to love life."

Masters speaks through the words of the dead to voice his own revelations of life's uncertain failures and rewards, and his generally cynical view has been cited by critics as an attack on the values of the small Midwestern town. Some of the names in the *Anthology* were taken from a cemetery in the area near Lewistown and Petersburg, Illinois, where he spent most of his boyhood. Other names he took from state papers of Illinois, and still others were products of his own imagination. The town he creates, however, is a combination of all his boyhood memories.

Masters studied law and established a successful practice in Chicago, but his enthusiasm for J. W. Mackail's *Select Epigrams from the Greek Anthology* (1890) stimulated his own literary talents. His poems appeared first in *Reedy's Mirror,* often under the pseudonym of Webster Ford. When the *Anthology* appeared in print in 1915, it caused an immediate sensation, since some of its characters were identified as real people who had been or were still influential in Masters' home region, and the scandalous behavior it described had great appeal. The first edition was more successful financially than any volume of American poetry previously published.

The epitaphs reprinted here include those of Chase Henry, the town drunkard; Deacon Taylor, a church member who drank in secret; Griffy the Cooper, who identifies the confinement of the small town; Mrs. Williams, the cause of much gossip; Yee Bow, the object of prejudice; Eugene Carman, who despairs of small-town conformity; Seth Compton, the last vestige of culture; and Lucinda Matlock, who exemplifies the spirit of the pioneer woman. The epitaphs were the basis of an opera that was performed in Italy in 1947, and, more recently, a Broadway production. Masters' other writings, including volumes of poetry, biography, fiction, and autobiography, were not received by readers and critics with much enthusiasm, so he is known today chiefly for one work.

from

SPOON RIVER ANTHOLOGY

CHASE HENRY

In life I was the town drunkard;
When I died the priest denied me burial
In holy ground.
The which redounded to my good fortune.
For the Protestants bought this lot,
And buried my body here,
Close to the grave of the banker Nicholas,
And of his wife Priscilla.
Take note, ye prudent and pious souls,
Of the cross-currents in life
Which bring honor to the dead, who lived in shame. [10]

Edgar Lee Masters, *Spoon River Anthology* (New York: The Macmillan Company. 1915). Reprinted by permission of Ellen C. Masters. Copyright 1914, 1942 by The Macmillan Company.

DEACON TAYLOR

I belonged to the church,
And to the party of prohibition;
And the villagers thought I died of eating watermelon.
In truth I had cirrhosis of the liver,
For every noon for thirty years,
I slipped behind the prescription partition
In Trainor's drug store
And poured a generous drink
From the bottle marked
"Spiritus frumenti." [50]

GRIFFY THE COOPER

The cooper should know about tubs.
But I learned about life as well,
And you who loiter around these graves
Think you know life.
You think your eye sweeps about a wide horizon, perhaps,
In truth you are only looking around the interior of your tub.
You cannot lift yourself to its rim
And see the outer world of things,
And at the same time see yourself.
You are submerged in the tub of yourself—
Taboos and rules and appearances,
Are the staves of your tub.
Break them and dispel the witchcraft
Of thinking your tub is life!
And that you know life! [59]

MRS. WILLIAMS

I was the milliner
Talked about, lied about,
Mother of Dora,
Whose strange disappearance

Was charged to her rearing.
My eye quick to beauty
Saw much beside ribbons
And buckles and feathers
And leghorns and felts,
To set off sweet faces,
And dark hair and gold.
One thing I will tell you
And one I will ask:
The stealers of husbands
Wear powder and trinkets,
And fashionable hats.
Wives, wear them yourselves.
Hats may make divorces—
They also prevent them.
Well now, let me ask you:
If all the children, born here in Spoon River
Had been reared by the County, somewhere on a farm; [62]
And the fathers and mothers had been given their freedom
To live and enjoy, change mates if they wished,
Do you think that Spoon River
Had been any the worse? [63]

YEE BOW

They got me into the Sunday-school
In Spoon River
And tried to get me to drop Confucius for Jesus.
I could have been no worse off
If I had tried to get them to drop Jesus for Confucius.
For, without any warning, as if it were a prank,
And sneaking up behind me, Harry Wiley,
The minister's son, caved my ribs into my lungs,
With a blow of his fist.
Now I shall never sleep with my ancestors in Pekin,
And no children shall worship at my grave. [88]

EUGENE CARMAN

Rhodes' slave! Selling shoes and gingham,
Flour and bacon, overalls, clothing, all day long
For fourteen hours a day for three hundred and thirteen days
For more than twenty years.
Saying "Yes'm" and "Yes, sir" and "Thank you"
A thousand times a day, and all for fifty dollars a month.
Living in this stinking room in the rattle-trap "Commercial."
And compelled to go to Sunday School, and to listen
To the Rev. Abner Peet one hundred and four times a year
For more than an hour at a time,
Because Thomas Rhodes ran the church
As well as the store and the bank.
So while I was tying my neck-tie that morning
I suddenly saw myself in the glass:
My hair all gray, my face like a sodden pie.
So I cursed and cursed: You damned old thing!
You cowardly dog! You rotten pauper! [116]
You Rhodes slave! Till Roger Baughman
Thought I was having a fight with some one,
And looked through the transom just in time
To see me fall on the floor in a heap
From a broken vein in my head. [117]

SETH COMPTON

When I died, the circulating library
Which I built up for Spoon River,
And managed for the good of inquiring minds,
Was sold at auction on the public square,
As if to destroy the last vestige
Of my memory and influence.
For those of you who could not see the virtue
Of knowing Volney's "Ruins" as well as Butler's "Analogy"
And "Faust" as well as "Evangeline,"
Were really the power in the village,
And often you asked me,
"What is the use of knowing the evil in the world?"
I am out of your way now, Spoon River,

Choose your own good and call it good.
For I could never make you see
That no one knows what is good
Who knows not what is evil;
And no one knows what is true
Who knows not what is false. [156]

LUCINDA MATLOCK

I went to the dances at Chandlerville,
And played snap-out at Winchester.
One time we changed partners,
Driving home in the moonlight of middle June,
And then I found Davis.
We were married and lived together for seventy years.
Enjoying, working, raising the twelve children,
Eight of whom we lost
Ere I had reached the age of sixty.
I spun, I wove, I kept the house, I nursed the sick,
I made the garden, and for holiday
Rambled over the fields where sang the larks,
And by Spoon River gathering many a shell,
And many a flower and medicinal weed—
Shouting to the wooded hills, singing to the green valleys.
At ninety-six I had lived enough, that is all,
And I passed to a sweet repose.
What is this I hear of sorrow and weariness,
Anger, discontent and drooping hopes?
Degenerate sons and daughters,
Life is too strong for you—
It takes life to love Life."[229]

SHERWOOD ANDERSON
1876–1941

Repression and Frustration

from

WINESBURG, OHIO

Sherwood Anderson's *Winesburg, Ohio* (1919) struck directly at the myth of the American small town. Its 21 short stories—or sketches—present a typical Midwestern town of the 1880s, but Anderson saw the town as narrow and ingrown, its inhabitants frustrated and repressed by the rigid limitations of their small-town lives. Anderson, who spent his own formative years in the small town of Clyde, Ohio, examines the buried lives, the secret selves of the little people of Winesburg, tracing their discontent, their lack of communication, their anguish, their fears. Yet it seems clear that Anderson has compassion for the frustrated and lonely of Winesburg; there is little in his stories of the cynicism of Masters's *Spoon River Anthology*.

Winesburg, Ohio was a radical move in literature. Denounced at publication as immoral, with many critics calling it nasty and dirty, the series of loosely connected stories became an important influence on American realistic writing. Anderson's frank appraisal of cramped spirits and social misfits, as well as his use of sex in normal situations, was an impressive example of America's revolt from the village. The new frankness was presented in a style that depended upon simple language, a straightforward approach, and a realistic-naturalistic treatment.

Anderson was most successful as a short-story writer, and *Winesburg, Ohio* is unquestionably his most significant work. Others of his well-known books are *Windy McPherson's Son* (1916), *Poor White* (1920), *The Triumph of the Egg* (1921), *Many Marriages* (1923), *Dark Laughter* (1925), *Beyond Desire* (1932), and *Kit Brandon* (1936).

The three stories from *Winesburg, Ohio* that follow are typical of Anderson's concern for the undersurface of life. "Hands" tells the story of a schoolteacher suspected of homosexuality. In Winesburg, Wing Biddlebaum is an eccentric, an object of gossip and misunderstanding. Anderson seems to stress that the schoolteacher's love for young boys was not overtly sexual. The loneliness of Alice Hindman is the subject of "Adventure." Seeking another human being to embrace, Alice in an act of passion removes her clothes and runs at night into the street naked. But the man she meets is deaf and is unable to respond. In "The Strength of God" the Reverend Curtis Hartman is a devout man who is led away from thoughts of God by temptations of the flesh and who must struggle to keep from being a peeping Tom.

from WINESBURG, OHIO

"HANDS"

Upon the half decayed veranda of a small frame house that stood near the edge of a ravine near the town of Winesburg, Ohio, a fat little old man walked nervously up and down. Across a long field that had been seeded for clover but that had produced only a dense crop of yellow mustard weeds, he could see the public highway along which went a wagon filled with berry pickers returning from the fields. The berry pickers, youths and maidens, laughed and shouted boisterously. A boy clad in a blue shirt leaped from the wagon and attempted to drag after him one of the maidens, who screamed and protested shrilly. The feet of the boy in the road kicked up a cloud of dust that floated across the face of the departing sun. Over the long field came a thin girlish voice. "Oh, you Wing Biddlebaum, comb your hair, it's falling into your eyes," commanded the voice to the man, who was [7] bald and whose nervous little hands fiddled about the bare white forehead as though arranging a mass of tangled locks.

Wing Biddlebaum, forever frightened and beset by a ghostly band of doubts, did not think of himself as in any way a part of the life of the town where he had lived for twenty years. Among all the people of Winesburg but one had come close to him. With George Willard, son of Tom

Willard, the proprietor of the New Willard House, he had formed something like a friendship. George Willard was the reporter on the *Winesburg Eagle* and sometimes in the evenings he walked out along the highway to Wing Biddlebaum's house. Now as the old man walked up and down on the veranda, his hands moving nervously about, he was hoping that George Willard would come and spend the evening with him. After the wagon containing the berry pickers had passed, he went across the field through the tall mustard weeds and climbing a rail fence peered anxiously along the road to the town. For a moment he stood thus, rubbing his hands together and looking up and down the road, and then, fear overcoming him, ran back to walk again upon the porch of his own house.

In the presence of George Willard, Wing Biddlebaum, who for twenty years had been the town mystery, lost something of his timidity, and [8] his shadowy personality, submerged in a sea of doubts, came forth to look at the world. With the young reporter at his side, he ventured in the light of day into Main Street or strode up and down on the rickety front porch of his own house, talking excitedly. The voice that had been low and trembling became shrill and loud. The bent figure straightened. With a kind of wiggle, like a fish returned to the brook by the fisherman, Biddlebaum the silent began to talk, striving to put into words the ideas that had been accumulated by his mind during long years of silence.

Wing Biddlebaum talked much with his hands. The slender expressive fingers, forever active, forever striving to conceal themselves in his pockets or behind his back, came forth and became the piston rods of his machinery of expression.

The story of Wing Biddlebaum is a story of hands. Their restless activity, like unto the beating of the wings of an imprisoned bird, had given him his name. Some obscure poet of the town had thought of it. The hands alarmed their owner. He wanted to keep them hidden away and looked with amazement at the quiet inexpressive hands of other men who worked beside him in the fields, or passed, driving sleepy teams on country roads.

When he talked to George Willard, Wing Biddlebaum closed his fists and beat with them [9] upon a table or on the walls of his house. The action made him more comfortable. If the desire to talk came to him when the two were walking in the fields, he sought out a stump or the top board of a fence and with his hands pounding busily talked with renewed ease.

The story of Wing Biddlebaum's hands is worth a book in itself. Sympathetically set forth it would tap many strange, beautiful qualities in obscure men. It is a job for a poet. In Winesburg the hands had attracted attention merely because of their activity. With them Wing Biddlebaum had picked as high as a hundred and forty quarts of strawberries in a day. They became his distinguishing feature, the source of his fame. Also they made more grotesque an already grotesque and elusive individuality. Winesburg was proud of the hands of Wing Biddlebaum in the same spirit in which it was proud of Banker White's new stone house and Wesley Moyer's bay stallion, Tony Tip, that had won the two-fifteen trot at the fall races in Cleveland.

As for George Willard, he had many times wanted to ask about the hands. At times an almost overwhelming curiosity had taken hold of him. He felt that there must be a reason for their strange activity and their inclination to keep hidden away and only a growing respect for [10] Wing Biddlebaum kept him from blurting out the questions that were often in his mind.

Once he had been on the point of asking. The two were walking in the fields on a summer afternoon and had stopped to sit upon a grassy bank. All afternoon Wing Biddlebaum had talked as one inspired. By a fence he had stopped and beating like a giant woodpecker upon the top board had shouted at George Willard, condemning his tendency to be too much influenced by the people about him. "You are destroying yourself," he cried. "You have the inclination to be alone and to dream and you are afraid of dreams. You want to be like others in town here. You hear them talk and you try to imitate them."

On the grassy bank Wing Biddlebaum had tried again to drive his point home. His voice became soft and reminiscent, and with a sigh of contentment he launched into a long rambling talk, speaking as one lost in a dream.

Out of the dream Wing Biddlebaum made a picture for George Willard. In the picture men lived again in a kind of pastoral golden age. Across a green open country came clean-limbed young men, some afoot, some mounted upon horses. In crowds the young men came to gather about the feet of an old man who sat beneath a tree in a tiny garden and who talked to them.

Wing Biddlebaum became wholly inspired. [11] For once he forgot the hands. Slowly they stole forth and lay upon George Willard's shoulders. Something new and bold came into the voice that talked. "You must try to forget all you have learned," said the old man. "You must begin to dream. From this time on you must shut your ears to the roaring of the voices."

Pausing in his speech, Wing Biddlebaum looked long and earnestly at George Willard. His eyes glowed. Again he raised the hands to caress the boy and then a look of horror swept over his face.

With a convulsive movement of his body, Wing Biddlebaum sprang to his feet and thrust his hands deep into his trousers pockets. Tears came to his eyes. "I must be getting along home. I can talk no more with you," he said nervously.

Without looking back, the old man had hurried down the hillside and across a meadow, leaving George Willard perplexed and frightened upon the grassy slope. With a shiver of dread the boy arose and went along the road toward town. "I'll not ask him about his hands," he thought, touched by the memory of the terror he had seen in the man's eyes. "There's something wrong, but I don't want to know what it is. His hands have something to do with his fear of me and of everyone."

And George Willard was right. Let us look [12] briefly into the story of his hands. Perhaps our talking of them will arouse the poet who will tell the hidden wonder story of the influence for which the hands were but fluttering pennants of promise.

In his youth Wing Biddlebaum had been a school teacher in a town in Pennsylvania. He was not then known as Wing Biddlebaum, but went by the less euphonic name of Adolph Myers. As Adolph Myers he was much loved by the boys of his school.

Adolph Myers was meant by nature to be a teacher of youth. He was one of those rare, little-understood men who rule by a power so gentle that it passes as a lovable weakness. In their feeling for the boys under their charge such men are not unlike the finer sort of women in their love of men.

And yet that is but crudely stated. It needs the poet there. With the boys of his school, Adolph Myers had walked in the evening or had sat talking until dusk upon the schoolhouse steps lost in a kind of dream. Here and there went his hands, caressing the shoulders of the boys, playing about the tousled heads. As he talked his voice became soft and musical. There was a caress in that also. In a way the voice and the hands, the stroking of the shoulders and the touching of the hair were a part of the schoolmaster's efforts to carry a dream into the young [13] minds. By the caress that was in his fingers he expressed himself. He was one of those men in whom the force that creates life is diffused, not centralized. Under the caress of his hands doubt and disbelief went out of the minds of the boys and they began also to dream.

And then the tragedy. A half-witted boy of the school became enamored of the young master. In his bed at night he imagined unspeakable things and in the morning went forth to tell his dreams as facts. Strange, hideous accusations fell from his loose-hung lips. Through the Pennsylvania town went a shiver. Hidden, shadowy doubts that had been in men's minds concerning Adolph Myers were galvanized into beliefs.

The tragedy did not linger. Trembling lads were jerked out of bed and questioned. "He put his arms about me," said one. "His fingers were always playing in my hair," said another.

One afternoon a man of the town, Henry Bradford, who kept a saloon, came to the schoolhouse door. Calling Adolph Myers into the school yard he began to beat him with his fists. As his hard knuckles beat down into the frightened face of the schoolmaster, his wrath became more and more terrible. Screaming with dismay, the children ran here and there like disturbed insects. "I'll teach you to put your hands on my boy, you beast," roared the saloon keeper, who, tired of [14] beating the master, had begun to kick him about the yard.

Adolph Myers was driven from the Pennsylvania town in the night. With lanterns in their hands a dozen men came to the door of the house where he lived alone and commanded that he dress and come forth. It was raining and one of the men had a rope in his hands. They had intended to hang the schoolmaster, but something in his figure, so small, white, and pitiful, touched their hearts and they let him escape. As he ran away into the darkness they repented of their weakness and ran after him, swearing and throwing sticks and great balls of soft mud at the figure that screamed and ran faster and faster into the darkness.

For twenty years Adolph Myers had lived alone in Winesburg. He was but forty but looked sixty-five. The name of Biddlebaum he got from a box of goods seen at a freight station as he hurried through an eastern Ohio town. He had an aunt in Winesburg, a black-toothed old woman who raised chickens, and with her he lived until she died. He had been ill for a year after the experience in Pennsylvania, and after his recovery worked as a day laborer in the fields, going timidly about and striving to conceal his hands. Although he did not understand what had happened he felt that the hands must be to blame. [15] Again and again the fathers of the boys had talked of the hands. "Keep your hands to yourself," the saloon keeper had roared, dancing with fury in the schoolhouse yard.

Upon the veranda of his house by the ravine, Wing Biddlebaum continued to walk up and down until the sun had disappeared and the road beyond the field was lost in the grey shadows. Going into his house he cut slices of bread and spread honey upon them. When the rumble of the evening train that took away the express cars loaded with the day's harvest of berries had passed and restored the silence of the summer night, he went again to walk upon the veranda. In the darkness he could not see the hands and they became quiet. Although he still hungered for the presence of the boy, who was the medium through which he expressed his love of man, the hunger became again a part of his loneliness and his waiting. Lighting a lamp, Wing Biddlebaum washed the few dishes soiled by his simple meal and, setting up a folding cot by the screen door that led to the porch, prepared to undress for the night. A few stray white bread crumbs lay on the cleanly washed floor by the table; putting the lamp upon a low stool he began to pick up the crumbs, carrying them to his mouth one by one with unbelievable rapidity. In the dense blotch of light beneath the table, the kneeling figure [16] looked like a priest engaged in some service of his church. The nervous expressive fingers, flashing in and out of the light, might well have been mistaken for the fingers of the devotee going swiftly through decade after decade of his rosary. [17]

"ADVENTURE"

Alice Hindman, a woman of twenty-seven when George Willard was a mere boy, had lived in Winesburg all her life. She clerked in Winney's Dry Goods Store and lived with her mother, who had married a second husband.

Alice's step-father was a carriage painter, and given to drink. His story is an odd one. It will be worth telling some day.

At twenty-seven Alice was tall and somewhat slight. Her head was large and overshadowed her body. Her shoulders were a little stooped and her hair and eyes brown. She was very quiet but beneath a placid exterior a continual ferment went on.

When she was a girl of sixteen and before she began to work in the store, Alice had an affair with a young man. The young man, named Ned Currie, was older than Alice. He, like George Willard, was employed on the *Winesburg Eagle* and for a long time he went to see Alice almost every evening. Together the two walked under the trees through the streets of the town and [123] talked of what they would do with their lives. Alice was then a very pretty girl and Ned Currie took her into his arms and kissed her. He became excited and said things he did not intend to say and Alice, betrayed by her desire to have something beautiful come into her rather narrow life, also grew excited. She also talked. The outer crust of her life, all of her natural diffidence and reserve, was torn away and she gave herself over to the emotions of love. When, late in the fall of her sixteenth year, Ned Currie went away to Cleveland where he hoped to get a place on a city newspaper and rise in the world, she wanted to go with him. With a trembling voice she told him what was in her mind. "I will work and you can work," she said. "I do not want to harness you to a needless expense that will prevent your making progress. Don't marry me now. We will get along without that and we can be together. Even though we live in the same house no one will say anything. In the city we will be unknown and people will pay no attention to us."

Ned Currie was puzzled by the determination and abandon of his sweetheart and was also deeply touched. He had wanted the girl to become his mistress but changed his mind. He wanted to protect and care for her. "You don't know what you're talking about," he said sharply; "you may be sure I'll let you do no such thing. As soon as I [124] get a good job I'll come back. For the present you'll have to stay here. It's the only thing we can do."

On the evening before he left Winesburg to take up his new life in the city, Ned Currie went to call on Alice. They walked about through the streets for an hour and then got a rig from Wesley Moyer's livery and went for a drive in the country. The moon came up and they found themselves unable to talk. In his sadness the young man forgot the resolutions he had made regarding his conduct with the girl.

They got out of the buggy at a place where a long meadow ran down to the bank of Wine Creek and there in the dim light became lovers. When at midnight they returned to town they were both glad. It did not seem to them that anything that could happen in the future could blot out the wonder and beauty of the thing that had happened. "Now we will have to stick to each other, whatever happens we will have to do that," Ned Currie said as he left the girl at her father's door.

The young newspaperman did not succeed in getting a place on a Cleveland paper and went west to Chicago. For a time he was lonely and wrote to Alice almost every day. Then he was caught up by the life of the city; he began to make friends and found new interests in life. In Chicago he boarded at a house where there were sev-[125]eral women. One of them attracted his attention and he forgot Alice in Winesburg. At the end of a year he had stopped writing letters, and only once in a long time, when he was lonely or when he went into one of the city parks and saw the moon shining on the grass as it had shone that night on the meadow by Wine Creek, did he think of her at all.

In Winesburg the girl who had been loved grew to be a woman. When she was twenty-two years old her father, who owned a harness repair shop, died suddenly. The harness maker was an old soldier, and after a few months his wife received a widow's pension. She used the first money she got to buy a loom and became a weaver of carpets, and Alice got a place in Winney's store. For a number of years nothing could have induced her to believe that Ned Currie would not in the end return to her.

She was glad to be employed because the daily round of toil in the store made the time of waiting seem less long and uninteresting. She began to save money, thinking that when she had saved two or three hundred dollars she would follow her lover to the city and try if her presence would not win back his affections.

Alice did not blame Ned Currie for what happened in the moonlight in the field, but felt that she could never marry another man. To her [126] the thought of giving to another what she felt could belong only to Ned seemed monstrous. When other young men tried to attract her attention she would have nothing to do with them. "I am his wife and shall remain his wife whether he comes back or not," she whispered to herself, and for all of her willingness to support herself could not have understood the growing modern idea of a woman's owning herself and giving and taking for her own ends in life.

Alice worked in the dry goods store from eight in the morning until six at night and on three evenings a week went back to the store to stay from seven until nine. As time passed and she became more and more lonely she began to practice the devices common to lonely people. When at night she went upstairs into her own room she knelt on the floor to pray and in her prayers whispered things she wanted to say to her lover. She became attached to inanimate objects, and because it was her own, could not bear to have anyone touch the furniture of her room. The trick of saving money, begun for a purpose, was carried on after the scheme of going to the city to find Ned Currie had been given up. It became a fixed habit, and when she needed new clothes she did not get them. Sometimes on rainy afternoons in the store she got out her bank book and, letting it lie open before her, spent hours dreaming impos-[127]sible dreams of saving money enough so that the interest would support both herself and her future husband.

"Ned always liked to travel about," she thought. "I'll give him the chance. Some day when we are married and I can save both his money and my own, we will be rich. Then we can travel together all over the world."

In the dry goods store weeks ran into months and months into years as Alice waited and dreamed of her lover's return. Her employer, a grey old man with false teeth and a thin grey mustache that drooped down over his mouth, was not given to conversation, and sometimes, on rainy days in the winter when a storm raged in Main Street, long hours passed when no customers came in. Alice arranged and rearranged the stock. She stood near the front window where she could look down the deserted street and thought of the evenings when she had walked with Ned Currie and of what he had said. "We will have to stick to each other now." The words echoed and re-echoed through the mind of the maturing woman. Tears came into her eyes. Sometimes when her employer had gone out and she was alone in the store she put her head on the counter and wept. "Oh, Ned, I am waiting," she whispered over and over, and all the time the [128] creeping fear that he would never come back grew stronger within her.

In the spring when the rains have passed and before the long hot days of summer have come, the country about Winesburg is delightful. The town lies in the midst of open fields, but beyond the fields are pleasant patches of woodlands. In the wooded places are many little cloistered nooks, quiet places where lovers go to sit on Sunday afternoons. Through the trees they look out across the fields and see farmers at work about the barns or people driving up and down on the roads. In the town bells ring and occasionally a train passes, looking like a toy thing in the distance.

For several years after Ned Currie went away Alice did not go into the wood with other young people on Sunday, but one day after he had been gone for two or three years and when her loneliness seemed unbearable, she put on her best dress and set out. Finding a little sheltered place from which she could see the town and a long stretch of the fields, she sat down. Fear of age and ineffectuality took possession of her. She could not sit still, and arose. As she stood looking out over the land something, perhaps the thought of never ceasing life as it expresses itself in the flow of the seasons, fixed her mind on the passing years. With a shiver of dread, she realized that for her [129] the beauty and freshness of youth had passed. For the first time she felt that she had been cheated. She did not blame Ned Currie and did not know what to blame. Sadness swept over her. Dropping to her knees, she tried to pray, but instead of prayers words of protest came to her lips. "It is not going to come to me. I will never find happiness. Why do I tell myself lies?" she cried, and an odd sense of relief came with this, her bold attempt to face the fear that had become a part of her everyday life.

In the year when Alice Hindman became twenty-five two things happened to disturb the dull uneventfulness of her days. Her mother married Bush Milton, the carriage painter of Winesburg, and she herself became a member of the Winesburg Methodist Church. Alice joined the church because she had become frightened by the loneliness of her position in life. Her mother's second marriage had emphasized her isolation. "I am becoming old and queer. If Ned comes he will not want me. In the city where he is living men are perpetually young. There is so much going on that they do not have time to grow old," she told herself with a grim little smile, and went resolutely about the business of becoming acquainted with people. Every Thursday evening when the store had closed she went to a prayer meeting in the basement of the church and on Sunday eve-[130]ning attended a meeting of an organization called The Epworth League.

When Will Hurley, a middle-aged man who clerked in a drug store and who also belonged to the church, offered to walk home with her she did not protest. "Of course I will not let him make a practice of being with me, but if he comes to see me once in a long time there can be no harm in that," she told herself, still determined in her loyalty to Ned Currie.

Without realizing what was happening, Alice was trying feebly at first, but with growing determination, to get a new hold upon life. Beside the drug clerk she walked in silence, but sometimes in the darkness as they went stolidly along she put out her hand and touched softly the folds of his coat. When he left her at the gate before her mother's house she did not go indoors, but stood for a moment by the door. She wanted to call to the drug clerk, to ask him to sit with her in the darkness on the porch before the house, but was afraid he would not understand. "It is not him that I want," she told herself; "I want to avoid being so much alone. If I am not careful I will grow unaccustomed to being with people."

During the early fall of her twenty-seventh year a passionate restlessness took possession of Alice. She could not bear to be in the company of the [131] drug clerk, and when, in the evening, he came to walk with her she sent him away. Her mind became intensely active and when, weary from the long hours of standing behind the counter in the store, she went home and crawled into bed, she could not sleep. With staring eyes she looked into the darkness. Her imagination, like a child awakened from long sleep, played about the room. Deep within her there was something that could not be cheated by phantasies and that demanded some definite answer from life.

Alice took a pillow into her arms and held it tightly against her breasts.

Getting out of bed, she arranged a blanket so that in the darkness it looked like a form lying between the sheets and, kneeling beside the bed, she caressed it, whispering words over and over, like a refrain. "Why doesn't something happen? Why am I left here alone?" she muttered. Although she sometimes thought of Ned Currie, she no longer depended on him. Her desire had grown vague. She did not want Ned Currie or any other man. She wanted to be loved, to have something answer the call that was growing louder and louder within her.

And then one night when it rained Alice had an adventure. It frightened and confused her. She had come home from the store at nine and found the house empty. Bush Milton had gone off to [132] town and her mother to the house of a neighbor. Alice went upstairs to her room and undressed in the darkness. For a moment she stood by the window hearing the rain beat against the glass and then a strange desire took possession of her. Without stopping to think of what she intended to do, she ran downstairs through the dark house and out into the rain. As she stood on the little grass plot before the house and felt the cold rain on her body a mad desire to run naked through the streets took possession of her.

She thought that the rain would have some creative and wonderful effect on her body. Not for years had she felt so full of youth and courage. She wanted to leap and run, to cry out, to find some other lonely human and embrace him. On the brick sidewalk before the house a man stumbled homeward. Alice started to run. A wild, desperate mood took possession of her. "What do I care who it is. He is alone, and I will go to him," she thought; and then without stopping to consider the possible result of her madness, called softly. "Wait!" she cried. "Don't go away. Whoever you are, you must wait."

The man on the sidewalk stopped and stood listening. He was an old man and somewhat deaf. Putting his hand to his mouth, he shouted. "What? What say?" he called.

Alice dropped to the ground and lay trembling. [133] She was so frightened at the thought of what she had done that when the man had gone on his way she did not dare get to her feet, but crawled on hands and knees through the grass to the house. When she got to her own room she bolted the door and drew her dressing table across the doorway. Her body shook as with a chill and her hands trembled so that she had difficulty getting into her nightdress. When she got into bed she buried her face in the pillow and wept brokenheartedly. "What is the matter with me? I will do something dreadful if I am not careful," she thought, and turning her face to the wall, began trying to force herself to face bravely the fact that many people must live and die alone, even in Winesburg. [134]

"THE STRENGTH OF GOD"

The Reverend Curtis Hartman was pastor of the Presbyterian Church of Winesburg, and had been in that position ten years. He was forty years old, and by his nature very silent and reticent. To preach, standing in the pulpit before the people, was always a hardship for him and from Wednesday morning until Saturday evening he thought of nothing but the two sermons that must be preached on Sunday. Early on Sunday morning he went into a little room called a study in the bell tower of the church and prayed. In his prayers there was one note that always predominated. "Give me strength and courage for Thy work, O Lord!" he pleaded, kneeling on the bare floor and bowing his head in the presence of the task that lay before him.

The Reverend Hartman was a tall man with a brown beard. His wife, a stout, nervous woman, was the daughter of a manufacturer of underwear at Cleveland, Ohio. The minister himself was rather a favorite in the town. The elders of the church liked him because he was quiet and unpretentious and Mrs. White, the banker's wife, thought him scholarly and refined. [171]

The Presbyterian Church held itself somewhat aloof from the other churches of Winesburg. It was larger and more imposing and its minister was better paid. He even had a carriage of his own and on summer evenings sometimes drove about town with his wife. Through Main Street and up and down Buckeye Street he went, bowing gravely to the people, while his wife, afire with secret pride, looked at him out of the corners of her eyes and worried lest the horse became frightened and run away.

For a good many years after he came to Winesburg things went well with Curtis Hartman. He was not one to arouse keen enthusiasm among the worshippers in his church but on the other hand he made no enemies. In reality he was much in earnest and sometimes suffered prolonged periods of remorse because he could not go crying the word of God in the highways and byways of the town. He wondered if the flame of the spirit really burned in him and dreamed of a day when a strong sweet new current of power would come like a great wind into his voice and his soul and that people would tremble before the spirit of God made manifest in him. "I am a poor stick and that will never really happen to me," he mused dejectedly, and then a patient smile lit up his features. "Oh well, I suppose I'm doing well enough," he added philosophically. [172]

The room in the bell tower of the church, where on Sunday mornings the minister prayed for an increase in him of the power of God, had but one window. It was long and narrow and swung outward on a hinge like a door. On the window, made of little leaded panes, was a design showing the Christ laying his hand upon the head of a child. One Sunday morning in the summer as he sat by his desk in the room with a large Bible opened before him, and the sheets of his sermon scatttered about, the minister was shocked to see, in the upper room of the house next door, a woman lying in her bed and smoking a cigarette while she read a book. Curtis Hartman went on tiptoe to the window and closed it softly. He was horror stricken at the thought of a woman smoking and trembled also to think that his eyes, just raised from the pages of the book of God, had looked upon the bare shoulders and white throat of a woman. With his brain in a whirl he went down into the pulpit and preached a long sermon without once thinking of his gesture or his voice. The sermon attracted unusual attention because of its power and clearness. "I wonder if she is listening, if my voice is carrying a message into her soul," he thought and began to hope that on future Sunday mornings he might be able to say words that would touch and awaken the woman apparently far gone in secret sin. [173]

The house next door to the Presbyterian Church, through the windows of which the minister had seen the sight that had so upset him, was occupied by two women. Aunt Elizabeth Swift, a grey competent-looking widow with money in the Winesburg National Bank, lived there with her daughter Kate Swift, a school teacher. The school teacher was thirty years old and had a neat trim-looking figure. She had few friends and bore a reputation of having a sharp tongue. When he began to think about her, Curtis Hartman remembered that she had been to Europe and had lived for two years in New York City. "Perhaps after all her smoking means nothing," he thought. He began to remember that when he was a student in college and occasionally read novels, good although somewhat worldly women had smoked through the pages of a book that had once fallen into his hands. With a rush of new determination he worked on his sermons all through the week and forgot, in his zeal to reach the ears and the soul of this new listener, both his embarrassment in the pulpit and the necessity of prayer in the study on Sunday mornings.

Reverend Hartman's experience with women had been somewhat limited. He was the son of a wagon maker from Muncie, Indiana, and had worked his way through college. The daughter of the underwear manufacturer had boarded in [174] a house where he lived during his school days and he had married her after a formal and prolonged courtship, carried on for the most part by the girl herself. On his marriage day the underwear manufacturer had given his daughter five thousand dollars and he promised to leave her at least twice that amount in his will. The minister had thought himself fortunate in marriage and had never permitted himself to think of other women. He did not want to think of other women. What he wanted was to do the work of God quietly and earnestly.

In the soul of the minister a struggle awoke. From wanting to reach the ears of Kate Swift, and through his sermons to delve into her soul, he began to want also to look again at the figure lying white and quiet in the bed. On a Sunday morning when he could not sleep because of his thoughts he arose and went to walk in the streets. When he had gone along Main Street almost to the old Richmond place he stopped and picking up a stone rushed off to the room in the bell tower. With the stone he broke out a corner of the window and then locked the door and sat down at the desk before the open Bible to wait. When the shade of the window to Kate Swift's room was raised he could see, through the hole, directly into her bed, but she was not there. She also had risen and had gone for a walk and the hand that [175] raised the shade was the hand of Aunt Elizabeth Swift.

The minister almost wept with joy at this deliverance from the carnal desire to "peep" and went back to his own house praising God. In an ill moment he forgot, however, to stop the hole in the window. The piece of glass broken out at the corner of the window just nipped off the bare heel of the boy standing motionless and looking with rapt eyes into the face of the Christ.

Curtis Hartman forgot his sermon on that Sunday morning. He talked to his congregation and in his talk said that it was a mistake for people to think of their minister as a man set aside and intended by nature to lead a blameless life. "Out of my own experience I know that we, who are the ministers of God's word, are beset by the same temptations that assail you," he declared. "I have been tempted and have surrendered to temptation. It is only the hand of God, placed beneath my head, that raised me up. As he has raised me so also will he raise you. Do not despair. In your hour of sin raise your eyes to the skies and you will be again and again saved."

Resolutely the minister put the thoughts of the woman in the bed out of his mind and began to be something like a lover in the presence of his wife. One evening when they drove out together he turned the horse out of Buckeye Street and in [176] the darkness on Gospel Hill, above Water-works Pond, put his arm around Sarah Hartman's waist. When he had eaten breakfast in the morning and was ready to retire to his study at the back of his house he went around the table and kissed his wife on the cheek. When thoughts of Kate Swift came into his head, he smiled and raised his eyes to the skies. "Intercede for me, Master," he muttered, "keep me in the narrow path intent on Thy work."

And now began the real struggle in the soul of the brown-bearded minister. By chance he discovered that Kate Swift was in the habit of lying in her bed in the evenings and reading a book. A lamp stood on a table by the side of the bed and the light streamed down upon her white shoulders and bare throat. On the evening when he made the discovery the minister sat at the desk in the study from nine until after eleven and when her light was put out stumbled out of the church to spend two more hours walking and praying in the streets. He did not want to kiss the shoulders and the throat of Kate Swift and had not allowed his mind to dwell on such thoughts. He did not know what he wanted. "I am God's child and he must save me from myself," he cried, in the darkness under the trees as he wandered in the streets. By a tree he stood and looked at the sky that was covered with hurrying clouds. He [177] began to talk to God intimately and closely. "Please, Father, do not forget me. Give me power to go tomorrow and repair the hole in the window. Lift my eyes again to the skies. Stay with me, Thy servant, in his hour of need."

Up and down through the silent streets walked the minister and for days and weeks his soul was troubled. He could not understand the temptation that had come to him nor could he fathom the reason for its coming. In a way he began to blame God, saying to himself that he had tried to keep his feet in the true path and had not run about seeking sin. "Through my days as a young man and all through my life here I have gone quietly about my work," he declared. "Why now should I be tempted? What have I done that this burden should be laid on me?"

Three times during the early fall and winter of that year Curtis Hartman crept out of his house to the room in the bell tower to sit in the darkness looking at the figure of Kate Swift lying in her bed and later went to walk and pray in the streets. He could not understand himself. For weeks he would go along scarcely thinking of the school teacher and telling himself that he had conquered the carnal desire to look at her body. And then something would happen. As he sat in the study of his own house, hard at work on a sermon, he would become nervous and begin to [178] walk up and down the room. "I will go out into the streets," he told himself and even as he let himself in at the church door he persistently denied to himself the cause of his being there. "I will not repair the hole in the window and I will train myself to come here at night and sit in the presence of this woman without raising my eyes. I will not be defeated in this thing. The Lord has devised this temptation as a test of my soul and I will grope my way out of darkness into the light of righteousness."

One night in January when it was bitter cold and snow lay deep on the streets of Winesburg Curtis Hartman paid his last visit to the room in the bell tower of the church. It was past nine o'clock when he left his own house and he set out so hurriedly that he forgot to put on his overshoes. In Main Street no one was aboard but Hop Higgins the night watchman and in the whole town no one was awake but the watchman and young George Willard, who sat in the office of the *Winesburg Eagle* trying to rewrite a story. Along the street to the church went the minister, plowing through the drifts and thinking that this time he would utterly give way to sin. "I want to look at the woman and to think of kissing her shoulders and I am going to let myself think what I choose," he declared bitterly and tears came into his eyes. He began to think that he would get out of the [179] ministry and try some other way of life. "I shall go to some city and get into business," he declared. "If my nature is such that I cannot resist sin, I shall give myself over to sin. At least I shall not be a hypocrite, preaching the word of God with my mind thinking of the shoulders and neck of a woman who does not belong to me."

It was cold in the room of the bell tower of the church on that January night and almost as soon as he came into the room Curtis Hartman knew that if he stayed he would be ill. His feet were wet from tramping in the snow and there was no fire. In the room in the house next door Kate Swift had not yet appeared. With grim determination the man sat down to wait. Sitting in the chair and gripping the edge of the desk on which lay the Bible he stared into the darkness thinking the blackest thoughts of his life. He thought of his wife and for the moment almost hated her. "She has always been ashamed of passion and has cheated me," he thought. "Man has a right to expect living passion and beauty in a woman. He has no right to forget that he is an animal and in me there is something that is Greek. I will throw off the woman of my bosom and seek other women. I will besiege this school teacher. I will fly in the face of all men and if I am a creature of carnal lusts I will live then for my lusts."

The distracted man trembled from head to [180] foot, partly from cold, partly from the struggle in which he was engaged. Hours passed and a fever assailed his body. His throat began to hurt and his teeth chattered. His feet on the study floor felt like two cakes of ice. Still he would not give up. "I will see this woman and will think the thoughts I have never dared to think," he told himself, gripping the edge of the desk and waiting.

Curtis Hartman came near dying from the effects of that night of waiting in the church, and also he found in the thing that happened what he took to be the way of life for him. On other evenings when he had waited he had not been able to see, through the little hole in the glass, any part of the school teacher's room except that occupied by her bed. In the darkness he had waited until the woman suddenly appeared sitting in the bed in her white night-robe. When the light was turned up she propped herself up among the pillows and read a book. Sometimes she smoked one of the cigarettes. Only her bare shoulders and throat were visible.

On the January night, after he had come near dying with cold and after his mind had two or three times actually slipped away into an odd land of fantasy so that he had by an exercise of will power to force himself back into consciousness, Kate Swift appeared. In the room next door a [181] lamp was lighted and the waiting man stared into an empty bed. Then upon the bed before his eyes a naked woman threw herself. Lying face downward she wept and beat with her fists upon the pillow. With a final outburst of weeping she half arose, and in the presence of the man who had waited to look and to think thoughts the woman of sin began to pray. In the lamplight her figure, slim and strong, looked like the figure of the boy in the presence of the Christ on the leaded window.

Curtis Hartman never remembered how he got out of the church. With a cry he arose, dragging the heavy desk along the floor. The Bible fell, making a great clatter in the silence. When the light in the house next door went out he stumbled down the stairway and into the street. Along the street he went and ran in at the door of the *Winesburg Eagle*. To George

Willard, who was tramping up and down in the office undergoing a struggle of his own, he began to talk half incoherently. "The ways of God are beyond human understanding,"he cried, running in quickly and closing the door. He began to advance upon the young man, his eyes glowing and his voice ringing with fervor. "I have found the light," he cried. "After ten years in this town, God has manifested himself to me in the body of a woman." His voice dropped and he began to whisper. "I did [182] not understand," he said. "What I took to be a trial of my soul was only a preparation for a new and more beautiful fervor of the spirit. God has appeared to me in the person of Kate Swift, the school teacher, kneeling naked on a bed. Do you know Kate Swift? Although she may not be aware of it, she is an instrument of God, bearing the message of truth."

Reverend Curtis Hartman turned and ran out of the office. At the door he stopped, and after looking up and down the deserted street, turned again to George Willard. "I am delivered. Have no fear." He held up a bleeding fist for the young man to see. "I smashed the glass of the window," he cried. "Now it will have to be wholly replaced. The strength of God was in me and I broke it with my fist." [183]

SINCLAIR LEWIS
1885–1951

The Village Virus

from

MAIN STREET

Although various pieces of American fiction had shown the small town to be provincial, cruel, and narrow rather than a kind and friendly place, Sinclair Lewis was the first writer to use predominantly the satirical method in his attack. He was born and raised in Sauk Center, Minnesota, the son of a country doctor, and people there considered him somewhat peculiar. He studied at Yale, traveled abroad, worked as a hack writer in New York, and wrote four novels and a play. His fifth novel, *Main Street* (1920), was his first real success. In this novel, with Sauk Center becoming Gopher Prairie, he was able to take revenge on his home town for its insular patterns of thinking. Lewis was critical of almost all aspects of small-town life, but especially its dullness and cultural deadness.

The idea for *Main Street* occurred to Lewis while he was a student at Yale, and the first draft was entitled *The Village Virus*, centering around the character of a village lawyer. The final version, appearing with Carol Kennicott as the central figure, established a reputation for its author and became the first smash hit of modern literature.

The characters in *Main Street* are representative of people in many small towns; as a result, they never quite come to life. The novel is filled with stereotypes or static classifications of people, events, and places. Some sense of reality, or at least verisimilitude, is achieved by Lewis's journalistic style as he accumulates great masses of minute details. But perhaps the technique of using stereotypes places emphasis on the central meaning of the novel—the spiritual malady of the people. The stereotypes are part of Lewis's insight into the human condition: at the center of their lives is a vacuum.

Carol Kennicott comes to Gopher Prairie as the bride of the town's

young doctor. She soon discovers the weaknesses of village life and sets
about on a program of reform, but without success. The passages that follow include a description of Carol's tour of Main Street just after her arrival; a party given by selected citizens to welcome Carol; a conversation
with a provincial, Raymond Wutherspoon; a meeting of elite society, the
Jolly Seventeen; a meeting of the women's study club, the Thanatopsis; a
visit with pioneer types, the Champ Perrys; and a conversation with a gossipy neighbor, Mrs. Bogart.

Lewis was a prolific writer; some of his work is first-rate, but he also
wrote much that is dull and shallow. His best work has been appreciated
both in this country and in Europe, and in 1930 he became the first American writer to receive the Nobel Prize. His best-known novels, in addition
to *Main Street,* are *Babbitt* (1922), *Arrowsmith* (1925), *Elmer Gantry* (1927),
and *Dodsworth* (1929).

from MAIN STREET

CHAPTER IV

. . .

When Carol had walked for thirty-two minutes she had completely
covered the town, east and west, north and south; and she stood at the
corner of Main Street and Washington Avenue and despaired.

Main Street with its two-story brick shops, its story-and-a-half wooden
residences, its muddy expanse from concrete walk to walk, its huddle of
Fords and lumber-wagons, was too small to absorb her. The broad, straight,
unenticing gashes of the streets let in the grasping prairie on every side.
. . . [33]

She glanced through the fly-specked windows of the most pretentious
building in sight, the one place which welcomed strangers and determined their opinion of the charm and luxury of Gopher Prairie—the
Minniemashie House. It was a tall lean shabby structure, three stories
of yellow-streaked wood, the corners covered with sanded pine slabs pur-
porting to symbolize stone. In the hotel office she could see a stretch of
bare unclean floor, a line of rickety chairs with brass cuspidors between,
a writing-desk with advertisements in mother-of-pearl letters upon the glass-
covered back. The dining-room beyond was a jungle of stained table-cloths
and catsup bottles.

She looked no more at the Minniemashie House.

A man in cuffless shirt-sleeves with pink arm-garters, wearing a linen collar but no tie, yawned his way from Dyer's Drug Store across to the hotel. He leaned against the wall, scratched a while, sighed, and in a bored way gossiped with a man tilted back in a chair. A lumber-wagon, its long green box filled with large spools of barbed-wire fencing, creaked down the block. A Ford, in reverse, sounded as though it were shaking to pieces, then recovered and rattled away. In the Greek candy-store was the whine of a peanut-roaster, and the oily smell of nuts.

There was no other sound nor sign of life.

She wanted to run, fleeing from the encroaching prairie, demanding the security of a great city. Her dreams of creating a beautiful town were ludicrous. Oozing out from every drab wall, she felt a forbidding spirit which she could never conquer.

She trailed down the street on one side, back on the other, glancing into the cross streets. It was a private Seeing Main Street tour. She was within ten minutes beholding not only the heart of a place called Gopher Prairie, but ten thousand towns from Albany to San Diego:

Dyer's Drug Store, a corner building of regular and unreal blocks of artificial stone. Inside the store, a greasy marble soda-fountain with an electric lamp of red and green and curdled-yellow mosaic shade. Pawed-over heaps of toothbrushes and combs and packages of shaving-soap. Shelves of soap-cartons, teething-rings, garden-seeds, and patent medicines in yellow packages—nostrums for consumption, for "women's diseases"—notorious mixtures of opium and alco-[34]hol, in the very shop to which her husband sent patients for the filling of prescriptions.

From a second-story window the sign "W. P. Kennicott, Phys. & Surgeon," gilt on black sand.

A small wooden motion-picture theater called "The Rosebud Movie Palace." Lithographs announcing a film called "Fatty in Love."

Howland & Gould's Grocery. In the display window, black, overripe bananas and lettuce on which a cat was sleeping. Shelves lined with red crêpe paper which was now faded and torn and concentrically spotted. Flat against the wall of the second story the signs of lodges—the Knights of Pythias, the Maccabees, the Woodmen, the Masons.

Dahl & Oleson's Meat Market—a reek of blood.

A jewelry shop with tinny-looking wrist-watches for women. In front of it, at the curb, a huge wooden clock which did not go.

A fly-buzzing saloon with a brilliant gold and enamel whiskey sign across the front. Other saloons down the block. From them a stink of stale beer, and thick voices bellowing pidgin German or trolling out dirty songs —vice gone feeble and unenterprising and dull—the delicacy of a mining-camp minus its vigor. In front of the saloons, farmwives sitting on the seats of wagons, waiting for their husbands to become drunk and ready to start home.

A tobacco shop called "The Smoke House," filled with young men shaking dice for cigarettes. Racks of magazines, and pictures of coy fat prostitutes in striped bathing-suits.

A clothing store with a display of "ox-blood-shade Oxfords with bull-dog toes." Suits which looked worn and glossless while they were still new, flabbily draped on dummies like corpses with painted cheeks.

The Bon Ton Store—Haydock & Simons'—the largest shop in town. The first-story front of clear glass, the plates cleverly bound at the edges with brass. The second story of pleasant tapestry brick. One window of excellent clothes for men, interspersed with collars of floral piqué which showed mauve daisies on a saffron ground. Newness and an obvious notion of neatness and service. Haydock & Simons. Haydock. She had met a Haydock at the station; Harry Haydock; an active person of thirty-five. He seemed great to her, now, and very like a saint. His shop was clean! [35]

Axel Egge's General Store, frequented by Scandinavian farmers. In the shallow dark window-space heaps of sleazy sateens, badly woven galateas, canvas shoes designed for women with bulging ankles, steel and red glass buttons upon cards with broken edges, a cottony blanket, a granite-ware frying-pan reposing on a sun-faded crêpe blouse.

Sam Clark's Hardware Store. An air of frankly metallic enterprise. Guns and churns and barrels of nails and beautiful shiny butcher knives.

Chester Dashaway's House Furnishing Emporium. A vista of heavy oak rockers with leather seats, asleep in a dismal row.

Billy's Lunch. Thick handleless cups on the wet oilcloth-covered counter. An odor of onions and the smoke of hot lard. In the doorway a young man audibly sucking a toothpick.

The warehouse of the buyer of cream and potatoes. The sour smell of a dairy.

The Ford Garage and the Buick Garage, competent one-story brick and cement buildings opposite each other. Old and new cars on grease-blackened concrete floors. Tire advertisements. The roaring of a tested motor; a racket which beat at the nerves. Surly young men in khaki union-overalls. The most energetic and vital places in town.

A large warehouse for agricultural implements. An impressive barricade of green and gold wheels, of shafts and sulky seats, belonging to machinery of which Carol knew nothing—potato-planters, manure-spreaders, silage-cutters, disk-harrows, breaking-plows.

A feed store, its windows opaque with the dust of bran, a patent medi-cine advertisement painted on its roof.

Ye Art Shoppe, Prop. Mrs. Mary Ellen Wilks, Christian Science Library open daily free. A touching fumble at beauty. A one-room shanty of boards recently covered with rough stucco. A show-window delicately rich in error: vases starting out to imitate tree-trunks but running off into blobs of gilt—an aluminum ash-tray labeled "Greetings from Gopher Prairie"—a Chris-tian Science magazine—a stamped sofa-cushion portraying a large ribbon tied to a small poppy, the correct skeins of embroidery-silk lying on the pillow. Inside the shop, a glimpse of bad carbon prints of bad and famous pictures, shelves of phonograph records and camera films, wooden toys, [36] and in the midst an anxious small woman sitting in a padded rocking chair.

A barber shop and pool room. A man in shirt sleeves, presumably Del Snafflin the proprietor, shaving a man who had a large Adam's apple.

Nat Hicks's Tailor Shop, on a side street off Main. A one-story building. A fashion-plate showing human pitchforks in garments which looked as hard as steel plate.

On another side street a raw red-brick Catholic Church with a varnished yellow door.

The post-office—merely a partition of glass and brass shutting off the rear of a mildewed room which must once have been a shop. A tilted writing-shelf against a wall rubbed black and scattered with official notices and army recruiting-posters.

The damp, yellow-brick schoolbuilding in its cindery grounds.

The State Bank, stucco masking wood.

The Farmers' National Bank. An Ionic temple of marble. Pure, exquisite, solitary. A brass plate with "Ezra Stowbody, Pres't."

A score of similar shops and establishments.

Behind them and mixed with them, the houses, meek cottages or large, comfortable, soundly uninteresting symbols of prosperity.

In all the town not one building save the Ionic bank which gave pleasure to Carol's eyes; not a dozen buildings which suggested that, in the fifty years of Gopher Prairie's existence, the citizens had realized that it was either desirable or possible to make this, their common home, amusing or attractive.

It was not only the unsparing unapologetic ugliness and the rigid straightness which overwhelmed her. It was the planlessness, the flimsy temporariness of the buildings, their faded unpleasant colors. The street was cluttered with electric-light poles, telephone poles, gasoline pumps for motor cars, boxes of goods. Each man had built with the most valiant disregard of all the others. Between a large new "block" of two-story brick shops on one side, and the fire-brick Overland garage on the other side, was a one-story cottage turned into a millinery shop. The white temple of the Farmers' Bank was elbowed back by a grocery of glaring yellow brick. One store-building had a patchy galvanized iron cornice; the building beside it was crowned with battlements and pyramids of brick capped with blocks of red sandstone. [37]

She escaped from Main Street, fled home.

She wouldn't have cared, she insisted, if the people had been comely. She had noted a young man loafing before a shop, one unwashed hand holding the cord of an awning; a middle-aged man who had a way of staring at women as though he had been married too long and too prosaically; an old farmer, solid, wholesome, but not clean—his face like a potato fresh from the earth. None of them had shaved for three days.

"If they can't build shrines, out here on the prairie, surely there's nothing to prevent their buying safety-razors!" she raged.

She fought herself: "I must be wrong. People do live here. It *can't* be as ugly as—as I know it is! I must be wrong. But I can't do it. I can't go through with it."

She came home too seriously worried for hysteria; and when she found Kennicott waiting for her, and exulting, "Have a walk? Well, like the town? Great lawns and trees, eh?" she was able to say, with a self-protective maturity new to her, "It's very interesting." [38]

. . .

The recently built house of Sam Clark, in which was given the party to welcome Carol, was one of the largest in Gopher Prairie. It had a clean sweep of clapboards, a solid squareness, a small tower, and a large screened porch. Inside, it was as shiny, as hard, and as cheerful as a new oak upright piano.

Carol looked imploringly at Sam Clark as he rolled to the door and shouted, "Welcome, little lady! The keys of the city are yourn!"

Beyond him, in the hallway and the living-room, sitting in [40] a vast prim circle as though they were attending a funeral, she saw the guests. They were *waiting* so! . . .

His arm about her, he led her in and bawled, "Ladies and worser halves, the bride! We won't introduce her round yet, because she'll never get your bum names straight anyway. Now bust up this star-chamber!"

They tittered politely, but they did not move from the social security of their circle, and they did not cease staring.

. . .

She was led about the circle. Her voice mechanically produced safe remarks:

"Oh, I'm sure I'm going to like it here ever so much," and "Yes, we did have the best time in Colorado—mountains," and "Yes, I lived in St. Paul several years. Euclid P. Tinker? No, I don't *remember* meeting him, but I'm pretty sure I've heard of him."

Kennicott took her aside and whispered, "Now I'll introduce you to them, one at a time." [41]

. . .

When the Dawsons and Mr. Mott had stated that they were "pleased to meet her," there seemed to be nothing else to say, but the conversation went on automatically.

"Do you like Gopher Prairie?" whimpered Mrs. Dawson.

"Oh, I'm sure I'm going to be ever so happy."

"There's so many nice people," Mrs. Dawson looked to Mr. Moot for social and intellectual aid. He lectured:

"There's a fine class of people. I don't like some of these retired farmers who come here to spend their last days—especially the Germans. They hate to pay school-taxes. They hate to spend a cent. But the rest are a fine class of people. Did you know that Percy Bresnahan came from here? Used to go to school right at the old building!"

"I heard he did."

"Yes. He's a prince. He and I went fishing together, last time he was here."

The Dawsons and Mr. Mott teetered upon weary feet, and smiled at Carol with crystallized expressions. She went on:

"Tell me, Mr. Mott: Have you ever tried any experiments [43] with any of the new educational systems? The modern kindergarten methods or the Gary system?"

"Oh. Those. Most of these would-be reformers are simply notoriety-seekers. I believe in manual training, but Latin and mathematics always will be the backbone of sound Americanism, no matter what these faddists advocate—heaven knows what they do want—knitting, I suppose, and classes in wiggling the ears!"

The Dawsons smiled their appreciation of listening to a savant. Carol waited till Kennicott should rescue her. The rest of the party waited for the miracle of being amused.

Harry and Juanita Haydock, Rita Simons and Dr. Terry Gould—the young smart set of Gopher Prairie. She was led to them. Juanita Haydock flung at her in a high, cackling, friendly voice:

"Well, this is *so* nice to have you here. We'll have some good parties—dances and everything. You'll have to join the Jolly Seventeen. We play bridge and we have a supper once a month. You play, of course?"

"N-no, I don't."

"Really? In St. Paul?"

"I've always been such a book-worm."

"We'll have to teach you. Bridge is half the fun of life." Juanita had become patronizing, and she glanced disrespectfully at Carol's golden sash, which she had previously admired. [44]

. . .

While others drifted to her group, Carol snatched up the conversation. She laughed and was frivolous and rather brittle. She could not distinguish their eyes. They were a blurry theater-audience before which she self-consciously enacted the comedy of being the Clever Little Bride of Doc Kennicott:

"These-here celebrated Open Spaces, that's what I'm going out for. I'll never read anything but the sporting-page again. Will converted me on our Colorado trip. There were so many mousey tourists who were afraid to get out of the motor 'bus that I decided to be Annie Oakley, the Wild Western Wampire, and I bought oh, a vociferous skirt which revealed my perfectly nice ankles to the Presbyterian glare of all the Ioway school-ma'ams, and I leaped from peak to peak like the nimble chamoys, and—— You may think that Herr Doctor Kennicott is a Nimrod, but you ought to have seen me daring him to strip to his B. V. D.'s and go swimming in an icy mountain brook."

She knew that they were thinking of becoming shocked, but Juanita Haydock was admiring, at least. . . . [45]

For fifteen minutes Carol kept it up. She asserted that she was going to stage a musical comedy, that she preferred café parfait to beefsteak, that she hoped Dr. Kennicott would never lose his ability to make love to charming women, and that she had a pair of gold stockings. They gaped for more. But she could not keep it up. She retired to a chair behind Sam Clark's bulk. The smile-wrinkles solemnly flattened out in the faces of all the other collaborators in having a party, and again they stood about hoping but not expecting to be amused.

Carol listened. She discovered that conversation did not exist in Gopher Prairie. Even at this affair, which brought out the young smart set, the hunting squire set, the respectable intellectual set, and the solid financial set, they sat up with gaiety as with a corpse.

Juanita Haydock talked a good deal in her rattling voice but it was invariably of personalities: the rumor that Raymie Wutherspoon was going to send for a pair of patent leather shoes with gray buttoned tops; the rheumatism of Champ Perry; the state of Guy Pollock's grippe; and the dementia of Jim Howland in painting his fence salmon-pink.

Sam Clark had been talking to Carol about motor cars, but he felt his duties as host. While he droned, his brows popped up and down. He interrupted himself, "Must stir 'em up." He worried at his wife, "Don't you think I better [46] stir 'em up?" He shouldered into the center of the room, and cried:

"Let's have some stunts, folks."

"Yes, let's!" shrieked Juanita Haydock.

"Say, Dave, give us that stunt about the Norwegian catching a hen."

"You bet; that's a slick stunt; do that, Dave!" cheered Chet Dashaway.

Mr. Dave Dyer obliged.

All the guests moved their lips in anticipation of being called on for their own stunts.

"Ella, come on and recite 'Old Sweetheart of Mine,' for us," demanded Sam.

Miss Ella Stowbody, the spinster daughter of the Ionic bank, scratched her dry palms and blushed. "Oh, you don't want to hear that old thing again."

Sure we do! You bet!" asserted Sam.

"My voice is in terrible shape tonight."

"Tut! Come on!"

Sam loudly explained to Carol, "Ella is our shark at elocuting. She's had professional training. She studied singing and oratory and dramatic art and shorthand for a year, in Milwaukee."

Miss Stowbody was reciting. As encore to "An Old Sweetheart of Mine," she gave a peculiarly optimistic poem regarding the value of smiles.

There were four other stunts: one Jewish, one Irish, one juvenile, and Nat Hick's parody of Mark Antony's funeral oration.

During the winter Carol was to hear Dave Dyer's hen-catching impersonation seven times, "An Old Sweetheart of Mine" nine times, the Jewish story and the funeral oration twice; but now she was ardent and, because she did so want to be happy and simple-hearted, she was as disappointed as the others when the stunts were finished, and the party instantly sank back into coma.

They gave up trying to be festive; they began to talk naturally, as they did at their shops and homes.

The men and women divided, as they had been tending to do all evening. Carol was deserted by the men, left to a group of matrons who steadily pattered of children, sickness, and cooks—their own shop-talk. She was piqued. She re-[47]membered visions of herself as a smart married woman in a drawing room, fencing with clever men. Her dejection was relieved by speculation as to what the men were discussing, in the corner between the piano and the phonograph. Did they rise from these housewifely personalities to a larger world of abstractions and affairs?

She made her best curtsy to Mrs. Dawson; she twittered, "I won't have my husband leaving me so soon! I'm going over and pull the wretch's ears." She rose with a *jeune fille* bow. She was self-absorbed and self-approving because she had attained that quality of sentimentality. She proudly dipped across the room and, to the interest and commendation of all beholders, sat on the arm of Kennicott's chair. [48]

. . .

As Carol defied decency by sitting down with the men, Mr. Stowbody was piping to Mr. Dawson, "Say, Luke, when was't Biggins first settled in Winnebago Township? Wa'n't it in 1879?"

"Why no 'twa'n't!" Mr. Dawson was indignant. "He come out from Vermont in 1867—no, wait, in 1868, it must have been—and took a claim on the Rum River, quite a ways above Anoka."

"He did not!" roared Mr. Stowbody. "He settled first in Blue Earth County, him and his father!"

("What's the point at issue?" Carol whispered to Kennicott.)

("Whether this old duck Biggins had an English setter or a Llewellyn. They've been arguing it all evening!")

Dave Dyer interrupted to give tidings, "D' tell you that Clara Biggins was in town couple days ago? She bought a hot-water bottle—expensive one, too—two dollars and thirty cents!"

"Yaaaaaah!" snarled Mr. Stowbody. "Course. She's just like her grandad was. Never save a cent. Two dollars and twenty—thirty, was it?—two dollars and thirty cents for a hot-water bottle! Brick wrapped up in a flannel petticoat just as good, anyway!"

"How's Ella's tonsils, Mr. Stowbody?" yawned Chet Dashaway.

While Mr. Stowbody gave a somatic and psychic study of them, Carol reflected, "Are they really so terribly interested in Ella's tonsils, or even in Ella's esophagus? I wonder if I could get them away from personalities? Let's risk damnation and try."

"There hasn't been much labor trouble around here, has there, Mr. Stowbody?" she asked innocently.

"No, ma'am, thank God, we've been free from that, except maybe with hired girls and farm-hands. Trouble enough with these foreign farmers; if you don't watch these Swedes they turn socialist or populist or some fool thing on you in a minute. Of course, if they have loans you can make 'em listen to reason. I just have 'em come into the bank for a talk and tell 'em a few things. I don't mind their being democrats, so much, but I won't stand having socialist around. [49] But thank God, we ain't got the labor trouble they have in these cities. Even Jack Elder here gets along pretty well, in the planing-mill, don't you, Jack?"

"Yep. Sure. Don't need so many skilled workmen in my place, and it's a lot of these cranky, wage-hogging, half-baked skilled mechanics that start trouble—reading a lot of this anarchist literature and union papers and all."

"Do you approve of union labor?" Carol inquired of Mr. Elder.

"Me? I should say not! It's like this: I don't mind dealing with my men if they think they've got any grievances—though Lord knows what's come over workmen, nowadays—don't appreciate a good job. But still, if they come to me honestly, as man to man, I'll talk things over with them. But I'm not going to have any outsider, any of these walking delegates, or whatever fancy names they call themselves now—bunch of rich grafters, living on the ignorant workmen! Not going to have any of those fellows butting in and telling *me* how to run *my* business!"

Mr. Elder was growing more excited, more belligerent and patriotic. "I stand for freedom and constitutional rights. If any man don't like my shop, he can get up and git. Same way, if I don't like him, he gits. And that's all there is to it. I simply can't understand all these complications and hoop-te-doodles and government reports and wage-scales and God knows what all that these fellows are balling up the labor situation with, when it's all perfectly simple. They like what I pay 'em, or they get out. That's all there is to it!"

"What do you think of profit-sharing?" Carol ventured.

Mr. Elder thundered his answer, while the others nodded, solemnly and in tune, like a shop-window of flexible toys, comic mandarins and judges and ducks and clowns, set quivering by a breeze from the open door:

"All this profit-sharing and welfare work and insurance and old-age pension is simply poppycock. Enfeebles a workman's independence—and wastes a lot of honest profit. The half-baked thinker that isn't dry behind the ears yet, and these suffragettes and God knows what all buttinskis there are that are trying to tell a business man how to run his business, and some of these college professors are about as bad, the whole kit and bilin' of 'em are nothing in God's world but socialism in disguise! And it's my bounden duty as a pro-[50]ducer to resist every attack on the integrity of American industry to the last ditch. Yes—SIR!"

Mr. Elder wiped his brow.

Dave Dyer added, "Sure! You bet! What they ought to do is simply to hang every one of these agitators, and that would settle the whole thing right off. Don't you think so, doc?"

"You bet," agreed Kennicott.

The conversation was at last relieved of the plague of Carol's intrusions and they settled down to the question of whether the justice of the peace had sent that hobo drunk to jail for ten days or twelve. It was a matter not readily determined. . . .

Once—only once—the presence of the alien Carol was recognized. Chet Dashaway leaned over and said asthmatically, "Say, uh, have you been reading this serial 'Two Out' in *Tingling Tales?* Corking yarn! Gosh, the fellow that wrote it certainly can sling baseball slang!"

The others tried to look literary. Harry Haydock offered, "Juanita is a great hand for reading high-class stuff, like 'Mid the Magnolias' by this Sara Hetwiggin Butts, and 'Riders of Ranch Reckless.' Books. But me," he glanced about importantly, as one convinced that no other hero had ever been in so strange a plight, "I'm so darn busy I don't have much time to read."

"I never read anything I can't check against," said Sam Clark. [51]

Thus ended the literary portion of the conversation, and for seven minutes Jackson Elder outlined reasons for believing that the pike-fishing was better on the west shore of Lake Minniemashie than on the east—though it was indeed quite true that on the east shore Nat Hicks had caught a pike altogther admirable.

. . .

Smiling as changelessly as an ivory figurine she sat quiescent, avoiding thought, glancing about the living-room and hall, noting their betrayal of unimaginative commercial prosperity. Kennicott said, "Dandy interior, eh? My idea of how a place ought to be furnished. Modern." She looked polite, and observed the oiled floors, hard-wood staircase, unused fireplace with tiles which resembled brown linoleum, cut-glass vases standing upon doilies, and the barred, shut, forbidding unit bookcases that were half filled with swashbuckler novels and unread-looking sets of Dickens, Kipling, O. Henry, and Elbert Hubbard.

She perceived that even personalities were failing to hold the party. The room filled with hesistancy as with a fog. People cleared their throats, tried to choke down yawns. The men shot their cuffs and the women stuck their combs more firmly into their back hair.

Then a rattle, a daring hope in every eye, the swinging of a door, the smell of strong coffee, Dave Dyer's mewing voice in a triumphant, "The eats!" They began to chatter. They had something to do. They could escape from themselves. They fell upon the food—chicken sandwiches, maple cake, drug-store ice cream. Even when the food was gone they remained cheerful. They could go home, any time now, and go to bed!

They went, with a flutter of coats, chiffon scarfs, and goodbys.

Carol and Kennicott walked home.

"Did you like them?" he asked.

"They were terribly sweet to me."

"Uh, Carrie—You ought to be more careful about [52] shocking folks. Talking about gold stockings, and about showing your ankles to school-teachers and all!" More mildly: "You gave 'em a good time, but I'd watch out for that, 'f I were you. Juanita Haydock is such a damn cat. I wouldn't give her a chance to criticize me."

"My poor effort to lift up the party! Was I wrong to try to amuse them?"

"No! No! Honey, I didn't mean——You were the only up-and-coming person in the bunch. I just mean——Don't get onto legs and all that immoral stuff. Pretty conservative crowd. [53]

. . .

CHAPTER V

. . .

Till they had a maid they took noon dinner and six o'clock supper at Mrs. Gurrey's boarding house.

. . .

In the line of unsmiling, methodically chewing guests, like horses at a manger, Carol came to distinguish one countenance: the pale, long, spectacled face and sandy pompadour hair of Mr. Raymond P. Wutherspoon, known as "Raymie," professional bachelor, manager and one half the sales-force in the shoe-department of the Bon Ton Store.

"You will enjoy Gopher Prairie very much, Mrs. Kennicott," petitioned Raymie. His eyes were like those of a dog waiting to be let in out of the cold. He passed the stewed apricots effusively. "There are a great many bright cultured people here. Mrs. Wilks, the Christian Science reader, is a very bright woman—though I am not a Scientist myself, in fact I sing in the Episcopal choir. And Miss Sherwin of the high school—she is such a pleas-ing, bright girl—I was fitting her to a pair of tan gaiters yesterday, I declare, it really was a pleasure."

"Gimme the butter, Currie," was Kennicott's comment. She defied him by encouraging Raymie:

"Do you have amateur dramatics and so on here?" [58]

"Oh yes! The town's just full of talent. The Knights of Pythias put on a dandy minstrel show last year."

"It's nice you're so enthusiastic."

"Oh, do you really think so? Lots of folks jolly me for trying to get up shows and so on. I tell them they have more artistic gifts than they know. Just yesterday I was saying to Harry Haydock: if he would read poetry, like Longfellow, or if he would join the band—I get so much pleasure out of playing the cornet, and our band-leader, Del Snafflin, is such a good musician, I often say he ought to give up his barbering and become a pro-fessional musician, he could play the clarinet in Minneapolis or New York or anywhere, but—but I couldn't get Harry to see it at all and—I hear you and the doctor went out hunting yesterday. Lovely country, isn't it. And did you make some calls? The mercantile life isn't inspiring like medicine. It must be wonderful to see how patients trust you, doctor."

"Huh. It's me that's got to do all the trusting. Be damn sight more won-derful 'f they'd pay their bills," grumbled Kennicott and, to Carol, he whispered something which sounded like "gentleman hen."

But Raymie's pale eyes were watering at her. She helped him with, "So you like to read poetry?"

"Oh yes, so much—though to tell the truth, I don't get much time for reading, we're always so busy at the store and——But we had the dandiest professional reciter at the Pythian Sisters sociable last winter."

Carol thought she heard a grunt from the traveling salesman at the end of the table, and Kennicott's jerking elbow was a grunt embodied. She persisted:

"Do you get to see many plays, Mr. Wutherspoon?"

He shone at her like a dim blue March moon, and sighed, "No, but I do love the movies. I'm a real fan. One trouble with books is that they're not so thoroughly safeguarded by intelligent censors as the movies are, and when you drop into the library and take out a book you never know what you're wasting your time on. What I like in books is a wholesome, really improving story, and sometimes—— Why, once I started a novel by this fellow Balzac that you read about, and it told how a lady wasn't with her husband, I mean she wasn't his wife. It went into details, disgustingly! And the English was real poor. I spoke to the library about it, and [59] they took it off the shelves. I'm not narrow, but I must say I don't see any use in this deliberately dragging in immorality! Life itself is so full of temptations that in literature one wants only that which is pure and uplifting." [60]

. . .

CHAPTER VII

. . .

The Jolly Seventeen (the membership of which ranged from fourteen to twenty-six) was the social cornice of Gopher Prairie. It was the country club, the diplomatic set, the St. Cecilia, the Ritz oval room, the Club de Vingt. To belong to it was to be "in." Though its membership partly coincided with that of the Thanatopsis study club, the Jolly Seventeen as a separate entity guffawed at the Thanatopsis, and considered it middle-class and even "highbrow." [86]

. . .

Though Juanita Haydock was highly advanced in the matters of finger-bowls, doilies, and bath-mats, her "refreshments" were typical of all afternoon-coffees. Juanita's best friends, Mrs. Dyer and Mrs. Dashaway, passed large dinner plates, each with a spoon, a fork, and a coffee cup without saucer. They apologized and discussed the afternoon's game as they passed through the thicket of women's feet. Then they distributed hot buttered rolls, coffee poured from an enamel-ware pot, stuffed olives, potato salad, and angel's-food cake. There was, even in the most strictly conforming Gopher Prairie circles, a certain option as to collations. The olives need not be stuffed. Doughnuts were in some houses well thought of as a substitute for the hot buttered rolls. But there was in all the town no heretic save Carol who omitted angel's-food. [88]

. . .

Vida Sherwin came in after school, with Miss Ethel Villets, the town librarian. Miss Sherwin's optimistic presence gave Carol more confidence. She talked. She informed the circle, "I drove almost down to Wahkeenyan with Will, a few days ago. Isn't the country lovely! And I do admire the

Scandinavian farmers down there so: their big red barns and silos and milking-machines and everything. Do you all know that lonely Lutheran church, with the tin-covered spire, that stands out alone on a hill? It's so bleak; somehow it seems so brave. I do think the Scandinavians are the hardiest and best people—"

"Oh, do you *think* so?" protested Mrs. Jackson Elder. "My husband says the Svenskas that work in the planing-mill are perfectly terrible—so silent and cranky, and so selfish, the way they keep demanding raises. If they had their way they'd simply ruin the business."

"Yes, and they're simply *ghastly* hired girls!" wailed Mrs. Dave Dyer. "I swear, I work myself to skin and bone trying to please my hired girls— when I can get them! I do everything in the world for them. They can have their gentleman friends call on them in the kitchen any time, and they get just the same to eat as we do, if there's any left over, and I practically never jump on them."

Juanita Haydock rattled, "They're ungrateful, all that class of people. I do think the domestic problem is simply becoming awful. I don't know what the country's coming to, with these Scandahoofian clodhoppers demanding every cent you can save, and so ignorant and impertinent, and on my word, demanding [89] bath-tubs and everything—as if they weren't mighty good and lucky at home if they got a bath in the wash-tub."

They were off, riding hard. Carol thought of Bea and waylaid them:

"But isn't it possibly the fault of the mistresses if the maids are ungrateful? For generations we've given them the leavings of food, and holes to live in. I don't want to boast, but I must say I don't have much trouble with Bea. She's so friendly. The Scandinavians are sturdy and honest——"

Mrs. Dave Dyer snapped, "Honest? Do you call it honest to hold us up for every cent of pay they can get? I can't say that I've had any of them steal anything (though you might call it stealing to eat so much that a roast beef hardly lasts three days), but just the same I don't intend to let them think they can put anything over on *me!* I always make them pack and unpack their trunks down-stairs, right under my eyes, and then I know they aren't being tempted to dishonesty by any slackness on *my* part!"

"How much do the maids get here?" Carol ventured.

Mrs. B. J. Gougerling, wife of the banker, stated in a shocked manner, "Any place from three-fifty to five-fifty a week! I know positively that Mrs. Clark, after swearing that she wouldn't weaken and encourage them in their outrageous demands, went and paid five-fifty—think of it! practically a dollar a day for unskilled work and, of course, her food and room and a chance to do her own washing right in with the rest of the wash. *How much do you pay, Mrs. Kennicott?*"

"Yes! How much do you pay?" insisted half a dozen.

"W-why, I pay six a week," she feebly confessed.

They gasped. Juanita protested, "Don't you think it's hard on the rest of us when you pay so much?" Juanita's demand was re-inforced by the universal glower.

Carol was angry. "I don't care! A maid has one of the hardest jobs on earth. She works from ten to eighteen hours a day. She has to wash slimy dishes and dirty clothes. She tends the children and runs to the door with wet chapped hands and ——" [90]

. . .

Carol felt guilty. She devoted herself to admiring the spinsterish Miss Villets—and immediately committed another offense against the laws of decency.

"We haven't seen you at the library yet," Miss Villets reproved.

"I've wanted to run in so much but I've been getting settled and—— I'll probably come in so often you'll get tired of me! I hear you have such a nice library."

"There are many who like it. We have two thousand more books than Wakamin."

"Isn't that fine. I'm sure you are largely responsible. I've had some experience, in St. Paul."

"So I have been informed. Not that I entirely approve of library methods in these large cities. So careless, letting tramps and all sorts of dirty persons practically sleep in the reading-rooms."

"I know, but the poor souls—— Well, I'm sure you will [91] agree with me in one thing: The chief task of a librarian is to get people to read."

"You feel so? My feeling, Mrs. Kennicott, and I am merely quoting the librarian of a very large college, is that the first duty of the *conscientious* librarian is to preserve the books."

"Oh!" Carol repented her "Oh." Miss Villets stiffened, and attacked:

"It may be all very well in cities, where they have unlimited funds, to let nasty children ruin books and just deliberately tear them up, and fresh young men take more books out than they are entitled to by the regulations, but I'm never going to permit it in this library!"

"What if some children are destructive? They learn to read. Books are cheaper than minds."

"Nothing is cheaper than the minds of some of these children that come in and bother me simply because their mothers don't keep them home where they belong. Some librarians may choose to be so wishy-washy and turn their libraries into nursing-homes and kindergartens, but as long as I'm in charge, the Gopher Prairie library is going to be quiet and decent, and the books well kept!" [92]

. . .

CHAPTER XI

She had often been invited to the weekly meetings of the Thanatopsis, the women's study club, but she had put it off. The Thanatopsis was, Vida Sherwin promised, "such a cozy group, and yet it puts you in touch with all the intellectual thoughts that are going on everywhere."

Early in March Mrs. Westlake, wife of the veteran physician, marched into Carol's living-room like an amiable old pussy and suggested, "My dear, you really must come to the Thanatopsis this afternoon. Mrs. Dawson is going to be leader and the poor soul is frightened to death. She wanted me to get you to come. She says she's sure you will brighten up the meeting with your knowledge of books and writings. (English poetry is our topic today.) So shoo! Put on your coat!"

"English poetry? Really? I'd love to go. I didn't realize you were reading poetry."

"Oh, we're not so slow!"

Mrs. Luke Dawson, wife of the richest man in town, gaped at them piteously when they appeared. Her expensive frock of beaver-colored satin with rows, plasters, and pendants of solemn brown beads was intended for a woman twice her size. She stood wringing her hands in front of nineteen folding chairs, in her front parlor with its faded photograph of Minnehaha Falls in 1890, its "colored enlargement" of Mr. Dawson, its bulbous lamp painted with sepia cows and mountains and standing on a mortuary marble column.

She creaked, "O Mrs. Kennicott, I'm in such a fix. I'm supposed to lead the discussion, and I wondered would you come and help?"

"What poet do you take up today?" demanded Carol, in her library tone of "What book do you wish to take out?"

"Why, the English ones."

"Not all of them?"

"W-why yes. We're learning all of European Literature [124] this year. The club gets such a nice magazine, *Culture Hints,* and we follow its programs. Last year our subject was Men and Women of the Bible, and next year we'll probably take up Furnishings and China. My, it does make a body hustle to keep up with all these new culture subjects, but it is improving. So will you help us with the discussion today?"

On her way over Carol had decided to use the Thanatopsis as the tool with which to liberalize the town. She had immediately conceived enormous enthusiasm; she had chanted, "These are the real people. When the housewives, who bear the burdens, are interested in poetry, it means something. I'll work with them—for them—anything!"

Her enthusiasm had become watery even before thirteen women resolutely removed their overshoes, sat down meatily, ate peppermints, dusted their fingers, folded their hands, composed their lower thoughts, and invited the naked muse of poetry to deliver her most improving message. . . .

Mrs. Dawson opened the meeting by sighing, "I'm sure I'm glad to see you all here today, and I understand that the ladies have prepared a number of very interesting papers, this is such an interesting subject, the poets, they have been an inspiration for higher thought, in fact wasn't it Reverend Benlick who said that some of the poets have been as much an inspiration as a good many of the ministers, and so we shall be glad to hear——"

The poor lady smiled neuralgically, panted with fright, scrabbled about the small oak table to find her eye-glasses, and continued, "We will first have the pleasure of hearing Mrs. Jenson on the subject 'Shakespeare and Milton.' "

Mrs. Ole Jenson said that Shakespeare was born in 1564 and died 1616. He lived in London, England, and in Stratford-[125]on-Avon, which many American tourists loved to visit, a lovely town with many curios and old houses well worth examination. Many people believed that Shakespeare was the greatest playwright who ever lived, also a fine poet. Not much was known about his life, but after all that did not really make so much difference, because they loved to read his numerous plays, several of the best known of which she would now criticize.

Perhaps the best known of his plays was "The Merchant of Venice," having a beautiful love story and a fine appreciation of a woman's brains, which a woman's club, even those who did not care to commit themselves on the question of suffrage, ought to appreciate. (Laughter.) Mrs. Jenson was sure that she, for one, would love to be like Portia. The play was about a Jew named Shylock, and he didn't want his daughter to marry a Venice gentleman named Antonio——

Mrs. Leonard Warren, a slender, gray, nervous woman, president of the Thanatopsis and wife of the Congregational pastor, reported the birth and death dates of Byron, Scott, Moore, Burns; and wound up:

"Burns was quite a poor boy and he did not enjoy the advantages we enjoy today, except for the advantages of the fine old Scotch kirk where he heard the Word of God preached more fearlessly than even in the finest big brick churches in the big and so-called advanced cities of today, but he did not have our educational advantages and Latin and the other treasures of the mind so richly strewn before the, alas, too ofttimes inattentive feet of our youth who do not always sufficiently appreciate the privileges freely granted to every American boy rich or poor. Burns had to work hard and was sometimes led by evil companionship into low habits. But it is morally instructive to know that he was a good student and educated himself, in striking contrast to the loose ways and so-called aristocratic society-life of Lord Byron, on which I have just spoken. And certainly though the lords and earls of his day may have looked down upon Burns as a humble person, many of us have greatly enjoyed his pieces about the mouse and other rustic subjects, with their message of humble beauty—I am so sorry I have not got the time to quote some of them."

Mrs. George Edwin Mott gave ten minutes to Tennyson and Browning.

Mrs. Nat Hicks, a wry-faced, curiously sweet woman, so [126] awed by her betters that Carol wanted to kiss her, completed the day's grim task by a paper on "Other Poets." The other poets worthy of consideration were Coleridge, Wordsworth, Shelley, Gray, Mrs. Hemans, and Kipling.

Miss Ella Stowbody obliged with a recital of "The Recessional" and extracts from "Lalla Rookh." By request, she gave "An Old Sweetheat of Mine" as encore.

Gopher Prairie had finished the poets. It was ready for the next week's labor: English Fiction and Essays.

Mrs. Dawson besought, "Now we will have a discussion of the papers, and I am sure we shall all enjoy hearing from one who we hope to have as a new member, Mrs. Kennicott, who with her splendid literary training and all should be able to give us many pointers and—many helpful pointers."

Carol had warned herself not to be so "beastly supercilious." She had insisted that in the belated quest of these work-stained women was an aspiration which ought to stir her tears. "But they're so self-satisfied. They think they're doing Burns a favor. They don't believe they have a 'belated quest.' They're sure that they have culture salted and hung up." It was out of this stupor of doubt that Mrs. Dawson's summons roused her. She was in a panic. How could she speak without hurting them?

Mrs. Champ Perry leaned over to stroke her hand and whisper, "You look tired, dearie. Don't you talk unless you want to."

Affection flooded Carol; she was on her feet, searching for words and courtesies:

"The only thing in the way of suggestion—— I know you are following a definite program, but I do wish that now you've had such a splendid introduction, instead of going on with some other subject next year you could return and take up the poets more in detail. Especially actual quotations— even though their lives are so interesting and, as Mrs. Warren said, so morally instructive. And perhaps there are several poets not mentioned today whom it might be worth while considering—Keats, for instance, and Matthew Arnold and Rossetti and Swinburne. Swinburne would be such a —well, that is, such a contrast to life as we all enjoy it in our beautiful Middlewest——"

She saw that Mrs. Leonard Warren was not with her. She captured her by innocently continuing: [127]

"Unless perhaps Swinburne tends to be, uh, more outspoken than you, than we really like. What do you think, Mrs. Warren?"

The pastor's wife decided, "Why, you've caught my very thoughts, Mrs. Kennicott. Of course I have never *read* Swinburne, but years ago, when he was in vogue, I remember Mr. Warren saying that Swinburne (or was it Oscar Wilde? but anyway:) he said that though many so-called intellectual people posed and pretended to find beauty in Swinburne, there can never be genuine beauty without the message from the heart. But at the same time I do think you have an excellent idea, and though we have talked about Furnishings and China as the probable subject for next year, I believe that it would be nice if the program committee would try to work in another day entirely devoted to English poetry! In fact, Madame Chairman, I so move you."

When Mrs. Dawson's coffee and angel's-food had helped them to recover from the depression caused by thoughts of Shakespeare's death they all told Carol that it was a pleasure to have her with them. The membership committee retired to the sitting-room for three minutes and elected her a member. [128]

. . .

Before the program committee adjourned they took three minutes to decide which of the subjects suggested by the magazine *Culture Hints,* Furnishings and China, or The Bible as Literature, would be better for the coming year. There was one annoying incident. Mrs. Dr. Kennicott interfered and showed off again. She commented, "Don't you think that we already get enough of the Bible in our churches and Sunday Schools?"

Mrs. Leonard Warren, somewhat out of order but much more out of temper, cried, "Well upon my word! I didn't suppose there was any one who felt that we could get enough of the Bible! I guess if the Grand Old Book has withstood the attacks of infidels for these two thousand years it is worth our *slight* consideration!"

"Oh, I didn't mean——" Carol begged. Inasmuch as she did mean, it was hard to be extremely lucid. "But I wish, instead of limiting ourselves either to the Bible, or to anecdotes about the Brothers Adam's wigs, which *Culture Hints* seems to regard as the significant point about furniture, we could study some of the really stirring ideas that are springing up today— whether it's chemistry or anthropology or labor problems—the things that are going to mean so terribly much."

Everybody cleared her polite throat.

Madam Chairman inquired, "Is there any other discussion? Will some one make a motion to adopt the suggestion of Vida Sherwin—to take up Furnishings and China?"

It was adopted, unanimously.

"Checkmate!" murmured Carol, as she held up her hand.

Had she actually believed that she could plant a seed of liberalism in the blank wall of mediocrity? How had she fallen into the folly of trying to plant anything whatever in a wall so smooth and sun-glazed, and so satisfying to the happy sleepers within? [144]

CHAPTER XII

. . .

Then she met Champ Perry in the post office—and decided that in the history of the pioneers was the panacea for Gopher Prairie, for all of America. We have lost their sturdiness, she told herself. We must restore the last of the veterans to power and follow them on the backward path to the integrity of Lincoln, to the gaiety of settlers dancing in a saw-mill. [150]

. . .

She called on the Perrys at their rooms above Howland & Gould's grocery.

When they were already old they had lost the money, [15] which they had invested in an elevator. They had given up their beloved yellow brick house and moved into these rooms over a store, which were the Gopher Prairie equivalent of a flat. A broad stairway led from the street to the upper hall, along which were the doors of a lawyer's office, a dentist's, a photographer's "studio," the lodge-rooms of the Affiliated Order of Spartans and, at the back, the Perrys' apartment.

They received her (their first caller in a month) with aged fluttering tenderness. Mrs. Perry confided, "My, it's a shame we got to entertain you in such a cramped place. And there ain't any water except that ole iron sink outside in the hall, but still, as I say to Champ, beggars can't be choosers. 'Sides, the brick house was too big for me to sweep, and it was way out, and it's nice to be living down here among folks. Yes, we're glad to be here. But—— Some day, maybe we can have a house of our own again. We're saving up—— Oh, dear, if we could have our own home! But these rooms are real nice, ain't they!"

As old people will, the world over, they had moved as much as possible of their familiar furniture into this small space. Carol had none of the superiority she felt toward Mrs. Lyman Cass's plutocratic parlor. She was at home here. She noted with tenderness all the makeshifts: the darned chair-arms, the patent rocker covered with sleazy cretonne, the pasted strips of paper mending the birch-bark napkin-rings labeled "Papa" and "Mama."

She hinted of her new enthusiasm. To find one of the "young folks" who took them seriously, heartened the Perrys, and she easily drew from them the principles by which Gopher Prairie should be born again—should again become amusing to live in.

This was their philosophy complete . . . in the era of aeroplanes and syndicalism:

The Baptist Church (and, somewhat less, the Methodist, Congregational, and Presbyterian Churches) is the perfect, the divinely ordained standard in music, oratory, philanthropy, and ethics. "We don't need all this new-fangled science, or this terrible Higher Criticism that's ruining our young men in colleges. What we need is to get back to the true Word of God, and a good sound belief in hell, like we used to have it preached to us."

The Republican Party, the Grand Old Party of Blaine and [152] McKinley, is the agent of the Lord and of the Baptist Church in temporal affairs.

All socialists ought to be hanged.

"Harold Bell Wright is a lovely writer, and he teaches such good morals in his novels, and folks say he's made prett' near a million dollars out of 'em."

People who make more than ten thousand a year or less than eight hundred are wicked.

Europeans are still wickeder.

It doesn't hurt any to drink a glass of beer on a warm day, but anybody who touches wine is headed straight for hell.

Virgins are not so virginal as they used to be.

Nobody needs drug-store ice cream; pie is good enough for anybody.

The farmers want too much for their wheat.

The owners of the elevator-company expect too much for the salaries they pay.

There would be no more trouble or discontent in the world if everybody worked as hard as Pa did when he cleared our first farm. [153]

. . .

CHAPTER XV

. . . She gave a reception for the Thanatopsis Club. But her real acquiring of merit was in calling upon that Mrs. Bogart whose gossipy opinion was so valuable to a doctor.

Though the Bogart house was next door she had entered it but three times. . . . [183]

The parlor was distinguished by an expanse of rag carpet from which, as they entered, Mrs. Bogart hastily picked one sad dead fly. In the center of the carpet was a rug depicting a red Newfoundland dog, reclining in a green and yellow daisy field and labeled "Our Friend." The parlor organ, tall and thin, was adorned with a mirror partly circular, partly square, and partly diamond-shaped, and with brackets holding a pot of geraniums, a mouth-organ, and a copy of "The Oldtime Hymnal." On the center table was a Sears-Roebuck mail-order catalogue, a silver frame with photographs of the Baptist Church and of an elderly clergyman, and an aluminum tray containing a rattlesnake's rattle and a broken spectacle-lens.

Mrs. Bogart spoke of the eloquence of the Reverend Mr. Zitterel, the coldness of cold days, the price of poplar wood, Dave Dyer's new hair-cut, and Cy Bogart's essential piety. "As I said to his Sunday School teacher, Cy may be a little wild, but that's because he's got so much better brains than a lot of these boys, and this farmer that claims he caught Cy stealing 'beggies, is a liar, and I ought to have the law on him."

Mrs. Bogart went thoroughly into the rumor that the girl waiter at Billy's Lunch was not all she might be—or, rather, was quite all she might be.

"My lands, what can you expect when everybody knows what her mother was? And if these traveling salesmen would let her alone she would be all right, though I certainly don't believe she ought to be allowed to think she can pull the wool over our eyes. The sooner she's sent to the school for incorrigible girls down at Sauk Centre, the better for all and—— Won't you just have a cup of coffee, Carol dearie, I'm sure you won't mind old Aunty Bogart calling you by your first name when you think how long I've known Will, and I was such a friend of his dear lovely mother when she lived here and—was that fur cap expensive? But—— Don't you think it's awful, the way folks talk in this town?" [184]

Mrs. Bogart hitched her chair nearer. Her large face, with its disturbing collection of moles and long black hairs, wrinkled cunningly. She showed her decayed teeth in a reproving smile, and in the confidential voice of one who scents stale bedroom scandal she breathed:

"Just don't see how folks can act like they do. You don't know the things that go on under cover. This town—why it's only the religious training I've given Cy that's kept him so innocent of things. Just the other day—— I never pay no attention to stories, but I heard it mighty good and straight that Harry Haydock is carrying on with a girl that clerks in a store down in Minneapolis, and poor Juanita not knowing anything about it—though maybe it's the judgment of God, because before she married Harry she acted up with more than one boy—— Well, I don't like to say it, and maybe I ain't up-to-date, like Cy says, but I always believe a lady shouldn't even give names to all sorts of dreadful things, but just the same I know there was at least one case where Juanita and a boy—well, they were just dreadful. And—and—— Then there's that Ole Jenson the grocer, that thinks he's so plaguey smart, and I know he made up to a farmer's wife and—— And this awful man Bjornstam that does chores, and Nat Hicks and ——"

There was, it seemed, no person in town who was not living a life of shame except Mrs. Bogart, and naturally she resented it.

She knew. She had always happened to be there. Once, she whispered, she was going by when an indiscreet window-shade had been left up a couple of inches. Once she had noticed a man and woman holding hands, and right at a Methodist sociable!

"Another thing—— Heaven knows I never want to start trouble, but I can't help what I see from my back steps, and I notice your hired girl Bea carrying on with the grocery boys and all——"

"Mrs. Bogart! I'd trust Bea as I would myself!"

"Oh, dearie, you don't understand me! I'm sure she's a good girl. I mean she's green, and I hope that none of these horrid young men that there are around town will get her into trouble! It's their parents' fault, letting them run wild and hear evil things. If I had my way there wouldn't be none of them, not boys nor girls neither, allowed to know anything [185] about—about things till they was married. It's terrible the bald way that some folks talk. It just shows and gives away what awful thoughts they got inside them, and there's nothing can cure them except coming right to God and kneeling down like I do at prayer-meeting every Wednesday evening, and saying, 'Oh God, I would be a miserable sinner except for thy grace.'

"I'd make every last one of these brats go to Sunday School and learn to think about nice things 'stead of about cigarettes and goings-on—and these dances they have at the lodges are the worst thing that ever happened to this town, lot of young men squeezing girls and finding out—— Oh, it's dreadful. I've told the mayor he ought to put a stop to them and—— There was one boy in this town, I don't want to be suspicious or uncharitable but——"

It was half an hour before Carol escaped. [186]

. . .

RING LARDNER
1885–1933

Barbershop Gossip

"HAIRCUT"

Ring Lardner knew the small town of America well. He was born in Niles, Michigan, and lived there until 1905, when he became a cub reporter for the South Bend (Indiana) *Times*. In time he joined other newspapers as a columnist, a sports writer, and an editor. One of his major interests, baseball, provided the inspiration for *You Know Me Al* (1916), the letters of an illiterate baseball player.

Lardner's reputation is based principally upon his naturalistic short fiction, in which he employs the most successful dialect since *The Adventures of Huckleberry Finn*. A folksy humor—achieved by odd syntax, misspellings, and mispronunciations—often softens what would seem to be harsh judgments of character.His character types and the vernacular they use place Lardner in the tradition of native American humorists and prompted H. L. Mencken, an authority on the varieties of language in America, to extol Lardner's mastery of idiom. Lardner himself explained his success by saying, "I just listen hard."

From 1925 until 1929 Lardner wrote a number of his most highly regarded short stories, many of them appearing in either *The Love Nest and Other Stories* (1926) or *Round Up* (1929).

Lardner has appeal for two kinds of readers—the uncritical, who accept his humor without recognizing any particular judgment, and the serious, who see in Lardner's satire and irony a revelation of an underlying evil. "Haircut," the selection that follows, provides something for both kinds of reader. The melodramatic plot, unfolded by a first-person narration in a small-town barber shop, is balanced by Lardner's attack on American folk humor through the barber-narrator's accounts of Jim Kendall's practical jokes. Typically for Lardner, there are no symbols, no unsual settings; the story concerns itself with exterior behavior as revealed by actions and speech. Irony appears in the barber's admiration for Jim Kendall and his sadistic practical jokes. The barber fails to see Kendall's viciousness, appreciating instead only the humor ("he certainly was a card") of his actions.

174

"HAIRCUT"

I got another barber that comes over from Carterville and helps me out Saturdays, but the rest of the time I can get along all right alone. You can see for yourself that this ain't no New York City and besides that, the most of the boys work all day and don't have no leisure to drop in here and get themselves prettied up.

You're a newcomer, ain't you? I thought I hadn't seen you round before. I hope you like it good enough to stay. As I say, we ain't no New York City or Chicago, but we have pretty good times. Not as good, though, since Jim Kendall got killed. When he was alive, him and Hod Myers used to keep this town in an uproar. I bet they was more laughin' done here than any town its size in America.

Jim was comical, and Hod was pretty near a match for him. Since Jim's gone, Hod tries to hold his end up just the same as ever, but [31] it's tough goin' when you ain't got nobody to kind of work with.

They used to be plenty fun in here Saturdays. This place is jam-packed Saturdays, from four o'clock on. Jim and Hod would show up right after their supper, round six o'clock. Jim would set himself down in that big chair, nearest the blue spittoon. Whoever had been settin' in that chair, why they'd get up when Jim come in and give it to him.

You'd of thought it was a reserved seat like they have sometimes in a theater. Hod would generally always stand or walk up and down, on some Saturdays, of course, he'd be settin' in this chair part of the time, gettin' a haircut.

Well, Jim would set here a w'ile without openin' his mouth only to spit, and then finally he'd say to me, "Whitey,"—my right name, that is, my first name, is Dick, but everybody round here calls me Whitey—Jim would say, "Whitey, your nose looks like a rosebud tonight. You must of been drinkin' some of your aw de cologne."

So I'd say, "No, Jim, but you look like [32] you'd been drinkin' somethin' of that kind or somethin' worse."

Jim would have to laugh at that, but then he'd speak up and say, "No, I ain't had nothin' to drink, but that ain't sayin' I wouldn't like somethin'. I wouldn't even mind if it was wood alcohol."

Then Hod Meyers would say, "Neither would your wife." That would set everybody to laughin' because Jim and his wife wasn't on very good terms. She'd of divorced him only they wasn't no chance to get alimony and she didn't have no way to take care of herself and the kids. She couldn't never understand Jim. He *was* kind of rough, but a good fella at heart.

Him and Hod had all kinds of sport with Milt Sheppard. I don't suppose you've seen Milt. Well, he's got an Adam's apple that looks more like a mushmelon. So I'd be shavin' Milt and when I'd start to shave down here on his neck, Hod would holler, "Hey, Whitey, wait a minute! Before you cut into it, let's make up a pool and see who can guess closest to the number of seeds." [33]

And Jim would say, "If Milt hadn't of been so hoggish, he'd of ordered a half a cantaloupe instead of a whole one and it might not of stuck in his throat."

All the boys would roar at this and Milt himself would force a smile, though the joke was on him. Jim certainly was a card!

There's his shavin' mug, settin' on the shelf, right next to Charley Vail's. "Charles M. Vail." That's the druggist. He comes in regular for his shave, three times a week. And Jim's is the cup next to Charley's. "James H. Kendall." Jim won't need no shavin' mug no more, but I'll leave it there just the same for old time's sake. Jim certainly was a character!

Years ago, Jim used to travel for a canned goods concern over in Carterville. They sold canned goods, Jim had the whole northern half of the State and was on the road five days out of every week. He'd drop in here Saturdays and tell his experiences for that week. It was rich.

I guess he paid more attention to playin' jokes than makin' sales. Finally the concern [34] let him out and he come right home here and told everybody he'd been fired instead of sayin' he'd resigned like most fellas would of.

It was a Saturday and the shop was full and Jim got up out of that chair and says, "Gentlemen, I got an important announcement to make. I been fired from my job."

Well, they asked him if he was in earnest and he said he was and nobody could think of nothin' to say till Jim finally broke the ice himself. He says, "I been sellin' canned goods and now I'm canned goods myself."

You see, the concern he'd been workin' for was a factory that made canned goods. Over in Carterville. And now Jim said he was canned himself. He was certainly a card!

Jim had a great trick that he used to play w'ile he was travelin'. For instance, he'd be ridin' on a train and they'd come to some little town like, well, like, we'll say, like Benton. Jim would look out the train window and read the signs on the stores.

For instance, they'd be a sign, "Henry Smith, Dry Goods." Well, Jim would write down the name and the name of the town and [35] when he got back to wherever he was goin' he'd mail back a postal card to Henry Smith at Benton and not sign no name to it, but he'd write on the card, well, somethin' like "Ask your wife about that book agent that spent the afternoon last week," or "Ask your Missus who kept her from gettin' lonesome the last time you was in Carterville." And he'd sign the card, "A Friend."

Of course, he never knew what really come of none of these jokes, but he could picture what *probably* happened and that was enough.

Jim didn't work very steady after he lost his position with the Carterville people. What he did earn, doin' odd jobs round town, why he spent pretty near all of it on gin and his family might of starved if the stores hadn't of carried them along. Jim's wife tried her hand at dressmakin', but they ain't nobody goin' to get rich makin' dresses in this town.

As I say, she'd of divorced Jim, only she seen that she couldn't support herself and the kids and she was always hopin' that some day Jim would cut out his habits and give her more than two or three dollars a week. [36]

They was a time when she would go to whoever he was workin' for and ask them to give her his wages, but after she done this once or twice, he beat her to it by borrowin' most of his pay in advance. He told it all round town, how he had outfoxed his Missus. He certainly was a caution!

But he wasn't satisfied with just outwittin' her. He was sore the way she had acted, tryin' to grab off his pay. And he made up his mind he'd get even. Well, he waited till Evans's Circus was advertised to come to town. Then he told his wife and two kiddies that he was goin' to take them to the circus. The day of the circus, he told them he would get the tickets and meet them outside the entrance to the tent.

Well, he didn't have no intentions of bein' there or buyin' tickets or nothin'. He got full of gin and laid round Wright's poolroom all day. His wife and the kids waited and waited and of course he didn't show up. His wife didn't have a dime with her, or nowhere else, I guess. So she finally had to tell the kids it was all off and they cried like they wasn't never goin' to stop. [37]

Well, it seems, w'ile they was cryin', Doc Stair came along and he asked what was the matter, but Mrs. Kendall was stubborn and wouldn't tell him, but the kids told him and he insisted on takin' them and their mother in the show. Jim found this out afterwards and it was one reason why he had it in for Doc Stair.

Doc Stair come here about a year and a half ago. He's mighty handsome young fella and his clothes always look like he has them made to order. He goes to Detroit two or three times a year and w'ile he's there he must have a tailor take his measure and then make him a suit to order. They cost pretty near twice as much, but they fit a whole lot better than if you just bought them in a store.

For a w'ile everbody was wonderin' why a young doctor like Doc Stair should come to a town like this where we already got Old Doc Gamble and Doc Foote that's both been here for years and all the practice in town was always divided between the two of them.

Then they was a story got around that Doc Stair's gal had throwed him over, a gal up in the Northern Peninsula somewheres, and the [38] reason he come here was to hide himself away and forget it. He said himself that he thought they wen't nothin' like general practice in a place like ours to fit a man to be a good all round doctor. And that's why he'd came.

Anyways, it wasn't long before he was makin enough to live on, though they tell me that he never dunned nobody for what they owed him, and the folks here certainly has got the owin' habit, even in my business. If I had all that was comin' to me for just shaves alone, I could go to Carterville and put up at the Mercer for a week and see a different picture every night. For instance, they's old George Purdy—but I guess I shouldn't ought to be gossipin'.

Well, last year, our coroner died, died of the flu. Ken Beatty, that was his name. He was the coroner. So they had to choose another man to be coroner in his place and they picked Doc Stair. He laughed at first and said he didn't want it, but they made him take it. It ain't no job than anybody would fight for and what a man makes out of it in a year would just buy seeds for their garden. Doc's [39] the kind, though, that can't say no to nothin' if you keep at him long enough.

But I was goin' to tell you about a poor boy we got here in town—Paul Dickson. He fell out of a tree when he was about ten years old. Lit on his head and it done somethin' to him and he ain't never been right. No harm in him, but just silly. Jim Kendall used to call him cuckoo; that's a name Jim had for anybody that was off his head, only he called people's head their bean. That was another of his gags, callin' head bean and callin' crazy people cuckoo. Only poor Paul ain't crazy, just silly.

You can imagine that Jim used to have all kinds of fun with Paul. He'd send him to the White Front Garage for a left-handed monkey wrench. Of course they ain't no such a thing as a left-handed monkey wrench.

And once we had a kind of a fair here and they was a baseball game between the fats and the leans and before the game started Jim called Paul over and sent him way down to Schrader's hardware store to get a key for the pitcher's box. [40]

They wasn't nothin' in the way of gags that Jim couldn't think up, when he put his mind to it.

Poor Paul was always kind of suspicious of people, maybe on account of how Jim had kept foolin' him. Paul wouldn't have much to do with anybody only his own mother and Doc Stair and a girl here in town named Julie Gregg. That is, she ain't a girl no more, but pretty near thirty or over.

When Doc first came to town, Paul seemed to feel like here was a real friend and he hung round Doc's office most of the w'ile; the only time he wasn't there was when he'd gone home to eat or sleep or when he seen Julie Gregg doin' her shoppin'.

When he looked out Doc's window and seen her, he'd run downstairs and join her and tag along with her to the different stores. The poor boy was crazy about Julie and she always treated him mighty nice and made him feel like he was welcome, though of course it wasn't nothin' but pity on her side.

Doc done all he could to improve Paul's mind and he told me once that he really [41] thought the boy was gettin' better, that they was times when he was as bright and sensible as anybody else.

But I was going' to tell you about Julie Gregg. Old Man Gregg was in the lumber business, but got to drinkin' and lost the most of his money and when he died, he didn't leave nothin' but the house and just enough insurance for the girl to skimp along on.

Her mother was a kind of a half invalid and didn't hardly ever leave the house. Julie wanted to sell the place and move somewhere else after the old man died, but the mother said she born here and would die here. It was tough on Julie, as the young people round this town—well, she's too good for them.

She's been away to school and Chicago and New York and different places and they ain't no subject she can't talk on, where you take the rest of the young folks here and you mention anything to them outside of Gloria Swanson or Tommy Meighan and they think you're delirious. Did you see Gloria in Wages of Virtue? You missed somethin'!

Well, Doc Stair hadn't been here more than [42] a week when he come in one day to get shaved and I recognized who he was as he had been pointed out to me, so I told him about my old lady. She's been ailin, for a couple of years and either Doc Gamble or Doc Foote, neither one, seemed to be helpin' her. So he said he would come out and see her, but if she was able to get out herself, it would be better to bring her to his office where he could make a completer examination.

So I took her to his office and w'ile I was waitin' for her in the reception room, in come Julie Gregg. When somebody comes in Doc Stair's office, they's a bell that rings in his inside office so as he can tell they's somebody to see him.

So he left my old lady inside and come out to the front office and that's the first time him and Julie met and I guess it was what they call love at first sight. But it wasn't fifty-fifty. This young fella was the slickest lookin' fella she'd ever seen in this town and she went wild over him. To him she was just a young lady that wanted to see the doctor.

She'd came on about the same business I [43] had. Her mother had been doctorin' for years with Doc Gamble and Doc Foote and without no result. So she'd heard they was a new doc in town and decided to give him a try. He promised to call and see her mother that same day.

I said a minute ago that it was love at first sight on her part. I'm not only judgin' by how she acted afterwards but how she looked at him that first day in his office. I ain't no mind reader, but it was wrote all over her face that she was gone.

Now Jim Kendall, besides bein' a jokesmith and a pretty good drinker, well, Jim was quite a lady-killer. I guess he run pretty wild durin' the time he was on the road for them Carterville people, and besides that, he'd had a couple little affairs of the heart right here in town. As I say, his wife could of divorced him, only she couldn't.

But Jim was like the majority of men, and women, too, I guess. He wanted what he couldn't get. He wanted Julie Gregg and worked his head off tryin' to land her. Only he'd of said bean instead of head. [44]

Well, Jim's habits and his jokes didn't appeal to Julie and of course he was a married man, so he didn't have no more chance than, well, than a rabbit. That's an expression of Jim's himself. When somebody didn't have no chance to get elected or somethin', Jim would always say they didn't have no more chance than a rabbit.

He didn't make no bones about how he felt. Right in here, more than once, in front of the whole crowd, he said he was stuck on Julie and anybody that could get her for him was welcome to his house and wife and kids included. But she wouldn't have nothin' to do with him; wouldn't even speak to him on the street. He finally seen he wasn't gettin' nowheres with his usual line so he decided to try the rough stuff. He went right up to her house one evenin' and when she opened the door he forced his way in and grabbed her. But she broke loose and before he could stop her, she run in the next room and locked the door and phoned to Joe Barnes. Joe's the marshal. Jim could hear who she was phonin' to and he beat it before Joe got there. [45]

Joe was an old friend of Julie's pa. Joe went to Jim the next day and told him what would happen if he ever done it again.

I don't know how the news of this little affair leaked out. Chances is that Joe Barnes told his wife and she told somebody else's wife and they told their husband. Anyways, it did leak out and Hod Meyers had the nerve to kid Jim about it, right here in this shop. Jim didn't deny nothin' and kind of laughed it off and said for us all to wait; that lots of people had tried to make a monkey out of him, but he always got even.

Meanw'ile everybody in town was wise to Julie's bein' wild mad over Doc. I don't suppose she had any idear how her face changed when him and her was together; of course she couldn't of, or she'd of kept away from him. And she didn't know that we was all noticin' how many times she made excuses to go up to his office or pass it on the other side of the street and look up in his window to see if he was there. I felt sorry for her and so did most other people.

Hod Meyers kept rubbin' it into Jim about [46] how the Doc had cut him out. Jim didn't pay no attention to the kiddin' and you could see he was plannin' one of his jokes.

One trick Jim had was the knack of changin' his voice. He could make you think he was a girl talkin' and he could mimic any man's voice. To show you how good he was along this line, I'll tell you the joke he played on me once.

You know, in most towns of any size, when a man is dead and needs a shave, why the barber that shaves him soaks him five dollars for the job; that is, he don't soak *him,* but whoever ordered the shave. I just charge three dollars because personally I don't mind much shaving a dead person. They lay a whole lot stiller than live customers. The only thing is that you don't feel like talkin' to them and you get kind of lonesome.

Well, about the coldest day we ever had here, two years ago last winter, the phone rung at the house w'ile I was home to dinner and I answered the phone and it was a woman's voice and she said she was Mrs. John Scott and her husband was dead and would I come out and shave him. [47]

Old John had always been a good customer of mine. But they live seven miles out in the country, on the Streeter road. Still I didn't see how I could say no.

So I said I would be there, but would have to come in a jitney and it might cost three or four dollars besides the price of the shave. So she, or the voice, it said that was all right, so I got Frank Abbott to drive me out to the place and when I got there, who should open the door but old John himself! He wasn't no more dead than, well, than a rabbit.

It didn't take no private detective to figure out who had played me this little joke. Nobody could of thought it up but Jim Kendall. He certainly was a card!

I tell you this incident just to show you how he could disguise his voice and make you believe it was somebody else talkin'. I'd of swore it was Mrs. Scott had called me. Anyways, some woman.

Well, Jim waited till he had Doc Stair's voice down pat; then he went after revenge.

He called Julie up on a night when he knew Doc was over in Carterville. She never questioned but what it was Doc's voice. Jim said he must [48] see her that night; he couldn't wait no longer to tell her somethin'. She was all excited and told him to come to the house. But he said he was expectin' an important long-distance call and wouldn't she please forget her manners for once and come to his office. He said they couldn't nothin' hurt her and nobody would see her and he just *must* talk to her a little w'ile. Well, poor Julie fell for it.

Doc always keeps a night light in his office, so it looked to Julie like they was somebody there.

Meanwhile Jim Kendall had went to Wrightson's poolroom, where they was a whole gang amusin' themselves. The most of them had drank plenty of gin, and they was a rough bunch when sober. They was always strong for Jim's jokes and when he told them to come with him and see some fun they give up their card games and pool games and followed along.

Doc's office is on the second floor. Right outside his door they's a flight of stairs leadin' [49] to the floor above. Jim and his gang hid in the dark behind these stairs.

Well, Julie come up to Doc's door and rung the bell and they was nothin' doin'. She rung it again and she rung it seven or eight times. Then she tried the door and found it locked. Then Jim made some kind of noise and she heard it and waited a minute, and then she says, "Is that you, Ralph?" Ralph is Doc's first name.

They was no answer and it must of came to her all of a sudden that she'd been bunked. She pretty near fell downstairs and the whole gang after her. They chased her all the way home, hollerin', "Is that you, Ralph?" and "Oh, Ralphie, dear, it that you?" Jim says he couldn't holler it himself, as he was laughin' too hard.

Poor Julie! She didn't show up here on Main Street for a long, long time afterward.

And of course Jim and his gang told everybody in town, everybody but Doc Stair. They was scared to tell him, and he might of never knowed only for Paul Dickson. The poor cuckoo, as Jim called him, he was here in the [50] shop one night when Jim was still gloatin' yet over what he'd done to Julie. And Paul took in as much of it as he could understand and he run to Doc with the story.

It's a cinch Doc went up in the air and swore he'd make Jim suffer. But it was a kind of a delicate thing, because if it got out that he had beat Jim up, Julie was bound to hear of it and then she'd know that Doc knew and of course knowin' that he knew would make it worse for her than ever. He was going' to do somethin', but it took a lot of figurin'.

Well, it was a couple days later when Jim was here in the shop again, and so was the cuckoo. Jim was goin' duck-shootin' the next day and had came in lookin' for Hod Meyers to go with him. I happened to know that Hod had went over to Carterville and wouldn't be home till the end of the week. So Jim said he hated to go alone and he guessed he would call it off. Then poor Paul spoke up and said if Jim would take him he would go along. Jim thought a w'ile and then he said, well, he guessed a half-wit was better than nothin'.

I suppose he was plottin' to get Paul out in [51] the boat and play some joke on him, like pushing him in the water. Anyways, he said Paul could go. He asked him had he ever shot a duck and Paul said no, he'd never even had a gun in his hands. So Jim said he could set in the boat and watch him and if he behaved himself, he might lend him his gun for a couple of shots. They made a date to meet in the mornin' and that's the last I seen of Jim alive.

Next mornin', I hadn't been open more than ten minutes when Doc Stair come in. He looked kind of nervous. He asked me had I seen Paul Dickson. I said no, but I knew where he was, out duck-shootin' with Jim Kendall. So Doc says that's what he had heard, and he couldn't understand it because Paul had told him he wouldn't never have no more to do with Jim as long as he lived.

He said Paul had told him about the joke Jim had played on Julie.

He said Paul had asked him what he thought of the joke and the Doc had told him that anybody that would do a thing like than ought not to be let live.

I said it had been a kind of a raw thing, but [52] Jim just couldn't resist no kind of a joke, no matter how raw. I said I thought he was all right at heart, but just bubblin' over with mischief. Doc turned and walked out.

At noon he got a phone call from old John Scott. The lake where Jim and Paul had went shootin' is on John's place. Paul had came runnin' up to the house a few minutes before and said they'd been an accident. Jim had shot a few ducks and then give the gun to Paul and told him to try his luck. Paul hadn't never handled a gun and he was nervous. He was shakin' so hard that he couldn't control the gun. He let fire and Jim sunk back in the boat, dead.

Doc Stair, bein' the coroner, jumped in Frank Abbott's flivver and rushed out to Scott's farm. Paul and old John was down on the shore of the lake. Paul had rowed the boat to shore, but they'd left the body in it, waitin' for Doc to come.

Doc examined the body and said they might as well fetch it back to town. They was no use leavin' it there or callin' a jury, as it was a plain case of accidental shootin'. [53]

Personally I wouldn't never leave a person shoot a gun in the same boat I was in unless I was sure they knew somethin' about guns. Jim was a sucker to leave a new beginner have his gun, let alone a half-wit. It probably served Jim right, what he got. But we still miss him round here. He certainly was a card!

Comb it wet or dry? [54]

ERSKINE CALDWELL
1903–

Boredom
in a Georgia Town

"SATURDAY
AFTERNOON"

Of the thousands of theatergoers who saw the adaptation of Erskine Caldwell's novel *Tobacco Road* in the seven years it ran on Broadway, many
left the theater convinced they had seen tragedy treated comically. And
many of the millions who have read Caldwell's books realize only occasionally how serious he is in presenting the less savory aspects of southern
rural life.

Yet Caldwell's strong sense of social justice is not negated by his presenting the brutal facts of the human condition with a grotesque humor or
with extreme candor. His subject is chiefly the Georgia folk he knows best—
the sharecroppers and poor whites of the South—and he vividly, sometimes
shockingly, depicts the decadence and degeneration of the South.

Caldwell was born in rural Georgia, the son of an itinerant Presbyterian minister. During his boyhood the family moved about from church
to church on a meager income. Caldwell attended the University of Virginia
and the University of Pennsylvania as well as Erskine College in South
Carolina. He has held a variety of jobs—professional football player, body-
guard, real estate agent—and has reported widely on trips abroad and
served as a war correspondent. A prolific writer, he has seen his books enjoy
enormous sales, particularly in the paperback market. Lynching, rape,
murder, and violence fill his books.

Because of his obsession with the South, Caldwell is thought of as a
regionalist, and because of *Tobacco Road* (1932), *God's Little Acre* (1933),
Tragic Ground (1944), *Georgia Boy* (1950), and other novels, he is thought
of as a novelist. But his real talent is for short fiction, as "Saturday Afternoon" amply illustrates. Here is the classic lynching story—macabre, nau-
seating, unforgettably painful, and real. The style of the story is its most

impressive feature, for Caldwell has, in his flat, deadpan emotionless manner of telling the tale, established his contempt for the flat, deadpan, emotionless manner in which these small-towners murder a fellow citizen.

"Saturday Afternoon" is told from the point of view of the town loafers, who are simply unconcerned about the victim. Murdering a Negro is one way to relieve the stifling boredom of a hot Saturday afternoon in a Georgia village.

"SATURDAY AFTERNOON"

Tom Denny shoved the hunk of meat out of his way and stretched out on the meatblock. He wanted to lie on his back and rest. The meatblock was the only comfortable place in the butcher-shop where a man could stretch out and Tom just had to rest every once in a while. He could prop his foot on the edge of the block, swing the other leg across his knee and be fairly comfortable with a hunk of rump steak under his head. The meat was nice and cool just after it came from the icehouse. Tom did that. He wanted to rest himself a while and he had to be comfortable on the meatblock. He kicked off his shoes so he could wiggle his toes.

Tom's butcher-shop did not have a very pleasant smell. Strangers who went in to buy Tom's meat for the first time were always asking him what it was that had died between the walls. The smell got worse and worse year after year.

Tom bit off a chew of tobacco and made himself comfortable on the meatblock.

There was a swarm of flies buzzing around the place: those lazy, stinging, fat and greasy flies that lived in Tom's butcher-shop. A screen door at the front kept out some of them that tried to get inside, but if they were used to coming in and filling up on fresh blood on the meatblock they knew how to fly around to the back door where there had never been a screen.

Everybody ate Tom's meat, and liked it. There was no other butcher-shop in town. You walked in and said, "Hello, Tom. How's everything today?" "Everything's slick as a whistle with me, but my old woman's got the chills and fever again." Then after Tom had finished telling how it felt to have chills and fever, you said, "I want a pound of pork chops, Tom." And Tom said, "By gosh, I'll git it for you right away." While you stood

Erskine Caldwell, "Saturday Afternoon," from *Jackpot* (New York: Duell, Sloan and Pearce, 1931). Copyright 1930 by Boris J. Israel; renewed 1957 by Erskine Caldwell. Reprinted by permission of Little, Brown and Co.

around waiting for the chops Tom turned the hunk of beef over two or three time businesslike and hacked off a pound of pork for you. If you wanted veal it was all the [643] same to Tom. He slammed the hunk of beef around several times making a great to-do, and got the veal for you. He pleased everybody. Ask Tom for any kind of meat you could name, and Tom had it right there on the meatblock waiting to be cut off and weighed.

Tom brushed the flies off his face and took a little snooze. It was mid-day. The country people had not yet got to town. It was laying-by season and everybody was working right up to twelve o'clock sun time, which was half an hour slower than railroad time. There was hardly anybody in town at this time of day, even though it was Saturday. All the town people who had wanted some of Tom's meat for Saturday dinner had already got what they needed, and it was too early in the day to buy Sunday meat. The best time of day to get meat from Tom if it was to be kept over until Sunday was about ten o'clock Saturday night. Then you could take it home and be fairly certain that it would not turn bad before noon the next day—if the weather was not too hot.

The flies buzzed and lit on Tom's mouth and nose and Tom knocked them away with his hand and tried to sleep on the meatblock with the cool hunk of rump steak under his head. The tobacco juice kept trying to trickle down his throat and Tom had to keep spitting it out. There was a cigar-box half full of sawdust in the corner behind the showcase where livers and brains were kept for display, but he could not quite spit that far from the position he was in. The tobacco juice splattered on the floor midway between the meatblock and cigar-box. What little of it dropped on the piece of rump steak did not really matter: most people cleaned their meat before they cooked and ate it, and it would all wash off.

But the danged flies! They kept on buzzing and stinging as mean as ever, and there is nothing any meaner than a lazy, well-fed, butcher-shop fly in the summer-time, anyway. Tom knocked them off his face and spat them off his mouth the best he could without having to move too much. After a while he let them alone.

Tom was enjoying a good little snooze when Jim Baxter came running through the back door from the barber-shop on the corner. Jim was Tom's partner and he came in sometimes on busy days to help out. He was a great big man, almost twice as large as Tom. He always wore a big wide-brimmed black hat and a blue shirt with the sleeves [644] rolled up above his elbows. He had a large egg-shaped belly over which his breeches were always slipping down. When he walked he tugged at his breeches all the time, pulling them up over the top of his belly. But they were always working down until it looked as if they were ready to drop to the ground any minute and trip him. Jim would not wear suspenders. A belt was more sporty-looking.

Tom was snoozing away when Jim ran in the back door and grabbed him by the shoulders. A big handful of flies had gone to sleep on Tom's mouth. Jim shooed them off.

"Hey, Tom, Tom!" Jim shouted breathlessly. "Wake up, Tom! Wake up quick!"

Tom jumped to the floor and pulled on his shoes. He had become so accustomed to people coming in and waking him up to buy a quarter's worth of steak or a quarter's worth of ham that he had mistaken Jim for a customer. He rubbed the back of his hands over his mouth to take away the fly-stings.

"What the hell!" he sputtered, looking up and seeing Jim standing there beside him. "What do you want?"

"Come on, Tom! Git your gun! We're going after a nigger down the creek a ways."

"God Almighty, Jim!" Tom shouted, now fully awake. He clutched Jim's arm and begged: "You going to git a nigger, sure enough?"

"You're damn right. Tom. You know that gingerbread nigger what used to work on the railroad a long time back? Him's the nigger we're going to git. And we're going to git him good and proper, the yellow-face coon. He said something to Fred Jackson's oldest gal down the road yonder about an hour ago. Fred told us all about it over at the barber-shop. Come on, Tom. We got to hurry. I expect we'll jerk him up pretty soon now."

Tom tied on his shoes and ran across the street behind Jim. Tom had his shotgun under his arm, and Jim had pulled the cleaver out of the meat-block. They'd get the God-damn nigger all right—God damn his yellow hide to hell!

Tom climbed into an automobile with some other men. Jim jumped on the running-board of another car just as it was leaving. There were thirty or forty cars headed for the creek bottom already and more getting ready to start. [645]

They had a place already picked out at the creek. There was a clearing in the woods by the road and there was just enough room to do the job like it should be done. Plenty of dry brushwood nearby and a good-sized sweet-gum tree in the middle of the clearing. The automobiles stopped and the men jumped out in a hurry. Some others had gone for Will Maxie. Will was the gingerbread Negro. They would probably find him at home laying by his cotton. Will could grow good cotton. He cut out all the grass first, and then he banked his rows with earth. Everybody else laid by his cotton without going to the trouble of taking out the grass. But Will was a pretty smart Negro. And he could raise a lot of corn too, to the acre. He always cut out the grass before he laid-by his corn. But nobody liked Will. He made too much money by taking out the grass before laying-by his cotton and corn. He made more money than Tom and Jim made in the butcher-shop selling people meat.

Doc Cromer had sent his boy down from the drugstore with half a dozen cases of Coca-Cola and a piece of ice in a washtub. The tub had some muddy water put in from the creek, then the chunk of ice, and then three cases of Coca-Cola. When they were gone the boy would put the other three cases in the tub and give the dopes a chance to cool. Everybody likes to drink a lot of dopes when they are nice and cold.

Tom went out in the woods to take a drink of corn with Jim and Hubert Wells. Hubert always carried a jug of corn with him wherever he happened to be going. He made the whiskey himself at his own still and got a fairly good living by selling it around the courthouse and the barber-shop. Hubert made the best corn in the county.

Will Maxie was coming up the big road in a hurry. A couple of dozen men were behind him poking him with sticks. Will was getting old. He had a wife and three grown daughters, all married and settled. Will was a pretty good Negro too, minding his own business, stepping out of the road when he met a white man, and otherwise behaving himself. But nobody liked Will. He made too much money by taking the grass out of his cotton before is was laid-by.

Will came running up the road and the men steered him into the clearing. It was all fixed. There was a big pile of brushwood and a [646] trace-chain for his neck and one for his feet. That would hold him. There were two or three cans of gasoline, too.

Doc Cromer's boy was doing a good business with his Coca-Colas. Only five or six bottles of the first three cases were left in the washtub. He was getting ready to put the other cases in now and give the dopes a chance to get nice and cool. Everybody likes to have a dope every once in a while.

The Cromer boy would probably sell out and have to go back to town and bring back several more cases. And yet there was not such a big crowd today, either. It was the hot weather that made people have to drink a lot of dopes to stay cool. There were only a hundred and fifty or seventy-five there today. There had not been enough time for the word to get passed around. Tom would have missed it if Jim had not run in and told him about it while he was taking a nap on the meatblock.

Will Maxie did not drink Coca-Cola. Will never spent his money on anything like that. That was what was wrong with him. He was too damn good for a Negro. He did not drink corn whiskey, nor make it; he did not carry a knife, nor a razor; he bared his head when he met a white man, and he lived with his own wife. But they had him now! God damn his ginger-bread hide to hell! They had him where he could not take any more grass out of his cotton before laying it by. They had him tied to a sweetgum tree in the clearing at the creek with a trace-chain around his neck and another around his knees.. Yes, sir, they had Will Maxie now, the yellow-face coon. He would not take any more grass out of his cotton before lay-ing it by!

Tom was feeling good. Hubert gave him another drink in the woods. Hubert was all right. He made good corn whiskey. Tom liked him for that. And Hubert always took his wife a big piece of meat Saturday night to use over Sunday. Nice meat, too. Tom cut off the meat and Hubert took it home and made a present of it to his wife.

Will Maxie was going up in smoke. When he was just about gone they gave him the lead. Tom stood back and took good aim and fired away at Will with his shotgun as fast as he could breech it and put in a new load. About forty or more of the other men had shotguns too. They filled him so full of lead that his body sagged from his neck where the trace-chain held him up. [647]

The Cromer boy had sold completely out. All of his ice and dopes were gone. Doc Cromer would feel pretty good when his boy brought back all that money. Six whole cases he sold, at a dime a bottle. If he had brought along another case or two he could have sold them easily enough. Everybody likes Coca-Cola. There is nothing better to drink on a hot day, if the dopes are nice and cool.

After a while the men got ready to draw the body up in the tree and tie it to a limb so it could hang there, but Tom and Jim could not wait and they went back to town the first chance they got to ride. They were in a big hurry. They had been gone several hours and it was almost four o'clock. A lot of people came downtown early Saturday aternoon to get their Sunday meat before it was picked over by the country people. Tom and Jim had to hurry back and open up the meat-market and get to work slicing steaks and chopping soup bones with the cleaver on the meatblock. Tom was the butcher. He did all the work with the meat. He went out and killed a cow and quartered her. Then he hauled the meat to the butcher-shop and hung it on the hooks in the ice-house. When somebody wanted to buy some meat, he took one of the quarters from the hook and threw it on the meatblock and cut what you ask for. You told Tom what you wanted and he gave it to you, no matter what it was you asked for.

Then you stepped over to the counter and paid Jim the money for it. Jim was the cashier. He did all the talking, too. Tom had to do the cutting and weighing. Jim's egg-shaped belly was too big for him to work around the meatblock. It got in his way when he tried to slice you a piece of tenderloin steak, so Tom did that and Jim took the money and put it into the cashbox under the counter.

Tom and Jim got back to town just in time. There was a big crowd standing around on the street getting ready to do their weekly trading, and they had to have some meat. You went in the butcher-shop and said, "Hello, Tom. I want two pounds and a half of pork chops." Tom said, "Hello, I'll get it for you right away." While you were waiting for Tom to cut the meat off the hunk of rump steak you asked him how was everything.

"Everything's slick as a whistle," he said, "except my old woman's got the chills and fever pretty bad again." [648]

Tom weighed the pork chops and wrapped them up for you and then you stepped over to Jim and paid him the money. Jim was the cashier. His egg-shaped belly was too big for him to work around the meatblock. Tom did that part, and Jim took the money and put it into the cashbox under the counter. [649]

e. e. cummings
1894–1962

The Broken Spirit

"any one lived in a pretty how town"

e. e. cummings was one of the American writers who contributed to the resurgence of serious literary activity after World War I. In the same manner that many people at that time revolted against long-established social traditions and values, cummings attempted to shock the complacency of his readers by making unusual technical innovations in his poems. Such devices as unconventional typographical arrangements, unusual spelling and punctuation, and unexpected use of vocabulary, however, reinforce both the rhythmical structure of his poems and their underlying meanings. cummings's experimentation with line, form, and syntax not only shock the reader's expectations but result in exceptional vividness.

In the poem reprinted here, the usual syntactical rules will not be helpful in an interpretation; nouns, verbs, adverbs, and adjectives are interchangeable. It may be helpful to understand that *anyone* and *noone* are the two central characters in the narrative. Various particular interpretations of the poem have been offered by critics—a story of lovers who died, a story of childhood and growing up—but in a more general sense the lines suggest the effects of the community upon the individual spirit. The poet suggests how difficult it is to maintain a free and spontaneous relationship with the natural world, the dreams of youth, and the freshness of human affections as individuals become assimilated into the adult world of conformity. The phrase "pretty how town" suggests that the setting is just any, or perhaps every, little town. The line "one day anyone died i guess" can best be interpreted as a spiritual rather than physical death. The rhythms of this poem are a significant part of the meaning. The harsher rhythms and sounds of the second stanza, suggesting the adult world, are in sharp contrast with the spontaneous flowing rhythms of the first stanza, suggesting the world of childhood. The use of the two refrains "spring summer autumn winter" and "sun moon stars rain," rearranged each time they appear, places the whole story within the natural cyclical pattern of time and nature. Consider the appropriateness of the image "and only the snow can begin to explain" in relation to the central meaning of the poem.

cummings wrote several volumes of poetry. His most widely acclaimed novel, *The Enormous Room* (1922), was his first published work. He is less well known as a painter.

"any one lived in a pretty how town"

anyone lived in a pretty how town
(with up so floating many bells down)
spring summer autumn winter
he sang his didn't he danced his did.

Women and men (both little and small)
cared for anyone not at all
they sowed their isn't they reaped their same
sun moons stars rain

children guessed (but only a few
and down they forgot as up they grew
autumn winter spring summer)
that no one loved him more by more

when by now and tree by leaf
she laughed his joy she cried his grief
bird by snow and stir by still
anyone's any was all to her

someones married their everyones
laughed their crying and did their dance
(sleep wake hope and then) they
said their nevers they slept their dream

stars rain sun moon
(and only the snow can begin to explain
how children are apt to forget to remember
with up so floating many bells down)

one day anyone died i guess
(and noone stooped to kiss his face)
busy folk buried them side by side
little by little and was by was [370]

all by all and deep by deep
and more by more they dream their sleep
noone and anyone earth by april
wish by spirit and if by yes.

Women and men (both dong and ding)
summer autumn winter spring
reaped their sowing and went their came
sun moon stars rain [371]

JOHN O'HARA
1905–1970

The Outsider

"DR. WYETH'S SON"

In his best writing John O'Hara often turns to the scenes of his boyhood for his material. The small town of Pottsville, located in south-central Pennsylvania, becomes the fictional town of Gibbsville. In story after story and novel after novel he explores various social and political aspects of the community. It is populated with a wide variety of people, but the middle-class and professional people claim the writer's chief interest. O'Hara created a complex mythical region in American literature, similar to what William Faulkner did with Yoknapatawpha County.

His first novel, *Appointment in Samarra* (1934), was an immediate success and remains the best example among his novels of a social analysis of a small Pennsylvania town. It emphasizes class distinctions, centering primarily on the country-club set. O'Hara sees the banality and hypocrisy of middle-class life, much like Sinclair Lewis, but he approaches his subject in a less satirical manner.

The Doctor's Son and Other Stories (1935) was O'Hara's first published collection of short stories, and in them he reveals many of the experiences he had when, as a boy, he accompanied his father on his rounds as a doctor. It was then that the writer gained many of his insights into the lives of the people who were later to populate his fiction. "Dr. Wyeth's Son" is less autobiographical than the title story in this collection, but it reveals clearly some of O'Hara's perceptions of small-town life: its treatment of outsiders, its prejudices, its attitudes toward drinking and language. In general, a picture of the provincial small town emerges.

O'Hara's many novels tend to be the same long story—fictional biographies of upper-middle-class families. Representative titles are *A Rage to Live* (1949), *Ten North Frederick* (1955), and *Ourselves to Know* (1960). He turned out numerous collections of short stories, probably the form for which his talents were best suited. Some of these collections are *Files on Parade* (1939), *The Hat on the Bed* (1963), and *The Horse Knows the Way* (1964).

"DR. WYETH'S SON"

There were many things that made Johnny Wyeth stand apart from the rest of our gang. For one thing, his accent. He had a Southern accent. He had come to our town only the winter before that summer, and his accent was unchanged, although he went to school with us and we all had at least traces of Pennsylvania Dutch inflections and sentence structure in our talk. But being with us did not change his accent, although being with him may have had its effect on ours. But besides his accent there was his way of dressing that made him different from the rest of us. We all wore, in the summer, a sort of uniform for all but dress-up occasions. When we had to dress, we wore white duck knickerbockers and blue Norfolk jackets, but other times in the evening we wore khaki (we pronounced it "kyky") knickerbockers and blue shirts and "Scout" shoes, which were ordinary brown high shoes except they had a cap on the toes. But Johnny, in the summer evenings, wore white linen suits and white buckskin Oxfords, which had the advantage of being noiseless when we [198] played games like Run, Sheepie, Run, and a game which we simply called Chase. Then, Johnny was different from the rest of us because he wore glasses. He was cross-eyed, and to boys of that age being cross-eyed is not unattractive. At least in Johnny's case it gave him a wild look which I supposed caused us to credit him with a lot more daring than we all had.

Johnny's father, like mine, was a doctor, and I used to hear my father say that Dr. Wyeth was the best diagnostician who had come to our town in years, but that "it was too bad he drank." This was a curious admission to come from my father, who was a total abstainer and a rabid dry. I knew Dr. Wyeth drank, all right. Nights he used to come home and leave his car with the engine running, in front of the Markwith house, where the Wyeths lived. (They didn't own their home, as we all knew.) He would sit in the car for a few minutes and then get out and stagger in, and Johnny would leave us—we hung around Victoria Jones's porch—and go up and turn off the motor. I remember the switch, a shiny Bosch switch it was, and Johnny never would let us turn it; he had to do it himself.

There was one other thing that kept Johnny from being like us, and that was his language. He cursed and [199] swore all the time. We were pretty clean of speech; the majority of us were Catholics and we had to tell it in confession when we used bad language, but Johnny was Presbyterian and he didn't care what he said. One of his favorite words was "baster." He did not know what it meant, and neither did we, but he said it was the worst thing you could call anybody, and he said his father had told him that if anyone ever called him that, to go right ahead and kill him, hit him with a rock or anything else. Johnny used it whenever he was extremely angry. The rest of the time he simply cursed and swore and used dirty words. The Holding twins, Gerald and Francis, in whose back yard we had our headquarters, in a dusty, dirt-smelling tool house, were the ones who most frequently told Johnny to cut out his language. But they had no effect on Johnny.

However, one afternoon that summer, late one afternoon, we were playing Million-Dollar Mystery in the Holdings' tool house. "The Million-Dollar Mystery" was the name of a movie serial which we were all following, and we would use the scenario of each episode to provide us with a game from Friday to Friday. It was quite late, almost supper time, and we were playing hard, and Gerald or Francis, I forget which, had an old, rusty Daisy air rifle, which he stuck in Johnny's [200] stomach with too much force behind it, and Johnny let out a yell you could have heard up at the courthouse. "God damn you! What's the idea you doing that?" And so on, with a lot of profanity.

"Oh, come on," we all said. "Don't get so sore about nothing. Quit swearing and put up your hands. He has you covered."

"No, sir, I won't do anything of the kind," said Johnny. "This no-good baster ain't gonna do that to me."

"Don't you call *me* that," said the Holding twin.

"Oh, I won't, eh? Who says I won't, you baster." Johnny raised his voice and the argument went on, everybody getting in it one way or another, but always Johnny's voice and the words he said were more distinguishable than anything else. And then suddenly we looked around as the door of the tool shed opened, and there was Mr. Holding. Mr. Holding in bedroom slippers, spectacles with a little gold chain reaching back to one ear, necktie held against his shirt by a little gold gold pincher.

"Who's using that language in this yard? John Wyeth, was that you?"

"What if it was? No baster ain't gonna hit me with any God-damn rifle." [201]

"Here, here! Stop that kind of talk this minute. Leave this yard or I'll take you by the ear. Leave this yard this minute, you young guttersnipe, using language like that. I'll show you—" He advanced toward Johnny, and Johnny moved back and grabbed an old garden rake.

"God damn you, don't you put a hand to me! I'll sure hit you with this, you put a finger on me."

"Oh, *ho!* Like father, like son," said Mr. Holding. "Well, we'll see who has the say about what goes on in this yard. Come on, you boys. Hurry up and go home. I'll settle with Johnny. Ought to know what to expect from his kind."

"Go on, *get* out!" Johnny screamed, and called Mr. Holding an old baster and a lot of other things which we did not make out, because we were out of the tool house. Mr. Holding went right to the house, and standing in the areaway beside the house we could hear him on the telephone. "Dr. Wyeth? This is Holding, next door. Will you come over and get that son of yours out of my yard, or will I have to call the police?" . . . Decent young boys . . . *my* sons hear talk like that . . . and keep him away from these boys or you'll hear from *all* the fathers in this neighborhood. We're all getting fed up with the goings-on since you moved [202] here." We heard no more because Mrs. Holding told us to go home.

But that night after supper we met early at Victoria Jones's porch and we all waited for the Holding twins, and at seven or so they came down the street together. Right away we asked them about what had happened after we were sent home.

"Oh, did he get his!" said one Holding.

"Did he get his!" said the other.

"What happened?" we said.

"Papa called up Mr. Wyeth and told him to come over and get Johnny or else he'd get the police to arrest him, and so pretty soon Mr. Wyeth—"

"Doctor Wyeth," I said.

"Aw, well, Doctor. He came over and got Johnny and took him out the back gate, and *then* you should of *heard* it. He had Johnny yelling and cursing. What he beat him with, it must of been at least a cane. He must of beat him with a cane for a half an hour."

"More than once. A couple of times," said the other Holding.

"Oh, a couple of times at least. He was still giving it to him when we sat down for supper. The worst I ever heard anybody get beaten."

We asked them more questions, but they did not [203] know many more details, and after that Victoria Jones came out and sat on the porch and the other girls came one by one, and the argument was about whether Johnny deserved it. Johnny did not show up that night, but along about nine o'clock, when it was just getting dark, we saw Dr. Wyeth drive up in his car and stop in front of his house, and this night he was the worst we'd ever seen him. He could hardly get out of the car. When he did finally get out and go in the house, none of us dared to go over and turn off the motor. [204]

WILLIAM SAROYAN
1908–

Relief
from Monotony
"LOCOMOTIVE 38, THE OJIBWAY"

William Saroyan began to write when he was nine, and since then he has produced an immense volume of work—short stories, novels, plays, and essays—all of them characterized by his particular brand of realism and cheerful hope. He writes as if he truly believes in the American dream.

Born in 1908 in Fresno, California, of Armenian parents, he worked as a newsboy at the age of eight and as a telegraph boy when he was 13. When he left school at 15, he took on various jobs, such as tree pruning and office work. He later served overseas during World War II.

In 1934, with the publication of "The Daring Young Man on the Flying Trapeze," an immensely successful short story, Saroyan came to the public's attention. Since then he has published many collections of short stories, including *Little Children* (1937), *Peace, It's Wonderful* (1939), and *My Name Is Aram* (1940). The best known among his eight novels is *The Human Comedy* (1943), which was made into a wartime movie. His major plays include *My Heart's in the Highlands* (1939), *The Beautiful People* (1941), and *The Time of Your Life* (1939), for which he won both a Pulitzer Prize and the New York Drama Critics Circle Award. More recent work includes a collection of eight plays, *The Dogs, or the Paris Comedy* (1969); an autobiography, *I used to believe I had forever, now I'm not so sure* (1968); a group of letters, *Letters from 74 Rue Taibout* (1969); and autobiographical essays, *Days of Life and Death and Escape to the Moon* (1970).

The short-story collection *My Name Is Aram* is semi-autobiographical, and from that collection comes "Locomotive 38, the Ojibway," reprinted here. Saroyan once wrote that "[the small town] is always a place of monotony but at the same time as you grow, change, go away, remember, return, and go away again, it is one of the most exhaustibly rich places."

"Locomotive 38, the Ojibway" describes a typical small California town in the 1920s—the drug store with its soda fountain, the trolley, the budding automobile agency—and the people. One of these, a 14-year-old boy bored with life there, finds the monotony relieved by the arrival of an Indian in the town. Saroyan's delightful humor gives a touch of the romantic to the story and to the relationship between the impressionable boy and the rich Indian.

"Locomotive 38, the Ojibway" describes the sense of longing of the youngster, recalling what Saroyan once asked: "Is the small town a place, truly of the world, or is it no more than something out of a boy's dreaming?" In this story and in all of his work Saroyan brings us the laughter and compassion and curiosity of life. For him, being human is an endless opportunity for pleasure and bafflement.

"LOCOMOTIVE 38, THE OJIBWAY"

One day a man came to town on a donkey and began loafing around in the public library where I used to spend most of my time in those days. He was a tall young Indian of the Ojibway tribe. He told me his name was Locomotive 38. Everybody in town believed he had escaped from an asylum.

Six days after he arrived in town his animal was struck by the Tulare Street trolley and seriously injured. The following day the animal passed away, most likely of internal injuries, on the corner of Mariposa and Fulton streets. The animal sank to the pavement, fell on the Indian's leg, groaned and died. When the Indian got his leg free he got up and limped into the drug store on the corner and made a long distance telephone call. He telephoned his brother in Oklahoma. The call cost him a lot of money, which he [169] dropped into the slot as requested by the operator as if he were in the habit of making such calls every day.

I was in the drug store at the time, eating a Royal Banana Special, with crushed walnuts.

When he came out of the telephone booth he saw me sitting at the soda fountain eating this fancy dish.

Hello, Willie, he said.

He knew my name wasn't Willie—he just liked to call me that.

William Saroyan, "Locomotive 38, the Ojibway," from *My Name is Aram* (New York: Harcourt Brace Jovanovich, 1940). Reprinted by permission of Harcourt Brace Jovanovich, Inc. Copyright 1940, 1968 by William Saroyan.

He limped to the front of the store where the gum was, and bought three packages of Juicy Fruit. Then he limped back to me and said, What's that you're eating, Willie? It looks good.

This is what they call a Royal Banana Special, I said.

The Indian got up on the stool next to me.

Give me the same, he said to the soda fountain girl.

That's too bad about your animal, I said.

There's no place for an animal in this world, he said. What kind of an automobile should I buy?

Are you going to buy an automobile? I said.

I've been thinking about it for several minutes now, he said. [170]

I didn't think you had any money, I said. I thought you were poor.

That's the impression people get, he said. Another impression they get is that I'm crazy.

I didn't get the impression that you were crazy, I said, but I didn't get the impression that you were rich, either.

Well, I am, the Indian said.

I wish I was rich, I said.

What for? he said.

Well, I said, I've been wanting to go fishing at Mendota for three years in a row now. I need some equipment and some kind of an automobile to get out there in.

Can you drive an automobile? the Indian said.

I can drive anything, I said.

Have you ever driven an automobile? he said.

Not yet, I said. So far I haven't had any automobile to drive, and it's against my family religion to steal an automobile.

Do you mean to tell me you believe you could get into an automobile and start driving? he said.

That's right, I said.

Remember what I was telling you on the steps of the public library the other evening? he said.

You mean about the machine age? I said. [171]

Yes, he said.

I remember, I said.

All right, he said. Indians are born with an instinct for riding, rowing, hunting, fishing, and swimming. Americans are born with an instinct for fooling around with machines.

I'm no American, I said.

I know, the Indian said. You're an Armenian. I remember. I asked you and you told me. You're an Armenian born in America. You're fourteen years old and already you know you'll be able to drive an automobile the minute you get into one. You're a typical American, although your complexion, like my own, is dark.

Driving a car is no trick, I said. There's nothing to it. It's easier than riding a donkey.

All right, the Indian said. Just as you say. If I go up the street and buy an automobile, will you drive for me?

Of course, I said.

How much in wages would you want? he said.

You mean you want to give me wages for driving an automobile? I said.

Of course, the Ojibway said.

Well, I said, that's very nice of you, but I don't want any money for driving an automobile. [172]

Some of the journeys may be long ones, he said.

The longer the better, I said.

Are you restless? he said.

I was born in this little old town, I said.

Don't you like it? he said.

I like mountains and streams and mountain lakes, I said.

Have you ever been in the mountains? he said.

Not yet, I said, but I'm going to reach them some day.

I see, he said. What kind of an automobile do you think I ought to buy?

How about a Ford roadster? I said.

Is that the best automobile? he said.

Do you want the *best?* I said.

Shouldn't I have the best? he said.

I don't know, I said. The best costs a lot of money.

What's the best? he said.

Well, I said, some people think the Cadillac is the best. Others like the Packard. They're both pretty good. I wouldn't know which is best. The Packard is beautiful to see going down the highway, but so is the Cadillac. I've watched a lot of them fine cars going down the highway.

How much is a Packard? he said. [173]

Around three thousand dollars, I said. Maybe a little more.

Can we get one right away? he said.

I got down off the stool. He sounded crazy, but I knew he wasn't.

Listen, Mr. Locomotive, I said, do you really want to buy a Packard right away?

You know my animal passed away a few minutes ago, he said.

I saw it happen, I said. They'll probably be arresting you any minute now for leaving the animal in the street.

They won't arrest me, he said.

They will if there's a law against leaving a dead donkey in the street, I said.

No, they won't, he said.

Why not? I said.

Well, he said, they won't after I show them a few papers I carry around with me all the time. The people of this country have a lot of respect for money, and I've got a lot of money.

I guess he is crazy after all, I thought.

Where'd you get all this money? I said.

I own some land in Oklahoma, he said. About fifty thousand acres.

Is it worth money? I said. [174]

No, he said. All but about twenty acres of it is worthless. I've got some oil wells on them twenty acres. My brother and I.

How did you Ojibways ever get down to Oklahoma? I said. I always thought the Ojibways lived up north, up around the Great Lakes.

That's right, the Indian said. We used to live up around the Great Lakes, but my grandfather was a pioneer. He moved west when everybody else did.

Oh, I said. Well, I guess they won't bother you about the dead donkey at that.

They won't bother me about anything, he said. It won't be because I've got money. It'll be because they think I'm crazy. Nobody in this town but you knows I've got money. Do you know where we can get one of them automobiles right away?

The Packard agency is up on Broadway, two blocks beyond the public library, I said.

All right, he said. If you're sure you won't mind driving for me, let's go get one of them. Something bright in color, he said. Red, if they've got red. Where would you like to drive to first?

Would you care to go fishing at Mendota? I said. [175]

I'll take the ride, he said. I'll watch you fish. Where can we get some equipment for you?

Right around the corner at Homan's, I said.

We went around the corner to Homan's and the Indian bought twenty-seven dollars' worth of fishing equipment for me. Then we went up to the Packard agency on Broadway. They didn't have a red Packard, but there was a beautiful green one. It was light green, the color of new grass. This was back there in 1922. The car was a beautiful sports touring model.

Do you think you could drive this great big car? the Indian said.

I *know* I can drive it, I said.

The police found us in the Packard agency and wanted to arrest the Indian for leaving the dead donkey in the street. He showed them the papers he had told me about and the police apologized and went away. They said they'd removed the animal and were sorry they'd troubled him about it.

It 's no trouble at all, he said.

He turned to the manager of the Packard agency, Jim Lewis, who used to run for Mayor every time election time came around.

I'll take this car, he said.

I'll draw up the papers immediately, Jim said. [176]

What papers? the Indian said. I'm going to pay for it now.

You mean you want to pay three thousand two hundred seventeen dollars and sixty-five cents *cash*? Jim said.

Yes, the Indian said. It's ready to drive, isn't it?

Of course, Jim said. I'll have the boys go over it with a cloth to take off any dust on it. I'll have them check the motor too, and fill the gasoline tank. It won't take more than ten minutes. If you'll step into the office I'll close the transaction immediately.

Jim and the Indian stepped into Jim's office.

About three minutes later Jim came over to me, a man shaken to the roots.

Aram, he said, who is this guy? I thought he was a nut. I had Johnny telephone the Pacific-Northwest and they said his bank account is being transferred from somewhere in Oklahoma. They said his account is something over a million dollars. I thought he was a nut. Do you know him?

He told me his name is Locomotive 38, I said. That's no name.

That's a translation of his Indian name, Jim said. We've got his full name on the contract. Do you know him? [177]

I've talked to him every day since he came to town on that donkey that died this morning, I said, but I never thought he had any money.

He says you're going to drive for him, Jim said. Are you sure you're the man to drive a great big car like this, son?

Wait a minute now, Mr. Lewis, I said. Don't try to push me out of this chance of a lifetime. I can drive this big Packard as well as anybody else in town.

I'm not trying to push you out of anything, Jim said. I just don't want you to drive out of here and run over six or seven innocent people and maybe smash the car. Get into the car and I'll give you a few pointers. Do you know anything about the gear shift?

I don't know anything about anything yet, I said, but I'll soon find out.

All right, Jim said. Just let me help you.

I got into the car and sat down behind the wheel. Jim got in beside me.

From now on, son, he said, I want you to regard me as a friend who will give you the shirt off his back. I want to thank you for bringing me this fine Indian gentleman.

He told me he wanted the best car on the mar-[178]ket, I said. You know I've always been crazy about driving a Packard. Now how do I do it?

Well, Jim said, let's see.

He looked down at my feet.

My God, son, he said, your feet don't reach the pedals.

Never mind that, I said. You just explain the gear shift.

Jim explained everything while the boys wiped the dust off the car and went over the motor and filled the gasoline tank. When the Indian came out and got into the car, in the back where I insisted he should sit, I had the motor going.

He says he knows how to drive, the Indian said to Jim Lewis. By instinct, he said. I believe him, too.

You needn't worry about Aram here, Jim said. He can drive all right. Clear the way there, boys, he shouted. Let him have all the room necessary.

I turned the big car around slowly, shifted, and shot out of the agency at about fifty miles an hour, with Jim Lewis running after the car and shouting. Take it easy, son. Don't open up until you get out on the highway. The speed limit in town is twenty-five miles an hour. [179]

The Indian wasn't at all excited, even though I was throwing him around a good deal.

I wasn't doing it on purpose, though. It was simply that I wasn't very familiar with the manner in which the automobile worked.

You're an excellent driver, Willie, he said. It's like I said. You're an American and you were born with an instinct for mechanical contraptions like this.

We'll be in Mendota in an hour, I said. You'll see some great fishing out there.

How far is Mendota? the Indian said.

About ninety miles, I said.

Ninety miles is too far to go in an hour, the Indian said. Take two hours. We're passing a lot of interesting scenery I'd like to look at a little more closely.

All right, I said, but I sure am anxious to get out there and fish.

Well, all right then, the Indian said. Go as fast as you like this time, but some time I'll expect you to drive a little more slowly, so I can see some of the scenery. I'm missing everything. I don't even get a chance to read the signs.

I'll travel slowly *now* if you want me to, I said. [180]

No, he insisted. Let her go. Let her go as fast as she'll go.

Well, we got out to Mendota in an hour and seventeen minutes. I would have made better time except for the long stretch of dirt road.

I drove the car right up to the river bank. The Indian asked if I knew how to get the top down, so he could sit in the open and watch me fish. I didn't know how to get the top down, but I got it down. It took me twenty minutes to do it.

I fished for about three hours, fell into the river twice, and finally landed a small one.

You don't know the first thing about fishing, the Indian said.

What am I doing wrong? I said.

Everything, he said. Have you ever fished before?

No, I said.

I didn't think so, he said.

What am I doing wrong? I said.

Well, he said, nothing in particular, only you're fishing at about the same rate of speed that you drive an automobile.

Is that wrong? I said.

It's not exactly wrong, he said, except that it'll [181] keep you from getting anything to speak of, and you'll go on falling into the river.

I'm not falling, I said. They're pulling me in. They've got an awful pull. This grass is mighty slippery, too. There ain't nothing around here to grab hold of.

I reeled in one more little one and then I asked if he'd like to go home. He said he would if I wanted to, too, so I put away the fishing equipment and two fish and got in the car and started driving back to town.

I drove that big Packard for this Ojibway Indian, Locomotive 38, as long as he stayed in town, which was all summer. He stayed at the hotel all the time. I tried to get him to learn to drive, but he said it was out of the question. I drove that Packard all over the San Joaquín Valley that summer, with the Indian in the back, chewing eight or nine sticks of gum. He told me to drive anywhere I cared to go, so it was either to some place where I could fish, or some place where I could hunt. He claimed I didn't know anything about fishing or hunting, but he was glad to see me trying. As long as I knew him he never laughed, except once. That was the time I shot at a jack-rabbit with a 12-gauge shotgun that [182] had a terrible kick, and killed a crow. He tried to tell me all the time that that was my average. To shoot at a jack-rabbit and kill a crow. You're an American, he said. Look at the way you took to this big automobile.

One day in November that year his brother came to town from Oklahoma, and the next day when I went down to the hotel to get him, they told me he'd gone back to Oklahoma with his brother.

Where's the Packard? I said.

They took the Packard, the hotel clerk said.

Who drove? I said.

The Indian, the clerk said.

They're both Indians, I said. Which of the brothers drove the car?

The one who lived at this hotel, the clerk said.

Are you sure? I said.

Well, I only saw him get into the car out front and drive away, the clerk said. That's all.

Do you mean to tell me he knew how to shift gears? I said.

It *looked* as if he did, the clerk said. He looked like an expert driver to me.

Thanks, I said.

On the way home I figured he'd just wanted [183] me to *believe* he couldn't drive, so *I* could drive all the time and feel good. He was just a young man who'd come to town on a donkey, bored to death or something, who'd taken advantage of the chance to be entertained by a small town kid who was bored to death, too. That's the only way I could figure it out without accepting the general theory that he was crazy. [184]

TENNESSEE WILLIAMS
1914–

Prim and Proper
"THE CASE OF THE CRUSHED PETUNIAS"

The name of Tennesee Williams is well known today as that of one of the leading dramatists to appear on the American scene since World War II. He first became known in theatrical circles with his one-act plays, such as the one included here. His first full-length play, *Battle of Angels* (1940), shocked and annoyed a Boston audience with its treatment of violence and sexual disorders. These themes, which have been present in a large part of Williams's work, have caused considerable controversy among theatergoers and critics. *The Glass Menagerie,* produced in 1945, was his first successful play and received the New York Drama Critics Circle Award. *A Streetcar Named Desire* received the Pulitzer Prize in 1947. These two plays are considered by many critics to be his best, although he received the Pulitzer Prize again in 1955 for *Cat on a Hot Tin Roof* and has written numerous other plays that have been successful on Broadway, including *The Rose Tatoo* (1950), *Sweet Bird of Youth* (1959), *Period of Adjustment* (1960), and *Night of the Iguana* (1961).

Williams's theatrical innovations and poetic style account in large part for his prominent place in the modern American theater. He makes use of modified realistic settings and relies upon verbal and physical symbolism to carry much of the meaning in his plays. Physical objects serve as symbols of the plight of the main character. In *The Glass Menagerie,* he uses the glass animals in such a manner, and in "The Case of the Crushed Petunias," the petunias themselves are only one of several physical symbols reflecting and commenting on the character of Dorothy Simple. The reader will quickly find other such symbols if he looks for them. Williams's language is poetic and highly evocative, which contributes much to the dramatic force of his plays; in fact, it is the only redeeming quality in some of his less successful ones.

The themes that emerge in Williams's plays reflect his rejection of American middle-class Protestant culture, with its puritan and hypocritical standards of respectability. The setting of "The Case of the Crushed Petunias" is Primanproper, Massachusetts, "within the cultural orbit of Boston." But this New England locale is representative of the routine of dullness and conformity that exists in most small towns across the nation. The Dorothy Simples with their "Simple Notions" are surrounded by crowds of Mrs. Dulls. An underlying theme in the play, of course, is the idea that sexual repression is the product of the conventional attitudes found in all such Primanpropers. People who live in these places are emotionally and spiritually dead.

"THE CASE OF THE CRUSHED PETUNIAS"

A LYRICAL FANTASY

This play is respectfully dedicated to the talent and charm of
Miss Helen Hayes—Key West, February, 1941

CHARACTERS

DOROTHY SIMPLE

POLICE OFFICER

YOUNG MAN

MRS. DULL

SCENE: *The action of the play takes place in the Simple Notion Shop, owned and operated by* MISS DOROTHY SIMPLE, *a New England maiden of twenty-six, who is physically very attractive but has barricaded her house and her heart behind a double row of petunias.*

The town is Primanproper, Massachusetts, which lies within the cultural orbit of Boston.

The play starts in the early morning. MISS SIMPLE, *very agitated for some reason, has just opened her little shop. She stands in the open door and in a flood of spring sunlight, but her face expresses grief and indignation. She is calling to a* POLICE OFFICER *on the corner.*

DOROTHY   Officer?—Officer!

OFFICER   (*Strolling up to her.*) Yes, Miss Simple?

DOROTHY   I wish to report a case of deliberate and malicious sabotage!

OFFICER   Sabotage of what, Miss Simple?

DOROTHY   Of my petunias! [22]

OFFICER   Well, well, well. Now what do you mean by that?

DOROTHY   Exactly what I said. You can see for yourself. Last night this house was surrounded by a beautiful double row of pink and lavender petunias. Look at them now! When I got up this morning I discovered them in this condition. Every single little petunia deliberately and maliciously crushed under foot!

OFFICER   My goodness! Well, well, well!

DOROTHY   "Well, well, well" is not going to catch the culprit!

OFFICER   What do you want me to do, Miss Simple?

DOROTHY   I want you to apprehend a petuniacidal maniac with a size eleven D foot.

OFFICER   Eleven D?

DOROTHY   Yes, that is the size of the footprint that crushed my petunias. I just now had them measured by a shoe clerk.

OFFICER   That's a pretty large foot, Miss Simple, but lots of men have got large feet.

DOROTHY   Not in Primanproper, Massachusetts. Mr. Knowzit, the shoe clerk, assured me that there isn't a man in town who wears a shoe that size. Of course you realize the danger of allowing this maniac to remain at large. Any man who would crush a sweet petunia is equally capable in my opinion of striking a helpless woman or kicking an innocent child!

OFFICER   I'll do my best, Miss Simple. See yuh later.

DOROTHY   (*Curtly.*) Yes, Good-bye. (*Slams door. She returns behind her notion counter and drums restively with her pale pink-polished nails. The canary cheeps timidly. Then tries an arpeggio.* DOROTHY, *to canary.*) Oh, hush up! (*Then contritely.*) Excuse me, please. My nerves are all to pieces! (*Blows her nose. The doorbell tinkles as a customer enters. He is a young man, shockingly large and aggressive looking in the flower-paper cubicle of the shop.*) Gracious, please be careful. You're bumping your head against my chandelier.

YOUNG MAN   (*Good-humoredly.*) Sorry, Miss Simple. I guess I'd better sit down. (*The delicate little chair collapses beneath him.*)

DOROTHY   Heaven have mercy upon us! You seem to have a genius for destruction! You've broken that little antique chair to smithereens!

YOUNG MAN   Sorry, Miss Simple.

DOROTHY   I appreciate your sorrow, but that won't mend my chair.—Is there anything I can show you in the way of notions? [23]

YOUNG MAN   I'd like to see that pair of wine-colored socks you have in the window.

DOROTHY   What size socks do you wear?

YOUNG MAN   I keep forgetting. But my shoes are eleven D.

DOROTHY (*Sharply.*) What size did you say? Eleven? Eleven D?

YOUNG MAN That's right, Miss Simple. Eleven D.

DOROTHY Oh. Your shoes are rather muddy, aren't they?

YOUNG MAN That's right, Miss Simple, I believe they are.

DOROTHY Quite muddy. It looks like you might have stepped in a freshly watered flower-bed last night.

YOUNG MAN Come to think of it, that's what I did.

DOROTHY I don't suppose you've heard about that horrible case of petunia crushing which occurred last night?

YOUNG MAN As a matter of fact, I have heard something about it.

DOROTHY From the policeman on the corner?

YOUNG MAN No, ma'am. Not from him.

DOROTHY Who from, then? He's the only man who knows about it except— except—except—the man who *did* it! (*Pause. The canary cheeps inquiringly.*) You—you—*you*—are the man who *did* it!

YOUNG MAN Yes, Miss Simple. I am the man who did it.

DOROTHY Don't try to get away!

YOUNG MAN I won't, Miss Simple.

DOROTHY Stand right where you are till the officer comes!

YOUNG MAN You're going to call the officer?

DOROTHY Yes, I am, I certainly am.—In a minute. First I'd like to ask you *why* you *did* it? Why did you crush my petunias?

YOUNG MAN Okay, I'll tell you why. First, because you'd barricaded your house—and also your heart—beyond that silly little double row of petunias!

DOROTHY Barricaded? My house—my heart—behind them? That's absurd. I don't know what you mean.

YOUNG MAN I know. They're apparently such delicate, fragile creatures, these petunias, but they have a terrible resistance.

DOROTHY Resistance to what, may I ask?

YOUNG MAN Anything big or important that happens to come by your house. Nothing big or important can ever get by a double row of petunias! That is the reason why you are living alone with your canary and beginning to dislike it.

DOROTHY Dislike my canary? I love it! [24]

YOUNG MAN Secretly, Miss Simple, you wish the bird-seed would choke it! You dislike it nearly as much as you secretly disliked your petunias.

DOROTHY Why should I, why should you, why should anybody dislike petunias!

YOUNG MAN Our animosity and its resultant action is best explained by a poem I once composed on the subject of petunias—and similar flora. Would you like to hear it?

DOROTHY I suppose I should, if it's relevant to the case.

YOUNG MAN Extremely relevant. It goes like this:

(LIGHT MUSIC.)

> How grimly do petunias look
>   on things not listed in the book
>
> For these dear creatures never move
>   outside the academic groove.
>
> They mark with sharp and moral eye
>   phenomena that pass them by
>
> And classify as good or evil
>   mammoth whale or tiny weevil.
>
> They note with consummate disdain
>   all that is masculine or plain
>
> They blush down to their tender roots
>   when men pass by in working boots
>
> All honest language shocks them so
>   they cringe to hear a rooster crow
>
> Of course they say that good clean fun's
>   permissible for *every* one
>
> But find that even Blindman's Bluff
>   is noisy and extremely rough
>
> AND—
>   (*Stage whisper.*)—Not quite innocent enough!

What do you think of it?

DOROTHY   Unfair! Completely unfair!

YOUNG MAN   (*Laughing.*) To organized petunias? [25]

DOROTHY   Yes, and besides, I don't think anyone has the right to impose his opinions in the form of footprints on other people's petunias!

YOUNG MAN   (*Removing small package from pocket.*) I'm prepared to make complete restitution.

DOROTHY   What with?

YOUNG MAN   With these.

DOROTHY   What are they?

YOUNG MAN   Seeds.

DOROTHY   Seeds of what? Sedition?

YOUNG MAN   No. Wild roses.

DOROTHY   Wild? I couldn't use them!

YOUNG MAN   Why not, Miss Simple?

DOROTHY   Flowers are like human beings. They can't be allowed to grow wild. They have to be——

YOUNG MAN   Regimented? Ahhh. I see. You're a horticultural fascist!

DOROTHY   (*With an indignant gasp.*) I ought to call the policeman about those petunias!

YOUNG MAN   Why don't you, then?

DOROTHY   Only because you made an honest confession.

YOUNG MAN   That's not why, Miss Simple.

DOROTHY   No?

YOUNG MAN   The actual reason is that you are fascinated.

DOROTHY   *AM* I? Indeed!

YOUNG MAN   Indeed you are, Miss Simple. In spite of your late unlamented petunias, you're charmed, you're intrigued—you're frightened!

DOROTHY   You're very conceited!

YOUNG MAN   Now, if you please, I'd like to ask you a question.

DOROTHY   You may. But I may not answer.

YOUNG MAN   You will if you can. But you probably won't be able. The question is this: What do you make of it all?

DOROTHY   I don't understand—— All *what?*

YOUNG MAN   The world? The universe? And your position in it? This miraculous accident of being alive! (SOFT MUSIC BACKGROUND.) Has it ever occurred to you how much the living are outnumbered by the dead? Their numerical superiority, Miss Simple, is so tremendous that you couldn't possibly find a ratio [26] with figures vast enough *above* the line, and small enough *below* to represent it.

DOROTHY   You sound like you were trying to sell me something.

YOUNG MAN   I am, I am, just wait!

DOROTHY   I'm not in the market for——

YOUNG MAN   Please! One minute of your infinitely valuable time!

DOROTHY   All right. One minute.

YOUNG MAN   *Look!*

DOROTHY   At what?

YOUNG MAN   Those little particles of dust in the shaft of April sunlight through that window.

DOROTHY   What about them?

YOUNG MAN   Just think. You might have been one of those instead of what you are. You might have been any one of those infinitesimal particles of dust. Or any one of millions and billions and trillions of other articles of mute, unconscious matter. Never capable of asking any questions. Never capable of giving any answers. Never capable of doing, thinking, feeling anything at all! But instead, dear lady, by the rarest and most improbable of accidents, you happened to be what you are. Miss Dorothy Simple from Boston! Beautiful. Human. Alive. Capable of thought and feeling and action. Now here comes the vital part of my question. What are you going to *do* about it, Miss Simple?

DOROTHY   (*Who is somewhat moved, in spite of her crushed petunias.*)

Well, goodness—gracious—sakes alive! I thought you came in here to buy some socks?

YOUNG MAN   Yes, but I've got to sell *you* something first.

DOROTHY   Sell me what?

YOUNG MAN   A wonderful bill of goods.

DOROTHY   I'll have to see it before I sign the order.

YOUNG MAN   That's impossible. I can't display my samples in this shoppe.

DOROTHY   Why not?

YOUNG MAN   They're much too precious. You have to make an appointment.

DOROTHY   (*Retreating.*) Sorry. But I do all my business in here.

YOUNG MAN   Too bad for you.—In fact, too bad for us both. Maybe you'll change your mind?

DOROTHY   I don't think so.

YOUNG MAN   Anyway, here's my card. [27]

DOROTHY   (*Reading it, bewildered.*)—LIFE—INCORPORATED. (*Looks up slowly.*)

YOUNG MAN   Yes. I represent that line.

DOROTHY   I see. You're a magazine salesman?

YOUNG MAN   No. It isn't printed matter.

DOROTHY   But it's matter, though?

YOUNG MAN   Oh, yes, and it's matter of tremendous importance, too. But it's neglected by people. Because of their ignorance they've been buying cheap substitute products. And lately a rival concern has sprung up outside the country. This firm is known as DEATH, UNLIMITED. Their product comes in a package labelled WAR. They're crowding us out with new aggressive methods of promotion. And one of their biggest sales-points is EXCITEMENT. Why does it work so well? Because you little people surround your houses and also your hearts with rows of tiresome, trivial little things like petunias! If we could substitute wild roses there wouldn't be wars! No, there'd be excitement enough in the world *without* having wars! That's why we've started this petunia-crushing campaign, Miss Simple. Life, Incorporated, has come to the realization that we have to use the same aggressive methods of promotion used by DEATH, UNLIMITED over there! We've got to show people that the malignantly trivial little petunias of the world can be eliminated more cleanly, permanently and completely by LIFE, IN-CORPORATED than by DEATH, UNLIMITED! Now what do you say, Miss Simple? Won't you try our product?

DOROTHY   (*Nervously.*) Well, you see it's like this—I do all my buying in Boston and——

YOUNG MAN   What do you buy in Boston?

DOROTHY   You can see for yourself. Look over the stock.

YOUNG MAN   (*Examining the shelves.*) Thimbles—threads—ladies' needlework—white gloves——

DOROTHY   Notions. Odds and ends.

YOUNG MAN   Odds and ends—of existence?

DOROTHY   Yes, that's it exactly.

YOUNG MAN   What do you do after hours?

DOROTHY   I carry on a lot of correspondence.

YOUNG MAN   Who with?

DOROTHY   With wholesale firms in Boston.

YOUNG MAN   How do you sign your letters? [28]

DOROTHY   "Sincerely." "As ever." "Very truly yours."

YOUNG MAN   But never with love?

DOROTHY   Love? To firms in Boston?

YOUNG MAN   I guess not. I think you ought to enlarge your correspondence.
    I'll tell you what I'll do. I'll meet you tonight on Highway No. 77!

DOROTHY   Oh, no! I have my correspondence!

YOUNG MAN   Delay your correspondence. Meet me there. We'll have a
    couple of beers at the Starlight Casino.

DOROTHY   (*With frantic evasion.*) But I don't drink!

YOUNG MAN   Then *eat*. Swiss cheese on rye. It doesn't matter, Afterwards
    I'll take you for a ride in an open car.

DOROTHY   Where to?

YOUNG MAN   To Cypress Hill.

DOROTHY   Why, that's the cemetery.

YOUNG MAN   Yes, I know.

DOROTHY   Why there?

YOUNG MAN   Because dead people give the best advice.

DOROTHY   Advice on what?

YOUNG MAN   The problems of the living.

DOROTHY   What advice do they give?

YOUNG MAN   Just one word: *Live!*

DOROTHY   Live?

YOUNG MAN   Yes, live, live, live! It's all they know, it's the only word left
    in their vocabulary!

DOROTHY   I don't see how——?

YOUNG MAN   I'll tell you how. There's one thing in Death's favor. It's a
    wonderful process of simplification. It rids the heart of all inconse-
    quentials. For instance, it goes through the dictionary with an abso-
    lutely merciless blue pencil. Finally all that you've got left's one page—
    and on that page one word!

DOROTHY   The word you hear at night on Cypress Hill?

YOUNG MAN   The word you hear at night on Cypress Hill!

DOROTHY   Ohhh. Oh, oh!

YOUNG MAN   But no one hears it till they deal with *me*. I have a secret
    patented device that makes it audible to them. Something never proc-
    essed by Du Pont. But none the less a marvelous invention. It's abso-
    lutely weightless and transparent. It fits inside the ear. Your friends

won't even know you have it on. But this I guar-[29]antee: you'll hear
that word, that sound much like the long, sweet sound of leaves in
motion!

DOROTHY   Leaves?

YOUNG MAN   Yes, willow leaves or leaves of cypresses or leaves of wind-
blown grass! And afterwards you'll never be the same. No, you'll be
changed forever!

DOROTHY   In what way?

YOUNG MAN   You'll live, live, *live!*—And not behind petunias. How about
it, Miss Simple? Dorothy? Is it a date? Tonight at half-past eight on
No. 77?

DOROTHY   Whereabouts on Highway No. 77

YOUNG MAN   By the wild plum-tree—at the broken place in the long stone
wall—where roots have cleft the rocks and made them crumble.

DOROTHY   It sounds so far. It sounds—uncivilized.

YOUNG MAN   It is uncivilized, but it isn't far.

DOROTHY   How would I get out there? What means of transportation?

YOUNG MAN   Borrow your kid brother's bike.

DOROTHY   Tonight's Scout meeting night; he wouldn't let me.

YOUNG MAN   Then walk, it wouldn't kill you!

DOROTHY   How do you know? It might. I come from Boston.

YOUNG MAN   Listen, lady. Boston's a state of mind that you'll grow out of.

DOROTHY   Not without some insulin shock treatments.

YOUNG MAN   Stop evading! Will you or will you not?

DOROTHY   I've got so much to do. I have to return some books to the public
library.

YOUNG MAN   Just one more time—will you or will you not?

DOROTHY   I can't give definite answers—I'm from Boston!

YOUNG MAN   Just one more mention of Boston's apt to be fatal! Well, Miss
Simple? I can't wait forever!

DOROTHY   I guess I—might.

YOUNG MAN   You guess you *might?*

DOROTHY   I mean I guess I will.

YOUNG MAN   You *guess* you will?

DOROTHY   I mean I will—I *will!*

YOUNG MAN   That's better—So long, Dorothy. (*He grins and goes out,
slamming door.*) [30]

DOROTHY   Good-bye. (*She stares dreamily into space for a moment.* MRS.
DULL *comes in.*)

MRS. DULL   (*Sharply.*) Miss Simple!

DOROTHY   Oh! Excuse me. What do you want?

MRS. DULL   I want a pair of wine-colored socks for my husband.

DOROTHY   I'm terribly sorry but the only pair in stock have been reserved.

MRS. DULL   Reserved for whom, Miss Simple?

DOROTHY   A gentleman who represents this line. (*Showing card.*)

MRS. DULL   Life, Incorporated? Huh, I never heard of it.

DOROTHY   Neither had I before. But now I have. And tomorrow the store will be closed for extensive alterations.

MRS. DULL   Alterations of what kind, Miss Simple?

DOROTHY   I'm going to knock out all four walls.

MRS. DULL   Knock out—what——? Incredible!

DOROTHY   Yes, to accommodate some brand-new merchandise. Things I never kept in stock before.

MRS. DULL   What kind of things? Things in bottles, Miss Simple, or things in boxes?

DOROTHY   Neither one nor the other, Mrs. Dull.

MRS. DULL   But everything comes in bottles or in boxes.

DOROTHY   Everything but Life, Incorporated.

MRS. DULL   What does it come in, then?

DOROTHY   I'm not sure yet. But I suspect it's something unconfined, something wild and open as the sky is!—Also I'm going to change the name of the store. It isn't going to be SIMPLE NOTIONS any more, it's going to be TREMENDOUS INSPIRATIONS!

MRS. DULL   Gracious! In that case you'll certainly lose my custom.

DOROTHY   I rather expected to.

MRS. DULL   And you're not sorry?

DOROTHY   Not the least bit sorry. I think I caught a slight skin rash from dealing with your silver. Also you sniff too much. You ought to blow your nose. Or better still, you ought to trim it down. I've often wondered how you get your nose through traffic. (MRS. DULL *gasps, looks desperately about her, rushes out.*) You forgot your groceries, Mrs. Dull! (*Heaves them out the door. Loud impact, sharp outcry. Music up.*) Officer?—Officer!

OFFICER   Did you say size eleven D, Miss Simple?

DOROTHY   Never mind that now, that's all been settled. [31]

OFFICER   Amicably? Out of court, you mean?

DOROTHY   Amicably and out of court. The saboteur has made full restitution and the case is dropped. Now what I want to ask of you is this: how do I get out to No. 77?

OFFICER   Highway No. 77? That road's abandoned.

DOROTHY   Not by me. Where is it?

OFFICER   It's in an awful condition, it's overgrown by brambles!

DOROTHY   I don't care! Where is it?

OFFICER   They say the rain has loosened half the stones. Also the wind has taken liberties with it. The moon at night makes such confusing shadows people lose their way, go dangerous places, do dangerous things!

DOROTHY   Things such as what?

OFFICER   Oh—senseless acrobatics, cart-wheels in mid-air, unheard of songs they sing, distil the midnight vapors into wine—do pagan dances!

DOROTHY   Marvelous! How do I get there?

OFFICER   I warn you, Miss Simple, once you go that way you can't come back to Primanproper, Massachusetts!

DOROTHY   Who wants to come back here? Not I! Never was anyone a more willing candidate for expatriation than I am tonight! All I want to know is where it is—— Is it north, south, or east or west of town?

OFFICER   That's just it, ma'am. It's in all four directions.

DOROTHY   Then I suppose that I could possibly miss it?

OFFICER   Hardly possible, if you want to find it. Is that all?

DOROTHY   Yes, sir, that's all.—Thanks very much.—Good-bye! (MUSIC UP. DOROTHY *softly*.) Good-bye forever! [32]

SHIRLEY JACKSON
1919–1966

Ritual and Violence

"THE LOTTERY"

Shirley Jackson lived in a small town in Vermont with her husband, critic Stanley Edgar Hyman, and much of her work is based on her observations and experiences there. Her writing contains various kinds of social commentary; *Life Among the Savages* (1953) and *Raising Demons* (1957), for instance, rather humorously chronicle family life in a small New England town.

Jackson's style combines somewhat paradoxically strong elements of realism and fantasy. The majority of her short pieces and novels contain segments that are terrifying. Common, ordinary people placed against common, ordinary backgrounds become involved in supernatural happenings or reveal morbid states of mind. This contrast heightens the dramatic tension of the pieces and make Jackson's underlying thesis more vivid.

"The Lottery," Jackson's best-known story, occupies a deserving place on a list of classic short stories. The setting of the story is any small American town. There is little traditional conflict in the plot, but the intense suspense is maintained by mysterious undertones and the reader's anxiety to discover the meaning of the lottery. The story opens in a casual, almost festive tone, a technique that intensifies the sense of horror when the last events of the story are revealed. In fact, the final event is so fantastic that the story is made more credible by the everyday and commonplace nature of the preceding events. There is considerable flexibility in interpreting this story, which most resembles the fable or allegory in type. The themes of small-town routine, cultural lag, and small-town ritual are emphasized by Jackson, but more significant is the psychological basis for cruelty committed by an entire community. Even though the citizens are generally kind, thoughtful, and decent, they participate enthusiastically in cruelty sanctioned by custom and tradition. Some details seem to refer to an earlier time in American history, but the story is really timeless and deals with current, live issues.

Some of Jackson's novels are *The Road Through the Wall* (1948), *Hangsaman* (1951), *The Bird's Nest* (1954), and *We Have Always Lived in the Castle* (1963). Most representative of her fantastic and allegorical short stories is the collection entitled *The Lottery or The Adventures of James Harris* (1949).

"THE LOTTERY"

The morning of June 27th was clear and sunny, with the fresh warmth of a full-summer day; the flowers were blossoming profusely and the grass was richly green. The people of the village began to gather in the square, between the post office and the bank, around ten o'clock; in some towns there were so many people that the lottery took two days and had to be started on June 26th, but in this village, where there were only about three hundred people, the whole lottery took less than two hours, so it could begin at ten o'clock in the morning and still be through in time to allow the villagers to get home for noon dinner.

The children assembled first, of course. School was recently over for the summer, and the feeling of liberty sat uneasily on most of them; they tended to gather together quietly for a while before they broke into boisterous play, and their talk was still of the classroom and the teacher, of books and reprimands. Bobby Martin had already stuffed his pockets full of stones, and the other boys soon followed his example, selecting the smoothest and roundest stones; Bobby and Harry Jones and Dickie Delacroix—the villagers pronounced this name "Dellacroy"—eventually made a great pile of stones in one corner of the square and guarded it against the raids of the other boys. The girls stood aside, talking among themselves, looking over their shoulders at the boys, and the very small children rolled in the dust or clung to the hands of their older brothers or sisters.

Soon the men began to gather, surveying their own children, speaking of planting and rain, tractors and taxes. They stood [291] together, away from the pile of stones in the corner, and their jokes were quiet and they smiled rather than laughed. The women, wearing faded house dresses and sweaters, came shortly after their menfolk. They greeted one another and exchanged bits of gossip as they went to join their husbands. Soon the women, standing by their husbands, began to call to their children, and the children came reluctantly, having to be called four or five times. Bobby Martin ducked under his mother's grasping hand and ran, laughing, back to the pile of stones. His father spoke up sharply, and Bobby came quickly and took his place between his father and his oldest brother.

The lottery was conducted—as were the square dances, the teen-age club, the Halloween program—by Mr. Summers, who had time and energy to devote to civic activities. He was a round-faced, jovial man and he ran the coal business, and people were sorry for him, because he had no children and his wife was a scold. When he arrived in the square, carrying the black wooden box, there was a murmur of conversation among the villagers, and he waved and called, "Little late today, folks." The postmaster, Mr. Graves, followed him, carrying a three-legged stool, and the stool was put in the center of the square and Mr. Summers set the black box down on it. The villagers kept their distance, leaving a space between themselves and the stool, and when Mr. Summers said, "Some of you fellows want to give me a hand?" there was a hesitation before two men, Mr. Martin and his oldest son, Baxter, came forward to hold the box steady on the stool while Mr. Summers stirred up the papers inside it.

The original paraphernalia for the lottery had been lost long ago, and the black box now resting on the stool had been put into use even before Old Man Warner, the oldest man in town, was born. Mr. Summers spoke frequently to the vil-[292]lagers about making a new box, but no one liked to upset even as much tradition as was represented by the black box. There was a story that the present box had been made with some pieces of the box that had preceded it, the one that had been constructed when the first people settled down to make a village here. Every year, after the lottery, Mr. Summers began talking again about a new box, but every year the subject was allowed to fade off without anything's being done. The black box grew shabbier each year; by now it was no longer completely black but splintered badly along one side to show the original wood color, and in some places faded or stained.

Mr. Martin and his oldest son, Baxter, held the black box securely on the stool until Mr. Summers had stirred the papers thoroughly with his hand. Because so much of the ritual had been forgotten or discarded, Mr. Summers had been successful in having slips of papers substituted for the chips of wood that had been used for generations. Chips of wood, Mr. Summers had argued, had been all very well when the village was tiny, but now that the population was more than three hundred and likely to keep on growing, it was necessary to use something that would fit more easily into the black box. The night before the lottery, Mr. Summers and Mr. Graves made up the slips of paper and put them in the box, and it was then taken to the safe of Mr. Summers' coal company and locked up until Mr. Summers was ready to take it to the square next morning. The rest of the year, the box was put away, sometimes one place, sometimes another; it had spent one year in Mr. Graves's barn and another year underfoot in the post office, and sometimes it was set on a shelf in the Martin grocery and left there.

There was a great deal of fussing to be done before Mr. Summers declared the lottery open. There were the lists to [293] make up—of heads of families, heads of households in each family, members of each household in each family. There was the proper swearing-in of Mr. Summers by the postmaster, as the official of the lottery; at one time, some people remembered, there had been a recital of some sort, performed by the official of the lottery, a perfunctory, tuneless chant that had been rattled off duly each year; some people believed that the official of the lottery used to stand just so when he said or sang it, others believed that he was supposed to walk among the people, but years and years ago this part of the ritual had been allowed to lapse. There had been, also, a ritual salute, which the official of the lottery had had to use in addressing each person who came up to draw from the box, but this also had changed with time, until now it was felt necessary only for the official to speak to each person approaching. Mr. Summers was very good at all this; in his clean white shirt and blue jeans, with one hand resting carelessly on the black box, he seemed very proper and important as he talked interminably to Mr. Graves and the Martins.

Just as Mr. Summers finally left off talking and turned to the assembled villagers, Mrs. Hutchinson came hurriedly along the path to the square, her sweater thrown over her shoulders, and slid into place in the back of the crowd. "Clean forgot what day it was," she said to Mrs. Delacroix, who stood next to her, and they both laughed softly. "Thought my old man was out back stacking wood," Mrs. Hutchinson went on, "and then I looked out the window and the kids were gone, and then I remembered it was the twenty-seventh and came a-running." She dried her hands on her apron, and Mrs. Delacroix said, "You're in time, though. They'll still talking away up there."

Mrs. Hutchinson craned her neck to see through the crowd and found her husband and children standing near the front. [294] She tapped Mrs. Delacroix on the arm as a farewell and began to make her way through the crowd. The people separated good-humoredly to let her through; two or three people said, in voices just loud enough to be heard across the crowd, "Here comes your Missus, Hutchinson," and "Bill, she made it after all." Mrs. Hutchinson reached her husband, and Mr. Summers, who had been waiting, said cheerfully, "Thought we were going to have to get on without you, Tessie." Mrs. Hutchinson said, grinning, "Wouldn't have me leave m'dishes in the sink, now, would you, Joe?," and soft laughter ran through the crowd as the people stirred back into position after Mrs. Hutchinson's arrival.

"Well, now," Mr. Summers said soberly, "guess we better get started, get this over with, so's we can go back to work. Anybody ain't here?"

"Dunbar," several people said. "Dunbar, Dunbar."

Mr. Summers consulted his list. "Clyde Dunbar," he said. "That's right. He's broke his leg, hasn't he? Who's drawing for him?"

"Me, I guess," a woman said, and Mr. Summers turned to look at her. "Wife draws for her husband," Mr. Summers said. "Don't you have a grown boy to do it for you, Janey?" Although Mr. Summers and everyone else in the village knew the answer perfectly well, it was the business of the official of the lottery to ask such questions, formally. Mr. Summers waited with an expression of polite interest while Mrs. Dunbar answered.

"Horace's not but sixteen yet," Mrs. Dunbar said regretfully. "Guess I gotta fill in for the old man this year."

"Right," Mr. Summers said. He made a note on the list he was holding. Then he asked, "Watson boy drawing this year?"

A tall boy in the crowd raised his hand. "Here," he said. "I'm [295] drawing for m'mother and me." He blinked his eyes nervously and ducked his head as several voices in the crowd said things like "Good fellow, Jack," and "Glad to see your mother's got a man to do it."

"Well," Mr. Summers said, "guess that's everyone. Old Man Warner make it?"

"Here," a voice said, and Mr. Summers nodded.

A sudden hush fell on the crowd as Mr. Summers cleared his throat and looked at the list. "All ready?" he called. "Now, I'll read the names—heads of families first—and the men come up and take a paper out of the box. Keep the paper folded in your hand without looking at it until everyone has had a turn. Everything clear?"

The people had done it so many times that they only half listened to the directions; most of them were quiet, wetting their lips, not looking around. Then Mr. Summers raised one hand high and said, "Adams." A man disengaged himself from the crowd and came forward. "Hi, Steve," Mr. Summers said, and Mr. Adams said, "Hi, Joe." They grinned at one another humorlessly and nervously. Then Mr. Adams reached into the black box and took out a folded paper. He held it firmly by one corner as he turned and went hastily back to his place in the crowd, where he stood a little apart from his family, not looking down at his hand.

"Allen," Mr. Summers said. "Andrews. . . . Bentham."

"Seems like there's no time at all between lotteries any more," Mrs. Delacroix said to Mrs. Graves in the back row. "Seems like we got through with the last one only last week."

"Time sure goes fast," Mrs. Graves said.

"Clark. . . . Delacroix." [296]

"There goes my old man," Mrs. Delacroix said. She held her breath while her husband went forward.

"Dunbar," Mr. Summers said, and Mrs. Dunbar went steadily to the box while one of the women said, "Go on, Janey," and another said, "There she goes."

"We're next," Mrs. Graves said. She watched while Mr. Graves came around from the side of the box, greeted Mr. Summers gravely, and selected a slip of paper from the box. By now, all through the crowd there were men holding the small folded papers in their large hands, turning them over and over nervously. Mrs. Dunbar and her two sons stood together, Mrs. Dunbar holding the slip of paper.

"Harburt. . . . Hutchinson."

"Get up there, Bill," Mrs. Hutchinson said, and the people near her laughed.

"Jones."

"They do say," Mr. Adams said to Old Man Warner, who stood next to him, "that over in the north village they're talking of giving up the lottery."

Old Man Warner snorted. "Pack of crazy fools," he said. "Listening to the young folks, nothing's good enough for *them*. Next thing you know, they'll be wanting to go back to living in caves, nobody work any more, live *that* way for a while. Used to be a saying about 'Lottery in June, corn be heavy soon.' First thing you know, we'd all be eating stewed chickweed and acorns. There's *always* been a lottery," he added petulantly. "Bad enough to see young Joe Summers up there joking with everybody."

"Some places have already quit lotteries," Mrs. Adams said.

"Nothing but trouble in *that*," Old Man Warner said stoutly. "Pack of young fools." [297]

"Martin." And Bobby Martin watched his father go forward. "Overdyke. . . . Percy."

"I wish they'd hurry," Mrs. Dunbar said to her older son. "I wish they'd hurry."

"They're almost through," her son said.

"You get ready to run tell Dad," Mrs. Dunbar said.

Mr. Summers called his own name and then stepped forward precisely and selected a slip from the box. Then he called, "Warner."

"Seventy-seventh year I been in the lottery," Old Man Warner said as he went through the crowd. "Seventy-seventh time."

"Watson." The tall boy came awkwardly through the crowd. Someone said, "Don't be nervous, Jack," and Mr. Summers said, "Take your time, son."

"Zanini."

After that, there was a long pause, a breathless pause, until Mr. Summers, holding his slip of paper in the air, said, "All right, fellows." For a minute, no one moved, and then all the slips of paper were opened. Suddenly, all women began to speak at once, saying, "Who is it?," "Who's got it?," "Is it the Dunbars?," "Is it the Watsons?" Then the voices began to say, "It's Hutchinson. It's Bill." "Bill Hutchinson got it."

"Go tell your father," Mrs. Dunbar said to her older son.

People began to look around to see the Hutchinsons. Bill Hutchinson was standing quiet, staring down at the paper in his hand. Suddenly, Tessie Hutchinson shouted to Mr. Summers, "You didn't give him time enough to take any paper he wanted. I saw you. It wasn't fair."

"Be a good sport, Tessie," Mrs. Delacroix called, and Mrs. Graves said, "All of us took the same chance." [298]

"Shut up, Tessie," Bill Hutchinson said.

"Well, everyone," Mr. Summers said, "that was done pretty fast, and now we've got to be hurrying a little more to get done in time." He consulted his next list. "Bill," he said, "you draw for the Hutchinson family. You got any other households in the Hutchinsons?"

"There's Don and Eva," Mrs. Hutchinson yelled. "Make *them* take their chance!"

"Daughters draw with their husbands' families, Tessie," Mr. Summers said gently. "You know that as well as anyone else."

"It wasn't *fair*," Tessie said.

"Guess not, Joe," Bill Hutchinson said regretfully. "My daughter draws with her husband's family, that's only fair. And I've got no other family except the kids."

"Then as far as drawing for families is concerned, it's you," Mr. Summers said in explanation, "and as far as drawing for households is concerned, that's you, too. Right?"

"Right," Bill Hutchinson said.

"How many kids, Bill?" Mr. Summers asked formally.

"Three," Bill Hutchinson said. "There's Bill, Jr., and Nancy, and little Dave. And Tessie and me."

"All right, then," Mr. Summers said. "Harry, you got their tickets back?"

Mr. Graves nodded and held up the slips of paper. "Put them in the box, then," Mr. Summers directed. "Take Bill's and put it in."

"I think we ought to start over," Mrs. Hutchinson said, as quietly as she could. "I tell you it wasn't *fair*. You didn't give him time enough to choose. *Every*body saw that."

Mr. Graves had selected the five slips and put them in the box, and he dropped all the papers but those onto the ground, where the breeze caught them and lifted them off. [299]

"Listen, everybody," Mrs. Hutchinson was saying to the people around her.

"Ready, Bill?" Mr. Summers asked, and Bill Hutchinson, with one quick glance around at his wife and children, nodded.

"Remember," Mr. Summers said, "take the slips and keep them folded until each person has taken one. Harry, you help little Dave." Mr. Graves took the hand of the little boy, who came willingly with him up to the box. "Take a paper out of the box, Davy," Mr. Summers said. Davy put his hand into the box and laughed. "Take just *one* paper," Mr. Summers said.

"Harry, you hold it for him." Mr. Graves took the child's hand and removed the folded paper from the tight fist and held it while little Dave stood next to him and looked up at him wonderingly.

"Nancy next," Mr. Summers said. Nancy was twelve, and her school friends breathed heavily as she went forward, switching her skirt, and took a slip daintily from the box. "Bill, Jr.," Mr. Summers said, and Billy, his face red and his feet over-large, nearly knocked the box over as he got a paper out. "Tessie," Mr. Summers said. She hesitated for a minute, looking around defiantly, and then set her lips and went up to the box. She snatched a paper out and held it behind her.

"Bill," Mr. Summers said, and Bill Hutchinson reached into the box and felt around, bringing his hand out at last with the slip of paper in it.

The crowd was quiet. A girl whispered, "I hope it's not Nancy," and the sound of the whisper reached the edges of the crowd.

"It's not the way it used to be," Old Man Warner said clearly. "People ain't the way they used to be."

"All right," Mr. Summers said. "Open the papers. Harry, you open little Dave's." [300]

Mr. Graves opened the slip of paper and there was a general sigh through the crowd as he held it up and everyone could see that it was blank. Nancy and Bill, Jr., opened theirs at the same time, and both beamed laughed, turning around to the crowd and holding their slips of paper above their heads.

"Tessie," Mr. Summers said. There was a pause, and then Mr. Summers looked at Bill Hutchinson, and Bill unfolded his paper and showed it. It was blank.

"It's Tessie," Mr. Summers said, and his voice was hushed. "Show us her paper, Bill."

Bill Hutchinson went over to his wife and forced the slip of paper out of her hand. It had a black spot on it, the black spot Mr. Summers had made the night before with the heavy pencil in the coal-company office. Bill Hutchinson held it up, and there was a stir in the crowd.

"All right, folks," Mr. Summers said, "Let's finish quickly."

Although the villagers had forgotten the ritual and lost the original black box, they still remembered to use stones. The pile of stones the boys had made earlier was ready; there were stones on the ground with the blowing scraps of paper that had come out of the box. Mrs. Delacroix selected a stone so large she had to pick it up with both hands and turned to Mrs. Dunbar. "Come on," she said. "Hurry up."

Mrs. Dunbar had small stones in both hands, and she said, gasping for breath, "I can't run at all. You'll have to go ahead and I'll catch up with you."

The children had stones already, and someone gave little Davy Hutchinson a few pebbles.

Tessie Hutchinson was in the center of a cleared space by now, and she held her hands out desperately as the villagers moved in on her. "It isn't fair," she said. A stone hit her on the side of the head. [301]

Old Man Warner was saying, "Come on, come on, everyone." Steve Adams was in the front of the crowd of villagers, with Mr. Graves beside him.

"It isn't fair, it isn't right," Mrs. Hutchinson screamed, and then they were upon her. [302]

RALPH ELLISON
1914–
Black Identity
from
INVISIBLE MAN

The emergence of the black writer dealing with the black identity has been one of the prominent characteristics of post-World War II American literature. Black writers before this time had certainly dealt with the black experience in America, and Richard Wright treated it quite realistically in *Native Son* (1940), but as the relations between blacks and whites became more troubled, it was inevitable that more and more black writers would deal frankly with the issues involved. Most notable among these new voices were James Baldwin, in his novels *Go Tell It on the Mountain* (1953), and *Another Country* (1962), and, of a more radical nature, Eldridge Cleaver, in his work *Soul on Ice* (1967).

Ralph Ellison's *Invisible Man* is the most comprehensive treatment of the problems related to blacks in America, and as the novel progresses it becomes apparent that the problems are everyone's problems. This novel may be considered as a history of the blacks in America—the various attitudes, poses, and attempted solutions to black-white conflicts from Uncle Tom-ism to the more recent black militants. As the central character confronts these conditions in a picaresque fashion he discovers that he has no identity; he is merely adapting himself to the identities other people attempt to impose upon him—thus he is an "invisible man." Ellison concludes that the only way he can emerge with visibility is through illumination of the inner self. This is not just a problem for blacks.

The selection included here is the first chapter of the novel and is sometimes printed separately as "Battle Royal"; in fact, it was first written as a separate story. The setting is a small southern town, where the narrator, along with a number of other Negro boys, is humiliated at a stag party attended by the leading citizens of the town. A number of unpleasant attitudes and patterns of behavior of middle-class American become apparent as the narrative develops. The effects of the experience on the narrator lead to the main thrust of the novel.

Although *Invisible Man* was written in the 1940s, it was not published in its complete form until 1952. It received the 1953 National Book Award for fiction, and since that time it has achieved the status of a classic in our literature. Ellison, an Oklahoman, received an education in music at Tuskegee Institute. He has written reviews, short stories, articles, and criticism, but *Invisible Man* is his only novel and the solid base of his reputation.

from INVISIBLE MAN

CHAPTER 1

It goes a long way back, some twenty years. All my life I had been looking for something, and everywhere I turned someone tried to tell me what it was. I accepted their answers too, though they were often in contradiction and even self-contradictory. I was naïve. I was looking for myself and asking everyone except myself questions which I, and only I, could answer. It took me a long time and much painful boomeranging of my expectations to achieve a realization everyone else appears to have been born with: That I am nobody but myself. But first I had to discover that I am an invisible man!

And yet I am no freak of nature, nor of history. I was in the cards, other things having been equal (or unequal) eighty-five years ago. I am not ashamed of my grandparents for having been slaves. I am only ashamed of myself for having at one time been ashamed. About eighty-five years ago they were told that they were free, united with others of our country in everything pertaining to the common good, and, in everything social, separate like the fingers of the hand. And they believed it. They exulted in it. They stayed in their place, worked hard, and brought up my father to do the same. But my grandfather is the one. He was an odd old guy, my grandfather, and I am told I take after him. It was he who caused the trouble. On his deathbed he called my father to him and said, "Son, after I'm gone I want you to keep up the good fight. I never told you, but our life is a war and I have been a traitor all my born days, a spy in the enemy's country ever since I give up my gun back in the Reconstruction. Live with your head in the lion's mouth. I want you to overcome 'em with yesses, undermine 'em with grins, agree 'em to death and destruction, let 'em swoller you till they vomit or bust [13] wide open." They thought the old man had

Ralph Ellison, *Invisible Man* (New York: Random House, 1952). Copyright 1947 by Ralph Ellison. Reprinted from *Invisible Man* by permission of Random House, Inc.

gone out of his mind. He had been the meekest of men. The younger children were rushed from the room, the shades drawn and the flame of the lamp turned so low that it sputtered on the wick like the old man's breathing. "Learn it to the younguns," he whispered fiercely; then he died.

But my folks were more alarmed over his last words than over his dying. It was as though he had not died at all, his words caused so much anxiety. I was warned emphatically to forget what he had said and, indeed, this is the first time it has been mentioned outside the family circle. It had a tremendous effect upon me, however. I could never be sure of what he meant. Grandfather had been a quiet old man who never made any trouble, yet on his deathbed he had called himself a traitor and a spy, and he had spoken of his meekness as a dangerous activity. It became a constant puzzle which lay unanswered in the back of my mind. And whenever things went well for me I remembered my grandfather and felt guilty and uncomfortable. It was as though I was carrying out his advice in spite of myself. And to make it worse, everyone loved me for it. I was praised by the most lily-white men of the town. I was considered an example of desirable conduct—just as my grandfather had been, And what puzzled me was that the old man had defined it as *treachery*. When I was praised for my conduct I felt a guilt that in some way I was doing something that was really against the wishes of the white folks, that if they had understood they would have desired me to act just the opposite, that I should have been sulky and mean, and that that really would have been what they wanted, even though they were fooled and thought they wanted me to act as I did. It made me afraid that some day they would look upon me as a traitor and I would be lost. Still I was more afraid to act any other way because they didn't like that at all. The old man's words were like a curse. On my graduation day I delivered an oration in which I showed that humility was the secret, indeed, the very essence of progress. (Not that I believed this—how could I, remembering my grandfather?—I only believed that it worked.) It was a great success. Everyone praised me and I was invited to give the speech at a gathering of the town's leading white citizens. It was a triumph for our whole community.

It was in the main ballroom of the leading hotel. When I got there I discovered that it was on the occasion of a smoker, and I was told that since I was to be there anyway I might as well take part [14] in the battle royal to be fought by some of my schoolmates as part of the entertainment. The battle royal came first.

All of the town's big shots were there in their tuxedoes, wolfing down the buffet foods, drinking beer and whiskey and smoking black cigars. It was a large room with a high ceiling. Chairs were arranged in neat rows around three sides of a portable boxing ring. The fourth side was clear, revealing a gleaming space of polished floor. I had some misgivings over the battle royal, by the way. Not from a distaste for fighting, but because I didn't care too much for the other fellows who were to take part. They were tough guys who seemed to have no grandfather's curse worrying their minds. No one could mistake their toughness. And besides, I suspected that fighting a battle royal might detract from the dignity of my speech. In those pre-invisible days I visualized myself as a potential Booker T. Washington. But the other fellows didn't care too much for me either, and there were nine of them. I felt superior to them in my way, and I didn't like the manner in which we were all crowded together into the servants' elevator. Nor did they like my being there. In fact, as the warmly lighted floors flashed past the elevator we had words over the fact that I, by taking part in the fight, had knocked one of their friends out of a night's work.

We were led out of the elevator through a rococo hall into an anteroom and told to get into our fighting togs. Each of us was issued a pair of boxing gloves and ushered out into the big mirrored hall, which we entered looking cautiously about us and whispering, lest we might accidentally be heard above the noise of the room. It was foggy with cigar smoke. And already the whiskey was taking effect. I was shocked to see some of the most important men of the town quite tipsy. They were all there—bankers, lawyers, judges, doctors, fire chiefs, teachers, merchants. Even one of the more fashionable pastors. Something we could not see was going on up front. A clarinet was vibrating sensuously and the men were standing up and moving eagerly forward. We were a small tight group, clustered together, our bare upper bodies touching and shining with anticipatory sweat; while up front the big shots were becoming increasingly excited over something we still could not see. Suddenly I heard the school superintendent, who had told me to come, yell, "Bring up the shines, gentlemen! Bring up the little shines!"

We were rushed up to the front of the ballroom, where it smelled even more strongly of tobacco and whiskey. Then we were pushed [15] into place. I almost wet my pants. A sea of faces, some hostile, some amused, ringed around us, and in the center, facing us, stood a magnificent blonde—stark naked. There was dead silence. I felt a blast of cold air chill me. I tried to back away, but they were behind me and around me. Some of the boys stood with lowered heads, trembling. I felt a wave of irrational guilt and fear. My teeth chattered, my skin turned to goose flesh, my knees knocked. Yet I was strongly attracted and looked in spite of myself. Had the price of looking been blindness, I would have looked. The hair was yellow like that of a circus kewpie doll, the face heavily powdered and rouged, as though to form an abstract mask, the eyes hollow and smeared a cool blue, the color of a baboon's butt. I felt a desire to spit upon her as my eyes brushed slowly over her body. Her breasts were firm and round as the domes of East Indian temples, and I stood so close as to see the fine skin texture and beads of pearly perspiration glistening like dew around the pink and erected buds of her nipples. I wanted at one and the same time to run from the room, to sink through the floor, or go to her and cover her from my eyes and the eyes of the others with my body; to feel the soft thighs, to caress her and destroy her, to love her and murder her, to hide from her, and yet to stroke where below the small American flag tattooed upon her belly her thighs formed a capital V. I had a notion that of all in the room she saw only me with her impersonal eyes.

And then she began to dance, a slow sensuous movement; the smoke of a hundred cigars clinging to her like the thinnest of veils. She seemed like a fair bird-girl girdled in veils calling to me from the angry surface of some gray and threatening sea. I was transported. Then I became aware of the clarinet playing and the big shots yelling at us. Some threatened us if we looked and others if we did not. On my right I saw one boy faint. And now a man grabbed a silver pitcher from a table and stepped close as he dashed ice water upon him and stood him up and forced two of us to support him as his head hung and moans issued from his thick bluish lips. Another boy began to plead to go home. He was the largest of the group, wearing dark red fighting trunks much too small to conceal the erection which projected from him as though in answer to the insinuating low-registered moaning of the clarinet. He tried to hide himself with his boxing gloves.

And all the while the blonde continued dancing, smiling faintly at the big shots who watched her with fascination, and faintly smil-[16]ing at our fear. I noticed a certain merchant who followed her hungrily, his lips loose and drooling. He was a large man who wore diamond studs in a shirtfront which swelled with the ample paunch underneath, and each time the blonde swayed her undulating hips he ran his hand through the thin hair of his bald head and, with his arms upheld, his posture clumsy like that of an intoxicated panda, wound his belly in a slow and obscene grind. This creature was completely hypnotized. The music had quickened. As the dancer flung herself about with a detached expression on her face, the men began reaching out to touch her. I could see their beefy fingers sink into the soft flesh. Some of the others tried to stop them and she began to move around the floor in graceful circles, as they gave chase, slipping and sliding over the polished floor. It was mad. Chairs went crashing, drinks were spilt, as they ran laughing and howling after her. They caught her just as she reached a door, raised her from the floor, and tossed her as college boys are tossed at a hazing, and above her red, fixed-smiling lips I saw the terror and disgust in her eyes, almost like my own terror and that which I saw in some of the other boys. As I watched, they tossed her twice and her soft breasts seemed to flatten against the air and her legs flung wildly as she spun. Some of the more sober ones helped her to escape. And I started off the floor, heading for the anteroom with the rest of the boys.

Some were still crying and in hysteria. But as we tried to leave we were stopped and ordered to get into the ring. There was nothing to do but what we were told. All ten of us climbed under the ropes and allowed ourselves to be blindfolded with broad bands of white cloth. One of the men seemed to feel a bit sympathetic and tried to cheer us up as we stood with our backs against the ropes. Some of us tried to grin. "See that boy over there?" one of the men said. "I want you to run across at the bell and give it to him right in the belly. If you don't get him, I'm going to get you. I don't like his looks." Each of us was told the same. The blindfolds were put on. Yet even then I had been going over my speech. In my mind each word was as bright as flame. I felt the cloth pressed into place, and frowned so that it would be loosened when I relaxed.

But now I felt a sudden fit of blind terror. I was unused to darkness. It was as though I had suddenly found myself in a dark room filled with poisonous cottonmouths. I could hear the bleary voices yelling insistently for the battle royal to begin.

"Get going in there!" [17]

"Let me at that big nigger!"

I strained to pick up the school superintendent's voice, as though to squeeze some security out of that slightly more familiar sound.

"Let me at those black sonsabitches!" someone yelled.

"No, Jackson, no!" another voice yelled. "Here, somebody, help me hold Jack."

"I want to get at that ginger-colored nigger. Tear him limb from limb," the first voice yelled.

I stood against the ropes trembling. For in those days I was what they called ginger-colored, and he sounded as though he might crunch me between his teeth like a crisp ginger cookie.

Quite a struggle was going on. Chairs were being kicked about and I could hear voices grunting as with a terrific effort. I wanted to see, to see more desperately than ever before. But the blindfold was tight as a thick skin-puckering scab and when I raised my gloved hands to push the layers of white aside a voice yelled, "Oh, no you don't, black bastard! Leave that alone!"

"Ring the bell before Jackson kills him a coon!" someone boomed in the sudden silence. And I heard the bell clang and the sound of the feet scuffling forward.

A glove smacked against my head. I pivoted, striking out stiffly as someone went past, and felt the jar ripple along the length of my arm to my shoulder. Then it seemed as though all nine of the boys had turned upon me at once. Blows pounded me from all sides while I struck out as best I could. So many blows landed upon me that I wondered if I were not the only blindfolded fighter in the ring, or if the man called Jackson hadn't succeeded in getting me after all.

Blindfolded, I could no longer control my emotions. I had no dignity. I stumbled about like a baby or a drunken man. The smoke had become thicker and with each new blow it seemed to sear and further restrict my lungs. My saliva became like hot bitter glue. A glove connected with my head, filling my mouth with warm blood. It was everywhere. I could not tell if the moisture I felt upon my body was sweat or blood. A blow landed hard against the nape of my neck. I felt myself going over, my head hitting the floor. Streaks of blue light filled the black world behind the blindfold. I lay prone, pretending that I was knocked out, but felt myself seized by hands and yanked to my feet. "Get going, black boy! Mix it up!" My arms were like lead, my head smarting from blows. I managed to feel my way to the ropes and held on, trying to catch my breath. A glove [18] landed in my midsection and I went over again, feeling as though the smoke had become a knife jabbed into my guts. Pushed this way and that by the legs milling around me, I finally pulled erect and discovered that I could see the black, sweat-washed forms weaving in the smoky-blue atmosphere like drunken dancers weaving to the rapid drum-like thuds of blows.

Everyone fought hysterically. It was complete anarchy. Everybody fought everybody else. No group fought together for long. Two, three, four, fought one, then turned to fight each other, were themselves attacked. Blows landed below the belt and in the kidney, with the gloves open as well as closed, and with my eye partly opened now there was not so much terror. I moved carefully, avoiding blows, although not too many to attract attention, fighting from group to group. The boys groped about like blind, cautious crabs crouching to protect their mid-sections, their heads pulled in short against their shoulders, their arms stretched nervously before them, with their fists testing the smoke-filled air like the knobbed feelers of hypersensitive snails. In one corner I glimpsed a boy violently punching the air and heard him scream in pain as he smashed his hand against a ring post. For a second I saw him bent over holding his hand, then going down as a blow caught his unprotected head. I played one group against the other, slipping in and throwing a punch then stepping out of range while pushing the others into the melee to take the blows blindly aimed at me. The smoke was agonizing and there were no rounds, no bells at three minute intervals to relieve our exhaustion. The room spun round me, a swirl of lights, smoke, sweating bodies surrounded by tense white faces. I bled from both nose and mouth, the blood spattering upon my chest.

The men kept yelling, "Slug him, black boy! Knock his guts out!"

"Uppercut him! Kill him! Kill that big boy!"

Taking a fake fall, I saw a boy going down heavily beside me as though we were felled by a single blow, saw a sneaker-clad foot shoot into his groin as the two who had knocked him down stumbled upon him. I rolled out of range, feeling a twinge of nausea.

The harder we fought the more threatening the men became. And yet, I had begun to worry about my speech again. How would it go? Would they recognize my ability? What would they give me?

I was fighting automatically when suddenly I noticed that one after another of the boys was leaving the ring. I was surprised, filled with panic, as though I had been left alone with an unknown danger. [19] Then I understood. The boys had arranged it among themselves. It was the custom for the two men left in the ring to slug it out for the winner's prize. I discovered this too late. When the bell sounded two men in tuxedoes leaped into the ring and removed the blindfold. I found myself facing Tatlock, the biggest of the gang. I felt sick at my stomach. Hardly had the bell stopped ringing in my ears than it clanged again and I saw him moving swiftly toward me. Thinking of nothing else to do I hit him smash on the nose. He kept coming, bringing the rank sharp violence of stale sweat. His face was a black blank of a face, only his eyes alive—with hate of me and aglow with a feverish terror from what had happened to us all. I became anxious. I wanted to deliver my speech and he came at me as though he meant to beat it out of me. I smashed him again and again, taking his blows as they came. Then on a sudden impulse I struck him lightly and as we clinched, I whispered, "Fake like I knocked you out, you can have the prize."

"I'll break your behind," he whispered hoarsely.

"For *them?*"

"For *me,* sonofabitch!"

They were yelling for us to break it up and Tatlock spun me half around with a blow, and as a joggled camera sweeps in a reeling scene, I saw the howling red faces crouching tense beneath the cloud of blue-gray smoke. For a moment the world wavered, unraveled, flowed, then my head cleared and Tatlock bounced before me. That fluttering shadow before my eyes was his jabbing left hand. Then falling forward, my head against his damp shoulder, I whispered,

"I'll make it five dollars more."

"Go to hell!"

But his muscles relaxed a trifle beneath my pressure and I breathed, "Seven?"

"Give it to your ma," he said, ripping me beneath the heart.

And while I still held him I butted him and moved away. I felt myself bombarded with punches. I fought back with hopeless desperation. I wanted to deliver my speech more than anything else in the world, because I felt that only these men could judge truly my ability, and now this stupid clown was ruining my chances. I began fighting carefully now, moving in to punch him and out again with my greater speed. A lucky blow to his chin and I had him going too—until I heard a loud voice yell, "I got my money on the big boy." [20]

Hearing this, I almost dropped my guard. I was confused: Should I try to win against the voice out there? Would not this go against my speech, and was not this a moment for humility, for nonresistance? A blow to my head as I danced about sent my right eye popping like a jack-in-the-box and settled my dilemma. The room went red as I fell. It was a dream fall, my body languid and fastidious as to where to land, until the floor became

impatient and smashed up to meet me. A moment later I came to. An hyp-
notic voice said FIVE emphatically. And I lay there, hazily watching a dark
red spot of my own blood shaping itself into a butterfly, glistening and soak-
ing into the soiled gray world of the canvas.

When the voice drawled TEN I was lifted up and dragged to a chair.
I sat dazed. My eye pained and swelled with each throb of my pounding
heart and I wondered if now I would be allowed to speak. I was wringing
wet, my mouth still bleeding. We were grouped along the wall now. The
other boys ignored me as they congratulated Tatlock and speculated as to
how much they would be paid. One boy whimpered over his smashed hand.
Looking up front, I saw attendants in white jackets rolling the portable ring
away and placing a small square rug in the vacant space surrounded by
chairs. Perhaps, I thought, I will stand on the rug to deliver my speech.

Then the M.C. called to us, "Come on up here boys and get your
money."

We ran forward to where the men laughed and talked in their chairs,
waiting. Everyone seemed friendly now.

"There it is on the rug," the man said. I saw the rug covered with coins
of all dimensions and a few crumpled bills. But what excited me, scattered
here and there, were the gold pieces.

"Boys, it's all yours," the man said. "You get all you grab."

"That's right, Sambo," a blond man said, winking at me confidentially.

I trembled with excitement, forgetting my pain. I would get the gold
and the bills, I thought. I would use both hands. I would throw my body
against the boys nearest me to block them from the gold.

"Get down around the rug now," the man commanded, "and don't
anyone touch it until I give the signal."

"This ought to be good," I heard.

As told, we got around the square rug on our knees. Slowly the man
raised his freckled hand as we followed it upward with our eyes.

I heard, "These niggers look like they're about to pray!" [21]

Then, "Ready," the man said. "Go!"

I lunged for a yellow coin lying on the blue design of the carpet, touching it and sending a surprised shriek to join those rising around me. I tried
frantically to remove my hand but could not let go. A hot, violent force tore
through my body, shaking me like a wet rat. The rug was electrified. The
hair bristled up on my head as I shook myself free. My muscles jumped, my
nerves jangled, writhed. But I saw that this was not stopping the other boys.
Laughing in fear and embarrassment, some were holding back and scooping
up the coins knocked off by the painful contortions of the others. The men
roared above us as we struggled.

"Pick it up, goddamnit, pick it up!" someone called like a bass-voiced
parrot. "Go on, get it!"

I crawled rapidly around the floor, picking up the coins, trying to avoid the coppers and get greenbacks and the gold. Ignoring the shock by laughing, as I brushed the coins off quickly, I discovered that I could contain the electricity—a contradiction, but it works. Then the men began to push us onto the rug. Laughing embarrassedly, we struggled out of their hands and kept after the coins. We were all wet and slippery and hard to hold. Suddenly I saw a boy lifted into the air, glistening with sweat like a circus seal, and dropped, his wet back landing flush upon the charged rug, heard him yell and saw him literally dance upon his back, his elbows beating a frenzied tattoo upon the floor, his muscles twitching like the flesh of a horse stung by many flies. When he finally rolled off, his face was gray and no one stopped him when he ran from the floor amid booming laughter.

"Get the money," the M.C. called. "That's good hard American cash!"

And we snatched and grabbed, snatched and grabbed. I was careful not to come too close to the rug now, and when I felt the hot whiskey breath descend upon me like a cloud of foul air I reached out and grabbed the leg of a chair. It was occupied and I held on desperately.

"Leggo, nigger! Leggo!"

The huge face wavered down to mine as he tried to push me free. But my body was slippery and he was too drunk. It was Mr. Colcord, who owned a chain of movie houses and "entertainment palaces." Each time he grabbed me I slipped out of his hands. It became a real struggle. I feared the rug more than I did the drunk, so I held on, surprising myself for a moment by trying to topple *him* upon [22] the rug. It was such an enormous idea that I found myself actually carrying it out. I tried not to be obvious, yet when I grabbed his leg, trying to tumble him out of the chair, he raised up roaring with laughter, and, looking at me with soberness dead in the eye, kicked me viciously in the chest. The chair leg flew out of my hand and I felt myself going and rolled. It was as though I had rolled through a bed of hot coals. It seemed a whole century would pass before I would roll free, a century in which I was seared through the deepest levels of my body to the fearful breath within me and the breath seared and heated to the point of explosion. It'll all be over in a flash, I thought and I rolled clear. It'll all be over in a flash.

But not yet, the men on the other side were waiting, red faces swollen as though from apoplexy as they bent forward in their chairs. Seeing their fingers coming toward me I rolled away as a fumbled football rolls off the receiver's fingertips, back into the coals. That time I luckily sent the rug sliding out of place and heard the coins ringing against the floor and the boys scuffling to pick them up and the M.C. calling, "All right, boys, that's all. Go get dressed and get your money."

I was limp as a dish rag. My back felt as though it had been beaten with wires.

When we had dressed the M.C. came in and gave us each five dollars, except Tatlock, who got ten for being last in the ring. Then he told us to leave. I was not to get a chance to deliver my speech, I thought. I was going out into the dim alley in despair when I was stopped and told to go back. I returned to the ballroom, where the men were pushing back their chairs and gathering in groups to talk.

The M.C. knocked on a table for quiet. "Gentlemen," he said "we almost forgot an important part of the program. A most serious part, gentlemen. This boy was brought here to deliver a speech which he made at his graduation yesterday . . ."

"Bravo!"

"I'm told that he is the smartest boy we've got out there in Greenwood. I'm told that he knows more big words than a pocket-sized dictionary."

Much applause and laughter.

"So now, gentlemen, I want you to give him your attention."

There was still laughter as I faced them, my mouth dry, my eye throbbing. I began slowly, but evidently my throat was tense, because they began shouting, "Louder! Louder!"

"We of the younger generation extol the wisdom of that great [23] leader and educator," I shouted, "who first spoke these flaming words of wisdom: 'A ship lost at sea for many days suddenly sighted a friendly vessel. From the mast of the unfortunate vessel was seen a signal: "Water, water; we die of thirst!" The answer from the friendly vessel came back: "Cast down your bucket where you are." The captain of the distressed vessel, at last heeding the injunction, cast down his bucket, and it came up full of fresh sparkling water from the mouth of the Amazon River.' And like him I say, and in his words, 'To those of my race who depend upon bettering their condition in a foreign land, or who underestimate the importance of cultivating friendly relations with the Southern white man, who is his next-door neighbor, I would say: "Cast down your bucket where you are"—cast it down in making friends in every manly way of the people of all races by whom we are surrounded . . .' "

I spoke automatically and with such fervor that I did not realize that the men were still talking and laughing until my dry mouth, filling up with blood from the cut, almost strangled me. I coughed, wanting to stop and go to one of the tall brass, sand-filled spittoons to relieve myself, but a few of the men, especially the superintendent, were listening and I was afraid. So I gulped it down, blood, saliva and all, and continued. (What powers of endurance I had during those days! What enthusiasm! What a belief in the rightness of things!) I spoke even louder in spite of the pain. But still they talked and still they laughed, as though deaf with cotton in dirty ears. So I spoke with greater emotional emphasis. I closed my ears and swallowed blood until I was nauseated. The speech seemed a hundred times as long as before, but I could not leave out a single word. All had to be said, each memorized nuance considered, rendered. Nor was that all. Whenever I uttered a word of three or more syllables a group of voices would yell for me to repeat it. I used the phrase "social responsibility" and they yelled:

"What's that word you say, boy?"

"Social responsibility," I said.

"What?"

"Social . . ."

"Louder."

". . . responsibility."

"More!"

"Respon—"

"Repeat!"

"—sibility." [24]

The room filled with the uproar of laughter until, no doubt, distracted by having to gulp down my blood, I made a mistake and yelled a phrase I had often seen denounced in newspaper editorials, heard debated in private.

"Social . . ."

"What?" they yelled.

". . . equality—"

The laughter hung smokelike in the sudden stillness. I opened my eyes, puzzled. Sounds of displeasure filled the room. The M.C. rushed forward. They shouted hostile phrases at me. But I did not understand.

A small dry mustached man in the front row blared out, "Say that slowly, son!"

"What, sir?"

"What you just said!"

"Social responsibility, sir," I said.

"You weren't being smart, were you, boy?" he said, not unkindly.

"No, sir!"

"You sure that about 'equality' was a mistake?"

"Oh, yes, sir," I said. "I was swallowing blood."

"Well, you had better speak more slowly so we can understand. We mean to do right by you, but you've got to know your place at all times. All right, now go on with your speech.

I was afraid. I wanted to leave but I wanted also to speak and I was afraid they'd snatch me down.

"Thank you, sir," I said, beginning where I had left off, and having them ignore me as before.

Yet when I finished there was a thunderous applause. I was surprised to see the superintendent come forth with a package wrapped in white tissue paper, and, gesturing for quiet, address the men.

"Gentlemen, you see that I did not overpraise this boy. He makes a good speech and some day he'll lead his people in the proper paths. And I don't have to tell you that that is important in these days and times. This is a good, smart boy, and so to encourage him in the right direction, in the name of the Board of Education I wish to present him a prize in the form of this . . ."

He paused, removing the tissue paper and revealing a gleaming calfskin brief case.

". . . in the form of this first-class article from Shad Whitmore's shop."

"Boy," he said, addressing me, "take this prize and keep it well. [25] Consider it a badge of office. Prize it. Keep developing as you are and some day it will be filled with important papers that will help shape the destiny of your people."

I was so moved that I could hardly express my thanks. A rope of bloody saliva forming a shape like an undiscovered continent drooled upon the leather and I wiped it quickly away. I felt an importance that I had never dreamed.

"Open it and see what's inside," I was told.

My fingers a-tremble, I complied, smelling the fresh leather and finding an official-looking document inside. It was a scholarship to the state college for Negroes. My eyes filled with tears and I ran awkwardly off the floor.

I was overjoyed; I did not even mind when I discovered that the gold pieces I had scrambled for were brass pocket tokens advertising a certain make of automobile.

When I reached home everyone was excited. Next day the neighbors came to congratulate me. I even felt safe from grandfather, whose deathbed curse usually spoiled my triumphs. I stood beneath his photograph with my brief case in hand and smiled triumphantly into his stolid black peasant's face. It was a face that fascinated me. The eyes seemed to follow everywhere I went.

That night I dreamed I was at a circus with him and that he refused to laugh at the clowns no matter what they did. Then later he told me to open my brief case and read what was inside and I did, finding an official envelope stamped with the state seal; and inside the envelope I found another and another, endlessly, and I thought I would fall of weariness. "Them's years," he said. "Now open that one." And I did and in it I found an engraved document containing a short message in letters of gold. "Read it," my grandfather said. "Out loud!"

"To Whom It May Concern," I intoned. "Keep This Nigger-Boy Running."

I awoke with the old man's laughter ringing in my ears.

(It was a dream I was to remember and dream again for many years after. But at that time I had no insight into its meaning. First I had to attend college.) [26]

JAMES AGEE
1909–1955

The Nostalgic View

from

A DEATH IN THE FAMILY

When James Agee died suddenly on May 16, 1955, he was not a well-known writer. Two years later his unfinished novel *A Death in the Family* won a Pulitzer Prize. In the years that followed his other work was reissued, and in time Agee became almost legend.

Agee was born of Anglo-Catholic parents in Knoxville, Tennessee, in 1909. When he was nine, his father died and his mother placed him in a monastery school. This religious training was to affect him profoundly in his attitudes toward God, faith, and death. He went on to attend some of the best schools—Exeter and Harvard. It was at Harvard that he was to develop his craft, writing poems and stories for the Harvard *Advocate*.

Agee obtained a job on the staff of *Fortune* magazine, where he settled down to years of anonymous writing. However, Archibald MacLeish, the editor, recognized his talent, and with MacLeish's encouragement Agee gathered together the best of his old poems, which were then published in the Yale Younger Poets series. While with *Fortune* Agee did a study of white southern tenant farmers, but the editors rejected it. Later, in 1941, Agee published it as a book entitled *Let Us Now Praise Famous Men*, with photographs by Walker Evans.

In 1951 Agee published a novella, *The Morning Watch*, a sensitive portrayal of a day in the life of a 12-year-old boy in a Tennessee school. This work was to point to his major work of fiction, *A Death in the Family*.

A Death in the Family (1957) is a partly autobiographical and poetic story of a happy, secure Tennessee family whose good life is shattered by the meaningless death of the father in an auto accident. In this novel are to be found the principal Agee themes—man's search for identity, religion as a sustaining force, the role of chance in our lives, and the parent-child relationship.

Other posthumous works include *Agee on Film* (1958), a collection of motion picture reviews for *Nation* and *Time*; *Agee on Film: II*, a collection of five of his screenplays, including Stephen Crane's "The Bride Comes to Yellow Sky" and "The Blue Hotel"; and *Letters to Father Flye* (1962), Agee's letters to his friendly old schoolteacher and mentor.

A Death in the Family had not been completed by Agee before his death. However, the only problem for the editors was the placement of several scenes outside the time span of the basic story. "Knoxville: Summer 1915," which is reprinted here, was not a part of the manuscript that Agee left, but the editors felt it to be entirely appropriate as a prologue to the novel. It provides an evocative picture of a small town in early twentieth-century America. Here is the town as it dreams through a summer evening; Agee writes of the streets and the houses and the people, of the affirmation of life, giving us a moving prelude to the story of childhood, family life, and love that is to come in his memorable novel.

from A DEATH IN THE FAMILY

"Knoxville: Summer 1915"

We are talking now of summer evenings in Knoxville, Tennessee in the time that I lived there so successfully disguised to myself as a child. It was a little bit mixed sort of block, fairly solidly lower middle class, with one or two juts apiece on either side of that. The houses corresponded: middle-sized gracefully fretted wood houses built in the late nineties and early nineteen hundreds, with small front and side and more spacious back yards, and trees in the yards, and porches. These were softwooded trees, poplars, tulip trees, cottonwoods. There were fences around one or two of the houses, but mainly the yards ran into each other with only now and then a low hedge that wasn't doing very well. There were few good friends among the grown people, and they were not poor enough for the other sort of intimate acquaintance, but everyone nodded and spoke, and even might talk short times, trivially, and at the two extremes of the general or the particular, and ordinarly nextdoor neighbors talked quite a bit when [3] they happened to run into each other, and never paid calls. The men were mostly small businessmen, one or two very modestly executives, one or two worked with their hands, most of them clerical, and most of them between thirty and forty-five.

But it is of these evenings, I speak.

Supper was at six and was over by half past. There was still daylight, shining softly and with a tarnish, like the lining of a shell; and the carbon lamps lifted at the corners were on in the light, and the locusts were started, and the fire flies were out, and a few frogs were flopping in the dewy grass, by the time the fathers and the children came out. The children ran out first hell bent and yelling those names by which they were known; then the fathers sank out leisurely in crossed suspenders, their collars removed and their necks looking tall and shy. The mothers stayed back in the kitchen washing and drying, putting things away, recrossing their traceless footsteps like the lifetime journeys of bees, measuring out the dry cocoa for breakfast. When they came out they had taken off their aprons and their skirts were dampened and they sat in rockers on their porches quietly.

It is not of the games children play in the evening that I want to speak now; it is of a contemporaneous atmosphere that has little to do with them: that of the fathers of families, each in his space of lawn, his shirt fishlike pale in the unnatural light and his face nearly anonymous, hosing their lawns. The hoses were attached at spiggots that stood out of the brick foundations of the houses. The nozzles were variously set but usually so there was a long sweet stream of spray, the nozzle wet in the hand, the water trickling the right forearm and the peeled-back cuff, and the water whishing out a long loose and low-curved cone, and so gentle a sound. First an insane noise of violence in the nozzle, then the still irregular sound of adjustment, then the smoothing into steadiness and a pitch [4] as accurately tuned to the size and style of streams as any violin. So many qualities of sound out of one hose: so many choral differences out of those several hoses that were in earshot. Out of any one hose, the almost dead silence of the release, and the short still arch of the separate big drops, silent as a held breath, and the only noise the flattering noise on leaves and the slapped grass at the fall of each big drop. That, and the intense hiss with the intense stream; that, and that same intensity not growing less but growing more quiet and delicate with the turn of the nozzle, up to that extreme tender whisper when the water was just a wide bell of film. Chiefly, though, the hoses were set much alike, in a compromise between distance and tenderness of spray (and quite surely a sense of art behind this compromise, and a quiet deep joy, too real to recognize itself), and the sounds therefore were pitched much alike; pointed by the snorting start of a new hose; decorated by some man playful with the nozzle; left empty, like God by the sparrow's fall, when any single one of them desists: and all, though near alike, of various pitch; and in this unison. These sweet pale streamings in the light lift out their pallors and their voices all together, mothers hushing their children, the hushing unnaturally prolonged, the men gentle and silent and each snail-like withdrawn into the quietude of what he singly is doing, the urination of huge children stood loosely military against an invisible wall, and gentle happy and peaceful, tasting the mean goodness of their liv-

ing like the last of their suppers in their mouths; while the locusts carry on this noise of hoses on their much higher and sharper key. The noise of the locust is dry, and its seems not be rasped or vibrated but urged from him as if through a small orifice by a breath that can never give out. Also there is never one locust but an illusion of at least a thousand. The noise of each locust is pitched in some classic locust range out of which none of them varies more than two full tones: and yet you seem to [5] hear each locust discrete from all the rest, and there is a long, slow, pulse in their noise, like the scarcely defined arch of a long and high set bridge. They are all around in every tree, so that the noise seems to come from nowhere and everywhere at once, from the whole shell heaven, shivering in your flesh and teasing your eardrums, the boldest of all the sounds of night. And yet it is habitual to summer nights, and is of the great order of noises, like the noises of the sea and of the blood her precocious grandchild, which you realize you are hearing only when you catch yourself listening. Meantime from low in the dark, just outside the swaying horizons of the hoses, conveying always grass in the damp of dew and its strong green-black smear of smell, the regular yet spaced noises of the crickets, each a sweet cold silver noise threenoted, like the slipping each time of three matched links of a small chain.

But the men by now, one by one, have silenced their hoses and drained and coiled them. Now only two, and now only one, is left, and you see only ghostlike shirt with the sleeve garters, and sober mystery of his mild face like the lifted face of large cattle enquiring of your presence in a pitchdark pool of meadow; and now he too is gone; and it has become that time of evening when people sit on their porches, rocking gently and talking gently and watching the street and the standing up into their sphere of possession of the trees, of birds hung havens, hangars. People go by; things go by. A horse, drawing a buggy, breaking his hollow iron music on the asphalt; a loud auto; a quiet auto; people in pairs, not in a hurry, scuffling, switching their weight of aestival body, talking casually, the taste hovering over them of vanilla, strawberry, pasteboard and starched milk, the image upon them of lovers and horsemen, squared with clowns in hueless amber. A street car raising its iron moan; stopping, belling and starting; stertorous; rousing and raising again its iron increasing moan and swimming its gold windows and straw seats on past [6] and past and past, the bleak spark crackling and cursing above it like a small malignant spirit set to dog its tracks; the iron whine rises on rising speed; still risen, faints; halts; the faint stinging bell; rises again, still fainter; fainting, lifting, lifts, faints forgone: forgotten. Now is the night one blue dew.

Now is the night one blue dew, my father has drained, he has coiled the hose.
Low on the length of lawns, a frailing of fire who breathes.

Content, silver, like peeps of light, each cricket makes his comment over
over and over in the drowned grass.
A cold toad thumpily flounders.
Within the edges of damp shadows of side yards are hovering children
nearly sick with joy of fear, who watch the unguarding of a tele-
phone pole.
Around white carbon corner lamps bugs of all sizes are lifted elliptic,
solar systems. Big hardshells bruise themselves, assailant: he is
fallen on his back, legs squiggling.
Parents on porches: rock and rock: From damp strings morning glories:
hang their ancient faces.
The dry and exalted noise of the locusts from all the air at once en-
chants my eardrums.

On the rough wet grass of the back yard my father and mother have
spread quilts. We all lie there, my mother, my father, my uncle, my aunt,
and I too am lying there. First we were sitting up, then one of us lay down,
and then we all lay down, on our stomachs, or on our sides, or on our backs,
and they have kept on talking. They are not talking much, and the talk is
quiet, of nothing in particular, of nothing at all in particular, of nothing
at all. The stars are wide and alive, they seem each like a smile of great
sweetness, and they seem very near. All my people are larger bodies than
mine, quiet, with voices gentle and meaningless like the voices of sleeping [7]
birds. One is an artist, he is living at home. One is a musician, she is living
at home. One is my mother who is good to me. One is my father who is
good to me. By some chance, here they are, all on this earth; and who shall
ever tell the sorrow of being on this earth, lying, on quilts, on the grass, in
a summer evening, among the sounds of the night. May God bless my
people, my uncle, my aunt, my mother, my good father, oh, remember
them kindly in their time of trouble; and in the hour of their taking away.

After a little I am taken in and put to bed. Sleep, soft smiling, draws
me unto her: and those receive me, who quietly treat me, as one familiar
and well-beloved in that home: but will not, oh, will not, not now, not
ever; but will not ever tell me who I am. [8]

JOHN UPDIKE
1932–

A Supermarket Soliloquy

"A & P"

.In the dedicatory epigraph of *Pigeon Feathers and Other Stories* (1962), John Updike suggests to the reader that he will find the theme of memory running through these short stories. Updike often reminisces in his stories to show that the past needs discovering. In doing so, he reaches back to his own adolescence in Shillington, Pennsylvania, to create accounts of small-town life, based upon life in Shillington (renamed "Olinger" in his fiction).

Updike is considered one of America's brilliant young writers. His style has been termed magical and poetic, sometimes dazzling. Certainly his language is lyrical. He is a graduate of Harvard, where he wrote for the Harvard *Lampoon*. Later his work began appearing in *The New Yorker*, a magazine that has published most of his short fiction.

Updike has written 11 books, including the novels *The Poorhouse Fair* (1959), *Rabbit, Run* (1960), *The Centaur* (1963), *Of the Farm* (1966), and *Couples* (1968). In addition to *Pigeon Feathers,* his stories have been collected in *The Same Door* (1959) and *The Music Room* (1966). Updike has also written verse (*The Carpentered Hen,* 1958) and essays (*Assorted Prose,* 1965).

"A & P," which appears in *Pigeon Feathers,* tells of an incident in a shopping center of a beach community. The narrator is a 19-year-old clerk who takes a stand on a moral issue when three girls are reproached by the store manager for their attire in the A & P. Updike presents the story as a soliloquy in which the clerk declares the girls' innocence in the face of the manager's judgment, the young boy finally quitting his job in his role as defender of the girls' morality. The incident suggests several significant aspects of the small town: morality, class differences, routine, and resistance to change.

"A & P"

In walks these three girls in nothing but bathing suits. I'm in the third checkout slot, with my back to the door, so I don't see them until they're over by the bread. The one that caught my eye first was the one in the plaid green two-piece. She was a chunky kid, with a good tan and a sweet broad soft-looking can with those two crescents of white just under it, where the sun never seems to hit, at the top of the backs of her legs. I stood there with my hand on a box of HiHo crackers trying to remember if I rang it up or not. I ring it up again and the customer starts giving me hell. She's one of these cash-register-watchers, a witch about fifty with rouge on her cheek-bones and no eyebrows, and I know it made her day to trip me up. She'd been watching cash registers for fifty years and probably never seen a mistake before.

By the time I got her feathers smoothed and her [187] goodies into a bag—she gives me a little snort in passing, if she'd been born at the right time they would have burned her over in Salem—by the time I get her on her way the girls had circled around the bread and were coming back, without a pushcart, back my way along the counters, in the aisle between the checkouts and the Special bins. They didn't even have shoes on. There was this chunky one, with the two-piece—it was bright green and the seams on the bra were still sharp and her belly was still pretty pale so I guessed she just got it (the suit)—there was this one, with one of those chubby berry-faces, the lips all bunched together under her nose, this one, and a tall one, with black hair that hadn't quite frizzed right, and one of these sunburns right across under the eyes, and a chin that was too long—you know, the kind of girl other girls think is "striking" and "attractive" but never quite makes it, as they very well know, which is why they like her so much—and then the third one, that wasn't quite so tall. She was the queen. She kind of led them, the other two peeking around and making their shoulders round. She didn't look around, not this queen, she just walked straight on slowly, on these long white prima-donna legs. She came down a little hard on her heels, as if she didn't walk in her bare feet that much, putting down her heels and then letting the weight move along to her toes as if she was test-ing the floor with every step, putting a little deliberate extra action into it. You never know for sure how girls' minds work (do you really think it's a mind in there or just a little buzz like a bee in a glass jar?) but you got the idea she had [188] talked the other two into coming in here with her, and now she was showing them how to do it, walk slow and hold yourself straight.

John Updike, "A & P," from *Pigeon Feathers and Other Stories* (New York: Alfred A. Knopf, 1962). © Copyright 1962 by John Updike. Reprinted by permission of Alfred A. Knopf, Inc. This story originally appeared in *The New Yorker*.

She had on a kind of dirty-pink—beige, maybe, I don't know—bathing suit with a little nubble all over it and, what got me, the straps were down. They were off her shoulders looped loose around the cool tops of her arms, and I guess as a result the suit had slipped a little on her, so all around the top of the cloth there was this shining rim. If it hadn't been there you wouldn't have known there could have been anything whiter than those shoulders. With the straps pushed off, there was nothing between the top of the suit and the top of her head except just *her,* this clear bare plane of the top of her chest down from the shoulder bones like a dented sheet of metal tilted in the light. I mean, it was more than pretty.

She had sort of oaky hair that the sun and salt had bleached, done up in a bun that was unravelling, and a kind of prim face. Walking into the A & P with your straps down, I suppose it's the only kind of face you *can* have. She held her head so high her neck, coming up out of those white shoulders, looked kind of stretched, but I didn't mind. The longer her neck was, the more of her there was.

She must have felt in the corner of her eye me and over my shoulder Stokesie in the second slot watching, but she didn't tip. Not this queen. She kept her eyes moving across the racks, and stopped, and turned so slow it made my stomach rub the inside of my apron, and buzzed to the other two, who kind of huddled against her for relief, and then they all three [189] of them went up the cat-and-dog-food-breakfast-cereal-macaroni-rice-raisins-seasoning-spreads-spaghetti-soft-drinks-crackers-and-cookies aisle. From the third slot I look straight up this aisle to the meat counter, and I watched them all the way. The fat one with the tan sort of fumbled with the cookies, but on second thought she put the package back. The sheep pushing their carts down the aisle—the girls were walking against the usual traffic (not that we have one-way signs or anything)—were pretty hilarious. You could see them, when Queenie's white shoulders dawned on them, kind of jerk, or hop, or hiccup, but their eyes snapped back to their own baskets and on they pushed. I bet you could set off dynamite in an A & P and the people would by and large keep reaching and checking oatmeal off their lists and muttering "Let me see, there was a third thing, began with A, asparagus, no, ah, yes, applesauce!" or whatever it is they do mutter. But there was no doubt, this jiggled them. A few houseslaves in pin curlers even looked around after pushing their carts past to make sure what they had seen was correct.

You know, it's one thing to have a girl in a bathing suit down on the beach, where what with the glare nobody can look at each other much anyway, and another thing in the cool of the A & P, under the fluorescent lights, against all those stacked packages, with her feet paddling along naked over our checkerboard green-and-cream rubber-tile floor.

"Oh, Daddy," Stokesie said beside me. "I feel so faint."

"Darling," I said. "Hold me tight." Stokesie's mar-[190]ried, with two babies chalked up on his fuselage already, but as far as I can tell that's the only difference. He's twenty-two, and I was nineteen this April.

"Is it done?" he asks, the responsible married man finding his voice. I forgot to say he thinks he's going to be manager some sunny day, maybe in 1990 when it's called the Great Alexandrov and Petrooshki Tea Company or something.

What he meant was, our town is five miles from a beach, with a big summer colony out on the Point, but we're right in the middle of town, and the women generally put on a shirt or shorts or something before they get out of the car into the street. And anyway these are usually women with six children and varicose veins mapping their legs and nobody, including them, could care less. As I say, we're right in the middle of town, and if you stand at our front doors you can see two banks and the Congregational church and the newspaper store and three real-estate offices and about twenty-seven old freeloaders tearing up Central Street because the sewer broke again. It's not as if we're on the Cape; we're north of Boston and there's people in this town haven't seen the ocean for twenty years.

The girls had reached the meat counter and were asking McMahon something. He pointed, they pointed, and they shuffled out of sight behind a pyramid of Diet Delight peaches. All that was left for us to see was old McMahon patting his mouth and looking after them sizing up their joints. Poor kids, I began to feel sorry for them, they couldn't help it. [191]

Now here comes the sad part of the story, at least my family says it's sad, but I don't think it's so sad myself. The store's pretty empty, it being Thursday afternoon, so there was nothing much to do except lean on the register and wait for the girls to show up again. The whole store was like a pinball machine and I didn't know which tunnel they'd come out of. After a while they come around out of the far aisle, around the light bulbs, records at discount of the Caribbean Six or Tony Martin Sings or some such gunk you wonder they waste the wax on, sixpacks of candy bars, and plastic toys done up in cellophane that fall apart when a kid looks at them anyway. Around they come, Queenie still leading the way, and holding a little gray jar in her hand. Slots Three through Seven are unmanned and I could see her wondering between Stokes and me, but Stokesie with his usual luck draws an old party in baggy gray pants who stumbles up with four giant cans of pineapple juice (what do these bums *do* with all that pineapple juice? I've often asked myself) so the girls come to me. Queenie puts down the jar and I take it into my fingers icy cold. Kingfish Fancy Herring Snacks in Pure Sour Cream: 49¢. Now her hands are empty, not a ring or a bracelet, bare as God made them, and I wonder where the money's coming from. Still with her prim look she lifts a folded dollar bill out of the hollow at the center of her nubbled pink top. The jar went heavy in my hand. Really, I thought that was so cute.

Then everybody's luck begins to run out. Lengel comes in from haggling with a truck full of cabbages [192] on the lot and is about to scuttle into the door marked MANAGER behind which he hides all day when the girls touch his eye. Lengel's pretty dreary, teaches Sunday school and the rest, but he doesn't miss that much. He comes over and says, "Girls, this isn't the beach."

Queenie blushes, though maybe it's just a brush of sunburn I was noticing for the first time, now that she was so close. "My mother asked me to pick up a jar of herring snacks." Her voice kind of startled me, the way voices do when you see the people first, coming out so flat and dumb yet kind of tony, too, the way it tickled over "pick up" and "snacks." All of a sudden I slid right down her voice into her living room. Her father and the other men were standing around in ice-cream coats and bow ties and the women were in sandals picking up herring snacks on toothpicks off a big glass plate and they were all holding drinks the color of water with olives and sprigs of mint in them. When my parents have somebody over they get lemonade and if it's a real racy affair Schlitz in tall glasses with "They'll Do It Every Time" cartoons stencilled on.

"That's all right," Lengel said. "But this isn't the beach." His repeating this struck me as funny, as if it had just occurred to him, and he had been thinking all these years the A & P was a great big dune and he was the head lifeguard. He didn't like my smiling—as I say he doesn't miss much—but he concentrates on giving the girls that sad Sunday-school-superintendent stare.

Queenie's blush is no sunburn now, and the plump [193] one in plaid, that I liked better from the back—a really sweet can—pipes up, "We weren't doing any shopping. We just came in for the one thing."

"That makes no difference," Lengel tells her, and I could see from the way his eyes went that he hadn't noticed she was wearing a two-piece before. "We want you decently dressed when you come in here."

"We *are* decent," Queenie says suddenly, her lower lip pushing, getting sore now that she remembers her place, a place from which the crowd that runs the A & P must look pretty crummy. Fancy Herring Snacks flashed in her very blue eyes.

"Girls, I don't want to argue with you. After this come in here with your shoulders covered. It's our policy." He turns his back. That's policy for you. Policy is what the kingpins want. What the others want is juvenile delinquency.

All this while, the customers had been showing up with their carts but, you know, sheep, seeing a scene, they had all bunched up on Stokesie, who shook open a paper bag as gently as peeling a peach, not wanting to miss a word. I could feel in the silence everybody getting nervous, most of all Lengel, who asks me, "Sammy, have you rung up their purchase?"

I thought and said "No" but it wasn't about that I was thinking. I go through the punches, 4, 9, GROC. TOT—it's more complicated than you think, and after you do it often enough, it begins to make a little song, that you hear words to, in my case "Hello (*bing*) there, you (*gung*) hap-py *pee*-pul (*splat*)!"—the *splat* being the drawer flying out. I uncrease the bill, tenderly as you may imagine, it just having come [194] from between the two smoothest scoops of vanilla I have ever known were there, and pass a half and a penny into her narrow pink palm, and nestle the herrings in a bag and twist its neck and hand it over, all the time thinking.

The girls, and who'd blame them, are in a hurry to get out, so I say "I quit" to Lengel quick enough for them to hear, hoping they'll stop and watch me, their unsuspected hero. They keep right on going, into the electric eye; the door flies open they flicker across the lot to their car, Queenie and Plaid and Big Tall Goony-Goony (not that as raw material she was so bad), leaving me with Lengel and a kink in his eyebrow.

"Did you say something, Sammy?"

"I said I quit."

"I thought you did."

"You didn't have to embarrass them."

"It was they who were embarrassing us."

I started to say something that came out "Fiddle-de-doo." It's a saying of my grandmother's, and I know she would have been pleased.

"I don't think you know what you're saying," Lengel said.

"I know you don't," I said, "But I do." I pull the bow at the back of my apron and start shrugging it off my shoulders. A couple customers that had been heading for my slot begin to knock against each other, like scared pigs in a chute.

Lengel sighs and begins to look very patient and old and gray. He's been a friend of my parents for years. "Sammy, you don't want to do this to your [195] Mom and Dad," he tells me. It's true, I don't. But it seems to me that once you begin a gesture it's fatal not to go through with it. I fold the apron, "Sammy" stitched in red on the pocket, and put it on the counter, and drop the bow tie on top of it. The bow tie is theirs, if you've ever wondered. "You'll feel this for the rest of your life," Lengel says, and I know that's true, too, but remembering how he made that pretty girl blush makes me so scrunchy inside I punch the No Sale tab and the machine whirs "peepul" and the drawer splats out. One advantage of this scene taking place in summer, I can follow this up with a clean exit, there's no fumbling around getting your coat and galoshes, I just saunter into the electric eye in my white shirt that my mother ironed the night before, and the door heaves itself open, and outside the sunshine is skating around on the asphalt.

I look around for my girls, but they're gone, of course. There wasn't anybody but some young married screaming with her children about some candy they didn't get by the door of a powder-blue Falcon station wagon. Looking back in the big windows, over the bags of peat moss and aluminum lawn furniture stacked on the pavement, I could see Lengel in my place in the slot, checking the sheep through. His face was dark gray and his back stiff, as if he'd just had an injection of iron, and my stomach kind of fell as I felt how hard the world was going to be to me hereafter. [196]

JOYCE CAROL OATES
1938–

The Trap
of Despair

"PUZZLE"

A prolific and incessant writer, Joyce Carol Oates, although only in her late thirties, has been a major figure in American fiction over the last decade. This energetic and dedicated craftsman has produced in her fiction what appears to be a world of violence. She has been called "Gothic," and the despair, the blood, and the nightmarish quality of her work seem to confirm this. Certainly she writes of the violent and the extreme; yet her stories always seem to put an emphasis on the ordinary, as if to say that violence is simply a natural part of the ordinary. What Oates seeks is to tell the whole truth about the way we live. "I want to get the whole world into a book," she once said.

The power of her imagination is the key to her work, for her narrative fiction—she is a superb storyteller—gives some coherence to the jumble of experience. She has a remarkable ability to create scenes that remain in the reader's mind.

Born in Lockport, New York, in 1938, Oates credits the rural life of the Upstate New York she knew in childhood as having influenced her writing. Her parents had little money and fewer personal opportunities. At Syracuse University she was a brilliant student, and later she pursued graduate work at the University of Wisconsin. She and her husband, Raymond Smith, now teach in the English Department at the University of Windsor.

In the past 13 years her production has been impressive. The output includes seven novels, five collections of short stories, three books of poems, four plays, a collection of essays on tragedies, and hundreds of book reviews and stories not yet collected. Among her novels are *With Shuddering Fall* (1964), *Expensive People* (1968), *them* (1969), and *Do With Me What You Will* (1973). Short story collections include *Upon the Sweeping Flood* (1966), *The Wheel of Love* (1970), *Marriages and Infidelities* (1972), *The Goddess and Other Women* (1974), and *The Seduction* (1975).

"Puzzle," the selection that follows, comes from *Marriages and Infidelities*, a collection conceived by Oates in the belief that "by putting together a sequence of marriages, one might see how this one succeeds and that one fails. And how *this* one leads to some meaning beyond the self." "Puzzle" is set in suburbia, which in some ways has become the contemporary form of the small town in our culture. Here are the homes of the middle class, with the same attitudes, frustrations, and problems that have been characteristic of the small town through the years.

"Puzzle" has as its central figure a woman who exhibits many of the same frustrations and fears and despair. She rejects others and is rejected. After she loses her five-year-old child in a meaningless accident, her own life seems to consist only of meaningless activity. *"I am not really here,"* she thinks.

Oates's descriptive details add to the impact of the story. She opens in a typical drugstore, a sense of place similar to that used by Updike in "A & P." The houses are alike, boxlike in their conformity. And the sounds—the voices, the children's cries, the music in the bar—reinforce the ordinariness surrounded by violence and despair. The emptiness of the woman's life is reflected in the emptiness of the house and its surroundings. The sounds of the house are normal, everything is so ordinary; yet she is caught in despair. Everything is meaningless. "There is no reason. . . . It is a puzzle."

"PUZZLE"

At the corner there is a bicycle rack with a few bicycles stuck in it. Several children stand around—the bicycle rack is outside a drugstore—tearing wrappers off popsicles. The popsicles are bright colors—orange, pink, green. The children's faces are bright. I feel a strange sensation rise in me as I approach them—will they look at me? Will they turn to look at me?

A big boy comes out of the drugstore and gets his bicycle. One of the smaller children follows him, whining. "Hey, Billy, Billy," it sounds like. "Gimme a ride back?" The boy waves him away without bothering to look around. The child stands on the sidewalk with his popsicle raised to his mouth and turned awkwardly, so that the inside of his wrist shows, pale, the bluish veins prominent. In this way the popsicle won't drip down his [37] arm. He sucks at it noisily. "Hey, Billy," he says in a high petulant whine, not loud enough for the boy to hear. He turns back. The other children, arguing over something, have not noticed me. This child notices

Joyce Carol Oates, "Puzzle," from *Marriages and Infidelities* (New York: Vanguard, 1972). By permission of Vanguard Press, Inc. Copyright © 1968, 1969, 1970, 1971, 1972 by Joyce Carol Oates.

me. He has a bright, sunburned face, stained around the lips. His eyes are startled and shrewd. I feel a sense of dizziness, a fear of fainting. *But I am not really here*, a voice rises in me, assuring me, my own voice and yet detached and innocent. The child stares at me. The popsicle in his hand has begun to melt. He fastens his lips to it and sucks noisily at it, staring at me.

He seems to know me. He knows something about me.

I hurry by him. It is a mistake for me to have come out this morning— my mind is not right on such hot, muggy days. The child, eyeing me, takes a few steps in my direction. I can hear his lips sucking thirstily at the popsicle. Something must show on my face or in the sudden urgency of my legs—I have to get away from him, from that look of his—and he follows alongside me, curiously, as if drawn to me, as if he has something to say that the other children must not hear.

"What do you want?" I say nervously.

He says nothing.

"I don't know you. I don't know what you want." I hurry to the drugstore. I have never seen this child before and he does not know me. His face is a stranger's face. He is the child of strangers, people I would never meet. And yet there is something familiar about him—his face—a boy of about five, knowing, condemning, sly.

The popsicle is melting, running in a green watery streak down his arm.

In the drugstore I realize that my body is wet with perspiration. The air around me is like my own body, like my breathing. Very close to me, no relief. It will suffocate me. I don't look back outside at that boy: I go over to the cosmetic counter where there is a mirror. My face is pale and alarmed. Yet it is clear to me that I am not really there, in the mirror or in this drugstore, hiding [38] from a child who seems to know me, to have a message for me, and yet who cannot know me because we are strangers . . . I am not really here at all, I am not hiding here.

Since last April I have had strange adventures.

Noises in the air converge upon me like flocks of birds. The birds are black, scrawny, invisible crows. Try to shoot a crow!—you have time only to raise the rifle and the crow is gone, invisible.

Many years ago, when I lived at home, my father and my brothers used to shoot crows. Once they gave me the rifle to shoot a crow, but I couldn't raise the barrel . . . I was afraid of raising the barrel and shooting. . . .

The noises in the air can't be frightened away. It is morning: I am cleaning the house. Beneath the noise of the vacuum cleaner there is another noise, not as constant, the sound of someone talking. Chattering, like a child. I try not to listen to it but then, suddenly, I switch off the vacuum cleaner with my foot and listen . . . but the chattering is gone. It has not been frightened away but it waits for me, patiently. When I turn on the cleaner it begins again, almost inaudible, a light chattering of words I can't make out. . . .

I rub furniture polish on the tables, on the arms and legs of chairs. I kneel on the floor to work. In the wood my own reflection is dark, vague. I would not be able to recognize myself. I am a married woman, a wife, an ex-mother, aged thirty. This is my house, I live here now. We lived in another house until a year ago, then we had to move here, to this particular house with a back yard that is unfenced and fades away into a field they haven't yet dug up. A big sign on the highway announces a new subdivision of homes to be built next year, but they haven't yet started digging the trees out . . . the field is nothing to look at, a few scrawny bushes and trees, mostly weeds, some piles of debris people have dumped there, and on the far end a large drainage ditch, dry now in October. It is a large, wide ditch that overflows with water in the spring, when everything is melting; now [39] it is dry. I think it is dry—I don't drive by it, I take another street when I drive. But it would be dry now, in October.

I rub furniture polish onto the dull, nicked wood of our coffee table. The table does not need to be cleaned; it is already clean. But I polish it again, slowly, because it is only eleven o'clock in the morning and the day is very long. I work slowly. Everything moves slowly for me now. The cloth I use is from an old sheet of ours that wore out, a yellowed white sheet. As I rub the table a voice comes into my head. I think it is singing a song. *I am not really here.* . . . I polish the table's legs, slowly, frightened. *I am not really here.* Is this a song I heard somewhere but can't remember?

I am not really here.

All day I wait for the words to continue, to explain themselves. I believe that there are more words, waiting. The song must have more lines.

Side by side in my mind are two places: the place I live in now, this small house, and the place I lived in when I was a child. That house was a little bigger than this, with an attic two of my brothers slept in but it was a poor house, falling apart. This house it too new to fall apart: it is on the corner of a street, at the end of a row of houses that are alike. One story, wood with brick on the front only, a garage, a picture window of moderate size. The brick is red. The rest of the house is painted white. In an airplane you would see this row of houses and other rows of houses, all alike. The streets are not yet paved; they will be paved next year. We are beside a highway that leads to the city twelve miles away. To the north of us are empty fields, waiting to be excavated so that more rows of houses can be built.

I am not really here.

There are large ditches around the fields, at the edge of our yards, cutting us off from the highway. The ditches are filled with leaves at this time of year. We played in a ditch back home [40]—I remember the weed-flowers, yellow and blue flowers, I remember the crickets and the frogs and the stink of scummy water. When we were very small we pretended the water in the ditch was a river; pretended to be afraid of it. In the winter the ditch froze. We walked on it. I remember snowdrifts along the road—twelve feet high. The snowplows along the road at night, their revolving lights, big rusted plows lifted, partly suspended by chains. . . . Upper New York State, the foothills of the Adirondacks. Wild country. A small, wild city five miles from us, too much wind, too much snow.

Sitting here, in this house, hundreds of mles from that memory, I can define clearly. I am an adult, a wife. I live now in a climate where the snow doesn't drift in the roads; there are rarely snowplows. I am free of the bitterness of those winters and the prowling blue lights of the snowplows and the fact of my parents, whom I don't see.

The last time my husband and I quarreled and I left him, my mother said *He's no good, we always knew that.* Then when I went back to him she said I was crazy; said I could go to hell. Later, of course, she changed her mind. She wanted to make up. But I kept hearing her words, the anger in her words, and I wouldn't go back. I kept hearing her tell me *He's no good, we always knew that.* Her words got into me, ringing in my head. Something is always getting into a woman, giving her a shape, pushing her out of shape.

Sounds in the air slowly pushing us out of shape: like a great flock of birds.

I sit here in the living room, by the coffee table, unable to remember what I was doing. The rag stained with furniture polish—the bottle of dark polish on the floor. I must have been polishing the table again. The time is stuck at eleven-fifteen. Except for the noise of children playing outside, always children playing outside, there is nothing for me to hear. I must get up, get working. I must put on the radio. I must not think of my parents, of [41] the time when I was their daughter. How does a daughter become a mother? How does a mother become turned inside-out again, back into being just a woman, a daughter?

I am not really here.

In the first days after Jackie died I could hear sounds vividly. The sound of traffic over on the highway—voices rising in the house next door—my husband's breathing. Sometimes he breathes heavily, grunting to himself. No reason for it. It is a puzzle to me, the sounds he makes when he thinks he is alone . . . his breath expelled in a kind of grunt as if he were pushing something from him. I could hear him in this house, the two of us living between the walls of this house, in a box. I heard him walking, I heard him out in the garage. I heard him drive into the driveway at night and I heard him slam the door of the car and I heard his footsteps on the gravel. In the kitchen he would bump into something and I would hear him mutter to himself.

He said to me, three days after the funeral, "Why don't you say something? I live here too."

Six years ago I walked around downtown wondering what to do. I wandered through the five-and-ten-cent stores, through the grubby little park, I sat in the old library and looked at magazines. The magazines had nothing to do with me. Time passed through my head, in and out of my head. I had become a married woman but nothing had happened to me. My husband worked for the siding company then, making good money. He had to climb ladders in the hot sun and nail siding onto houses and garages, his strong legs carrying him anywhere. Even then he was a big man. His face was tanned to an olivish dark, his eyes were light and jumpy in his face, his skin always looked a little greasy. When he grinned it was sudden, like a shout; like someone calling your name.

He had never been a child himself, he told me bitterly, be-[42]cause his parents were too old. He was the seventh child—coming at the end, for his parents' old age. But his father had died when he was two.

He had that dark face some men have—quizzical and dark but ready to grin—you must surprise them into grinning.

We met at a beach. Kids everywhere milling around, cars with their doors left open, seats too hot to sit on because of the sun. . . . Late Sunday afternoon. The odor of beer. The noise of radios. We were all in our bathing suits. I had been swimming and my long hair was piled on top of my head, I was a little dizzy from the heat, I kept giggling . . . he, my future husband, a man seven years older than I, kept fooling around on the beach, doing tricks. He was at the center of men like himself. Everyone liked him. He stood on his hands until the veins in his throat bulged . . . he brought his legs down again, hard, spraying sand. . . . There was sand on his chest, drying in the matted dark hair. I felt the sharp angry pain of love for him in my own chest; deep in my chest.

The straps of my bathing suit left vivid pale lines on my shoulders, and the skin of my shoulders was burned to a bright red. I lay awake for nights after that Sunday, crying because of the sunburn, because I couldn't sleep.

We were married and he worked for a siding company. Then we moved out, after the trouble with my parents; we moved to another state. He worked for another siding company. The manager liked him, went out drinking with him. He made good money and kept saying—*I'm making good money, right?* I walked downtown or sat on the edge of our bed, alone. I wanted to leave him. I did not love him. I loved him, yes, but he didn't love me. I loved him but I couldn't believe him, couldn't trust him, I wasn't ready for marriage, I couldn't stand his noises . . . his bullying . . . his plans for borrowing money and starting a company of his own. *I want to go in business for myself,* he kept saying. When I began to realize I must be pregnant, [43] that it had happened to me at last, I did not want to tell him.

We had a fight and he moved out; threw his clothes in a suitcase and moved out.

In the back of my mind I loved him but I couldn't live with him. I wasn't ready to be married. I went to the movies in the afternoon and did not think about being married, about being pregnant. I did not think about myself at all. Pregnant? How could I be pregnant? My husband drove back and I went out to him; we went for a drive down along the river, not talking. I began to cry. He said nothing, his face was dark. I thought it was dark because of the blood held back, all the hatred he was holding back.

"I'm going to have a baby," I said.

I did not look at him.

"A baby? . . ."

We lived then upstairs in the house on Sloan Street. He moved back in with me. Now the house is torn down, to make way for the new telephone building. This happened in 1963, in the summer. Jackie was born in April of 1964.

When he was three years old Jackie ran into the house crying. I asked, "What's happened? What's wrong?"

He showed me his bleeding hand—the palm of his hand had been scraped.

"How did you do that? It isn't bad! Did you hurt it on something dirty?" I patted the blood away with a tissue. He stopped crying hard; he pressed against me with his wet face.

My husband said, coming into the kitchen, "Let's see what happened—"

He took Jackie's hand and stared down at it. Jackie's hand was very small in his; his own hand was not clean. He had been working on the lawn mower. "Should this be washed out or what?" he said, looking at me. "You think there's some germs in it?" [44]

"I'd better wash it out."

I turned on the hot water.

"Maybe it should be sterilized. It should be washed out good," my husband said slowly. He stared down at Jackie's hand and for a few seconds he was silent. He loved Jackie very much; he was always afraid of Jackie getting hit by a car. Now Jackie tried to get away from him, uneasy. My husband looked strange, as if the sight of blood frightened him.

"I can wash it out. I'll put a bandage on it," I said.

He paid no attention to me. Instead, he turned on one of the electric

burners of the stove, still holding Jackie's hand. "If it was something rusty
. . . if it was some dirt, some filth, he could get very sick," my husband said.
"The germs should be all killed."

"What? What are you going to do?"

"I know what to do," he said irritably, vaguely.

"All it needs is a bandage. . . ."

Jackie began to cry, afraid of his father. He tried to get away.

"Goddamn it, hold still! You want to get lockjaw or something? Why
is this kid always crying?" He pulled Jackie to the stove and before I could
stop him he pressed his palm down onto the burner—Jackie screamed,
kicked, broke away—it was all over in a second.

"You're crazy! You burned him!" I cried.

My husband stared at me. Jackie was screaming, gasping for breath,
he had backed away against the kitchen table. His screams rose higher and
higher. My husband stared at him and at me, very pale.

"You're crazy!" I shouted at him.

I ran cold water for Jackie to stick his hand under. The burn was not
bad—the stove hadn't been hot enough.

"I didn't mean to hurt him," my husband said slowly, "I . . . I don't
know what. . . ."

"Putting his hand on the stove! God, you must be crazy!"

There was something pulsating in me, a bright, thrilling nerve [45]
—I wanted to laugh in my husband's face, I wanted to claw at him, I
wanted to gather Jackie up in my arms and run out of the house with him!
I hated my husband and I was glad that he had made such a stupid mistake. I was glad he had burned Jackie and that Jackie was crying in my
arms, pressing against me, terrified of his father.

"I don't know what I was thinking of," he said. His voice was vague
and slow and surprised. "I didn't mean . . . I'm sorry. . . ."

"Don't scare him any more!"

"I'm sorry. I must be going crazy. . . ."

"Where did you ever get such an idea?"

He rubbed his hands violently across his face, across his eyes. "Jesus,
I must be going crazy," he said.

"You're just lucky the stove wasn't hot."

Jackie kept crying, frightened. I took him into the bathroom and put a
bandage on the cut—only a small scratch—no real burn at all.

We live in a boxlike house, a coop for people. My brothers had coops
for rabbits back home. And, back home, we lived in a boxlike house, a coop
for people. I sit in this little house between the walls and think of that
other house, where I was born, where I lived before I knew what would
happen to me. I think about the puzzle I live in. My life is constructed like

a series of boxes, rooms in which I did certain things. I then left the rooms and moved on to other rooms. Now I am in a particular room, between these walls, sitting on the sofa in front of the turned-off television set. My husband is late coming home from work and I think I am waiting for him.

At the cemetery the coffins are out of sight. On top of most of the graves there is a covering of grass; good. Nothing will heave up those coffins because they are buried quite deep. Nothing will pry them loose. They are little boxes, only big enough for one person. [46]

My son had two fathers. One lived with us and the other lived away somewhere, a ghost-father, a stranger. I kept thinking of that other man. I remembered the day on the beach, the early days we went out together . . . sitting around in taverns, driving late at night. I hugged Jackie and thought about his other father, his real father. The man who lived in the house with us coughed in the bathroom every morning. He coughed violently, angrily. I could hear him: that coughing would tear out his insides.

My other husband, Jackie's other father, was a younger man. If he coughed, the coughing did not bend him in two, did not sound as if it were tearing at his insides.

I loved that man, but the man who lived with us, the man who slept with me, I hated. I did not hate him but I was afraid of him. I loved him sometimes, but most of the time I hated him. I wished he was dead. I said to Jackie, "Your father will be home soon so clean up that mess in the driveway. He'll give you hell." I walked through the house angrily, talking to myself. "Going into business for yourself . . . now you owe three thousand dollars . . . goddamn you, you should shoot yourself, you should drop dead! I took Jackie with me when I drove out, the two of us alone together; sometimes I continued my argument with my husband, out in the car, laughing and sobbing so that Jackie was frightened of me.

"Your father is crazy! He's crazy! Why doesn't he die!" I cried.

Outside, children's cries. It is autumn now, six months since Jackie died. The cries are like a swarm of birds rushing at me. I press my hands against my ears but still the noise is with me, rushing at me. Children outside? Always children playing outside?

I run into the back bedroom, where it is dark. Shades pulled; everything closed up. Muggy air. Still a child is crying out in front of the house . . . my head pounds with his cries. Six months ago Joey Baxter, a boy who lives up the street, ran shouting to my back door. I saw him running from the field. He was [47] running in a panic, crazily. He was shouting something to me but he couldn't even see me yet, in the house, watching him.

"The ditch!—" he was shouting.

I ran outside to meet him. His face was not a child's face.

It is October now and everything is rustling with wind and leaves. A child is crying outside. I hear the cries of children every day and I want to scream at them *No, I am not here, not really here, go home to your mothers!* But my hands, pressed against my ears, make me realize that I am losing my mind, I am going crazy, I must stop. I hold my pounding head between my hands, all that is myself, my soul, held panicked between my hands. I must not stay back here, hiding. I must see what is going on outside, I must be an adult, I must see if someone needs me. . . .

I run out the front door. Children by the curb, playing in the leaves. "What's wrong? Is someone hurt?" I ask them. The children break away guiltily and run across the street. But there is one child left behind, lying in the gutter, in a pile of leaves. . . . I kneel down beside him. They have covered him with leaves and rolled him around, a boy of about three. There are bits of leaves in his eyes, even. He cries helplessly. He seems blind, rubbing his eyes with his fists, terrified. *Don't cry, don't cry like that!*

The other children have run away. This child is left behind, squirming in the dirty leaves, half-buried beneath them, gone blind. When he stares at me, sucking in his breath to scream, he does not seem to see me. When I try to help him up he kicks at me. His screams climb in my head until I have the crazy wish that they had really buried him, silenced him, stuffed leaves into his mouth. . . .

"Don't cry like that! I'm not your mother!"

Joey Baxter, in clothes too heavy for this warm April afternoon, is running to my back door. He and Jackie play together all the time. He runs shouting into the air. The back yard of our [48] house has no fence but runs out into a field, and on the far edge of the field there are piles of lumber, concrete blocks, bricks, a drainage ditch. The ditch is swollen with water. Shading my eyes I can barely see it, the sun is so bright, and Joey's shouts make my vision blotch. Why is he shouting so?

Joey Baxter runs shouting to my back door.

Joey runs shouting from the field into our back yard.

Joey runs stumbling, shouting something to me.

"The ditch!—he fell in the ditch!" Joey shouts.

The drainage ditch has a twenty-four-inch pipe at one end, leading under the street. The grating in front of the pipe, they said, was pried off by children. But there was a grating there; a grating was definitely there at one time.

When the ditch is dry it is nothing to look at—lined with dead weeds, popsicle wrappers, junk. Nothing to catch the eye. The opening of the pipe is visible. It is dark and coated with last year's slime. It leads under the street, into darkness.

When the ditch is filled with water, when water rushes into it, the opening of the pipe is not visible. Branches and debris carried along by the rushing water are sucked into the pipe and out of sight, under the muddy street, vanished.

In the newspaper the contractor was quoted: *We definitely put a grating on that pipe. But children must have pried it off.*

He used to run in front of cars on our street—once a driver stopped and came in to tell me. Jackie was hiding. I went looking for him and found him in the garage, hiding. He was giggling. Then he started to cry. I dragged him in the house and slammed the door and took him into the bathroom, my heart pounding, and there I could not think what I wanted to do—spank him? But I did not want to hurt him. I did not want him to cry. I knelt by him, hugging him, and the two of us cried together. "You shouldn't play in the street! What if you get hit by a car! What if something happens to you!" [49]

He twisted into my arms, closer into my arms.

But he kept playing in the street; he played with other, older boys down by the row of new houses, crawling in the foundations, getting into trouble. He fell and cut himself, just beneath the chin, so that blood streamed down his neck and onto his shirt. . . . I wept over him, but I never punished him. All I could do was cry, bewildered and frightened.

"What are you trying to do? Are you trying to kill yourself?"

After he stopped crying we would lie together, the two of us, on the bed. My husband would not be home. We would lie together, quiet, on top of the bedspread, and I would touch his hot forehead until he fell asleep.

I never told my husband about these things: I was afraid of his anger.

Someone sent an envelope to me, my name and address printed in pencil, and inside was the clipping: BOY DROWNS IN DRAINAGE DITCH. No other message.

My husband and I go out with another couple, it is Saturday night, we end up at the usual place. We sit drinking. The other man eats potato chips and wipes his hands on his thighs, in a very good mood tonight. He works at Ford's where my husband works now. He and my husband talk about men at work, about their foreman. The union. In the back of my husband's head are words he won't let out about how he hates this job, about how he is ashamed of it and of himself, losing so much money, being in debt. He had tried to start a siding company for himself but had lost it —too many bills, surprises, the weather, bad customers. But this couple doesn't know about that part of his life—they only know about the bad luck with Jackie, last spring. They never talk about it or about their own children with us.

Music is piped in from the bar. I can't hear the words but only the music. Then the words come out of my own head, surprising [50] me. *I am not really here*, these words say. But I can't remember the rest of the song.

My husband's face is slack and heavy; Saturday night; he has worked for time-and-a-half pay today, until three o'clock in the afternoon. His skin is olive-tan, dark. Beneath his chin there is a roll of flesh, squeezed against his neck when he brings his chin back, talking. He and the other man smirk about someone—a name I don't know—they drink beer—they settle themselves in their chairs. There are three very sharp lines leading outward from my husband's eyes that I have not noticed before. Creases in his skin. He is squinting. He squints and rubs his hand across his face, up and down over his eyes, then lets his hand fall and laughs along with the other man.

The music clicks off but my own words keep on: *I am not really here.* I want to hear the next line of the song, I want desperately to know what it is! *I am not really here.* But the words are stuck, they won't go any farther, I can't remember. . . . My husband and his friend are trying to remember something too. The name of a man who died? A heart attack in the plant? *I am not really here.* Watching them, pretending to listen to them, I think of Jackie and of how he would not have grown up to be a man like these men. I know that. Sucked into the pipe, carried along on that rushing, violent, filthy water, drowned and mangled inside the pipe, his face smashed in, a five-year-old who would never have grown up into a man . . . he is with me here in the tavern as much as these three adults are with me. He is still with me. We are all present to one another like that —here and not here, remembered or not remembered. My husband breaks off, staring at me. He must see something awful in my face. Then he looks back to his friend again and the conversation continues. . . .

I am not really here.

We return home around two o'clock. We are reluctant to go home, a little afraid. I can hear my husband breathing hard. He [51] grunts sometimes for no reason—doing something that takes no effort, like rolling up the car window. We go into the house where one light is burning, in the living room, and we are frightened to enter it. We do not look at each other. The house is filled with emptiness. With nothing. It is a kind of hole, smelling of damp, of nothing. You keep waiting for a noise. Something is going to happen, and yet it does not happen.

My husband opens the refrigerator and takes out a can of beer.

"Sit down for a minute," he says.

The window beside him is dark and shows us both his reflection. If it were daylight we could see the back yard, the field, the heaps of debris, the line that is the drainage ditch, so far away.

My husband wipes his forehead with both hands. "Can't you sit down for a minute?" he says.

"I'm tired."

"I want to tell you something," he says slowly. When he expels his breath it is too loud, labored. His eyes are dull but the creases around them are sharp. He frightens me, sitting like this. It is not really my husband. It is not that other man, either, my real husband. It is no one at all. I am in the doorway, standing, and I can feel the warmth from the refrigerator, its slight vibrations. I think suddenly *He will want to leave me now. . . .*

"Before he—before it happened—the accident—just a few days before, I thought about it, that ditch. The ditch," he says quickly. "Not the pipe but the ditch. I didn't know about the pipe. I was driving by it, coming home the back way, where some kids were playing in the water, and I thought—Jesus, what if a kid falls in there and drowns, there'll be hell to pay for somebody, what if Jackie fools around there! But then I forgot about it.—I don't know why—I just forgot about it."

He stares at me. I can feel the nausea in him.

"I forgot all about it. If I hadn't forgot he'd be alive now, wouldn't he?"

I look away from him. I put my hand out against the refrigerator; it is vibrating gently, invisibly. All the sounds of the house [52] are normal. Now I will tell this man the things I must tell him. It is time. It is time for me to tell him of my hatred for him, and my love, and the terrible anger that has wanted to scream its way out of me for years, screaming into his face, into his body. It is time for me to tell him that the death was my fault. Jackie died because I wanted his father dead.

My husband turns abruptly in his chair, scraping the floor. "If we hadn't moved to this goddamn house, he wouldn't be dead. That was my fault. Moving here. He wouldn't be dead if we hadn't moved, would he?"

His face is anxious and sweaty, an aging face. I have an impulse to touch it—is it warm? What does it feel like to live behind that particular face? But I cannot move. The moment is too heavy upon me. I cannot believe that I am really here, listening to these words, that I am really here in this room, this kitchen, staring at a man I met on the beach so many years ago, another man. A stranger. This man, my husband, is getting heavy; his body is heavy and exhausted.

"It was my fault, wasn't it?" he says, questioning, staring at me.

"No."

"You want me to get out? I will. I don't blame you." His face is greasy. There are tears in his eyes.

I shake my head no, no. No. I go to him and put my arms around him, his head and his shoulders, and he presses himself against me, exhausted, hot, breathing hard. He hides his face against me and I can't see him. What is this puzzle of people!—what have they to do with one another? They can't help one another. They are better alone. Jackie did not die because my husband forgot about the ditch . . . he did not die because we had to move here, because my husband was a failure . . . he did not die because I wanted his father dead. There is no reason. He died.

But I can't think of it any longer—this puzzle we live in, the boxes, the walls, the hot dry sand that fell from my husband's [53] body that Sunday, the pain of my loins, my backbone vivid with pain at that birth, that wonderful birth. And what came of it? A **son**, a death. Drowning. A drainage ditch. A small coffin.

How do these things come together—what do they mean? It is a puzzle I cannot understand. I am here in my husband's embrace, in the silence of our marriage, and there is nothing outside of this moment, this love I have been allotted, that I can understand. [54]

RICHARD BRAUTIGAN
1935–

The Lost Vision

from

TROUT FISHING
IN AMERICA

Richard Brautigan belongs to the West Coast. Born in Tacoma, Washington, he lived in Oregon and Montana before arriving in San Francisco in 1958, when the beat generation was in full swing. San Francisco has been his home since then, so he has been affected by the various youth movements of the sixties that were generated from that part of the country. Although considered reticent, Brautigan is very much a part of the current San Francisco literary scene.

Brautigan's style is rather inventive, and the structure of his novels is quite loose; in fact, it is difficult to classify his work in conventional terms. Even though *Trout Fishing in America* does not have a clearly defined narrative line, it is held together by a broad pattern and by thematic development. A young man first attempts to find a place to go trout fishing; later he and his family try to find a life of freedom and independence in a pastoral setting; and finally they come to realize that such a life is no longer possible in America and doubt if it ever was. The agrarian myth is just that—a myth.

The words "trout fishing in America" are the title of the book, an act, a place, an attitude, and a person, so they become a broad symbol uniting and giving meaning to the various episodes in the work. In "Prologue to Grider Creek" the Midwestern small town of Mooresville, Indiana, is revealed to be the home of violence, suggesting that violence is at the heart of middle-class life. After the narrator as a young boy has tried with great difficulty to find a place to go trout fishing, he finally reaches a stream in "Tom Martin Creek." But he soon discovers it "to be a real son-of-a-bitch . . . brush, poison oak and hardly any good places to fish. . . ." America's love of camping, discovering the great outdoors, is treated ironically in "The Teddy Roosevelt Chingader'" with a family from New York in their ten-room trailer and trailer camps with all the modern conveniences, and again in "A Note on the Camping Craze that is Currently Sweeping America." In "The Last Time I Saw Trout Fishing in America" the theme is tied in with Hemingway and his search for the agrarian myth. "The Cleveland Wrecking Yard" somewhat humorously identifies the commercialism of anything that might be considered agrarian in our culture. The juxtaposition is ironic.

Trout Fishing in America is Brautigan's most popular work, especially with college students. He has written a number of other books, including *A Confederate General from Big Sur* (1964), *In Watermelon Sugar* (1968), *The Abortion* (1971), and a volume of rather terse verse, *The Pill Versus the Spring-hill Mine Disaster* (1968).

from TROUT FISHING IN AMERICA

PROLOGUE TO GRIDER CREEK

Mooresville, Indiana, is the town that John Dillinger came from, and the town has a John Dillinger Museum. You can go in and look around.

Some towns are known as the peach capital of America or the cherry capital or the oyster capital, and there's always a festival and the photograph of a pretty girl in a bathing suit.

Mooresville, Indiana, is the John Dillinger capital of America.

Recently a man moved there with his wife, and he discovered hundreds of rats in his basement. They were huge, slow-moving child-eyed rats.

When his wife had to visit some of her relatives for a few days, the man went out and bought a .38 revolver and a lot of ammunition. Then he went down to the basement where the rats were, and he started shooting them. It didn't bother the rats at all. They acted as if it were a movie and started eating their dead companions for popcorn.

The man walked over to a rat that was busy eating a friend and placed the pistol against the rat's head. The rat did not move and continued eating away. When the hammer clicked back, the rat paused between bites and looked out of the corner of its eye. First at the pistol and then at the man. It was a kind of friendly look as if to say, "When my mother was young she sang like Deanna Durbin."

The man pulled the trigger.

He had no sense of humor.

There's always a single feature, a double feature and an eternal feature playing at the Great Theater in Mooresville, Indiana: the John Dillinger capital of America. [13]

TOM MARTIN CREEK

I walked down one morning from Steelhead, following the Klamath River that was high and murky and had the intelligence of a dinosaur. Tom Martin Creek was a small creek with cold, clear water and poured out of a canyon and through a culvert under the highway and then into the Klamath.

I dropped a fly in a small pool just below where the creek flowed out of the culvert and took a nine-inch trout. It was a good-looking fish and fought all over the top of the pool.

Even though the creek was very small and poured out of a steep brushy canyon filled with poison oak, I decided to follow the creek up a ways because I like the feel and motion of the creek.

I liked the name, too.

Tom Martin Creek.

It's good to name creeks after people and then later to follow them for a while seeing what they have to offer, what they know and have made of themselves.

But that creek turned out to be a real son-of-a-bitch. I had to fight it all the God-damn way: brush, poison oak and hardly any good places to fish, and sometimes the canyon was so narrow the creek poured out like water from a faucet. Sometimes it was so bad that it just left me standing there, not knowing which way to jump.

You had to be a plumber to fish that creek.

After that first trout I was alone in there. But I didn't know it until later. [19]

THE TEDDY ROOSEVELT CHINGADER'

The Challis National Forest was created July 1, 1908, by Executive Order of President Theodore Roosevelt . . . Twenty Million years ago, scientists tell us, three-toed horses, camels, and possibly rhinoceroses were plentiful in this section of the country.

This is part of my history in the Challis National Forest. We came over through Lowman after spending a little time with my woman's Mormon relatives at McCall, where we learned about Spirit Prison and couldn't find Duck Lake.

I carried the baby up the mountain. The sign said 1½ miles. There was a green sports car parked on the road. We walked up the trail until we met a man with a green sports car hat on and a girl in a light summer dress.

She had her dress rolled above her knees and when she saw us coming, she rolled her dress down. The man had a bottle of wine in his back pocket. The wine was in a long green bottle. It looked funny sticking out of his back pocket.

"How far is it to Spirit Prison?" I asked.

"You're about half way," he said.

The girl smiled. She had blonde hair and they went on down. Bounce, bounce, bounce, like a pair of birthday balls, down through the trees and boulders.

I put the baby down in a patch of snow lying in the hollow behind a big stump. She played in the snow and then started eating it. I remembered something from a book by Justice of the Supreme Court, William O. Douglas. DON'T EAT SNOW. IT'S BAD FOR YOU AND WILL GIVE YOU A STOMACH ACHE.

"Stop eating that snow!" I said to the baby.

I put her on my shoulders and continued up the path toward Spirit Prison. That's where everybody who isn't a Mormon [58] goes when they die. All Catholics, Buddhists, Moslems, Jews, Baptists, Methodists and International Jewel Thieves. Everybody who isn't a Mormon goes to the Spirit Slammer.

The sign said 1½ miles. The path was easy to follow, then it just stopped. We lost it near a creek. I looked all around. I looked on both sides of the creek. but the path had just vanished.

Could be the fact that we were still alive had something to do with it. Hard to tell.

We turned around and started back down the mountain. The baby cried when she saw the snow again, holding out her hands for the snow. We didn't have time to stop. It was getting late.

We got in our car and drove back to McCall. That evening we talked about Communism. The Mormon girl read aloud to us from a book called *The Naked Communist* written by an ex-police chief of Salt Lake City.

My woman asked the girl if she believed the book were written under the influence of Divine Power, if she considered the book to be a religious text of some sort.

The girl said, "No."

I bought a pair of tennis shoes and three pairs of socks at a store in McCall. The socks had a written guarantee. I tried to save the guarantee, but I put it in my pocket and lost it. The guarantee said that if anything happened to the socks within three months time, I would get new socks. It seemed like a good idea.

I was supposed to launder the old socks and send them in with the guarantee. Right off the bat, new socks would be on their way, traveling across America with my name on the package. Then all I would have to do, would be to open the package, take those new socks out and put them on. They would look good on my feet.

I wish I hadn't lost that guarantee. That was a shame. I've had to face the fact that new socks are not going to be a family heirloom. Losing the guarantee took care of that. All future generations are on their own.

We left McCall the next day, the day after I lost the sock guarantee, following the muddy water of the North Fork of the Payette down and the clear water of the South Fork up.

We stopped at Lowman and had a strawberry milkshake and then drove back into the mountains along Clear Creek and over the summit to Bear Creek. [59]

There were signs nailed to the trees all along Bear Creek, the signs said, "IF YOU FISH IN THIS CREEK, WE'LL HIT YOU IN THE HEAD." I didn't want to be hit in the head, so I kept my fishing tackle right there in the car.

We saw a flock of sheep. There's a sound that the baby makes when she sees furry animals. She also makes that sound when she sees her mother and me naked. She made that sound and we drove out of the sheep like an airplane flies out of the clouds.

We entered Challis National Forest about five miles away from that sound. Driving now along Valley Creek, we saw the Sawtooth Mountains for the first time. It was clouding over and we thought it was going to rain.

"Looks like it's raining in Stanley," I said, though I had never been in Stanley before. It is easy to say things about Stanley when you have never been there. We saw the road to Bull Trout Lake. The road looked good. When we reached Stanley, the streets were white and dry like a collision at a high rate of speed between a cemetery and a truck loaded with sacks of flour.

We stopped at a store in Stanley. I bought a candy bar and asked how the trout fishing was in Cuba. The woman at the store said, "You're better off dead, you Commie bastard." I got a receipt for the candy bar to be used for income tax purposes.

The old ten-cent deduction.

I didn't learn anything about fishing in that store. The people were awfully nervous, especially a young man who was folding overalls. He had about a hundred pairs left to fold and he was really nervous.

We went over to a restaurant and I had a hamburger and my woman had a cheeseburger and the baby ran in circles like a bat at the World's Fair.

There was a girl there in her early teens or maybe she was only ten years old. She wore lipstick and had a loud voice and seemed to be aware of boys. She got a lot of fun out of sweeping the front porch of the restaurant.

She came in and played around with the baby. She was very good with the baby. Her voice dropped down and got soft with the baby. She told us that her father'd had a heart attack and was still in bed. "He can't get up and around," she said. [60]

We had some more coffee and I thought about the Mormons. That very morning we had said good-bye to them, after having drunk coffee in their house.

The smell of coffee had been like a spider web in the house. It had not been an easy smell. It had not lent itself to religious contemplation, thoughts of temple work to be done in Salt Lake, dead relatives to be discovered among ancient papers in Illinois and Germany. Then more temple work to be done in Salt Lake.

The Mormon woman told us that when she had been married in the temple at Salt Lake, a mosquito had bitten her on the wrist just before the ceremony and her wrist had swollen up and become huge and just awful. It could've been seen through the lace by a blindman. She had been so embarrassed.

She told us that those Salt Lake mosquitoes always made her swell up when they bit her. Last year, she had told us, she'd been in Salt Lake, doing some temple work for a dead relative when a mosquito had bitten her and her whole body had swollen up. "I felt so embarrassed," she had told us. "Walking around like a balloon."

We finished our coffee and left. Not a drop of rain had fallen in Stanley. It was about an hour before sundown.

We drove up to Big Redfish Lake, about four miles from Stanley and looked it over. Big Redfish Lake is the Forest Lawn of camping in Idaho, laid out for maximum comfort. There were a lot of people camped there, and some of them looked as if they had been camped there for a long time.

We decided that we were too young to camp at Big Redfish Lake, and besides they charged fifty cents a day, three dollars a week like a skidrow hotel, and there were just too many people there. There were too many trailers and campers parked in the halls. We couldn't get to the elevator because there was a family from New York parked there in a ten-room trailer.

Three children came by drinking rub-a-dub and pulling an old granny by her legs. Her legs were straight out and stiff and her butt was banging on the carpet. Those kids were pretty drunk and the old granny wasn't too sober either, shouting something like, "Let the Civil War come again, I'm ready to fuck!"

We went down to Little Redfish Lake. The campgrounds there were just about abandoned. There were so many people [61] up at Big Redfish Lake and practically nobody camping at Little Redfish Lake, and it was free, too.

We wondered what was wrong with the camp. If perhaps a camping plague, a sure destroyer that leaves all your camping equipment, your car and your sex organs in tatters like old sails, had swept the camp just a few days before, and those few people who were staying at the camp now, were staying there because they didn't have any sense.

We joined them enthusiastically. The camp had a beautiful view of the mountains. We found a place that really looked good, right on the lake.

Unit 4 had a stove. It was a square metal box mounted on a cement block. There was a stove pipe on top of the box, but there were no bullet holes in the pipe. I was amazed. Almost all the camp stoves we had seen in Idaho had been full of bullet holes. I guess it's only reasonable that people, when they get the chance, would want to shoot some old stove sitting in the woods.

Unit 4 had a big wooden table with benches attached to it like a pair of those old Benjamin Franklin glasses. the ones with those funny square lenses. I sat down on the left lens, facing the Sawtooth Mountains. Like astigmatism, I made myself at home. [62]

A NOTE ON THE CAMPING CRAZE
THAT IS CURRENTLY SWEEPING AMERICA

As much as anything else, the Coleman lantern is the symbol of the camping craze that is currently sweeping America, with its unholy white light burning in the forests of America.

Last summer, a Mr. Norris was drinking at a bar in San Francisco. It was Sunday night and he'd had six or seven. Turning to the guy on the next stool, he said, "What are you up to?"

"Just having a few," the guy said.

"That's what I'm doing," Mr. Norris said. "I like it."

"I know what you mean," the guy said. "I had to lay off for a couple years. I'm just starting up again."

"What was wrong?" Mr. Norris said.

"I had a hole in my liver," the guy said.

"In your liver?"

"Yeah, the doctor said it was big enough to wave a flag in. It's better now. I can have a couple once in a while. I'm not supposed to, but it won't kill me."

"Well, I'm thirty-two years old," Mr. Norris said. "I've had three wives and I can't remember the names of my children."

The guy on the next stool, like a bird on the next island, took a sip from his Scotch and soda. The guy liked the sound of the alcohol in his drink. He put the glass back on the bar.

"That's no problem," he said to Mr. Norris. "The best thing I know for remembering the names of children from previous marriages, is to go out camping, try a little trout fishing. Trout fishing is one of the best things in the world for remembering children's names."

"Is that right?" Mr. Norris said.

"Yeah," the guy said.

"That sounds like an idea," Mr. Norris said. "I've got to do something. Sometimes I think one of them is named Carl, [73] but that's impossible. My third-ex hated the name Carl."

"You try some camping and that trout fishing," the guy on the next stool said. "And you'll remember the names of your unborn children."

"Carl! Carl! Your mother wants you!" Mr. Norris yelled as a kind of joke, then he realized that it wasn't very funny. He was getting there.

He'd have a couple more and then his head would always fall forward and hit the bar like a gunshot. He'd always miss his glass, so he wouldn't cut his face. His head would always jump up and look startled around the bar, people staring at it. He'd get up then, and take it home.

The next morning Mr. Norris went down to a sporting goods store and charged his equipment. He charged a 9 x 9 foot dry finish tent with an aluminum center pole. Then he charged an Arctic sleeping bag filled with eiderdown and an air mattress and an air pillow to go with the sleeping bag. He also charged an air alarm clock to go along with the idea of night and waking in the morning.

He charged a two-burner Coleman stove and a Coleman lantern and a folding aluminum table and a big set of interlocking aluminum cookware and a portable ice box.

The last things he charged were his fishing tackle and a bottle of insect repellent.

He left the next day for the mountains.

Hours later, when he arrived in the mountains, the first sixteen campgrounds he stopped at were filled with people. He was a little surprised. He had no idea the mountains would be so crowded.

At the seventeenth campground, a man had just died of a heart attack and the ambulance attendants were taking down his tent. They lowered the center pole and then pulled up the corner stakes. They folded the tent neatly and put it in the back of the ambulance, right beside the man's body.

They drove off down the road, leaving behind them in the air, a cloud of brilliant white dust. The dust looked like the light from a Coleman lantern.

Mr. Norris pitched his tent right there and set up all his equipment and soon had it all going at once. After he finished eating a dehydrated beef Stroganoff dinner, he turned off all his equipment with the master air switch and went to sleep, for it was now dark. [74]

It was about midnight when they brought the body and placed it beside the tent, less than a foot away from where Mr. Norris was sleeping in his Arctic sleeping bag.

He was awakened when they brought the body. They weren't exactly the quietest body bringers in the world. Mr. Norris could see the bulge of the body against the side of the tent. The only thing that separated him from the dead body was a thin layer of 6 oz. water resistant and mildew resistant DRY FINISH green AMERIFLEX poplin.

Mr. Norris un-zipped his sleeping bag and went outside with a gigantic hound-like flashlight. He saw the body bringers walking down the path toward the creek.

"Hey, you guys!" Mr. Norris shouted. "Come back here. You forgot something."

"What do you mean?" one of them said. They both looked very sheepish, caught in the teeth of the flashlight.

"You know what I mean," Mr. Norris said. "Right now!"

The body bringers shrugged their shoulders, looked at each other and then reluctantly went back, dragging their feet like children all the way. They picked up the body. It was heavy and one of them had trouble getting hold of the feet.

That one said, kind of hopelessly to Mr. Norris, "You won't change your mind?"

"Goodnight and good-bye," Mr. Norris said.

They went off down the path toward the creek, carrying the body between them. Mr. Norris turned his flashlight off and he could hear them, stumbling over the rocks along the bank of the creek. He could hear them swearing at each other. He heard one of them say, "Hold your end up." Then he couldn't hear anything.

About ten minutes later he saw all sorts of lights go on at another campsite down along the creek. He heard a distant voice shouting, "The answer is no! You already woke up the kids. They have to have their rest. We're going on a four-mile hike tomorrow up to Fish Konk Lake. Try someplace else." [75]

THE LAST TIME I SAW TROUT FISHING IN AMERICA

The last time we met was in July on the Big Wood River, ten miles away from Ketchum. It was just after Hemingway had killed himself there, but I didn't know about his death at the time. I didn't know about it until I got back to San Francisco weeks after the thing had happened and picked up a copy of *Life* magazine. There was a photograph of Hemingway on the cover.

"I wonder what Hemingway's up to," I said to myself. I looked inside the magazine and turned the pages to his death. Trout Fishing in America forgot to tell me about it. I'm certain he knew. It must have slipped his mind.

The woman who travels with me had menstrual cramps. She wanted to rest for a while, so I took the baby and my spinning rod and went down to the Big Wood River. That's where I met Trout Fishing in America.

I was casting a Super-Duper out into the river and letting it swing down with the current and then ride on the water up close to the shore. It fluttered there slowly and Trout Fishing in America watched the baby while we talked.

I remember that he gave her some colored rocks to play with. She liked him and climbed up onto his lap and she started putting the rocks in his shirt pocket.

We talked about Great Falls, Montana. I told Trout Fishing in America about a winter I spent as a child in Great Falls. "It was during the war and I saw a Deanna Durbin movie seven times," I said.

The baby put a blue rock in Trout Fishing in America's shirt pocket and he said, "I've been to Great Falls many times. I remember Indians and fur traders. I remember Lewis and Clark, but I don't remember ever seeing a Deanna Durbin movie in Great Falls." [89]

"I know what you mean," I said. "The other people in Great Falls did not share my enthusiasm for Deanna Durbin. The theater was always empty. There was a darkness to that theater different from any theater I've been in since. Maybe it was the snow outside and Deanna Durbin inside. I don't know what it was."

"What was the name of the movie?" Trout Fishing in America said.

"I don't know," I said. "She sang a lot. Maybe she was a chorus girl who wanted to go to college or she was a rich girl or they needed money for something or she did something. Whatever it was about, she sang! and sang! but I can't remember a God-damn word of it.

"One afternoon after I had seen the Deanna Durbin movie again, I went down to the Missouri River. Part of the Missouri was frozen over. There was a railroad bridge there. I was very relieved to see that the Missouri River had not changed and begun to look like Deanna Durbin.

"I'd had a childhood fancy that I would walk down to the Missouri River and it would look just like a Deanna Durbin movie—a chorus girl who wanted to go to college or she was a rich girl or they needed money for something or she did something.

"To this day I don't know why I saw that movie seven times. It was just as deadly as *The Cabinet of Doctor Caligari*. I wonder if the Missouri River is still there?" I said.

"It is," Trout Fishing in America said smiling. "But it doesn't look like Deanna Durbin."

The baby by this time had put a dozen or so of the colored rocks in Trout Fishing in America's shirt pocket. He looked at me and smiled and waited for me to on about Great Falls, but just then I had a fair strike on my Super-Duper. I jerked the rod back and missed the fish.

Trout Fishing in America said, "I know that fish who just struck. You'll never catch him."

"Oh," I said.

"Forgive me," Trout Fishing in America said. "Go on ahead and try for him. He'll hit a couple of times more, but you won't catch him. He's not a particularly smart fish. Just lucky. Sometimes that's all you need."

"Yeah," I said. "You're right there."

I cast out again and continued talking about Great Falls. [90]

Then in correct order I recited the twelve least important things ever said about Great Falls, Montana. For the twelfth and least important thing of all, I said, "Yeah, the telephone would ring in the morning. I'd get out of bed. I didn't have to answer the telephone. That had all been taken care of, years in advance.

"It would still be dark outside and the yellow wallpaper in the hotel room would be running back off the light bulb. I'd put my clothes on and go down to the restaurant where my stepfather cooked all night.

"I'd have breakfast, hot cakes, eggs and whatnot. Then he'd make my lunch for me and it would always be the same thing: a piece of pie and a stone-cold pork sandwich. Afterwards I'd walk to school. I mean the three of us, the Holy Trinity: me, a piece of pie, and a stone-cold pork sandwich. This went on for months.

"Fortunately it stopped one day without my having to do anything serious like grow up. We packed our stuff and left town on a bus. That was Great Falls, Montana. You say the Missouri River is still there?"

"Yes, but it doesn't look like Deanna Durbin," Trout Fishing in America said. "I remember the day Lewis discovered the falls. They left their camp at sunrise and a few hours later they came upon a beautiful plain and on the plain were more buffalo than they had ever seen before in one place.

"They kept on going until they heard the faraway sound of a waterfall and saw a distant column of spray rising and disappearing. They followed the sound as it got louder and louder. After a while the sound was tremendous and they were at the great falls of the Missouri River. It was about noon when they got there.

"A nice thing happened that afternoon, they went fishing below the falls and caught half a dozen trout, good ones, too, from sixteen to twenty-three inches long.

"That was June 13, 1805.

"No, I don't think Lewis would have understood it if the Missouri River had suddenly begun to look like a Deanna Durbin movie, like a chorus girl who wanted to go to college," Trout Fishing in America said. [91]

THE CLEVELAND WRECKING YARD

Until recently my knowledge about the Cleveland Wrecking Yard had come from a couple of friends who'd bought things there. One of them bought a huge window: the frame, glass and everything for just a few dollars. It was a fine-looking window.

Then he chopped a hole in the side of his house up on Potrero Hill and put the window in. Now he has a panoramic view of the San Francisco County Hospital.

He can practically look right down into the wards and see old magazines eroded like the Grand Canyon from endless readings. He can practically hear the patients thinking about breakfast: *I hate milk,* and thinking about dinner: *I hate peas,* and then he can watch the hospital slowly drown at night, hopelessly entangled in huge bunches of brick seaweed.

He bought that window at the Cleveland Wrecking Yard.

My other friend bought an iron roof at the Cleveland Wrecking Yard and took the roof down to Big Sur in an old station wagon and then he carried the iron roof on his back up the side of a mountain. He carried up half the roof on his back. It was no picnic. Then he bought a mule, George, from Pleasanton. George carried up the other half of the roof.

The mule didn't like what was happening at all. He lost a lot of weight because of the ticks, and the smell of the wildcats up on the plateau made him too nervous to graze there. My friend said jokingly that George had lost around two hundred pounds. The good wine country around Pleasanton in the Livermore Valley probably had looked a lot better to George than the wild side of the Santa Lucia Mountains.

My friend's place was a shack right beside a huge fireplace where there had once been a great mansion during the 1920s, built by a famous movie actor. The mansion was built [102] before there was even a road down at Big Sur. The mansion had been brought over the mountains on the backs of mules, strung out like ants, bringing visions of the good life to the poison oak, the ticks, and the salmon.

The mansion was on a promontory, high over the Pacific. Money could see farther in the 1920s, and one could look out and see whales and the Hawaiian Island and the Kuomintang in China.

The mansion burned down years ago.

The actor died.

His mules were made into soap.

His mistresses became bird nests of wrinkles.

Now only the fireplace remains as a sort of Carthaginian homage to Hollywood.

I was down there a few weeks ago to see my friend's roof. I wouldn't have passed up the chance for a million dollars, as they say. The roof looked like a colander to me. If that roof and the rain were running against each other at Bay Meadows, I'd bet on the rain and plan to spend my winnings at the World's Fair in Seattle.

My own experience with the Cleveland Wrecking Yard began two days ago when I heard about a used trout stream they had on sale out at the Yard. So I caught the Number 15 bus on Columbus Avenue and went out there for the first time.

There were two Negro boys sitting behind me on the bus. They were talking about Chubby Checker and the Twist. They thought that Chubby Checker was only fifteen years old because he didn't have a mustache. Then they talked about some other guy who did the twist forty-four hours in a row until he saw George Washington crossing the Delaware.

"Man, that's what I call twisting," one of the kids said.

"I don't think I could twist no forty-four hours in a row," the other kid said. "That's a lot of twisting."

I got off the bus right next to an abandoned Time Gasoline filling station and an abandoned fifty-cent self-service car wash. There was a long field on one side of the filling station. The field had once been covered with a housing project during the war, put there for the shipyard workers.

On the other side of the Time filling station was the Cleveland Wrecking Yard. I walked down there to have a look at the used trout stream. The Cleveland Wrecking Yard has a very long front window filled with signs and merchandise. [103]

There was a sign in the window advertising a laundry marking machine for $65.00. The original cost of the machine was $175.00. Quite a saving.

There was another sign advertising new and used two and three ton hoists. I wondered how many hoists it would take to move a trout stream.

There was another sign that said:

THE FAMILY GIFT CENTER
GIFT SUGGESTIONS FOR THE ENTIRE FAMILY

The window was filled with hundreds of items for the entire family. *Daddy, do you know what I want for Christmas? What, son? A bathroom. Mommy, do you know what I want for Christmas? What, Patricia? Some roofing material.*

There were jungle hammocks in the window for distant relatives and dollar-ten-cent gallons of earth-brown enamel paint for other loved ones.

There was also a big sign that said:

USED TROUT STREAM FOR SALE
MUST BE SEEN TO BE APPRECIATED

I went inside and looked at some ship's lanterns that were for sale next to the door. Then a salesman came up to me and said in a pleasant voice, "Can I help you?"

"Yes," I said. "I'm curious about the trout stream you have for sale. Can you tell me something about it? How are you selling it?"

"We're selling it by the foot length. You can buy as little as you want or you can buy all we've got left. A man came in here this morning and bought 563 feet. He's going to give it to his niece for a birthday present," the salesman said.

"We're selling the waterfalls separately of course, and the trees and birds, flowers, grass and ferns we're also selling extra. The insects we're giving away free with a minimum purchase of ten feet of stream."

"How much are you selling the stream for?" I asked.

"Six dollars and fifty-cents a foot," he said. "That's for the first hundred feet. After that it's five dollars a foot."

"How much are the birds?" I asked.

"Thirty-five cents apiece," he said. "But of course they're used. We can't guarantee anything."

"How wide is the stream?" I asked. "You said you were [104] selling it by the length, didn't you?"

"Yes," he said. "We're selling it by the length. Its width runs between five and eleven feet. You don't have to pay anything extra for width. It's not a big stream, but it's very pleasant."

"What kinds of animals do you have?" I asked.

"We only have three deer left," he said.

"Oh . . . What about flowers?"

"By the dozen," he said.

"Is the stream clear?" I asked.

"Sir," the salesman said. "I wouldn't want you to think that we would ever sell a murky trout stream here. We always make sure they're running crystal clear before we even think about moving them."

"Where did the stream come from?" I asked.

"Colorado," he said. "We moved it with loving care. We've never damaged a trout stream yet. We treat them all as if they were china."

"You're probably asked this all the time, but how's fishing in the stream?" I asked.

"Very good," he said. "Mostly German browns, but there are a few rainbows."

"What do the trout cost?" I asked.

"They come with the stream,' he said. "Of course it's all luck. You never know how many you're going to get or how big they are. But the fishing's very good, you might say it's excellent. Both bait and dry fly," he said smiling.

"Where's the stream at?" I asked. "I'd iike to take a look at it."

"It's around in back," he said. "You go straight through that door and then turn right until you're outside. It's stacked in lengths. You can't miss it. The waterfalls are upstairs in the used plumbing department."

"What about the animals?"

"Well, what's left of the animals are straight back from the stream. You'll see a bunch of our trucks parked on a road by the railroad tracks. Turn right on the road and follow it down past the piles of lumber. The animal shed's right at the end of the lot."

"Thanks," I said. "I think I'll look at the waterfalls first. You don't have to come with me. Just tell me how to get there and I'll find my own way." [105]

"All right," he said. "Go up those stairs. You'll see a bunch of doors and windows, turn left and you'll find the used plumbing department. Here's my card if you need any help."

"Okay," I said. "You've been a great help already. Thanks a lot. I'll take a look around."

"Good luck," he said.

I went upstairs and there were thousands of doors there. I'd never seen so many doors before in my life. You could have built an entire city out of those doors. Doorstown. And there were enough windows up there to build a little suburb entirely out of windows. Windowville.

I turned left and went back and saw the faint glow of pearl-colored light. The light got stronger and stronger as I went farther back, and then I was in the used plumbing department, surrounded by hundreds of toilets.

The toilets were stacked on shelves. They were stacked five toilets high. There was a skylight above the toilets that made them glow like the Great Taboo Pearl of the South Sea movies.

Stacked over against the wall were the waterfalls. There were about a dozen of them, ranging from a drop of a few feet to a drop of ten or fifteen feet.

There was one waterfall that was over sixty feet long. There were tags on the pieces of the big falls describing the correct order for putting the falls back together again.

The waterfalls all had price tags on them. They were more expensive than the stream. The waterfalls were selling for $19.00 a foot.

I went into another room where there were piles of sweet-smelling lumber, glowing a soft yellow from a different color skylight above the lumber. In the shadows at the edge of the room under the sloping roof of the building were many sinks and urinals covered with dust, and there was also another waterfall about seventeen feet long, lying there in two lengths and already beginning to gather dust.

I had seen all I wanted of the waterfalls, and now I was very curious about the trout stream, so I followed the salesman's directions and ended up outside the building.

O I had never in my life seen anything like that trout stream. It was stacked in piles of various lengths: ten, fifteen, twenty feet. etc. There was one pile of hundred-foot [106] lengths. There was also a box of scraps. The scraps were in odd sizes ranging from six inches to a couple of feet.

There was a loudspeaker on the side of the building and soft music was coming out. It was a cloudy day and seagulls were circling high overhead.

Behind the stream were big bundles of trees and bushes. They were covered with sheets of patched canvas. You could see the tops and roots sticking out the ends of the bundles.

I went up close and looked at the lengths of stream. I could see some trout in them. I saw one good fish. I saw some crawdads crawling around the rocks at the bottom.

It looked like a fine stream. I put my hand in the water. It was cold and felt good.

I decided to go around to the side and look at the animals. I saw where the trucks were parked beside the railroad tracks. I followed the road down past the piles of lumber, back to the shed where the animals were.

The salesman had been right. They were practically out of animals. About the only thing they had left in any abundance were mice. There were hundreds of mice.

Beside the shed was a huge wire birdcage, maybe fifty feet high, filled with many kinds of birds. The top of the cage had a piece of canvas over it, so the birds wouldn't get wet when it rained. There were woodpeckers and wild canaries and sparrows.

On my way back to where the trout stream was piled, I found the insects. They were inside a prefabricated steel building that was selling for eighty-cents a square foot. There was a sign over the door. It said

INSECTS [107]

Suggested Areas
of Research

As the primary sources included in this text are examined, topics for research will occur to the student. The editors furnish the following list of areas of research only as suggestions. Many of the areas below would require limiting in order to fit the length and scope of the assigned research project.

1. family life in the small town
2. occupations and professions in the small town
3. growing up in a small town
4. small-town humor
5. small-town morality
6. speech and dialect, idiom
7. communication lines
8. cultural poverty
9. discontent in the small town
10. the small-town migration
11. forces of poverty in the small town
12. complacency in the small town
13. the vitality of frontier living
14. the romantic ideal of the small town
15. urban influences on the small town
16. recreational opportunities in the small town
17. gossip
18. law enforcement
19. small-town characters
20. stereotypes
21. crime in the small town
22. university influences on the small town
23. clubs and social organizations
24. industry

25. architecture
26. slums
27. class distinctions
28. politics
29. church and religious life
30. the schoolteacher
31. gregariousness of the small town (in contrast to isolation)
32. resistance to change
33. function of the business section
34. the minister
35. the routine of the small town
36. the small town newspaper and its editor
37. prejudices of race, nationality, and religion
38. educational opportunities
39. friendliness or nosiness
40. attitudes in the home
41. changes in the treatment of the small town in literature
42. realism in depicting the small town
43. prophesying a new age through analysis of the small town
44. psychological evaluations of people and the small town
45. literary techniques used to depict the small town
46. satirical treatment of the small town

Sample Thesis Statements

An important step in preparing a research paper is writing an adequate thesis statement—one that limits and controls the subsequent development of the paper. The following samples are offered to suggest a variety of subject approaches that can be used after examination of the materials included in this text, as well as any outside sources the instructor may wish to include.

1. Writers of American fiction usually present a kind of "double vision" of sex behavior in the small town—a public view based on Victorian standards and the actual, contradictory practice.
2. American fiction writers, in treating the small town, tend to show great class distinctions resulting from financial status. In these fictional situations the rich always seem to dominate the poor and to control such institutions in the town as its government and business.
3. Writers of American fiction often include gossip as a major ingredient of small-town life. Although gossip can be a means of destroying a person's reputation, it can also be an effective means of communication.
4. Writers of American fiction often portray the small-town schoolteacher of the late nineteenth and early twentieth centuries as an exemplary figure. His personal life as well as his public life must at all times create the impression of a person to be admired and respected by everyone.
5. The culture of the small town, as viewed by the American writer, is changing at a slower rate than that of the big city and has therefore developed a cultural lag. The dress, conversation, and reading habits of the small town have contributed to this cultural lag.
6. Writers of American fiction often portray the class distinctions that exist in the small town. People are classified by their wealth, occupation, education, family record, club membership, religious affiliation, and residence area. One or more of these status values usually determine the level people occupy on the social ladder.

7. Writers of American literature who deal with small towns identify complacency and resistance to change as characteristics of the small town.
8. In American literature the small-town schoolteacher is often depicted as a lonely person who has much contact with society but few intimate friends.
9. Several writers of American fiction have illustrated how the everyday routine of a small town leads to discontent.
10. In American fiction two sets of morals, public and private, are reflected by the people of the small town.
11. Realistic writers of American literature have a tendency to destroy the romantic image of the small town.
12. Two sociologists, Arthur J. Vidich and Joseph Bensman, in *Small Town in Mass Society* (1958), are concerned with "the techniques of personal and social adjustment that enable the community members to live constructive and meaningful lives in the face of an environment which is hostile to their values, aspirations, and illusions." Writers of American fiction have similar concerns.
13. The role of the schoolteacher in American fiction in the twentieth century is presented realistically in contrast to the stereotype of the nineteeth century.
14. Writers of American fiction often see the small town as creating cultural poverty.
15. There is a strong tendency on the part of American writers to treat the small town in satiric terms.

Additional
Primary Sources

ANDERSON, SHERWOOD. *Poor White*. New York: B. W. Huebsch, 1920. A small town becomes a manufacturing center.

ANDERSON, SHERWOOD. *The Triumph of the Egg*. New York: B. W. Huebsch, 1921. Small-town types who lead inhibited lives.

BRADSTREET, ANNE. "The Prologue" to "The Tenth Muse." In *Poems of Anne Bradstreet*. Edited by Robert Hutchinson. New York: Dover, 1969. The "carping tongues" of her New England community think that the author should put her hand to a needle rather than a pen.

CABLE, GEORGE WASHINGTON. *John March, Southerner*. New York: Scribner, 1894. New industrialism takes over this old southern town.

CAPOTE, TRUMAN. "Children on Their Birthdays." In *The Grass Harp, A Tree of Night and Other Stories*. New York: New American Library, 1956. In a small southern town a group of youngsters gather to celebrate another's birthday, and dishonesty, jealousy, gossip, and lack of religion are revealed.

CAPOTE, TRUMAN. *In Cold Blood*. New York: Random House, 1966. A small town in Kansas reacts to the murder of one of its families.

CHOPIN, KATE. "The Maid of Saint Phillippe." In *The Complete Works of Kate Chopin*. Baton Rouge: Louisiana University Press, 1969. When the little village of Saint Phillippe is abandoned to the English in the nineteenth century, a stalwart 17-year-old French girl refuses marriage to a wealthy French captain and joins an Indian tribe.

CLARK, WALTER VAN TILBURG. *The Ox-Bow Incident*. New York: Random House, 1940. Citizens of a western town lynch three innocent men—supposed cattle rustlers.

COOKE, JOHN ESTEN. *The Virginia Comedians*. New York: Prentice-Hall, 1954. A picture of Williamsburg, Virginia, as a capital town.

COZZENS, JAMES GOULD. *By Love Possessed*. New York: Harcourt Brace Jovanovich, 1957. An exposure of the immorality, loneliness, fraud, and frustration that lie beneath the small-town social facade.

CRANE, STEPHEN. "The Bride Comes to Yellow Sky." In *The Open Boat and Other Tales of Adventure*. New York: Doubleday, 1898. A small-town character reacts to change.

DELAND, MARGARET. *Around Old Chester*. New York: Harper & Row, 1915. Stories of small-town life in western Pennsylvania.

DELL, FLOYD. *Runaway*. New York: George H. Doran Co., 1925. The protagonist runs away from the narrow life of a small Midwestern town.

FAULKNER, WILLIAM. *Intruder in the Dust*. New York: Random House, 1948. A youngster and an old maid in a Mississippi small town prove the innocence of a Negro accused of murder.

FAULKNER, WILLIAM. *Light in August*. New York: H. Harrison Smith & Robert Haas, 1932. A small town is concerned with racial origins and the glorification of the past.

FAULKNER, WILLIAM. *Sartoris*. New York: Harcourt Brace Jovanovich, 1929. A small-town aristocratic family in Mississippi tries to hold on to tradition.

FAULKNER, WILLIAM. *Soldier's Pay*. New York: Liveright, 1926. A wounded World War I soldier returns to a small town, his family, and his fiancée.

FAULKNER, WILLIAM. *The Sound and the Fury*. New York: Jonathan Cape and Harrison Smith, 1929. A decaying aristocratic family in a small Mississippi town.

FAULKNER, WILLIAM. "That Evening Sun." In *Collected Stories of William Faulkner*. New York: Random House, 1950. A small-town Nergo servant, fearing her husband will kill her, finds little help from her employer and family.

FITZGERALD, F. SCOTT. "Winter Dreams." In *All the Sad Young Men*. New York: Scribner, 1926. An adolescent in a small town is disillusioned when he grows to manhood.

FREDERIC, HAROLD. *The Damnation of Theron Ware*. Chicago: Stone & Kimball, 1896. A young clergyman in a small town deals with religious problems.

FREEMAN, MARY E. WILKINS. *A New England Nun and Other Stories*. New York: Harper & Row, 1891. Realistic and ironic stories of New England villages.

FRENCH, ALICE. *Stories of a Western Town*. New York: Scribner, 1893. The everyday routine in an Iowa town is given a local-color treatment.

GALE, ZONA. *Friendship Village*. New York: Macmillan, 1908. A sentimental view of a little home town.

GALE, ZONA. *Miss Lulu Bett*. New York: Prentice-Hall, 1920. The study of a figure of revolt in the village.

GARLAND, HAMLIN. *Main-Travelled Roads*. Boston: Arena Publishing Co., 1891. Local-color stories of the grim lives of rural folk in the Dakotas and Iowa.

GARLAND, HAMLIN. *Money Magic*. New York: Harper & Row, 1907. Life in a farming town is affected by the Cripple Creek gold rush.

GLASGOW, ELLEN. *The Voice of the People*. New York: Doubleday, 1900. An old town fights new influences in a story of class distinctions.

HARRIS, JOEL CHANDLER. *Free Joe and Other Georgian Sketches*. New York: Scribner, 1887. An analysis of southern prewar small-town life.

HARTE, BRET. *The Luck of Roaring Camp and Other Sketches*. New York: Houghton Mifflin, 1869. Descriptions of nineteenth-century frontier life.

HAWTHORNE, NATHANIEL. "Main Street." In *The Snow Image and Other Twice-Told Tales*. Boston: Tichner, Reed & Fields, 1852. A description of an early nineteenth-century New England town.

HAWTHORNE, NATHANIEL. *The Scarlet Letter.* Boston: Ticknor, Reed & Fields, 1850. Hester Prynne, because she violates the community's code, is punished by the people of Salem, Massachusetts, and finds herself outside the "magnetic chain of humanity."

HEMINGWAY, ERNEST. "The Killers." In *Men Without Women.* New York: Scribner, 1927. A boy in a small town is alarmed at the lack of concern people have for others.

HEMINGWAY, ERNEST. "Soldier's Home." In *In Our Time.* New York: Liveright, 1927. A returning World War I soldier finds small-town life depressing and unexciting.

HOUGH, EMERSON. *The Story of the Cowboy.* New York: Prentice-Hall, 1897. Chapter 13—"Society in the Cow Country"—contains descriptions of early cow towns.

HOWELLS, WILLIAM DEAN. *A Boy's Town.* New York: Harper & Row, 1890. An autobiographical account of the writer's boyhood in Ohio.

HUGHES, LANGSTON. *Not Without Laughter.* New York: Knopf, 1930. Negro life in the small town.

HUGHES, RUPERT. *The Old Home Town.* New York: Harper & Row, 1926. The dull routine of a Mississippi River town.

INGE, WILLIAM. *Picnic.* New York: Random House, 1953. A stranger in the town causes citizens to reveal prejudices and hypocrisy.

IRVING, WASHINGTON. "Legend of Sleepy Hollow." From *The Sketch Book of Geoffrey Crayon, Gent.* New York: C. S. Van Winkle, 1820. A sketch of a rural schoolteacher in the early nineteenth century.

IRVING, WASHINGTON. "Rip Van Winkle." In *The Sketch Book of Geoffrey Crayon, Gent.* New York: C. S. Van Winkle, 1820. A nostalgic view of an early nineteenth-century small town.

JEWETT, SARAH ORNE. *The Country of the Pointed Firs.* New York: Houghton Mifflin, 1896. Local-color sketches of an isolated seaport town in Maine.

LEE, HARPER. *To Kill a Mockingbird.* Philadelphia: Lippincott, 1960. Racial prejudice, class distinctions, and stereotypes in a small Alabama town in the 1930s.

LEWIS, ALFRED HENRY. *Wolfville.* New York: Lippincott, 1897. Life in a small cattle town in the frontier Southwest.

LOCKRIDGE, ROSS, JR. *Raintree County.* Boston: Houghton Mifflin, 1948. Flashbacks to episodes in the life of a high school principal in a small town illuminate the history of the county.

LONGSTREET, AUGUSTUS. *Georgia Scenes.* Augusta, Georgia: S. R. sentinel office, 1835. Sketches of small towns and rural folk in Georgia.

MASTERS, EDGAR LEE. *The New Spoon River.* New York: Liveright, 1924. A river town is changed by standardization.

METALIOUS, GRACE. *Peyton Place.* New York: Julian Messner, 1956. A small New England town is shown to be filled with scandal.

MILLER, ARTHUR. *The Crucible.* New York: Viking Press, 1953. A play about Salem at the time of the witch trials.

O'HARA, JOHN. *Appointment in Samarra.* New York: Harcourt Brace Jovanovich, 1934. Class levels and attitudes in a Pennsylvania town.

O'NEILL, EUGENE. *Ah, Wilderness!* New York: Random House, 1933. A humorous play about an adolescent boy.

PORTER, KATHERINE ANNE. "The Grave." In *The Leaning Tower and Other Stories*. New York: Harcourt Brace Jovanovich, 1934. A nine-year-old girl who, with her older brother, explores a family cemetery, gains an understanding of the life cycle, and accepts her role as a woman.

RICHTER, CONRAD. *The Town*. New York: Knopf, 1950. A frontier village grows into a small city, yet citizens retain small-town characteristics.

SAROYAN, WILLIAM. *The Human Comedy*. New York: Harcourt Brace Jovanovich, 1942. The day-to-day drama of family life in a small California town.

STEINBECK, JOHN. *Pastures of Heaven*. New York: Viking Press, 1932. What appears to outsiders to be an ideal agrarian village is revealed through a number of stories to be a place of conflict, pain, and suffering.

STOWE, HARRIET BEECHER. *Oldtown Folks*. Boston: Osgood Fields, 1869. Old-fashioned provincial life in a small town near Boston.

STRIBLING, T. S. *The Store*. New York: Doubleday, 1932. This Pulitzer Prize-winning novel depicts a southern town after the Civil War.

SUCKOW, RUTH. *Iowa Interiors*. New York: Knopf, 1926. A collection of stories of frustrated older people in little towns.

SUCKOW, RUTH. *The Odyssey of a Nice Girl*. New York: Knopf, 1925. A young girl hemmed in by the restrictive village life.

TARKINGTON, BOOTH. *The Gentleman from Indiana*. New York: Doubleday, 1899. The virtuous life as opposed to political corruption in an Indiana town.

TARKINGTON, BOOTH. *The Magnificent Ambersons*. New York: Doubleday, 1918. Focuses on the lives of an aristocratic class of people in a small town.

TURNBULL, AGNES SLIGH. *The Rolling Years*. New York: Macmillan, 1936. An account of life in a western Pennsylvania farming community.

TWAIN, MARK. *The Man That Corrupted Hadleyburg and Other Stories and Essays*. New York: Doubleday, 1900. A small town's reputation for virtue is wiped out when the inhabitants are tempted by money.

WHARTON, EDITH. *Ethan Frome*. New York: Scribner, 1911. In a typical New England village, tragedy ends a love affair.

WHITE, WILLIAM ALLEN. *In Our Town*. New York: McClure, Phillips & Co., 1906. Sketches of Emporia, Kansas, by a newspaper editor.

WISTER, OWEN. *The Virginian*. New York: Macmillan, 1902. Lively western action in a nineteenth-century Wyoming cattle town.

WOLFE, THOMAS. *Look Homeward, Angel*. New York: Scribner, 1929. Growing up in a southern town.

76 77 78 79 80 9 8 7 6 5 4 3 2 1